CONSTRUCTING INTERNATIONAL RELATIONS

International Relations in a Constructed World

CONSTRUCTING INTERNATIONAL RELATIONS

the next generation

KARIN M. FIERKE AND
KNUD ERIK JØRGENSEN

Routledge
Taylor & Francis Group
LONDON AND NEW YORK

First published 2001 by M.E. Sharpe

Published 2015 by Routledge
2 Park Square, Milton Park, Abingdon, Oxon OX14 4RN
711 Third Avenue, New York, NY 10017, USA

Routledge is an imprint of the Taylor & Francis Group, an informa business

Library of Congress Cataloging-in-Publication Data

Constructing international relations : the next generation / edited by Karin M. Fierke and
Knud Erik Jørgensen.
    p. cm. — (international relations in a constructed world)
Includes bibliographical references and index.
ISBN 0-7656-0738-7 (cloth : alk. paper)—ISBN 0-7656-0739-5 (pbk. : alk. paper)
   1. International relations—Methodology. 2. International relations—Philosophy.
3. Constructivism (Philosophy) I. Fierke, K. M. (Karin M.) II. Jørgensen, Knud Erik.
III. Series.

JZ1305 .C665 2001   00-067135
327.1′01—dc21   CIP

ISBN 13: 9780765607393 (pbk)
ISBN 13: 9780765607386 (hbk)

Contents

About the Editors and the Contributors   vii

Acknowledgements   x

Introduction
K.M. Fierke and Knud Erik Jørgensen   3

PART I: RECONSIDERING CONSTRUCTIVISM

1.   **Constructivism as an Approach to Interdisciplinary Study**
     Friedrich V. Kratochwil   13

2.   **Four Levels and a Discipline**
     Knud Erik Jørgensen   36

3.   **Constructivisms in International Relations:**
     Wendt, Onuf, and Kratochwil
     Maja Zehfuss   54

4.   **Feminism: Constructivism's Other Pedigree**
     Birgit Locher and Elisabeth Prügl   76

5.   **What Systems Theory Can Tell Us About Constructivism**
     Mathias Albert   93

PART II: PRACTICING CONSTRUCTIVISM

6.   **Critical Methodology and Constructivism**
     K.M. Fierke   115

7. Discourse Study: Bringing Rigor to Critical Theory
    Jennifer Milliken   136

8. International Relations as Communicative Action
    Harald Müller   160

9. Communicative Action and the World of Diplomacy
    Lars G. Lose   179

10. Constructing Globalization
    Ben Rosamond   201

EPILOGUE

11. Can We Speak a Common Constructivist Language?
    Audie Klotz   223

12. The Politics of Constructivism
    Nicholas G. Onuf   236

Bibliography   255

Index   281

About the Editors and the Contributors

Mathias Albert is an assistant professor at Darmstadt University of Technology. His main areas of research include international relations theory, the theory of world society, and the evolution of transnational law. He has recently co-edited (with L. Brock and K.D. Wolf) *Civilizing World Politics. Society and Community Beyond the State* (Rowman and Littlefield, 2000) and (with D. Jacobson and Y. Lapid) *Identities, Borders, Orders: New Directions in IR Theory* (University of Minnesota Press, 2000) and is currently preparing a monograph on *The Politics of World Society.*

K.M. Fierke is a lecturer in the School of Politics, Queen's University Belfast, and has also worked at the Amsterdam School of Social Science Research, University of Amsterdam, and Nuffield College, Oxford University. She is the author of *Changing Games, Changing Strategies: Critical Investigations in Security* (Manchester University Press and St. Martin's Press, 1998), and numerous articles about constructivism and changing security relations, appearing in the *European Journal of International Relations, Millennium, Global Society, International Feminist Journal of International Relations,* and *Journal of European Public Policy.*

Knud Erik Jørgensen is an associate professor in the Department of Political Science at the University of Aarhus. He specializes in European integration studies, foreign policy, security studies, and international theory. He has edited *Reflective Approaches to European Governance* (Macmillan, 1997), *European Approaches to Crisis Management* (Kluwer, 1997) and co-edited (with Thomas Christiansen and Antje Wiener) *The Social Construction of Europe* (Sage, forthcoming 2001). He is currently preparing a book on the nexus between globalization and European integration.

Audie Klotz is an associate professor in the Department of Political Science at the University of Illinois-Chicago. Her book, *Norms in Interna-*

tional Relations (Cornell, 1995) won the Edgar S. Furniss Prize in security studies. She is co-author, with Cecelia Lynch, of *Constructing Global Politics: Strategies for Research in a Postpositivist World* (Cornell University Press, 2001) and has written additional pieces on international relations theory, sanctions policies, and southern African politics.

Friedrich V. Kratochwil is a professor of International Politics at the Geschwister-Scholl-Institut of the University of Munich (Ludwig-Maximilians-Universität). His research interests include international organization and international law. He is author of *International Order and Foreign Policy* (Westview Press, 1978); *Rules, Norms and Decisions: On the Conditions of Practical and Legal Reasoning in International Relations and Domestic Society* (Cambridge University Press, 1989) as well as numerous articles. He has edited with Yosef Lapid, *The Return of Culture and Identity in International Relations Theory* (Lynne Riener, 1996). As of May 1, 1999, he has taken over the editorship of *The European Journal of International Relations*.

Birgit Locher is a researcher and Ph.D. student at the University of Bremen, Germany. She holds an M.A. from the University of Konstanz and has studied at Rutgers and Cornell. Her publications include several articles and book chapters on gender in international relations. She is currently completing her dissertation on trafficking in women in the European Union.

Lars G. Lose holds a Masters Degree in International Studies from the University of Warwick (1995) and a Masters Degree in Political Science from the Department of Political Science at the University of Aarhus (1997). Lose has since 1997 been employed at the Royal Danish Ministry of Foreign Affairs.

Jennifer Milliken is the author of *Conflict Possibilities: The Social Construction of the Korean War* (Manchester University Press, 2001), as well as a number of articles and book chapters on constructivist methology and topics in the social construction of international relations. Dr. Milliken is on the faculty of the Graduate Institute of International Studies in Geneva, Switzerland; prior to that, she was on the faculty of York University in Toronto, Canada.

Harald Müller is director of the Peace Research Institute Frankfurt and professor of International Relations at Frankfurt University. His research interests include nuclear weapons politics, issues of proliferation, and disarmament. He has published numerous books, including *Europe and Nuclear Disarmament. Debates and Political Attitudes in 16 European Countries* (European Interuniversity Press, 1998); chapters in edited volumes, reports and articles, including *Nuclear Weapons and German Interests: An Attempt at Redefinition*, Frankfurt, PRIF Report 55, 2000. His most recent book is *Das Zusammenleben der Kulturen. Ein Gegenentwurf zu Huntington* (Fischer 1998). Harald Müller served as a member of the German Defence Review Commission and is on the UN Secretary General's Advisory Board on Disarmament Matters.

Nicholas G. Onuf is a professor in the Department of International Relations at Florida International University. His most recent book is *The Republican Legacy in International Thought* (Cambridge University Press, 1998). He has published *World of Our Making* (University of South Carolina Press, 1989) and edited with Vendulka Kubálková and Paul Kowert, *International Relations in a Constructed World* (Sharpe, 1998).

Elisabeth Prügl is an associate professor of International Relations at Florida International University in Miami. She is the author of *The Global Construction of Gender: Home-based Work in the Political Economy of the 20th Century* (Columbia University Press, 1999) and co-editor of *Gender Politics in Global Governance* (Rowman and Littlefield, 1999). Her current research focuses on the politics of agricultural reform in the European Union.

Ben Rosamond is a senior research fellow in the Centre for the Study of Globalisation and Regionalisation at the University of Warwick. He is the author of *Theories of European Integration* (Macmillan and St. Martin's Press, 2000) and co-author of *Politics: An Introduction* (Routledge 1997). He has published widely on the theoretical analysis of European integration, globalisation and the European Union, and international relations theory. He holds an award under the ESRC's 'One Europe or Several' Research Programme (Award number L213 252 024). He is currently preparing edited or co-edited volumes on regional integration in a globalised world, globalisation, and British political economy and political sociology.

Maja Zehfuss is a lecturer in the Department of Politics and International Studies at the University of Warwick. She has published in *Zeitschrift für Internationale Beziehungen*.

Acknowledgements

This book would not have been possible without the support and cooperation of a large number of people. We would like to thank the Danish Social Science Research Council for funding the original workshops where many of the chapters were first presented as papers, and the contributors to this volume for their patience during the long process of putting the book together. We owe a special debt to Vendulka Kubálková and Nicholas Onuf, editors of the Constructivism in International Relations series, for their enthusiasm for the project and for the extraordinary commitment of time and effort they devoted to rendering a consistent and highly readable text. Several students in the Political Science Department at the University of Aarhus also played an important role. Tenna Lundum Jensen, Lars Ploug Møller and Anja Nielsen put together the bibliography and the index and generally assisted in the preparation of the final manuscript. The students in the course, Social Construction in International Relations, read the text and commented on its accessibility. Last, but by no means least, we thank Anne-Grethe Gammelgaard for her efforts in standardizing the text and creating the final version of the manuscript.

CONSTRUCTING INTERNATIONAL RELATIONS

Introduction

K.M. Fierke and
Knud Erik Jørgensen

Two trends mark discussions of constructivism and international relations at the turn of the century. First, the debate between constructivists and rationalists has supplanted the age-old debate between realists and liberals. Instead of its marginal position in the early 1990s constructivism now occupies a central place in the discipline (Katzenstein, Keohane, and Krasner 1998). Second, rather than the "celebration of difference" declared by postpositivists a decade ago (Lapid 1989; Ashley and Walker 1990b; George and Campbell 1990), there are efforts to define constructivism, not only to distinguish it clearly from rationalism, but from other postpositivist approaches as well. A spate of articles has, in different ways, distinguished constructivists from rationalists, poststructuralists or critical theorists (Ruggie 1998a, 1998b; Hopf 1998; Adler 1997; Campbell 1998a; Price and Reus-Smit 1998; Checkel 1998). However, as Ole Waever (1998) points out, both of these trends are primarily American phenomena and, as evidenced by the 1998 anniversary issue of the journal *International Organization*, the referencing within this debate has been largely confined to American scholars. Yet, interestingly, constructivism and other postpositivist approaches have received a warmer reception in various European contexts;[1] indeed, given the emphasis on history and the social nature of state relations, constructivism has, arguably, always been part of the European tradition of thinking about international relations (Garnett 1984; Dunne 1995, 1998; Risse 1998). This book is an attempt to look more broadly at the place of constructivism in International Relations theory, raising critical questions about the meaning that constructivism has acquired in International Relations debates and the various philosophical traditions from which it emerged.

3

The project began at a meeting in Aarhus-Norsminde, Denmark, at the end of 1997 which was organized around the question "What is Constructivism?" Many of the participants, coming from different countries, brought a more or less clear answer to this question with them; however, by the end of a fruitful and lively dialogue, the only consensus was that we did not know the meaning of constructivism. One reason for the growing confusion at the meeting was the contrast between the dominant constructivism of the American context, represented by, among others, Alexander Wendt or Peter Katzenstein, and the various constructivisms represented at the workshop, constructivisms with origins in diverse traditions drawing on Ludwig Wittgenstein, Jürgen Habermas, Niklas Luhmann, or Michel Foucault. The dialogue revealed that the current fashion in International Relations obscures the roots of constructivism and ignores the rich variety of philosophical traditions from which this approach emerged.

To the likely disappointment of some readers, this collection does not provide a concise definition of constructivism. Instead, it explores the philosophical roots of several constructivisms, as well as the boundaries these place on constructivist practice. Rather than providing concise definitions or rigid "research programs," we hope the book will provide more of a map of the diverse branches of this family tree, identifying the areas of overlap between the various constructivisms, as well as the differences. At one and the same time, we challenge the idea that constructivism "is what IR scholars make of it"—which suggests that anything might qualify as constructivist.

Genealogies of Constructivism

A fruitful distinction can be made between the genealogy of constructivism philosophically and its genealogy within the discipline of International Relations. Philosophically, the linguistic turn, which began with Wittgenstein's *Tractatus Logico-Philosophicus* (1961) and came to fruition with the *Philosophical Investigations* (1958), is one of the most important roots of the approaches identified with constructivism.[2] The linguistic turn gave rise to a reorientation in the philosophical presuppositions underlying Western philosophy since Descartes, replacing the distinction between subjective and objective realms of experience with the social nature of language. Wittgenstein's later work countered assumptions that language originates either in the mind or is a mirror of an objective reality, arguing instead that language use is a form of action that is constitutive of the world.

Wittgenstein's philosophy of language provided one point of departure for later philosophers and theorists, from J.L. Austin, Peter Berger and Thomas Luckmann, John Searle, Anthony Giddens, Jürgen Habermas, Richard

Rorty, and Francois Lyotard—to name just a few strange bedfellows—who have inspired the various modern and postmodern constructivisms. For instance, Habermas was influenced by Wittgenstein's ideas about the social nature of language and communication and in particular the idea that human subjects are already united with one another through language (Honneth 1995, 86). Also, Wittgenstein's argument that individual speech is dependent on a pre-given system of linguistic meaning, which precedes intentionality, contributed to what has been seen as the postmodern crisis of the human subject. These ideas about language, along with Freud and Nietzsche's emphasis on the unconscious forces and motives underlying individual action, provided a challenge to the classical notion of autonomy and the idea that rational agents have control over their actions (Honneth 1995, 261). These various approaches have taken on a life of their own, evolving in distinct ways and engaging in contentious debates between one another; the dispute between Habermas and Foucault is one of the more famous.

While the genealogy of constructivism in philosophy reveals roots and a larger family tree, constructivism in International Relations has evolved from two quite distinct branches. When Onuf (1989) introduced the term constructivism to International Relations, he began with Wittgenstein. However, the constructivism that emerged into the limelight—now referred to as "conventional" constructivism—drew inspiration from Berger and Luckman or Giddens, among others, and defined itself in opposition to more radical constructivists, drawing on postmodern thinkers such as Foucault, Lyotard, or Derrida. One purpose of this book is to rethink what has become a stark dichotomy, a dichotomy that is specific to the genealogy of constructivism within the discipline of international relations.

This genealogy begins roughly in the 1980s, with the "Third Debate," which engaged theorists in a metatheoretical critique of mainstream international relations. In the mid-1980s, in North America, critical or postmodern theorists, such as Richard Ashley (1986), Robert Cox (1981) and R.B.J. Walker (1993) began to deconstruct some of the basic assumptions of international relations as a world of states trapped in an objective structure of anarchy. Scholars from the geographical "margins" of Europe and Australia, and scholars in the post-colonial tradition in other parts of the world, also engaged in these critical endeavors but without the clear lines of demarcation that marked the theoretical debate in North America.

In the late 1980s, as the first signs of the demise of the Cold War became visible, Alexander Wendt (1987) introduced the agent-structure problem to IR scholarship, John Ruggie (1989) questioned the inability of traditional international relations theory to deal with historical transformations, and Onuf (1989), as stated above, introduced the term constructivism. By this time, the metatheoretical critique of the Third Debate had created spaces for a "celebration of difference," resulting in a range of modern and postmodern constructivisms. Feminist scholars, such as J. Ann Tickner (1995), V. Spike Peterson (1992), and Christine Sylvester (1994), marginalized within the larger postpositivist debate, were also raising significant questions about the epistemological underpinnings of the dominant theoretical traditions and the relationship to the gendering of international relations.

In the 1990s, traditional "positivist" approaches in the field began to lose the high ground, faced with their failure to account for the end of the Cold War or dramatic changes taking place in the world of international politics (see Koslowski and Kratochwil 1995; Ruggie 1998b; Fierke 1998). Two further developments emerged around this weak spot. On the one hand, more mainstream scholars went on the offensive, accusing constructivists of being incapable of undertaking empirical research or of thinking like naive political utopians (see Keohane 1989; Goldstein and Keohane 1993; Mearsheimer 1995). On the other hand, a generation of younger scholars, particularly in the area of security studies, was applying these metatheoretical lessons to analyses of international politics (see Krause and Williams 1996). At the same time, the "postpositivists," previously united in their "celebration of difference" and challenge to the mainstream, began to more clearly distinguish between themselves, and specifically around the issue of how closely to engage the mainstream (see Fierke in this volume).

Wendt's agent-structure article (1987) had been an important impetus to the "third debate" between positivists and postpositivists in international relations. It was later overshadowed by the tremendous popularity of his "Anarchy Is What States Make of It" (1992a), a piece that has arguably replaced Kenneth Waltz's *Theory of International Politics* (1979) as the most frequently quoted article in the field of international relations theory. "Anarchy Is What States Make of It" was a major landmark in defining a constructivist approach to international relations; it has also been widely criticized for adopting too many of the assumptions of the mainstream it was criticizing, including the continuing emphasis on states as unitary actors and the failure to deal with the role of language in constituting intersubjective structures. Similarly, Barry Buzan and Ole Waever's work on security was criticized for giving up some of their previous insights (see McSweeney 1996, Buzan, Waever, and de Wilde 1998). Wendt was later joined in his 'bridge-building' enterprise with the mainstream by Peter Katzenstein whose collection *The Culture of National Security* (1996) has become another landmark, as have the works of many of his former students (e.g., Audie Klotz and Richard Price). The diluted constructivism of the bridge-builders was called into question at a 1994 workshop at the University of Minnesota by scholars, including Jutta Weldes, Mark Laffey, and Raymond Duvall, who defined themselves as "critical constructivists." Poststructuralists, and in particular David Campbell, one of the editors of a University of Minnesota Press series on international relations, took the criticism further: constructivists, he argued, have a tendency to become trapped in the protocols of empiricist social science at the expense of critical practice (Campbell 1998a, 225).

Reconsidering Constructivism

The first section of this book reconsiders constructivism in International Relations in light of its philosophical origins. In Chapter One, Friedrich Kratochwil explores the significance of the linguistic turn, especially as it relates to the boundary between International Relations and International Law. The linguistic turn signaled the transition from a positivist view of language as mirroring an objective reality, to language as constitutive of a social world. The former is a necessary point of departure for notions of hypotheses testing or the idea that theoretical statements can be compared with the world to see whether they correspond. This view of language is assumed by conventional constructivists who argue that constructivism is in essence no more than a method within the dominant nomological-deductive model of doing science (Checkel 1998).

From this perspective first order theory is an important end of constructivist practice, and constructivists should be concerned with developing theories that will provide an alternative to extant positivist theories. In Chapter Two, Knud Erik Jørgensen discusses the status of constructivism in relation to four different levels of scientific discourse, that is, philosophy, metatheory, first order theory and empirical research. He argues that constructivism can and should provide a foundation for theories of international relations—much as positivism does for mainstream theories—even though constructivism is not in and of itself a theory (see also Jørgensen 1997).

The implicit acceptance of a mirror view of language is a reflection of a tendency to ignore questions of language, in part out of a desire to distance constructivism from the discourse analysis of poststructuralists or to short circuit arguments from the mainstream that they are dealing "merely" with language. Maja Zehfuss, in Chapter Three, tackles the language question through a critical analysis of three leading constructivists in International Relations theory: Wendt, Onuf, and Kratochwil. She argues that Wendt's failure to deal with language represents a major weakness; by contrast, it is a major strength of Onuf and Kratochwil's constructivism that they do account for the role of language.

The distancing of conventional constructivists from more radical approaches, which have been marginalized by the mainstream, has also included analysts of gender. This is peculiar if one considers the important role that feminists have played in introducing questions about the social nature of identity, in contrast to prevailing assumptions about material determination. In Chapter Four, Birgit Locher and Elisabeth Prügl attempt to bridge this artificial chasm between constructivists and feminists. They analyze the constructivist pedigree of feminism and how constructivists and scholars of gender can further build on each other's work relating to issues of identity and institutions.

The distinction between constructivists, poststructuralists, and gender analysts disguises the extent to which all of these categories are constructivist in so far as they, in contrast to the more positivist approaches, assume that identities and interests are contingent and changeable. In Chapter Five, Mathias Albert examines the proliferation of constructivisms in International Relations through the lens of Niklas Luhmann's modern systems theory. He argues that attempts to distinguish 'ontological' constructivists from 'epistemological' constructivists reinforce a contrast that in fact evaporated with the linguistic turn. In contrast to constructivism's placement in a middle ground (Adler 1997) between positivism and poststructuralism, Albert argues that the different constructivisms are distinguished by varying degrees of reflexivity.

Constructivist Method and Practice

While the first section raised issues related to the philosophical origins of constructivism, the second section deepens the discussion to think about questions of method and application. Zehfuss ended her contribution, in Chapter Three, by asking what it would mean to do empirical research as a constructivist. This is taken up in Chapter Six, by K.M. Fierke, who explores a number of methodological inconsistencies in the conventional constructivist and poststructuralist positions, as a foundation for developing explicitly constructivist criteria for constructing "better" accounts of international politics.

The question of whether we should be trying to provide a better account, and if so how, has been a subject of controversy. In a special issue of the *Journal of European Public Policy* on Constructivism and European Integration (Christiansen, Jørgensen, and Wiener, 1999), Andrew Moravcsik (1999) criticized some of the contributors for claiming to test hypotheses, much in the tradition of positivism, yet failing to do so adequately (see also response from Risse and Wiener 1999).[3] In contrast to the poststructuralists, Fierke argues that the question of criteria is key; however, in contrast to the constructivists criticized by Moravcsik, these criteria necessarily differ from positivist criteria of hypothesis testing and falsification. The latter rely on a correspondence theory of truth, and it was precisely this claim that was undermined by the linguistic turn.

While conventional constructivists have tended to bend too far toward the methods of positivism, poststructuralists have been reluctant to take questions of method seriously. In Chapter Seven, Jennifer Milliken counters this conventional wisdom of poststructuralists, arguing that the development of sound methods of analysis should be taken seriously. While both Zehfuss and Fierke point to the key role of language in constructivist research, Milliken explores a particular method of discourse analysis and how it might be put to use in the analysis of actual cases.

The final three chapters explore some of the themes of the book in relation to specific subjects within International Relations. In Chapter Eight, Harald Müller demonstrates that constructivist methods and criteria are more useful than neo-utilitarian ones for the analysis of interstate negotiations. In Chapter Nine, Lars Lose looks to the international society literature and Habermas' theory of communicative action as a basis for developing a first order constructivist theory of diplomacy. In Chapter Ten, Ben Rosamond examines the relative absence of constructivist thought in the globalization literature and what this 'turn' might contribute to the analysis of global processes of integration and communication.

Finally, the book ends with commentaries on the text by two leading constructivists: Audie Klotz and Nicholas G. Onuf.

Notes

1. One indicator is the unusually large number of constructivists—in most cases with a critical bent—who have emigrated from North American to European Universities. These include Tarak Barkawi, David Campbell, Jeff Checkel, K.M. Fierke, Friedrich Kratochwil, Keith Krause, Mark Laffey, Lilly Ling, Jennifer Milliken, David Sylvan, R.B.J. Walker, Cindy Weber, Jutta Weldes, and Michael Williams. Several of these were granted Chairs while still in their thirties.

2. As Hacker (1996) elaborates, the linguistic turn actually began with the *Tractatus,* which added a mirror or picture view of language, to ideas, building on the tradition of metaphysics, that logical structures are properties of an objective world. The view that language provides labels for an objective reality was later adopted by the logical positivists of the Vienna Circle. The *Philosophical Investigations* turned this view of language on its head, demonstrating the social basis of language and meaning. In this respect,

Wittgentstein's early work introduced the importance of language and his later work re-placed the earlier mirror view of language with a constitutive one.

3. The Special Issue, including the debating section, has been published as Thomas Christiansen, Knud Erik Jørgensen, Antje Wiener eds., *The Social Construction of Europe* (London: Sage, 2001).

Part I
Reconsidering Constructivism

Constructivism as an Approach to Interdisciplinary Study

Friedrich V. Kratochwil

It is not surprising that the increasing specialization that characterizes our society and our understanding of the world leads to calls for "bridge building" and interdisciplinary studies. But if the progress of science consists in knowing more and more about less and less, then it becomes clear why scientific inquiry dissolves traditional, holistic worldviews, whether religious or philosophical. To that extent the success of science in providing us with warranted knowledge depends crucially on the disciplinary character and the often incompatible fundamental assumptions underlying the various disciplines. Thus, an economist is not helped in his efforts to build an economic theory by suggestions that the question of justice, or even of that of just price, should be included in economic analysis, even if philosophers and historians of economic thought might point to some interesting issues connected with such a suggestion.

It is perhaps for this reason that many attempts at interdisciplinary research are less based on a new perspective, or a new set of puzzles, than on the application of a new methodology taken from another field. While the fruitfulness of the latter strategy is, of course, an open question—to be appraised only by the substantive results that emerge from such a transfer— there is a danger. After all, the "law of the hammer" not only implies that we will find things to nail down—even if the problems we encounter would call for the use of a screw driver, or some other more suitable instrument; it also suggest that the need for other instruments, be they drill, plane, or even saw, will often be denied. As one representative of "rational choice" once humorously quipped, when the dangers of nailing down too many things were pointed out to him: "Listen, when you are equipped with my hammer, the whole world looks like a nail."

The upshot of these initial remarks is that a new fruitful cooperation between International Relations (IR) specialists and international lawyers cannot be based on the demand that lawyers measure up to the canon of "scientific" explanation, that they beef up on causes, and on independent, intervening and dependent variables; and that political scientist should learn how to argue a case. Given the lack of agreement as to the proper methods or theoretical standards in the field of international politics, and that even those who opt for a scientific explanation in the fashion of logical positivism do not measure up to their own canon, such a demand by social scientists seems hollow indeed.

In short, the positivist understanding of how "warranted knowledge" is produced might be more a problem than an answer when the puzzles significantly differ from those of classical physics, which provides the template for the orthodox understanding of science among IR specialists. Furthermore, since law clearly deals with "ought" statements and scientists restrict themselves to "is" statements, all in accordance with the presumably neutral and established epistemological principle articulated by Hume, lawyers have been quite successful in rebutting the imperialist claims of scientists. Thus, learning how to argue a case and reflecting on this practice prudentially in light of higher order principles seems to encompass all the necessary and appropriate tools for a lawyer.

When we ask ourselves why certain types of interdisciplinary investigation seem to have been successful, we notice that none of them was based on some form of disciplinary imperialism, be it methodological or substantive. Rather, these investigations started with a substantive problem that did not fit the standard disciplinary accounts. It seems, therefore, reasonable not to prejudice the possibilities of interdisciplinary work by simply adopting a particular methodology instead of starting with a specific substantive problem to which a variety of approaches and methodological orientations can contribute.

The last assertion might raise the objection that this is, indeed, a curious stance in a chapter that explicitly undertakes to outline the "constructivist" position. Given that constructivists are supposed to be "reflexivists,"[1] "idealists," etc., who are engaged in "understanding" rather than "explaining," and given that most of the discussion in political science to date has centered on methodological issues, the espoused position seems rather odd. However, it is odd only if we accept what needs to be proven in the first place, that is, that the issue can indeed be reduced to one of methodology. In other words, were constructivism only a methodological orientation, it could neither avoid the pitfalls of methodological imperialism, nor serve as a new basis for interdisciplinary research.

In short, I shall argue that constructivism is an approach, that is, it is characterized by certain "ontological" assumptions concerning human action, or "praxis" to use the classical concept, as well as by (some) methodological assumptions resulting from this commitment. I will have to show that the rather motley crew of researchers who was defined as the "out group" by the present day hegemonic discourse share some common ground, although not so much as is usually assumed. Furthermore, I will have to show the substantive contributions such an approach makes to the understanding of praxis. Finally, I want to flag some promising avenues for future research suggested by the constructivist approach.

In order to make good on these claims, my argument below takes the following steps. In section two I outline the "core position" of constructivism. Indeed most, if not all, of those who were designated "reflexivists" share these commitments. In this context it might come as a surprise to some readers that these positions come very close to the classical Aristotelian teachings as developed in his substantive treatises on ethics and politics, and in his methodological writings (*Rhetoric*, *Analytics*), as I shall show.

In the third section I focus on the "critical" element of the constructivist contribution. Here, I want to proceed by casting doubt on the appropriateness of the "anarchy problematique" and by a critical re-reading of E.H. Carr's classic *The Twenty Years' Crisis* (1964), which established IR as a field of study in its own right. Precisely because Carr's distinction between realism and utopianism has subsequently been so successful in buttressing certain substantive commitments, it gave rise to "realism" and "legalism" as disciplinary understandings informing international law and international politics. Deconstructing this disciplinary history is, therefore, one of the first steps towards a more fruitful theoretical inquiry into international politics and international law alike.

The fourth section is devoted to an exploration of the positive heuristics of constructivism, that is, to the elaboration of the argument that man is not only a language-endowed animal, but to the idea that meaning is use and that communication among a set of people is governed by conventions and criteria. This thought in turn provides a new set of puzzles, new avenues for research, and rather distinct methodological preferences for constructivists strongly influenced by ordinary language philosophy and pragmatism. In this context, I also shall briefly review some of the methodological issues, particularly that of interpretation, and hopefully lay to rest some of the more egregious errors that have plagued the discussion of *verstehen* and the allegedly antiscientific stance that adherents of interpretative approaches have taken. A short summary in the fifth section concludes the paper.

The Constructivist "Core"

One of the characteristics of a hegemonic discourse is that the classification of various existing approaches occurs on the basis of a simple exclusion. The "other" category usually gets filled with rather disparate alternatives that often differ from one another perhaps even more than from the normal case represented by the hegemonic position. While they certainly share a critical element vis à vis the orthodox teachings, they often vary fundamentally as to the respective substantive and methodological assumptions. If one wants to claim, therefore, that "constructivism" represents an identifiable approach, one has to point to some basic theoretically relevant assumptions and to a fuller articulation of their implications for the methods employed, as for example Nicholas Onuf (1989) has done in his study on rules and rule in international relations. These epistemological corollaries can, in turn, serve as a criterion for evaluating the heuristic power of the approach rather than simply indicate the points of disagreement with the hegemonic discourse.

Many of the contemporary controversies surrounding the constructivist approach have historical roots in nineteenth century debates concerning the epistemology of the *Kulturwissenschaften* as opposed to the natural sciences. There is no need to rehearse these arguments at length here, a controversy which goes back even further, that is, to Vico's and Herder's opposition to the Cartesian program. Nevertheless, we have to keep in mind that the most radical version of constructivism was formulated by the Chilean physiologist, Humberto Maturana during the last decades.[2] Maturana's *Biology of Cognition* (1970) soon became a type of cult book that engendered heated debate in the natural and social sciences, as well as in philosophy (epistemology), particularly on the continent. It attempted to integrate the results of three separate disciplines: cybernetics, psychology of language and of language acquisition, and biology.[3] Without wanting to enter into a discussion of the complexities of "autopoetic systems" (but see ch. 5 in this volume), we had better be aware that the standard positivist model of science has increasingly come under fire in the sciences themselves because of the recognition of the importance of recursiveness. But this means that arguments attacking the "reflexivist" program as unscientific are as problematic as the assertion that because of the reflexivity of human action, an incommensurably different epistemology is required for the *Kulturwissenschaften*.[4] Whether a consensus is emerging that reestablishes the "unity of science" position on a new basis remains to be seen.

For the more limited purposes of this paper, it seems to me that all constructivists in these fields base their research program on the assumption that the human world is not simply given and/or natural but that, on the contrary, the human world is one of artifice; that it is "constructed" through the actions of the actors themselves. While such a stance rules out any form of naive empiricism or naturalism, as well as most forms of structuralism, the specific thrust of constructivism consists in this fundamental assumption and its corollaries.

First, given that the human world is the result of "praxis," what are the methods and criteria appropriate for the elucidation of human action? In this context the question arises whether and what type of theory of action is possible, that is, whether the knowledge we obtain for examining actions will differ significantly in its form from that of nature. I do not want to rehearse the important philosophical issues of intentionality, of ascription, of determinism and free will, or even of the traditional mind/body problem that are relevant here. I only want to point out two things: a) that it seems possible to agree with the first substantive point above and still argue for an "empirically" based study of regularities based on some observationally oriented research program and/or the standard accounts of science exemplified in logical positivism; b) that the decision on this last point necessarily raises some hoary "metatheoretical" issues.

Second, given the problematic raised by corollary 1 b) above, constructivists at a minimum argue that the metatheoretical issue has to be treated as an "open question." At a maximum, they contend that specific elements for explicating actions require methodological tools for which the standard model of science is of little help because most accounts of action do not fit well with the standard version of causal imputation based on the model of antecedent causes. Even more important is the problem that what serves as an explanation for an action is extremely context dependent. Questions of "purposiveness" in action accounts (Aristotle's *hou heneka*), or explaining an action in terms of the attribution of responsibility, etc., require an "internal point of view," as Hart (1968) has put it aptly. They also raise the issue of the role of intersubjective understandings, which makes an appraisal of the action in question possible. In one of the key passages of his *Politics*, Aristotle (1962, Book 1, ch. 2, 28) addresses these issue with exemplary clarity:

> It follows that . . . man is by nature a political animal; it is in his nature to live in a state (polis). He who by his nature and not simply by ill luck has no city, no state is either too bad or too good, either sub-human or super human—sub-human like the war mad man condemned in Homer's words "having no family, no morals, no home"; for such a person is by his nature mad on war, he is a non-cooperator. . . . But it is not simply a matter of cooperation, for obviously man is a political animal in a sense in which a bee is not,

or any gregarious animal. Nature, as we say, does nothing without some purpose; and for the purpose of making man a political animal she has endowed him alone of the animals with the power of reasoned speech. Speech is something different from voice, which is possessed by other animals also, and used by them to express pain or pleasure; for the natural powers of some animals do indeed enable them both to feel pleasure and pain and to communicate these to each other. Speech, on the other hand, serves to indicate what is useful and what is harmful, and also what is right and what is wrong. For the real difference between man and other animals is that humans alone have the perception of good and evil, right and wrong, just and unjust. And it is the sharing of a common view in these matters that makes a household or a city.

Even if we no longer share with Aristotle the belief in the "purposes of nature," the above passage remains an argument of considerable force. Fundamental for his analysis is the distinction of man's sociality from that of "gregarious animals," which, in turn, is related to the opposition of "voice" and "speech." The latter pair is paralleled by the distinction between pain and pleasure, on the one hand, and the intersubjectively shared notions of "right" and "wrong," on the other hand. Each of these oppositional pairs deserves some brief comment.

The first distinction concerns the specific character of human sociality. While systems of gregarious animals are also open, self-reproducing systems, their reproduction is regulated by genetically coded specialization, as, for example, in the case of bees. However, the further we ascend the ladder of evolution, the lesser becomes the importance of genetically coded specializations when compared to "positions" or roles, as, for example, in a pack of wolves. Occupants of these positions have to be selected on the basis of individual properties, usually through fights. Nevertheless, in both types of biological systems the signaling systems are of decisive importance. Thus, the biologist Karl Ritter von Frisch has demonstrated how bees utilize such a system in order to communicate with other bees about food supplies, and Konrad Lorenz has, among other things, studied the signals in a pack of wolves. Wolves must not only recognize other members by scent and through howls when they hunt. But beyond that, the "signals" of a tightly coupled stimulus response system are necessary for the social order in the group. If two animals are fighting for positions in the pecking order, they must not kill each other; otherwise the proverbial Hobbesian state of *homo homini lupus* would obtain. As Lorenz has observed, the underdog inhibits the winning wolf from biting his throat by exposing his jugular and making himself vulnerable.

But the world disclosed by signals—Aristotle's "voice"—is quite different from that of speech, even if "pain or pleasure" are already part of it.

Different from the world of signals, which keeps their beings dependent on the here and now, speech not only frees humans from the immediacy of the situation—we can talk about a situation that has already passed, or has not even arisen—it also allows us to make choices rather than merely respond to a stimulus. With speech, an assessment of actions and events in terms of common values and through recollection and comparison becomes possible. We also can now "learn" not only from our own experiences, but—through our conceptual grasp—even from those of others. Thus, although the human world is one of artifice, it is not an idiosyncratic or subjective creation. Rather, it is through the intersubjectivity of language, and its shared meanings that social order is created. The person who does not participate in such a community constituted by common meanings, who utilizes a language of his own, is the person who lives in his own private world, that is, the "idiot" in the original sense of the term.

With these last remarks we have approached the point of the "linguistic turn," where some constructivists part company. Nevertheless, there is no doubt that the development of ordinary language philosophy has deeply influenced theory building in the social sciences and that this turn provides the decisive conceptual link between social theory and law. Since both disciplines are concerned with issues of praxis, the focus on rules serves not only as a natural bridge; it also liberates both disciplines from many of the conventional fetters. Epistemologically, the approach is critical of the dubious empiricism that has characterized some of work in the social sciences, but it also suggests a fecund alternative heuristic. It is the task of the next section to elaborate on the critical element of the approach, while the subsequent section will take up the issue of the positive heuristic in greater detail.

Points of Departure: the Role of Criticism

The emphasis on language and its conventional character has given the major impetus to the constructivist program in the postwar era. While the argument about the importance of conventions dates back to Hume, much of our standard understanding about the function of language was based, until recently, on a conception of language as a mirror of reality.[5] If language was supposed to be meaningful, it was so in virtue of its ability to depict accurately the things, actions, and properties of the "outer world." Thus, nouns stood for things, verbs for actions, and adjectives for properties. This led to rather complicated issues in the theory of meaning and reference, and the controversies surrounding the Frege/Russell and early Wittgensteinian attempts to resolve the mounting difficulties.

These problems need not concern us here. It is sufficient to point out that the decisive impulse for constructivism came from Wittgenstein's "linguistic turn" in his *Philosophical Investigations* (1953), where the problem of meaning found a new solution. The meaning of a term consisted no longer in its exact correspondence to an object in the "outer world" but in its use in speech. In other words, the later Wittgenstein directed our attention to the conventional and pragmatic character of language. Concepts meant something, not because they captured the ontological essences of "things"—the old Cartesian issue of how the "harmony" between the *res cogitans* and the *res extensa* was to be achieved had become problematic when God had been eliminated as the guarantor—but because they were used in a certain way among speakers who thereby communicated with one another. Gone was the attempt to approach the problem of truth and meaning via the construction of artificial, idealized languages, which supposedly told us how communication was possible. Instead of these formal calculi, everyday language, as elicited from competent speakers, served as the authoritative guide to determining the bounds of sense.

The emphasis on language as a "form of life" (not simply as a description of some mysterious things or properties attached to them in the outer world), the argument about family resemblances, and the idea that understanding proceeds via translation from one language to the other was crucial for the further development of constructivism. With it came some old baggage of the traditional distinctions between the *Kultur-* and *Naturwissenschaften*. But despite some similarities in the controversies, the emphasis on the pragmatic (rather than merely semantic) dimension of language, on "language games" and speech acts (rather than merely on interpretation) showed that one was not simply pouring old wine in new bottles. Besides, while the move from objects to their constitution was already part of the Kantian program, Kant rooted these constructions in the structure of human consciousness (*Bewußtsein überhaupt*). It was "consciousness in itself" that provided the trans-historically valid categorical framework within which our perceptions could be organized.

Part of the constructivist program consisted, therefore, in the demonstration that even these principles of construction were historically formed, and that as historical understandings, rather than neutral categories, they could no longer provide the ultimate foundations on which we were supposed to build our theories. In this sense, constructivism necessarily becomes a "critical theory" in the sense of Cox's categorization (Cox and Sinclair 1996, ch. 6). The careful analysis of the elements that constitute our disciplinary understandings is one of its important tasks. This analysis not only involves deconstruction and investigations into the archaeology of our present forms of knowledge.[6] In particular, all constructivists took issue with the unreflective adoption of the notion of anarchy as a starting point for analysis. Anarchy might only be what the states make of it, as Alexander Wendt (1992a) has reminded us, but the rigid dichotomy between hierarchy and anarchy might, indeed, be a blunt instrument for the analysis of order, even if we accept the concomitant conceptual distinction concerning the domestic, or international, arenas. After all, modern organization theory, and the study of various organizational forms and their advantages and liabilities, only became possible after our analysis was liberated from the anarchy-hierarchy dichotomy.[7] Since this dichotomy is not founded upon the nature of things, it is not surprising that it only recently came to represent the dominant tradition of political thought. After all, the old "republican" tradition had emphasized the need for various compound political organizations in order to safeguard against the twin dangers of anarchy and tyranny. This not only led to arguments about separation of powers and checks and balances; it also had several implications for international politics, as Daniel Deudney (1995) so nicely demonstrated in his essay on the American founding.

The impoverishment of the research agenda of structural realism is all the more astonishing as the original realists seem to have been well aware that the introduction of such simplifications—for the sake of methodological rigor—were not likely to lead to a fecund research program, but rather to sterility. True, the first modern realist manifesto, E.H. Carr's *The Twenty Years' Crisis* (1964) took the optimism of the Enlightenment, as well as the attempt to reform international relations fundamentally through the organization of a collective security system, severely to task. Carr was highly critical of the particular organizational answers to the—in his view—misdiagnosed problems, and he blamed a style of thought, that is utopianism, for this misdiagnosis. Nevertheless, he explicitly rejected the idea that within political discourse the bounds of sense coincided with those of "realism," since he believed that politics without utopia was impossible. Thus, he saw realism and utopianism as necessary conceptual opposites and interpreted them as cultural forms of high generality. They then served as the foundation for several further pairs of important oppositions in the analysis of political praxis (Carr 1964, ch. 1). In this context, the issue of determinism vs. free will, theory vs. practice, of intellectual vs. bureaucratic modes of problem solving, of left vs. right in the political spectrum, and of ethics vs. politics, make their appearance and are discussed against the background of the original division. Far from attempting to found a theory in which "realism" emerges as the guarantor of scientific status for the new field of international politics, Carr seems to be satisfied with this list of antinomies that characterize the political sphere.

While the criticism of inconsistency might be of lesser importance for the historian Carr, such criticism does have considerably more bite in the case of Morgenthau. Morgenthau (1967) not only wanted to establish the autonomy of the field of international politics, but to provide an objective and scientific theory that suggests that politics in general, and international politics in particular, consists in the pursuit of power. But in dealing with the analytic and historical complexities of political praxis, he relies on some logically incompatible assumptions. Smack against the principle of power maximization (Principle 1 of realism) stands the hortatory remarks about "prudence," about the need for policy which is "rational in view of its own *moral* and practical purposes" (Principle 2, emphasis added), for a "policy of compromise" to be pursued through the rules and maxims of classical diplomacy, rather than through a "crusade," or by chasing the "shadow of worthless rights," or even through the "surrender" of governmental policy to mass "public opinion" (ch. 32).

While we might want to dismiss such incoherence in the foundational assumptions of both "law" and "politics" as simple derailments of logic, and as the personal failings of particular theorists, I think there is more to the story than simple mistakes. Given some uncanny similarities in the flaws of the disciplinary understandings, a further question becomes relevant, that is, whether these mistakes are not also interconnected and, thereby, somehow codependent.[8] Could it be that there exists, despite the surface opposition, a symbiosis between the disciplinary understandings of "realism" in politics and the liberal vision in international law? A brief recapitulation of the history of both fields proves to be instructive.

On the surface, realism and international law became fully separate disciplines when, with the victory of realism in defining the boundaries of a new field, international politics attained the status of a subdiscipline of political science. It became increasingly difficult for a practitioner to cross disciplinary lines, and for the different cohorts to collaborate, even if representatives of both still populated an academic department. As already mentioned, the original division between utopia and reality proved to be a powerful aggregator of additional distinctions. The behavioral revolution contributed to it by superimposing the division of science and non-science (or humbug). Attempts to narrow the gap via the program of "policy science," and the New Haven approach to legal decision making, engendered, after some short lived enthusiasm, general scepticism in both camps. After all, one had reached the Humean fork, and there is no compelling proof that the is-ought distinction could be overcome by either logical or scientific means. Consequently, lawyers were supposed to take care of the "ought" side, and political scientists the "is" side of things.

Nevertheless, some attentive observers of these developments noticed the successive impoverishment of the puzzles that such disciplinary understandings engendered. Realism was elaborated in ever finer studies of deterrence and the causes of war, and legal analysis focused on increasingly arcane discussions of legal doctrine, if it was at all relevant to the legal enterprise, which became more and more concerned with "lawyering" and the professional side of law. While international lawyers had once served as the great conceptualizers of the international game, the newer breed of lawyers were less and less interested in the big picture, or in issues of jurisprudence, and more and more in the international dimension of corporate law, of taxation, of contract etc., and in doing the jobs for which law school as a professional school had trained its students. If there were theoretical pretensions at all, "what the law is" defined now what could be said and what made sense.

As Judith Shklar already noted in her study of *Legalism* (1964), and R.B.J. Walker later elaborated, both disciplines needed each other to generate their respective controversies. Like a couple with dovetailing neuroses, realists and legalists depended on each other for their own validation. The result was that an increasingly anemic conception of law was paralleled by an equally implausible conception of politics. There was either "justice," or there was "anarchy." Lawyers worried about the outlawing of war, about human rights, and often seemed to suggest that unless all politics was transformed into the paradigm of just action, no stabilization of expectations, which is crucial for social order, would occur, or even if it did, did not deserve the name of order. Political scientists, on the other hand, dealt with reality, that is they maintained, in the case of international politics, that "force" was no longer the *ultima ratio* of politics but the "first and foremost" one (Waltz 1979, 113). This change entailed such not too subtle shifts in meaning of crucial terms as, for example, from anarchy in the technical sense, defined as the absence of central institutions, to "anarchy" in the sense of the war of all against all.

Thus, an "entirely extravagant image of politics, as essentially a species of war," had emerged (Shklar 1964, 122), which, in turn, implied that rule following was a non-problem for the science of politics and was gladly handed over to the lawyers. They, in turn, worried largely how one would recognize rules as part of a system, or how different rules could be mapped in their logical relationships. At least the concept of law had to be kept separate from bargaining, or from other forms of unprincipled adjustments that are part of social life. Of course, there were always, on both sides, exceptions. But painting these developments with a broad brush does not mean that everything is thereby captured. And even if we consider the

above characterization to be a caricature, we should not forget that carica-
tures are not wrong in the sense that they depict something imaginary, or
nonexistent. Rather, their merit is to highlight and emphasize the most striking characteristic features while neglecting others.

As illuminating as these observations concerning the disciplinary histories and their symbiosis might be, constructivism as an approach would not
be able to provide a serious challenge to these disciplinary understandings
if its contribution were limited to criticism only. In the next section, therefore, I attempt to specify a set of positive heuristics for the study of international law and politics that seems to follow from a constructivist approach.

The Positive Heuristics of Constructivism

If Hobbes is truly the father of modern political theory, and if his "domestic
analogy" has been constitutive of our understanding of internal order and
external anarchy, then a constructivist perspective can throw considerable
light on the problem of order by taking the Hobbesian problematic as a
point of departure. After all, the prevailing interpretation of Hobbes only
became dominant in the late nineteenth century by displacing other readings
which emphasized the role of the "laws of nature" in the constitution of order, and the role of the sovereign, not only as the enforcer, but as the "fixer
of signs." In both interpretations, analysis shifts away from the preoccupation with force to the problem of common meanings.

In any case, contrary to the vulgar interpretation of his work, Hobbes
himself saw social order as dependent on expectations. Even if Hobbes
seems to have suggested that force is the most efficient way to structure
these expectations, it is not force pure and simple but the presumptions underlying action that are important. Furthermore, contrary to the conventional wisdom about Hobbes's naturalism, and the fundamental role of self-
preservation and "interest," Hobbes political psychology is far richer than
that of a standard utilitarian. In some of the most telling passages of his *Behemoth*, Hobbes (1990) deals with the power of imagination, prophecy, fan-
tasy and folly. Despite his alleged materialism, Hobbes pays particular attention to the role of ideas, even if he often dismisses them as conceptual
quibbles. He emphasizes the powerful force of "names" (e.g., whom to call
a "traitor," or to the success of sloganeering which identified "ship money"
with "tyranny"). Furthermore, he is well aware that norms such as, for example, traditional legitimacy, engender loyalty (towards the Stuarts), and
have to be overcome by appeals to other legitimizing sources. In short,
"equipped with imagination and language human beings respond to the pos-

sible as well as to the actual, to the dreaded or anticipated future as well as to the experienced present" (Holmes 1990, 122).

Thus, an entirely new picture of Hobbes emerges.[9] Quite contrary to the conventional interpretation of self-interest and fear as the foundations of Hobbes's political philosophy, a closer reading of the text reveals that neither fear nor interest were absolutes that could simply be presupposed as the unproblematic foundations upon which the edifice of the *Leviathan* could be erected. As a disciple of Bacon, and familiar with the code of honor and the concomitant folly of constantly endangering one's life by trying to win recognition, Hobbes knew very well that the fear of violent death was not simply the *summum malum* for the politically relevant actors. Modern interpretations of Hobbes, such as those of Holmes (1990) and Johnston (1986) have, therefore, suggested that Hobbes's writings should be seen as part of a rhetorical effort in promulgating new ideals, as the new way of life would lead to a more secure and peaceful political order. Hobbes was well aware that, far from designating natural conditions, interest and the fear of violent death are powerfully influenced by a variety of cultural factors. Even the basic fear of violent death is part of a historical tradition and of a political controversy in Hobbes's time.

The historical tradition concerns the power of "passions" that could easily undo any rational pursuit of self-interest and override even the desire for self-preservation.[10] As Sir Francis Bacon remarked, "There is no passion in the minds of man, so weak, but it Mates and Masters, the Feare of Death" (as quoted in Holmes 1990, 132). Hobbes himself reflected carefully on the impact of such passions as envy, revenge, love, honor, shame, pity, as they give rise to self-destructive courses of action. Even "boredom" leads, in the case of "seditious blockheads" (Hobbes 1990, 113) to the mindless overthrow of political order for the sole purpose of wanting change for the sake of change. Seen as a whole, the actions of people—and it is no accident that Hobbes's shrewdest remarks on the passions and motivations occur when he reflects on the history of the recent past—are characterized more by impulsiveness and compulsions, frenzy and hysteria than by the "rational" pursuit of interest, and their concomitant dilemmas. As Stephen Holmes (1990, 122–123) put it: "You cannot explain (much less foresee) social outcomes by reference to the postulate of universal self-interest. Human behavior, no matter how self-interested, remains unpredictable because it is guided partly by the assessment of the future—assessments that, in turn, result from irrational traits of the mind . . . not from the calculations of a rational maximizer."

When viewed from this perspective, the perhaps at first rather strange interpretation of the Leviathan as a "rhetorical" piece attains not only considerable force, it shows us also that interests are constructed, are part of a "discipline" in the double sense of the meaning, that is as understanding and as a type of regime in leading one's life. Even the emotions are not simply natural but part of a specific cultural milieu whose influence becomes visible only when we reflect upon the particular political tradition and contemporary controversies. Even in the case of the fear of violent death, Hobbes obviously does not refer to something that is unproblematically given. Rather he is engaged in a deeper political struggle concerning public authority and the effectiveness of the secular sanctions buttressing that political order. After all, St. Augustine had already remarked that it was eternal damnation, and not fear of violent death, that represents the *summum malum*. Such a belief, if accepted, tends, however, to weaken the deterrent power of secular punishment. In drawing clear lessons from the English Civil War, Hobbes argues that, "[a]s much as eternal torture is more terrible than death, so much [the people] would fear the clergy more than the King" (Hobbes 1990, 14–15).

Furthermore, part of the human predicament is not only that we have interests and preferences and might be able to rank various alternatives, but that we can also feel regret or pride in our preferences and rankings themselves. In other words, while we can be clear about our preferences, we also often know that they are problematic, and that we wished we had others. For example, while I might prefer smoking to abstention, I might very well wish, without calling such a wish irrational, that I had different desires. The preferences, upon which we act, are not simply unidimensional, to be treated as exogenously determined by the various "tastes," which are no longer susceptible to analysis. Rather, a theory that does not account for these metapreferences is a theory of "rational fools," as Amartya Sen (1978) once called it.

This idea of metapreferences indicates that humans as agents are "strong" evaluators, in Charles Taylor's (1989) parlance. Such evaluations are connected with our identities, which link emotions systematically to shared meanings expressed in a common language. This makes it possible for us to share, as Hume would have it, the feelings of approval and disapproval which are a basis of our moral assessments.

With these last remarks two problems are flagged: first, moral assessments do not involve purely cognitive issues. Second, our feelings or sentiments, which we usually consider to be purely personal or private, as well as separate from our rational faculties, are not simply idiosyncratic indications of pleasure and pain, as utilitarianism suggests. If our moral sense were nothing but the indication of private preferences of just how I or you separately as individuals "feel" about something, no such common appraisals would be possible. In a way, we have returned to one of our core arguments about constructivism: Aristotle's distinction between the indication of pain and pleasure, which belong to mere voice, and the sharing of common notions about the right and wrong, the base and the dignified, the just and unjust, characteristic of language. But each of these issues deserves further discussion.

First, how are emotions, or feelings, related to language, and how does such a perspective correct our standard account of motivation? After all, since Hume, reason has been seen as the "slave" of passion. But there is certainly something amiss in this argument. Not only is it on all fours with our experience; it is also logically faulty. If this account were correct, and "passion" were indeed always "complete" and sufficient for motivating action, then no actor could maximize the expected utility. The fact that I can somehow imagine other states of affairs, which promise stronger delights than the present desire, indicates that the classical utilitarian motivational account is untenable. Without my imagination, my conjuring up of alternatives, and without my ability to reason in calculating probabilities to counteract the Humean completeness of present passion, no delay of gratification could occur. While these objections pertain only to the classical rigid separation of reasons and passions, and to the need to introduce second order considerations into our calculus, we have thereby not yet shown the intersubjective character of our assessments, based on feelings of approbation and disapprobation.

This leads us to the second issue mentioned above: the public nature of appraisals. For this purpose, it is important to distinguish certain "language dependent feelings" from other emotions. While certain feelings seem to correspond to our standard notions of immediacy—as when we dread the person approaching us with a gun, or the fear that a overhanging rock might hit us while climbing—other feelings seem to be more complicated. Thus, in contrast to the experience of dread, feelings of remorse, shame, admiration, dignity, etc., have to do with who and what we are, that is they are dependent upon judgments and interpretations rather than on purely factual descriptions of situations. They are not objectively ascertainable because they can be explicated only in experience dependent terms. Their "imports" in Taylor's language, that is, the way a situation is of relevance to our purposes and aspirations, show a certain reflexivity. In other words, they involve "us" as persons with particular identities. This has important implications for the issue of their communicability and their role in intersubjective assessments. As Taylor (1985, 55) suggests:

> To feel shame is related to an import ascription....But to ascribe an import is
> to make a judgment about the way things are, which cannot simply be re-

duced to the way we feel about them, ... Beyond the question whether I feel ashamed is the question whether the situation is really shameful, whether I am rightly or wrongly, rationally or irrationally, ashamed.

But precisely because there is always the "further" question of why one feels the way one does, we usually can provide reasons for feelings of shame, dignity, or guilt. These feelings are not simply responses to situations, or indications of pain and pleasure in Aristotle's language. They are, in a way, language dependent in that the articulation of imports is intrinsic to the experience of the emotion. Thus, adopting a different formulation, expressing what happened in a situation in a different way, often changes how we feel about it. When I realize that my action was a response to provocation, my feelings of guilt are alleviated; when it becomes clear to me that my feelings of love were self-delusions, the emotions themselves—pathological cases excepted—change.

These observations are by no means of only academic interest. The problem of "motivated biases" is beginning only slowly to make inroads into cognitive psychology, despite the fact that we know how emotions distort the perceptions of participants in crisis situations. Even worse, one of the most telling criticisms of rational deterrence theory was provided by Lebow and Stein (1987, 1994) who systematically investigated crisis behavior. While it had been conventional wisdom during the 1960s that deterrence fails when either the threat is not communicated well or when the "commitment" of an actor is in doubt, Lebow and Stein's showed that many of the deductions of classical bargaining theory only hold when we assume that actors are opportunistically driven maximizers. Unfortunately, precisely the measures adopted to increase the effectiveness of deterrence will fail, however, if actors are motivated by fear. In the latter case, the only promising strategy was to talk them out of their increasing hostility by reassuring them rather than reinforcing their need to believe in an ever increasing hostile world. James Davis (1995) has shown how the need disposition that initiates escalatory cycles is crucially related to the initial assessment that the opponent must be invidious and hostile, since they attempted to deter "legitimate" demands.

The objections to such arguments are legion. After all, might not reasonable people fundamentally disagree what constitutes a legitimate demand, and was it not this indeterminacy in applying a concept to a situation, and being unable to objectively judge its fit or misfit that led to the elimination of such "fuzzy" concepts from the vocabulary of a science of politics? The point is not that even reasonable people disagree on what is legitimate—these concepts are "contestable," and they cannot be otherwise (Connolly 1983). But by eliminating them from our analysis for the sake of clarity, we not only fundamentally misunderstand politics, we also forego important insights that might provide us with some clues as to the decisive turning points in the escalation of conflicts. If we attempt to found a theory of politics on a neutral observational language, we have to realize that we cannot avoid even there the issue of interpreting and judging events. What counts as a case of deterrence, of self-defense or aggression, is not simply derived from pure observation, but is part of a complex appraisal. Furthermore, the claim that the fuzzy character of the concepts makes them useless obviously proves too much. There will be easy cases and there will be hard cases, but it does not follow that no agreement at all is possible. After all, there must be criteria for the use of a term that can be elucidated through analysis, even if we cannot neatly subsume everything under one particular concept.

Ultimately, the argument about fuzziness is similar to the argument about the uselessness of arguments in the normative sphere. Both are beholden to an epistemology that is based on a "mirror" image of language. Again, an implausible conclusion is reached: either concepts fit hand in glove, or they are useless. Experience tells us otherwise, as we do argue about these matters and the "fuzziness" seems crucial for persuasion. Thus, while these questions are open questions that cannot be answered in a straightforward fashion, there is little to be gained by forcing them in the Procrustean bed of a standard model of science. Such an attempt would be even less justified, if we could show that the old paradigm of science is based on rather problematic reconstruction of the development of one science, that is, physics, and if we could further show that the whole ideal of language as a precise mirror leads to internal contradictions and/or triviality. It is to these problems I want to turn now. Let us begin with the issue of whether "meaning" can be reduced to reference, as the mirror theory of language suggests.

The problem that the meaning of a sentence is not simply the sum of the correspondences of various words utilized in it can be illustrated. First, it is not the structure (syntax) alone that has decisive influence on the meaning of a sentence, there are also certain important modifiers such as connectives and conditionals—what does "although" correspond to?—that play a role in what a sentence means. Even worse for the mirror theory, as soon as certain modalities of actions are at issue, such as "may," "can," "cannot," etc., the traditional logic based on the dichotomy of "is"/"is not" is no longer adequate. Furthermore, the meaning of a sentence is often neither contained in the reference, nor the structure of the sentence. Rather, it is the context that determines the meaning entirely. For example, if someone calls and asks, "Is Jim there," and I answered, "Yes," and hang up, taking the caller's inquiry as a genuine question rather than a request, I obviously have not understood the meaning of the utterance. To that extent my response is "wrong" even if the answer is "right" (Jim is present). It is precisely by calling attention to the pragmatic dimension of our statements that constructivism makes its most important contribution to the analysis of communication, and, thereby, to a fuller understanding of social reality.

One brief remark on truth and triviality! One of the constitutive assumptions of the constructivist program is the view that to understand an action we not only need to take the actor's perspective, but that we also must be familiar with the intersubjective understandings that tell us something about the meaning of an act. For example, kicking a ball into a goal means something if I consider it in terms of the background conditions of a game of soccer. If I provide only an account in terms of the intentions of the actor, I might miss the mark as much as when I am satisfied with a description of the act in terms of the underlying physical laws. The meaning of "kicking a goal" is antecedent to the actor's intention and understandable only in terms of the "game" that is being played.

I have elaborated on those points by distinguishing between "observational," "intentional," and rule constituted "institutional facts" in another paper (Kratochwil 1988a). There is no need to rehearse those arguments once more at length. Here I want only to make one additional point. As the last example shows, what serves as an explanation is context dependent, that is, an event such as a kick is "explained" when it is understood as a move within a game. Consequently, attempts to specify the logical conditions of "scientific explanation" without considerations of context are problematic. If I claim to have explained the above action by providing, for example, the appropriate equations describing the physical actions of kicking, or even of kicking a ball, such an explanation would be virtually nonsensical, even if it is "true." Although such an account would provide a complete mathematical description of the action, its truth is at best trivial.

This argument has important implications for delineating the set of substantive problems that we investigate in the social sciences, as well as for the confidence we have in science to produce warranted knowledge in those cases. The case for the scientific approach hinges crucially on whether Hume was justified in dividing all sentences into "is" or "ought" statements, whereby true knowledge can only be gained about matters of fact (is-statements). Hume's "fork" not only seemed to exhaust all the possibilities, he also proved that there was also no way to bridge the logical chasm between the two. If I could now find a type of sentence that was meaningful but fitted neither category, my confidence in the initial division would have to be questioned, as the set no longer satisfied the criterion of exhaustiveness. Even worse, the concomitant presumption that meaningful discourses are only possible about factual statements, while norms and values are beyond rational inquiry, would at least have to be rethought and the entire epistemology and its ideals would seriously have to be reconsidered.

While the sufficiency of the Humean fork was accepted for two centuries, J.L. Austin's William James Lectures in 1955 at Harvard (1962; see also Searle 1969) demonstrated that there exists at least one more type of sentence that is meaningful but which fits neither of the two Humean sets. When I say, for example, in a marriage ceremony "I do," I neither describe something, nor do I state a value or engage in a normative debate. As a matter of fact, here the notion of a description breaks down entirely since I am "doing" something. But different from fishing, or painting, this "doing" does not exist aside from the utterance, and the meaning lies not in some descriptive accuracy or in some indication of preferences, but in the rule governed practice underlying the utterance.

The discovery of speech acts has had revolutionary implications not only for linguistic theory but also for social science in general. Since it can be shown that speech acts are incredibly numerous, ranging from demanding, to appointing, to apologizing, to asserting, and threatening, etc., its relevance for the analysis of social life is hardly controversial. The other point is that speech acts are constituted by norms, that is, they fit precisely the model of "institutional fact" elaborated above. Only within a practice governed by institutional rules will a certain utterance have a meaning. Finally, we can show that it is through such institutional arrangements that we, as members of a society, constantly bridge the gap between the "is" and the "ought," even if such a bridging does not occur on the basis of purely logical patterns of inference.

The advantage of such institutions like promise, or contract, or whatever, lies precisely in our ability to draw normative conclusions from (seemingly) factual premises, thus simplifying tremendously our normative dilemmas. If, for example, I claim that I do not owe Bill any money, and he can show that I signed a paper with the heading of "Contract" on it, then the conclusion that I have an obligation follows rather nicely from the fact that there was a contract. Even if the normative force of such a conclusion does not necessarily follow from a logical entailment but from the general (usually hidden) proposition that contracts are binding, it, nevertheless, becomes clear how arguments utilizing institutional rules in the major premise simplify our choices by providing trumps for arguments that can be beaten only with great difficulty.

From this sketchy account of the importance of institutions, and their rule based character, we can also see where and how interdisciplinary research would be useful. Obviously, since lawyers have been arguing about rules all their lives, their style of argument as well as their methodologies deserve far greater attention than they have received from social scientists. Beyond the legal argument, however, it also would be necessary to further investigate other types of discourses in which norms play a decisive role. In particular, logical formalizations of the inferences in persuasive arguments, and the nature of what serves as a "proof," deserve greater attention. Although constructivists as "reflexivists" have been charged with the neglect of "empirical tests" (Keohane 1988), the argument in this article should have demonstrated that this charge is rather scurrilous, given the fact that it is exactly the metatheoretical issue of what can count as a test that is usually the crucial issue. In this vein, the revival of practical reason in contemporary philosophical debates on the continent provides much food for thought. It could also improve considerably the rather sterile debate on the role of ideas that is limping along in IR journals.

Finally, as the research focus is on institutions, it should also be clear that such a program will involve us in historical as well as in comparative research. As the law student quickly learns in his class on property, there is not much sense in attempting to distill the concept of property out of various historical forms, or even to "test" a general concept across history in order to get at a valid generalization. The search for transhistorical laws is, of course, part of the methodology of logical positivism, and the attempt to reserve the label of explanation for nomological deductive explanations and their variations, is a clever gambit for preserving the high ground. But quite apart from the reasons expounded above, the search for general laws in the social science has been disappointing, as none has been discovered yet. The generalizations that we distill from extensive data analysis do not satisfy the logical requirements, which are required to endow the scientific explanation scheme proposed by Popper, or Hempel, with the necessary cogency.

Besides, even if such an enterprise were to yield some law-like regularity, it is not difficult to fathom that it would in all likelihood be trivial. The late William T. R. Fox once made the point more generally that things that are transhistorically valid are perhaps not the really interesting ones. Thus, it is hardly interesting—and cold comfort to boot—to know that someone drowned in a lake that is "on the average" only three feet deep. The moral of this example is clear: what we should be interested in for theoretical as well as for practical purposes is the "pocket" and "holes," rather than in the averages or generalities. This does not preclude historical research, but it does suggest that the image of history as storehouse of objective data is bound to court disaster. It is likely to result in poor social science, and even poorer historical work, as the phantasmagorical histories that have become the rage so amply demonstrate.[11] Not only do such allegedly historical excursions represent the worst type of "confirmatory" research, they also show a naiveté" in evaluating sources and assessing their importance that is rather breathtaking.

If history teaches us anything, then it is that we can no longer presume to get the story of how things really happened, as Ranke still could believe, or that history is able to instruct us through appropriate examples that have timeless validity. The idea that history can be a teacher, an idea that gave rise to pragmatic historiography from Thucydides to Machiavelli, until far into the nineteenth century, has been utterly discredited by modern historiography. To that extent, the radical historicity we encounter in modern historical works, where not only diachronic and synchronic levels of representation have ceased to coexist, where in tracing the development of a particular story we no longer encounter the already familiar, is somewhat unsettling. Gone are the familiar references to human nature, the paradigmatic examples of timeless greatness,[12] or the promise of salvation, even when pseudohistorical works suggest that we have reached the "end of history."

When the past has largely ceased "to throw light on the future"—as de Toqueville once so aptly put it when reflecting on the radical newness that accompanied the French Revolution—the search for historical understanding can only be understood from the vantage point of attempting to make sense of events which are unintelligible unless embedded in, and interpreted in, a narrative.[13] As the individual has to continuously rewrite his or her history, by relating within a biographical frame the events relating to the identity of the person, so the historical search is connected with the construction and reconstruction of collective meanings and with the identities of various actors, be they states, nations, classes, or marginalized groups.

Thus, in a way, we have reached again the point of our departure, that is, the artificiality of the human world, although this time from a different, not to say rather (post)modern perspective: the concern with identity. However, the further elaboration of this point will have to wait for another occasion.

Conclusion

This paper was concerned with an elaboration of the constructivist perspective for purposes of social inquiry. It attempted to achieve this through criticism as well as through an outline of the positive heuristics of the approach. In its critical part I argued that calls for interdisplinary work are as understandable as they are often misguided. Interdisciplinary work is not only difficult in a practical sense, it is conceptually challenging, as a new set of substantive puzzles has to be formulated. Otherwise, interdisciplinary research is hampered by incompatibilities, the colonizing tendencies of particular methodologies (remember "the law of the hammer"), or the elaboration of some vague similarities or high level abstractions that are, because of their generality, often quite uninformative.

As against this approach, I attempted to take a few steps back, and to develop the argument for an interdisciplinary research program through a common "core" of problems. This core is not only provided by the artificiality of the human world, it is also given by the language dependence of social order, exemplified by Aristotle's remarks about man as a political and language endowed animal. The constructivist move, however, was not only prepared by such classical understandings, but by the recognition of language as a rule governed activity. Precisely because both classical as well as "modern" (Cartesian) epistemology had insisted on the mirror quality of language, serious problems in the analysis of reference and meaning persisted. As soon as meaning was no longer determined merely by reference, but was seen as part of the structure of language itself, and of ongoing practices of actual speakers, a new paradigm emerged that could provide a common set of puzzles to both law and the social sciences.

In its more constructive part, I attempted to outline the positive heuristics of the constructivist program by focusing in greater detail on the context of ideas, interests, and identity, and their conceptual connections. This, in turn, made it necessary to discuss briefly the methodological implications of such an approach as it seems to be incompatible, not only with empiricism and logical positivism, but with any type of epistemology that proceeds from the crucial Humean distinction between "is" and "ought."

Against the Humean position that informs our scientific understanding, I argued that a research program based on more pragmatic grounds, which outflanks the Humean fork rather than denying its existence, is likely to be not only more fecund, but also better able to avoid the twin dangers of triviality and logical incoherence. Such a program opens up the research agenda through the inclusion of speech acts and institutions and also allows for the systematic inclusion of history, which we need for building better theories.

Notes

1. For a distinction along those lines see Robert Keohane (1988).
2. For a good introduction, see the volume of collected essays by Schmidt (1987).
3. For the psychological roots of constructivism, see von Glasersfeld (1987).
4. For a good discussion of these epistemological problems and debates, see Polkinghorne (1983).
5. For a critique of this conception, see Rorty (1979, 1991).
6. For an extensive treatment of Foucault's archeological approach, see Gutting (1989).

7. On this point and its implication for international organization, see my remarks in Kratochwil and Mansfield (1994, Preface). See also the growing literature on "governance." To name just a few, Young (1994); Ostrom (1990); Lake (1996).

8. For a more extensive discussion of this point, see Kratochwil (1998).

9. For a new interpretation of Hobbes that makes some of the same points, see Williams (1996).

10. For discussion, see Hirschman (1977); Mansbridge (1990), ch. 1; Holmes (1990b).

11. See, for example, Fischer (1992). For a critique, see Hall and Kratochwil (1993).

12. For an excellent analysis of the problem of "historicity" and its impact on historiography, see Koselleck (1985).

13. For the importance of the narrative form for an understanding of history, see Polkinghorne (1988).

2

Four Levels and a Discipline

Knud Erik Jørgensen

By engaging ourselves in debates on constructivism and related matters, we inevitably run the risk of forgetting or neglecting what obviously should remain the substance of International Relations (IR), namely international relations.[1] This risk notwithstanding, it is both necessary and useful to make a digression into the landscape of philosophical and metatheoretical issues, particularly because such a digression can help illuminate the strengths of constructivist approaches. It is necessary because IR otherwise may degenerate into a monoculture of rationalist methodologies, and useful because constructivism holds the promise of significantly increasing our knowledge about some of the key aspects of world politics.

Yet, there are many skeptics around and it would be downright foolish to deny that constructivism sometimes triggers very skeptical attitudes. Some raise, implicitly or explicitly, the good old existentialist question: does it exist?[2] And indeed, consulting textbooks on the philosophy of the social sciences often implies looking in vain for an entry "constructivism," meaning that, apparently, it is justified skepticism. A closer examination, however, reveals, as we shall see, that several variants exist. Even if the existence of constructivism is acknowledged, hurdles are not withering away, in part because acknowledgments typically have been followed by the apparently innocent but in reality inquisitorial question, "Have you ever read Sokal. . . ?"[3]

The aim of the present chapter is to provide an interpretation of constructivism. It is currently one of these topics which, to use Charles Taylor's words, "in some way is confused, incomplete, cloudy, seemingly con-

tradictory—in one way or another, unclear." According to Taylor, "[i]nter-
pretation, in the sense relevant to hermeneutics, is an attempt to make clear,
to make sense of an object of study" (1978, 156) that is "in some way confused," etc. Furthermore, the aim of the chapter is to demonstrate that some
of the skeptical attitudes among IR scholars are largely unfounded. In my
view, the best way to demonstrate how unfounded this criticism is, is to argue that constructivism is represented at four different levels of reasoning
and, furthermore, that at each level we can identify multiple versions of
constructivism. The four levels are: philosophy of science (including the
philosophy of the social sciences), metatheory, theory, and empirical analysis. This view implies necessarily that characterizing constructivism as
merely a theory or a metatheory is profoundly mistaken. A figure presenting these levels helps explain how the status of constructivism is different at
different levels.

philosophical constructivism
metatheoretical constructivism
constructivist theorizing
constructivist empirical research

FIGURE 1. CONSTRUCTIVISM AT FOUR LEVELS

At each level I present the key problematics and point out consequences for
research on international relations. I begin with the most abstract and philosophical issues, outlining some of the basic distinctions, problems, and
controversies that inevitably come with a particular constructivist stance—
for instance philosophical idealism vs. realism, the issue of multiple realities, etc. Later on, I move down the ladder of abstraction pointing out the
status of constructivism at less abstract levels. Approaching key problematics from this angle enables me to point out a number of misunderstandings
that characterize responses to the constructivist turn in international theory.
This approach is not necessarily in contradiction to the one proposed by
Finn Collin, who argues that "anyone proposing to embark on a serious examination of the social construction thesis as applied to social reality should
adhere closely to actual work in social science; which is to say that the
study should draw on the kinds of constructivist positions that have actually
been presented in the social science literature, rather than starting out from
vague philosophical speculation as to what a construction thesis might
amount to in this field" (1997, x).[4] I very much share the view that "vague
philosophical speculation" is to be avoided. What should not be avoided,
however, are the philosophical distinctions and categories.

Level One: Constructivism as a Philosophical Category

The simple truth is that at the most abstract level, constructivism has a status as a philosophical category comparable to philosophical realism, idealism, and solipsism. What does "philosophical" mean in this context? According to Shanyang Zhao, "Philosophical study is commonly defined as the study of ontological and epistemological issues concerning the nature of given phenomena and the way in which the nature of the phenomena comes to be known" (1991, 379). On the one hand, Zhao seems here to grossly reduce philosophy to merely some of its aspects. On the other hand, much depends on what is put into the categories of "ontology," "epistemology," and "given phenomena." In fact, many philosophical issues can be derived from questions concerning the nature of being and how we can know about those phenomena that are. According to a pragmatic understanding, Zhao employs his definition in order to make a distinction among philosophical study and meta-study, the latter being theories or reflections about theory, that is, having a markedly less abstract status than philosophical study. Though often conflated into one level and to some degree being connected, I agree with Zhao that it is very useful to keep philosophical and metatheoretical study separate.

It is unfortunate but true that it is seldom rewarding to rely solely on IR scholars when one wants to understand the substance and scope of these philosophical issues. IR scholars seldom have an interest in the issues *as such*, more often the interest is purely instrumental and thus somehow biased or unduly simplified. Among philosophers with a highly developed interest in the issues, we find, among others, John Searle (1995), Collin (1997), Heinz von Foerster et al. (1997), and Aron Ben-Ze'ev (1995). Searle's project is to outline what he calls "a general theory of the ontology of social facts and social institutions" (1995, *xii*). Three key concepts constitute the building blocks of Searle's theory: collective intentionality, the assignment by humans of functions to things, and constitutive rules. Put differently, Searle wants to provide a solid foundation of the social sciences. Collin's procedure is also to philosophically dissect arguments that have been heard around "constructivism." He makes a key distinction between "broad" and "narrow" arguments. In the category of broad arguments Collin includes ethnomethodology, cultural relativism, Peter Berger and Thomas Luckmann's version of the sociology of knowledge, and linguistic relativity. He claims that such arguments are philosophically untenable. In the category of narrow arguments Collin includes phenomenology, hermeneutics, the argument from the symbolic nature of social facts, and the argument from convention. Collin concludes that such arguments can be accepted.[5] Von Foerster et al. and Ben-Ze'ev are all primarily interested in the epistemological dimension of constructivism. I have found Ben-Ze'ev's (1995) explication of the philosophical realism/idealism and constructivism/non-constructivism controversies very helpful. Figure 2 summarizes the four possible positions.

	non-constructivism	*constructivism*
realism	naive realism	constructive realism
idealism	(naive idealism)	constructive idealism

FIGURE 2. PHILOSOPHY OF SCIENCE POSITIONS

Ben-Ze'ev explains the ontological and epistemological disputes:

> It is important not to confuse (as often occurs) the epistemological dispute of whether cognition is constructive with the ontological dispute about the independent existence of known objects. The epistemological dispute questions whether cognition (or knowledge) is loaded with the agents' contributions. The two positions on this issue may be termed "constructivism" and "non-constructivism" (or the "naive" paradigm). The ontological dispute questions whether the known objects exist independently of the knower. The two opposing positions with respect to this issue may be termed "realism" and "idealism." There appears to be three possible positions in this regard: (a) *naive realism*, according to which the agent has neither an epistemic nor an ontological influence on the known world; (b) *constructive realism*, according to which the agent has an epistemic but not an ontological influence, that is, knowledge is constructive in nature, but the existence of the world does not depend on the existence of an agent; (c) *constructive idealism*, according to which the agent has both an epistemic and an ontological influence on the known world. From a pure logical point of view, *naive idealism* represents still another possible position. But such a view, which assumes ontological but not epistemic dependency, is implausible, since ontological dependency is the stronger and seems to entail epistemic dependency. (1995, 50)

The three (or four) positions are very helpful in getting key claims about the philosophical status of constructivism right. As Figure 2 makes clear, Ben-Ze-ev's taxonomy suggests the existence of two most different constructivisms, one "realist" and the other "idealist." Clearly, the positions have different consequences for how research programs or research designs can be conceived of and, to some degree, also the possible impact of research depends on the options. Nevertheless, as will be demonstrated in more detail in sections below, communication lines between philosophical options and concrete research questions are long and winding.

One of the key issues concerns the question whether we have to choose among the positions described by Ben-Ze'ev. In the literature, we often meet an apparent dilemma between the two versions of constructivism. At one end of the spectrum, one finds the most radical variants of constructivism, rejecting philosophical realism. In the extreme solipsist understanding, reality only exists if we know about it. From the antirealist stance follows that, in the final analysis, everything is socially constructed. Furthermore, we contribute, through our scientific practice, to the construction of the reality we are investigating and describing. Whether deliberate or not, we may even change the social world that we are interested in understanding. At the other end of the spectrum, one finds versions of constructivism that do not reject philosophical realism but subscribe to a view the agent has an epistemic influence, that is, knowledge is constructive. But do we have to choose—categorically, once and for all—between the positions? Is it by necessity one or the other? It is indicative that social theorists such as Pierre Bourdieu (see Bourdieu and Wacquant, 1992), Anthony Giddens (1984) and Niklas Luhmann (1992) refuse to choose a fundamental position. Perhaps we are dealing with a false dilemma. It turns out that both positions are imaginable and if we want to, we can employ both.

It is clear that there is a notable difference between *The Social Construction of Reality* (Berger and Luckmann, 1966) and *The Construction of Social Reality* (Searle, 1995).[6] Social reality, after all, is nothing but in a sense, a subset of "reality" as such. One should assume (naively perhaps) that for social scientists this subset is of considerable interest. Hence, we have institutional facts and not merely brute facts. Hence, we have collective intentionality and not merely individual intentionality.[7] In other words, it is claimed that constructions of social reality exist and that features of social reality requires theories or concepts that are developed in order to help us understand social "world[s] of our making" (cf. Nicholas Onuf's famous book title, 1989). We can identify numerous social constructions "out there" in the social world and these constructions can be analyzed in a neutral, detached fashion.

Edward Said's book *Orientalism* can serve as an example. Said claims that "orientalism" is not what it appears to be. Rather, orientalism was constructed in western Europe through a long historical process. Said's aim is to unmask the cluster of constructions that goes under the name of orientalism, that is, collective perceptions of what it means to be "oriental" or what "orientals" basically are like (Said 1995, Afterword). Yet, by pointing out the constructedness of the term "oriental" as powerfully as he did, it seems to me that he also managed to reduce the power of the socially constructed image of orientalism, thus having an impact on one world of our making.

So far, certain issues about reality have been addressed. Yet issues about our representation of reality have not been. Among those that have not been addressed are the issues of objectivity and truth claims. I have avoided these issues because they are not necessarily part of the constructivist "package deal." To be sure, Searle's general theory of the ontology of social facts and social institutions *is* supplemented by a correspondence theory of truth, but it is perfectly possible to accept the first part of Searle's argument without accepting the second part.

It is no coincidence that what has been presented so far has nothing directly to do with IR. It comes from the fact that one of the multiple identities of constructivism is that of a philosophical category. All perspectives at the top level function the way the operating system of a computer does for theorizing at lower levels. Constructivism is empty as far as assumptions, propositions, or hypotheses about international relations are concerned.[8] The philosophers whom constructivists in IR refer to in order to explicate a given constructivist stance have probably never thought about international relations. In other words, IR scholars have to translate abstract philosophical categories and positions into their own theoretical reflections. How such translations are made is of course tricky business. In the present context it suffices to point out that a particular constructivist stance makes some IR theories possible, others less possible, and still others downright impossible. In Alexander Wendt and Raymond Duvall's succinct formulation: "Although social ontologies do not directly dictate the content of substantive theories, they do have conceptual and methodological consequences for how theorists approach those phenomena they seek to explain, and thus for the development of their theories" (1989, 55). A similar view is presented in the following statement: "social theories do not determine the content of our international theorizing, but they do structure the questions we ask about world politics and our approaches to answering these questions" (Wendt, 1992a, 422). In continuation of these observations, it seems to me that most constructivist IR theories have not yet been developed, invented, or (re)constructed. I return to this issue in the section on theory below.

If we investigate which philosophers IR scholars use as inspiration, it turns out to be a fairly long list, including among others, Berger and Luckmann, Searle, Taylor, Fred Dallmayr, Donald Campbell, Richard Rorty, Stephen Toulmin, Ronald Giere, Michael Gibbons, and several more.[9] Of course, being inspired by different names does not constitute a major problem—if it were not for the fact that the contents, approaches and meanings of constructivism *differ* considerably among these philosophers. In this sense, it would be more appropriate to talk about constructivisms—in the plural.

If constructivism's philosophical status is not realized from the beginning, debates will be likely to lead to severe misunderstandings. It simply does not make sense to compare substantive IR theories, say, neorealism and neoliberal institutionalism to constructivism.[10] If these constructs nevertheless are compared, one should be aware that at least two different levels of reasoning are represented, that is, those of philosophical position and of substantive IR theory. In my view, the proper procedure is comparison at similar levels of abstraction, that is, comparing constructivism to, say, materialism or rationalism, and, more specifically, constructivist theories of international institutions with materialist or rationalist theories of international institutions.

Level Two: Constructivism Going Metatheoretical

Leaving philosophical categories and issues behind, we arrive at the level of metatheory. According to Zhao, "metatheory in sociology is the study of extant sociological theory"; it "theorizes about theories of the social world" (1991, 378). In a similar fashion, metatheory in IR is the study of extant international theory. Zhao also explains that "If primary study is a long journey to an unfamiliar place, then meta-study involves frequent pauses for rest, identifying directions, revising travel plans, or even having second thoughts on the final destination" (1991, 381). To claim that IR is a discipline inhabited by scholars with a strong commitment to empirical research can hardly be an offense to anyone or, put differently, most IR scholars actually are on the long journey to an unfamiliar place. They see their mission as an endless struggle with data, and thus few have an interest in metatheory.

Yet the function of metatheory, as described by Zhao, makes it compulsory to consider the status of constructivism at the metatheoretical level. No matter whether constructivism is regarded as constituting a major reorientation vis à vis the subject matter (from a predominantly materialist ontology to a balance between material and ideational or social ontologies), or as also having consequences for epistemology, it does constitute a major turn in the discipline. The magnitude of the constructivist project—we assume here that there is only one—makes it pure nonsense to focus exclusively on theoretical or methodological matters, meaning in turn that for those with a highly developed interest in such things, constructivism cannot be anything but an unwelcome distraction if not a source of profound irritation. On the other hand, it is well known that generals with deep feelings for strategy do not like being charged for not delivering a doctrine on tactics.

However, apart from skeptical attitudes, reflections on constructivism's status at the metatheoretical level is also connected to certain other problems. It is a well publicized secret that the first generation of constructivist scholarship in IR has been rather inactive concerning development of theories. This relative absence of first order theorizing has the logical consequence that it is difficult but not impossible to examine the role of constructivism at the metatheoretical level. In the absence of theories, metatheorizing can easily go abstract, that is, focus on fairly abstract issues like the levels of analysis problem, the agent-structure problem or the like. In the following I attempt to demonstrate that this risk can be avoided. Five options are available.

First, the constructivist turn can be seen as one current within a huge exercise in developing metatheory of extant international theory. One of the major characteristics of the decade 1983-1993 was the veritable wave of metatheoretical criticism, directed particularly against neorealism. Constructivists, constituting an important current within the wave, have their specific reasons for cultivating constructivism, and often these reasons have to do with disappointment with existing theories or with what is seen as a bias concerning what is being researched and what is not. Thus, Friedrich Kratochwil and John Ruggie's (1986) criticism of inconsistencies in regime theory was accompanied with the development of a new philosophical footing for regime theory. Unfortunately, the (non)response of rationalist scholars has been to exorcise rather than refute this criticism (see Behnke, 1996). Ruggie has also helped to redefine our conception of structure and transformation.

> [H]ow we think about transformation fundamentally shapes what we look for; what we look for obviously has an effect on what we find; if we look for signs of transformation through the lenses of the conventional structural approach of our discipline we are unlikely to conclude that anything much is happening out there, but we cannot say whether or not that conclusion is correct because the epistemological biases of that approach are such that it is ill-equipped to detect signs of transformation. (1989, 32)

Likewise, the predominant materialist and utilitarian deep structures of mainstream IR theories have been criticized or complemented with an emphasis on the role of norms in international society by some, and an emphasis on the importance of identity by others. Norms, of course, have always constituted part of the English School's research agenda. Instead of a new turn in the discipline, it is more adequate to argue that American political science constructivists have discovered and picked up ideas that never were absent in European IR. Ronald Jepperson, Wendt, and Peter Katzenstein's

(1996) cautiously pragmatic approach is further evidence. In general, ideational factors and other social matters have been added to the research agenda. Robert Keohane's turn from explicit skepticism vis-à-vis the constructivist project (1988) to some degree of acceptance ten years later (1998) is in my view quite representative for most IR scholars.

Second, the constructivist turn is often associated with extant *social* theory. Given that at the philosophical and metatheoretical levels, constructivism is a cross-disciplinary category, it follows that insights reached from metatheoretical debates in other disciplines are often of considerable relevance for IR. It can therefore be very fruitful to examine constructivist research designs in other disciplines, compare, and maybe even import some of the insights into IR. Constructivism has a prominent presence in several disciplines, including sociology (Alfred Schütz [1967], Berger and Luckmann [1966], Giddens [1984], Luhmann [1997] and Bourdieu and Wacquant [1992]), history (Hayden White [1987]), psychology (Jean Piaget; see Glaserfeld [1995, 53–75]), and anthropology (Benedict Anderson [1983]).[11] Outstanding examples of constructivist metatheorizing are Wendt's (1987) and Onuf's (1989) work on structuration theory, that is, a second order social theory that contains no claims about international society but nevertheless presents interesting ideas concerning relations between agency, structure, and process—categories that are not at all unknown in or irrelevant to international studies.

Third, a metatheoretical issue *par excellence* concerns the question what *is* a theory? Both Raymond Aron (1967) and Martin Wight (1966) raised the issue. Since then many scholars seem to believe that the issue has been settled, arguing implicitly or explicitly that genuine IR theory *is* so and so. For others, it is a well known fact that answers to this question continue to differ considerably. They can refer to Reinhard Meyers (1990) who convincingly demonstrates that there are several types of theory in any social science discipline, and that different theories often serve different functions. A somewhat different differentiation between types of theory is provided by Chris Brown (1997,13) who makes a distinction between *explanatory, normative/prescriptive,* and *interpretative* theory.[12] Steve Smith (1995, 26–30) makes two crucial distinctions: between *constitutive* and *explanatory* theory, and between *foundationalist* and *anti-foundationalist* theory. In the present context, there is no reason to dig further into these different conceptions of theory. What remains, however, is to point out that certain philosophical and metatheoretical versions of constructivism are more compatible with or supportive of certain types of theory than of others. If, on the one hand, the hypothetico-deductive mode of theorizing is considered the only genuine mode, then it is easy to predict that constructivism will be regarded as a fairly weak and therefore unwarranted philosophical foundation. If, on the other hand, the pluralistic answer to the question "what is a theory?" is accepted, then it remains a considerable task to point out how various philosophical or metatheoretical versions of constructivism serve different types of theory differently. In other words, it remains a task to consider possible connections between different levels of abstraction.

A fourth metatheoretical issue concerns the strategy of reconstruction. Notably it deals with different objects for reconstruction. While Onuf (1989) wants to reconstruct the entire IR discipline, Timothy Dunne (1995, 1998) wants to reconstruct the international society tradition. While the strategy certainly promises a great deal for our understanding of the discipline and, in the case of the English School, provokes a reconsideration of both the old School and the genealogy of constructivism's presence in IR, there are nonetheless certain problems involved as well. One problem associated with the strategy of reconstruction is that we merely repeat and therefore reproduce previous debates in IR, though often in a different manner and in a different light. Thus, Jutta Weldes (1996, 1999) certainly has a point in her criticism of Wendt: his social theory of international politics *is* state-centric, yet does that imply that her plea for a bureaucratic politics model is always the better choice? Similarly, Jaeger (1996) claims that Wendt's state-centric approach demonstrates that he is a "realist constructivist." Possibly. However, I think his argument merely underlines my point (see below) that almost every possible paradigm in IR can be cast in a constructivist mode. If we want to, we can replay the great debates in IR, no matter whether there have been three, four or ten (Smith 1995). In my view, the problem of such a reconsideration is unavoidable, even desirable. What else is a discipline if not a set of key problematics?

It is possible to point out some examples of constructivist IR metatheorizing. Even if it is true that only few constructivist theories have been developed, a certain constructivist research practice has been developed, and this practice has in turn become the object of "metastudy." The wave of synthesizing reviews published during the late 1990s clearly constitutes a first wave of constructivist metastudy (Adler 1997, Checkel 1998, Hopf 1998, Ruggie 1998, and this volume). Thus, Jeffrey Checkel (1998) holds that structural approaches have been overemphasized in constructivist research in IR and he makes a plea for bringing agency back in; Ruggie has criticized the "barefoot empiricist manner" (1998, 18) in which constructivism has been developed, and Wendt (1994, 384) has cautioned against tendencies towards an "over-socialized" approach.

As I have attempted to demonstrate in this section, constructivism has an important role to play at the metatheoretical level. Thus, constructivists

played a prominent role in kicking off the Third Debate and thus contributed to opening what tended to be a rather closed research agenda; they
have been very active in importing insights from the field of social theory
to IR; they have reconsidered the concept of theory; and they have begun to
critically evaluate their own research practice. That is by no means a meager result of work during a decade. Constructivism's successful intervention
in IR has been noted with interest and subsequently awarded "recognition"
by an American troika of theorists with agenda-setting capabilities (Katzenstein, Keohane, and Krasner 1998). Despite this remarkable recognition by
three eminent scholars, there is an unspoken feeling that more has to come
and that the "more" in question has to do with theory building.

Level Three: Constructivist Theorizing

Leaving the philosophical and metatheoretical levels behind, or, rather,
changing focus, we arrive at the theoretical level and have thus reached a
territory that is more or less familiar to most IR scholars. It is of utmost importance to realize that at this level constructivism acquires a role that is
significantly different from the one it has at the philosophical and metatheoretical levels. To be sure, it still provides the backbone of various theories
but, crucially, it retreats somewhat into the background. Put differently, it
functions behind the scenes and may stop to flag the term "constructivism."
Why? After all, Kenneth Waltz (1979) did not present his theory as a "positivist theory of international politics," and Keohane (1989) did not market
his theory as a "rationalist, utilitarian theory of neoliberal institutionalism."
The categories "positivism," "rationalism," and "utilitarianism" are nevertheless features that provide Waltz's and Keohane's theories with a deep
philosophical and metatheoretical structure. And it is also noteworthy that
Joseph Nye's (1988) metatheoretical analysis pointed to the neo-neo synthesis, even if, at the theoretical level, in some quarters the neo-neo debate
continued (Baldwin 1993).

Paradigms. Before we come to first order theories proper, it is illuminating to pause at paradigms, being aggregates of international theory. I claim
that every possible paradigm in IR can be cast in constructivist terms, to a
degree. If we, for the sake of the argument, take the three paradigms presented in Paul Viotti and Mark Kauppi's popular textbook—that is, realism,
pluralism, and globalism—it follows that each of these paradigms can be
cast in a constructivist mode. Audie Klotz and Cecelia Lynch (1998) rightly
suggest that "there can be realist and liberal variants of constructivism,
since it offers an ontological and epistemological approach, rather than an
explanatory theory of international politics." Similarly, there is nothing in

constructivism that, in the words of Kubálková, Onuf, and Kowert, "mandates an "emancipatory" or "critical" politics" (1998, 4). As they explicate, "[c]ontructivism is normative in the sense that it takes normative phenomena—rules—as the foundation of society but Onuf's claim that rules always result in a condition of rule has earned him criticism from scholars who believe that a post-positivist position is necessarily 'critical'" (1998, 19-20).[13] Thus, even if constructivism is more open—compared to various a-historical approaches—to aspects of change or transformation in world politics, it does not follow that the change in question necessarily will be progressive, that is, constitute a change for the better.

This said, it is a sociology of science fact that for some reason liberal scholars have been more active than realists and globalists in promoting the constructivist turn. Wendt has rightly "argued that proponents of strong liberalism and the constructivists can and should join forces in contributing to a process oriented international theory . . . [they] have much to learn from each other if they can come to see this through the smoke and heat of epistemology" (1992a, 425). While I see no reason not to agree with Wendt on this issue, I do note that numerous aspects of realist theorizing also are compatible with constructivism, meaning that realists and constructivists have much to learn from each other if they can come to see that after constructivists' strategic strike on neorealism during the 1980s. It may be difficult to give Waltz's (1979) systemic theory a constructivist twist (see, however, Wendt 1999), but Stephen Walt's (1987) realist balance of threats theory is a likely candidate. Furthermore, the realist notion of security complexes has been given a constructivist twist, even by its own inventors (compare Buzan 1991 to Buzan, Waever, and de Wilde 1998). Finally, the classic realist notion of security dilemmas, developed by John Herz, is a prime candidate element of a constructivist realist theory of international politics. In this context, Ole Waever's (1995) conceptualization of processes of securitization are likely to empower a new conceptual package about security dilemmas. Katzenstein (1996) has convincingly demonstrated that constructivism and the study of norms is a very fruitful point of departure in security studies. What more can a modern realist wish for? Neither John Mearsheimer (1995) nor Robert Jervis (1998) seem to be aware of or interested in this potential for a reformulation of realism. Instead they see liberal arguments in constructivist clothes and because of the liberal contents they argue against the constructivist form. I would welcome it if constructivists would take the lead in examining the thinking present in research, rather than contributing to "tribal" theoretical warfare (for a good beginning, see Jepperson, Wendt, and Katzenstein 1996; on the current unflattering discursive climate in IR, see also Holsti 1996).

That IR paradigms can be cast in a constructivist mode ought not to come as a surprise. After all, it is a well known fact that nothing in the behavioral revolution determined either political realism or idealism. As pointed out by Vasquez (1983), many behavioralists reproduced the key assumptions of realism during the behavioral revolution. Along with this reproduction of realist assumptions within a new epistemological framework, it is worth noting also that world society theorists like John Burton and peace researchers—from David Singer to the Scandinavians—found behavioralism attractive as a weapon against what they perceived to be traditionalism in IR.

First Order Theory

Turning now from paradigms to first order theories, that is, theories about international phenomena, we reach first the disappointing but nevertheless true observation that, currently, constructivist research in IR has an unfortunate deficit when it comes to theory building. Constructivism as such is theoretically empty (for a similar view, see Checkel 1998, Risse 1998, Ruggie 1998b). In other words, constructivism does not, by itself, tell us anything, whatsoever, about international events, developments or any other international phenomena. Martha Finnemore explicitly declares that "[i]t is precisely the failure of Wendt and others to investigate the substantive content of social structures and marry constructivism with substantive theory that motivates my book" (1996a, 47). By cultivating this idea, Finnemore has proven to be a trendsetter by providing a bridge between first and second generation constructivists.

Why is it that IR scholars with constructivist leanings have been so predominantly a-theoretical? One possible answer is that theory building is not really the name of the game. Reconceptualization is. Weldes (1999), Kratochwil (1982), Ruggie (1993), and Antje Wiener (1998), among others, engage in reconceptualization of key concepts like "national interest," "state," "sovereignty," and "citizenship." Because concepts make part of the world of our making, it is a tempting approach. Indeed, the first thing first year Political Science students should learn to understand is the nature of "essentially contested concepts." Additionally, the strategy of reconstruction has the clear advantage that we do not have to begin entirely from scratch. Among other things, reconceptualization implies that well known, neglected, or apparently irrelevant materials can be looked at from a different perspective and sometimes gain new relevance for our attempts at making sense of world politics. Obviously, the strategy of reconceptualization does not allow a strict separation between the world out there and the world of our making. The strategy is, simultaneously, part of the process of understanding world politics, and a precondition for understanding world politics differently from previous understandings. Such a dual function is precisely what disturbs scholars who believe that their concepts, theories, and research designs are more innocent or neutral vis à vis the subject matter of their research than is often the case. Though reconceptualization is a necessary part of theory building, it cannot substitute theory building.

Since constructivism is not a theory, what sense does it make to continue investigating the status of constructivism at the theoretical level? The answer is, put simply, that theories informed by constructivism are absolutely feasible. Such a solution, however, opens a veritable Pandora's Box of new problems. How should theory building be conducted? If not all types of theory are feasible, which type of theory *is* feasible? Do we proceed in a deductive or inductive mode, or does the philosophical and metatheoretical underpinnings of constructivism transcend this distinction?

When viewed in relation to the different philosophical and metatheoretical statuses of constructivism, one should expect that each specific "constructivism" potentially contains *multiple* substantive theories, each characterized by its specific strongholds and limitations. Remembering here the differentiation of types of theory implies that generic calls for theory building are less than helpful. In this respect Checkel's (1998) conception of constructivist theory building turns out to be very narrowly conceived—with its strong emphasis on microfoundations, causal mechanisms, and standard midrange theory. Question driven research cannot and should not always end up with theorizing in the explanatory, causal, midrange mode. Thus Finnemore correctly points out that while different groups of scholars focus on social structures, "there has been little published discussion among these groups" (1996a, 21). This fact is really to be deplored since it is such debates that potentially would trigger substantive constructivist theorizing.

In principle, first order theorizing can follow two major avenues. The first option is to examine constructivism and existing IR theory, in some cases leading to a reformulation of existing theories. This is the approach chosen by Kratochwil and Ruggie (1986) in their path breaking reformulation of regime theory. A similar approach is adopted by Wendt when he transforms an existing (material) systemic theory into a social systemic theory (1994, 1995, 1999). Also Jutta Weldes (1996, 1999) adopts a reformulation strategy in her attempt to rethink the bureaucratic politics model.

The second option is to employ various constructivist "generic" theories—that is, theories like J.L. Austin (1962) and Searle's (1969) theory of speech acts, Jürgen Habermas's (1981) theory of communicative action,[14] and Luhmann's (1997) version of modern systems theory,[15] sociological interactionist theory, and many more theories of a similar stature—in the development of analytical frameworks. For instance, studies on diplomacy can incorporate notions of communication, signaling, communicative action, and identity and interest formation. Surely such notions have for a long time been present in studies of diplomacy but by employing constructivist perspectives, they can be given a novel and elaborated theoretical grounding.

In general, it makes sense to encourage constructivist scholars to become more active in "thinking theory thoroughly," to borrow James Rosenau and Mary Durfee's (1995) book title, but in this context not their positivism. So far we have not been able to really consider situations in which similar theories result in dissimilar conclusions. Presumably because we have seen relatively few constructivist studies of the same topic, meaning that we do not have a critical mass of studies on *specific* topics. So far, constructivist research has been characterized by a pronounced "go West" atmosphere in which virgin territory has been conquered step by step. An example suggests that this situation may soon change. Thus, British discourses on Europe have been studied by both Henrik Larsen (1997) and Thomas Diez (1999), both employing a linguistic discourse analysis yet arriving at different conclusions. This is how great debates are likely to begin, precisely because we can begin to compare propositions, scope conditions, and methods, and the like, without having to demarcate one's approach in relation to perspectives which are light years away.

So far, the role of constructivism at the theoretical level has not been prominent. Thus, instead of accounting for prominence, I had first to emphasize the obvious: Constructivism is not a theory. Expectations to the contrary are based on severe misunderstandings and can only lead to unnecessary deep frustrations. I also pointed out that constructivism is largely neutral vis-à-vis dominant paradigms in IR, and that wishful thinking among some realists equating constructivism with naive peaceloving democrats is largely misplaced. Furthermore, I noted that reconceptualization is a necessary but not sufficient part of the constructivist game. Finally, I pointed-ed out that some first order theorizing has been delivered but also that more should be developed, most likely as a result of competition between, complementarity or addition of other first order theories, constructivist or not.

Level Four: Constructivism and Empirical Research

When constructivism was launched (or relaunched), it was easy to dismiss it with reference to its meager empirical publishing record. Put differently, even if several points of constructivists' metatheoretical critique of extant international theory were considered legitimate, constructivism could not be expected to have a future unless it delivered empirical studies (Keohane 1988, Goldstein and Keohane 1993; see also Jørgensen 1997). Constructivists have delivered ever since, making it a downright impossible task to summarize studies published during the last decade of the twentieth century. Instead, I am going to address three issues having crucial relevance for extant and future empirical studies.

Many would regard the notion "applied constructivism" as a contradiction in terms, and it is. It is not possible to apply constructivism as such. It is possible, however, to apply a given constructivist substantive theory. The problem is rather, as we have just seen, that only relatively few constructivist substantive theories have been developed. The relative absence of such theories implies that we have a missing link between, on the one hand, our sophisticated philosophical, metatheoretical, and conceptual constructs and, on the other hand, a form of empirical analysis that transcends empiricism. This is an adequate description of the state of the (constructivist) art, and it is widely agreed on among leading constructivists. Thus, to present but one example, Finnemore argues that "[d]emonstrating the utility of a constructivist approach vis-à-vis dominant, interest based paradigms is the first step in establishing a constructivist research program. The second step will be to elaborate that set of normative arguments in ways that provide more, and more easily testable, hypotheses and research questions for the future. Simply claiming that 'norms matter' is not enough for constructivists. They must provide substantive arguments about which norms matter as well as how, where and why they matter" (1996a,130). The same goes for research on discourse (see Milliken's chapter in this volume) and identity.

Furthermore, it follows from the constructivist theoretical deficit that procedures for empirical research often seem to have been some sort of deduction from—or bridgebuilding between—philosophy of science positions and real world empirical problematics, potentially leading to the same sort of problems as when Giddens's structuration theory is applied without theoretical mediation, specification, or methodological operationalization.[16]

Finally, it is telling that, on the one hand, Jepperson, Wendt, and Katzenstein (1996) write about "methodological non-issues," arguing that a constructivist stance does not disturb the standard operating procedures of a "normal science." Besides a shift in the social ontology of research, scholars are invited to use the same procedures they did last year. On the other hand, Kratochwil and Ruggie (1986; see also Ruggie 1998b), among others, argue that just as ontology rules over epistemology, theory rules over method, meaning that not any method goes with any theory. Finnemore puts it very succinctly: "method should serve theory, not the reverse"

(1996a, 26). The question then remains which criteria, standards, and conventions exist for constructivist empirical research? Some criteria, which some assumed to be positivist, seem, in reality, to be rather accepted standards.[17]

Conclusion and Perspectives

Constructivism in IR is alive and doing well. An increasing number of articles and books are being published. It seems to be a safe prediction that constructivism is now in the hands of a second generation of constructivist scholars, a generation that presumably will be less confused, less preoccupied with strategic moves vis-à-vis competing perspectives, and less motivated to do everything at once. Instead, constructivist scholarship will be more diverse—in the sense of acknowledging and cultivating different currents of constructivism, more oriented towards theory building, and yet somehow more modest in its ambitions. Until we reach a mature constructivism in IR, it is satisfying to note that our knowledge of international relations has been significantly improved by employment of constructivism, and that IR, as a discipline, has become a more pluralistic enterprise.

Indeed, the introduction of constructivism constitutes nothing less than a major turning point in the discipline. Though certain similarities can be detected with the classical approach, constructivist research is based on philosophical and metatheoretical categories that are radically different from a considerable part of previous IR research. The approach opens a door to research programs unthinkable within positivist inspired research. Furthermore, the constructivist research programs under construction, so to speak, will be closer to the substance of international relations. The risk referred to at the beginning of this chapter—the risk of forgetting about international relations—has thus turned out to be not a risk but an advantage for our improved understanding of world politics. Constructivism ought therefore to become full part of the standard repertoire of a science which does not hesitate to use "social" as an adjective in front of the noun "science."

Notes

.1. For helpful comments on a previous version of this chapter, I am grateful to K.M. Fierke, Georg Sørensen, and Colin Wight.

2. Among prominent international theorists, Steve Smith has consistently argued that constructivism is an unfeasible position, see Smith (1997, 1999a, 2000).

3. The Sokal affair began with the publication of a phoney article in the journal *Social Text* (Sokal, 1996). The publication of *Intellectual Impostures* (see Sokal and Bricmont, 1998) escalated the affair into a transatlantic squabble. In my view, Sokal's

charges of anti-realism are irrelevant for most versions of constructivisms that I discuss in the present chapter.

4. Collin's *Social Reality* (1997) is to be recommended for its discussion of linkages between philosophy and the social sciences.

5. Were Collin's thorough critique of constructivist arguments to be accepted in full, it would have severe ramifications for the positions of several IR constructivist scholars. Thus, Collin does not find Berger and Luckmann's argument convincing, yet precisely that argument plays a crucial role in one of Alexander Wendt's articles (1992). Similarly, Searle's criticism of Humberto Maturana and Francisco Varela's anti-realism has implications, if accepted, for the contribution Niklas Luhmann's modern systems theory can provide for international theory (see Albert's contribution to this volume).

6. While the titles certainly are Berger and Luckmann, and Searle's respectively, it does not follow that they represent the position indicated by their titles.

7. The fact that there are different types of facts is far from unknown in international theory; see for instance Kratochwil (1989, 21–28).

8. See Finnemore (1996b, 27). Constructivism shares this feature with other categories in the same philosophical league, such as philosophical realism, positivism (which, it should be noted, also exists in various versions), and scientific realism. For writings on philosophical realism, see Searle (1995); on positivism, see Smith (1996) and King, Keohane, and Verba (1994); on scientific realism, see Bhaskar (1979), Dessler (1989).

9. Rarely do so-called science constructivists like Harry M. Collins, David Bloor, Barry Barnes, Bruno Latour, Michel Callon, Karin Knorr-Cetina, or Steve Fuller serve as a source of inspiration for IR scholars. On the science constructivists, see Collin (1997).

10. Consequently, at the philosophical level, constructivism is completely immune to frequent charges of representing political idealism, a phenomenon that can be coupled easily with all philosophical categories.

11. The field of sociology of science constructivism constitutes a specific area within sociological studies, including Berger and Luckmann (1966), Steier (1991), and Krohn, Küppers, and Nowotny (1990).

12. See also Mervyn Frost (1996) who has developed what he calls a constitutive theory.

13. A similar view is presented by Martha Finnemore who argues that "there is nothing inherently 'good' about social norms. Social norms can prescribe ethically reprehensible behavior, slavery, violence, intolerance—as well as charity and kindness—" (1996a, 32). In this context it is of course tempting to note that Finnemore (1996b) regards violence as "ethically reprehensible behavior." For the view that interpretive approaches ought be "progressive" or "emancipatory," see Neufeld (1993).

14. For assessments of the theory of communicative action, see Outhwaite (1994, 109–120); Honneth and Joas (1991); Dallmayr (1987, 73–100). For persuasive attempts to link Jürgen Habermas's theory with studies of international relations, see chapters by Harald Müller and Lars Lose in this volume.

15. See Albert's introduction to modern systems theory in this volume.

16. On the problems of applying Giddens's structuration theory to empirical research, see Gregson (1989); also see Giddens (1984).

17. Cf. Berger's remark: "I don't see why an insistence on the falsifiability of sociological propositions makes one a "Popperite." I rather think that, while the term is Popper's, the methodological principle is one accepted by the vast majority of social scientists" (Berger 1986, 233).

3

Constructivisms in International Relations: Wendt, Onuf, and Kratochwil

Maja Zehfuss

"Social construction," a term used by Peter Berger and Thomas Luckmann (1966), has become a buzzword in the discipline of International Relations (IR).[1] Some, but by no means all, who claim that social reality is constructed, call their work "constructivist." The growing interest in this approach is reflected in the increasing number of articles that attempt to locate, evaluate, or define constructivism (see Adler 1997; Checkel 1998; Hopf 1998; Price and Reus-Smit 1998; Walt 1998; Ruggie 1998b). In a move that seems at odds with the ongoing debate about what constructivism really "is," this chapter engages with the claims of three scholars who have, in more or less detail, put forward explicit constructivist approaches to the study of international relations: Alexander Wendt, Nicholas Onuf, and Friedrich Kratochwil and explores the differences between them.

Although these three scholars reference each other, and Kratochwil and Wendt claim to use the term "constructivist" in Onuf's sense, their theories differ in important ways. Talking about "constructivism" in IR as a homogenous concept, therefore, obscures the variety of approaches that come under this label. In particular, it is unhelpful to equate constructivism in IR with Wendt's approach and now with the contributions to the Katzenstein book (1996). This chapter argues that there is more than one constructivism in IR. It provides an introduction to the approaches of the three scholars. A closer look at their conceptualizations of intersubjectivity shows that Onuf's and Kratochwil's approaches are fundamentally different from Wendt's. For them language is central for the analysis of politics. This has important implications with respect to issues of epistemology and normativity.

Wendt

With his article, "Anarchy Is What States Make of It," Wendt (1992a) popularized constructivism—first introduced by Onuf—within IR (Smith 1997, 183; Waever 1997, 4).[2] In another article, Wendt (1992b, 183) neatly summarizes the gist of his argument:

> A world in which identities and interests are learned and sustained by intersubjectively grounded practice, by what states think and do, is one in which "anarchy is what states make of it." States may have made that system a competitive, self-help one in the past, but by the same token they might "unmake" those dynamics in the future.

This claim follows from recognizing the significance of structuration theory and scientific realism for the analysis of international relations.[3] Wendt therefore approaches constructivism from a social theory perspective. He uses notions from sociology and social psychology. His approach revolves around the problematic of identity. Our ideas about ourselves and our environment shape our interactions and are shaped by our interactions; thereby they create social reality.

That Wendt's thinking developed from an éngagement with Anthony Giddens's structuration theory is significant in two respects. Firstly, Wendt wants to follow Giddens with respect to the resolution of the agent-structure problem; that is, he takes agents and structures as mutually constitutive entities with equal ontological status (Wendt 1987, 339). Insofar as this implies that social reality is created only through social action, he hints at his later turn toward constructivism. Secondly, the claim that structures "really" exist—although they cannot be observed—makes necessary a departure from empiricism. Wendt introduces scientific realism as the philosophical basis of structuration theory (350). "Commonsense realism is the belief that the world of everyday objects exists independently of the mind. Scientific realism is the additional conviction that the unobservable entities and causal mechanisms often posited by scientific theories exist" (Shapiro and Wendt 1992, 210). Crucially, Wendt believes in the existence of a reality "out there" not only in terms of the natural, but also the social world, although this seems at odds with constructivist claims. Thus "the basic realist idea that scientific explanation consists in the identification of underlying causal mechanisms ... *does apply to the social sciences*" (Wendt 1987, 355, emphasis added). In other words, there is a social reality out there, independent of our thoughts about it, and Wendt is committed to explaining it (also see Wendt 1991, 391).

Structuration theory calls for social science to focus on the study of social practices (Giddens 1984, 2). Wendt takes this invitation a step further in developing a constructivist approach. He defines constructivism with reference to two fundamental principles of constructivist social theory. Firstly, people's actions are based on meanings (Wendt 1992a, 396–397) and, secondly, meaning arises out of interaction (403). The argument in "Anarchy Is What States Make of It" is sufficiently known. However, the context in which Wendt presents it is frequently forgotten. He starts by locating his position in relation to the debate between liberal and realist theories of international politics. Both sides to this debate are rationalist and therefore agree with the assumption that the interests and identities of actors are exogenously given. There is, however, a tradition of liberal scholarship that investigates processes of complex learning and therefore changes in interests and identities (393). Wendt aims to "build a bridge" between the liberal and the constructivist tradition (394) and therefore to position himself *between* the rationalist and reflectivist camps, as defined by Robert Keohane (1989, 158-179; Smith 1997, 183-187).

Wendt constructs his argument against the background of neorealism as formulated by Kenneth Waltz (1979). Wendt, like Waltz, presents a structural theory based on a state-centered ontology (Wendt 1994, 385; 1995, 72; 1996, 47-64). However, Wendt's conception of structure differs fundamentally from Waltz's. Structure only exists and has causal powers as process (Wendt 1992a, 395), that is, through actors' practices. Wendt thus argues against the neorealist claim that self-help is given by anarchic structure independently of processes of interaction (394). Rather self-help and power politics are institutions that have developed out of interaction in the international system and are sustained by such interaction. Wendt therefore does not dispute the anarchic character of contemporary international politics; he does, however, reject the explanations neorealists offer.

Wendt develops his constructivist argument in relation to the claim that, in a situation of anarchy, conceptions of security do not necessarily have to be self-interested. It is the intersubjective, rather than the material, aspect of structures that influences behavior. Wendt argues that it "is collective meanings that constitute the structures which organize our actions" (1992a, 397). Actors acquire identities, which Wendt defines as "relatively stable, role-specific understandings and expectations about self" (397), by participating in collective meanings. Identities provide the basis for interests, and these are defined in the process of defining situations (398). A "relatively stable set or 'structure' of identities and interests" is an institution (399). Self-help is such an institution; it is not a "constitutive feature of anarchy" (402). Under anarchy identity formation relates to the preservation of the self, in other words, security (399), but this does not necessarily entail self-interested conceptions of security. Notions of security "differ in the extent to which and the manner in which the self is identified cognitively with the other" (399–400). Conceptions of self and other, and consequently security interests, develop only in interaction.

Having established these claims, Wendt goes on to describe how a self-help situation may, but need not, develop out of the interaction of two actors who both want to survive and who have material capabilities. He holds that "[c]onceptions of self and interest tend to 'mirror' the practices of significant others over time" (Wendt 1992a, 404). This process is illustrated in two stories, one of which is worth quoting at length:

> Consider two actors—ego and alter—encountering each other for the first time. Each wants to survive and has certain material capabilities, but neither actor has biological or domestic imperatives for power, glory, or conquest . . . and there is no history of security or insecurity between the two. What should they do? . . . [M]ost decisions are and should be made on the basis of probabilities, and these are produced by interaction, by what actors *do.*
>
> In the beginning is ego's gesture, which may consist, for example, of an advance, a retreat, a brandishing of arms, a laying down of arms, or an attack. For ego, this gesture represents the basis on which it is prepared to respond to alter. This basis is unknown to alter, however, and so it must make an inference or "attribution" about ego's intentions and, in particular, given that this is anarchy, about whether ego is a threat. . . . Alter may make an attributional "error" in its inference about ego's intent, but there is no reason for it to assume a priori—before the gesture—that ego is threatening, since it is only through a process of signaling and interpreting that the costs and probabilities of being wrong can be determined. Social threats are constructed, not natural. (Wendt 1992a, 404–405)

Wendt goes on to illustrate this process in a second story. If aliens were to contact earth, we would not, presumably, feel threatened right away. If "they appear with one spaceship, saying what seems to be 'we come in peace,' we will feel 'reassured' and will probably respond with a gesture intended to reassure them, even if this gesture is not necessarily interpreted by them as such" (1992a, 405). Hence, a self-help situation need not follow.

The described "process of signaling, interpreting, and responding completes 'a social act'" (Wendt 1992a, 405), which leads to the creation of intersubjective meaning. Repetition of the process will lead to "reciprocal typifications" (Berger and Luckmann 1966, 54–58, 74) and to the creation of stable identities and expectations about future behavior. Thereby actors create and sustain social structures (Wendt 1992a: 405–406). Once structures of identity and interests have been created through typifications, they are not easy to transform because the social system becomes an objective social fact to the actors, and they may have a stake in maintaining stable identities (411). Change is, among other things, possible when actors alter their identities because of critical reflection upon the self (419). Thus, identity seems to be the key concept in Wendt's constructivism as it sits at the nexus between reproducing and changing a situation.[4] Therefore, identity must be crucially significant if anarchy is what states make of it. Self-interested conceptions of the self lie at the heart of a self-help system. Therefore, through identity change, other patterns of interaction, and thus other realities, can be created. Accordingly, Wendt calls for research to focus on "the relationship between what actors *do* and what they *are*" (424, emphasis in original). He himself has since turned his attention to the problem of the creation of collective identities (Wendt 1994, 385). For what states make of anarchy is related to their conception of identity.

Onuf

Wendt has been reproached time and again with not being a real constructivist, or at least merely a "reluctant" one (Ringmar 1997, 282). There is certainly one aspect which distinguishes Wendt's approach from Onuf's: the significance attributed to language within it. While Wendt only recently acknowledged its significance in a footnote (Jepperson, Wendt, and Katzenstein 1996, 64, fn. 98), it is a central aspect of the creation of reality to Onuf.

With his *World of Our Making* (1989), Onuf presented the first formulation of a constructivist approach to international relations.[5] Onuf's project is to "reconstruct" the discipline of IR by analyzing how people construct social reality (1). This involves questioning the traditional boundaries of the discipline. He aims to create a new paradigm of international relations which takes account of the political character of these boundaries and makes them a part of social theory (1, 22, 27, 36). This is more than an academic exercise since the social world is created by human practices. According to Onuf, "[c]onstitutive claims on behalf of social science disciplines, and the projects they engender, are among these practices" (15; also see 106). In his terms, Onuf is, therefore, also engaged in shaping international reality. Onuf's definition of a constructivist theory rests on the idea that "people *and* society construct, or constitute, each other" (36), which he takes from Giddens's work on structuration theory. The processes of construction and their institutionalization are crucial to Onuf's notion of reality. In very basic terms, human beings construct reality through their deeds, which may be speech acts. Speech acts in turn may be institutionalized into rules and thereby provide the context and basis of meaning for further human action. This process is deeply political as rules distribute benefits unevenly. In other words, rules privilege some people over others. The effect is rule.

Onuf's constructivism is based on deeds: "I begin with Goethe's aphorism, which for Wittgenstein seemed to express a philosophical position: In the beginning was the deed. I call this position constructivism" (1989, 36). Deeds may consist in physical actions or the speaking of words. There are no facts beyond deeds (36). Deeds are thus the starting point for Onuf's constructivism even if they cannot provide a secure foundation;[6] for there cannot be a philosophical foundation for constructivism that does not itself develop from the construction of reality and therefore from human practice (46). Deeds, however, are only capable of establishing a social reality if they carry meaning. Onuf argues that meaning in human social relationships depends on the existence of rules (21–22). Accordingly, Onuf's constructivism asserts the fundamental significance of rules for social reality and consequently the significance of rules for a constructivist social theory (66). Rules are essentially social. On the one hand, they provide guidance for human behavior and thereby make shared meaning possible. On the other hand, they create the possibility of agency in the first place (Onuf 1994, 6; 1997a, 8). Agency, in turn, influences rules because "[E]very time agents choose to follow a rule, they *change* it" (Onuf 1994: 18, emphasis in original), either by reinforcing or by weakening it. Onuf's response to the agency-structure problem consists in making rules central to the analysis (1997a, 7–8).

The notion that the social world is constructed by deeds where deeds may consist in the speaking of words rather than some physical activity is developed in speech act theory. As Onuf argues:

> The distinctive claim of the theory of speech acts is that language is both representative and performative. People use words to represent deeds and they can use words, and words alone, to perform deeds (1989, 82).

Rules are statements telling us how to carry on (Onuf 1989, 51). They develop from speech acts and the theory of speech acts can be brought to bear upon them. According to Onuf, a distinction between regulative and constitutive rules is impossible. They are always both (51–52, 86). Regulation and constitution cannot be separated in a socially constructed world because "what people take to be possible and what society makes permissible depend on vantage point, one's relation to practice" (51; Onuf 1997a, 11). As rules are always statements, Onuf's categorization of rules rather depends on their relation to types of speech acts (Onuf 1989, 79). He identifies three categories of rules which are based on three types of speech acts: assertive, directive, and commissive (23). Onuf asserts that categorization into instruction-rules, directive-rules, and commitment-rules provides "an inclusive classificatory scheme for *all* social rules" (91, emphasis in original). Not all speech acts are rules, however; only certain speech acts come to be accepted as rules. Onuf argues:

> When assertive speech acts are successful (their reception confirmed, with normativity attaching), they produce rules, however fragile their constitution and tenuous their normativity. When any such rule becomes a convention, constitution of the rule by speech acts accepting its status as a rule begins to supplant its constitution by the repetition of speech acts with complementary propositional content. Then the rule is normatively stronger, its regulative character supporting its independent constitution, and conversely. The change in condition is signified by a change in nomenclature: constitution becomes institution (86).

The texture of the social world is therefore made up of rules. They provide orientation for people. "Rules do indeed tell us how to carry on," but they "cannot provide closure for the purposes of carrying on because rules are not the sufficient agency whereby intentions become equivalent to causes" (51). Rules provide guidance but do not determine human behavior. Accordingly, based on the analysis of rules, Onuf can only make the most general statements about social action. Therefore, he introduces the additional concept of judgment.

Judgment arises from knowledge about the context of rules involved in a situation and about the consequences of following or violating them (Onuf 1989, 110). It is closely linked to the process of reasoning, and speech acts can be seen as "instances of applied reasoning" (99). According to Onuf, a "constructivist interpretation of reasoning extends to learning and knowing, not just in the sense of acquiring propositional knowledge, but learning and knowing how to use that knowledge, including knowledge of rules" (96–97). When people learn how to use rules, rather than just to know their content, they learn how to exercise judgment (110–111). Thus, it is the combination of practice and consciousness which creates judgment (119). Judgment leads to the choice of the actual course of action that makes sense within the context of rules.

Through their function in social life, rules provide the basis for Onuf's definition of the political. According to Onuf, political society has two general properties. There are always rules that make human activity meaningful. Secondly, rules result in an uneven distribution of benefits. This leads to a condition of rule (Onuf 1989, 21–22, 128). Through the rules-rule nexus society and politics are closely linked. Society is based on rules; politics always deals with asymmetric social relations generated by rules, that is rule (22). The political therefore is always potentially about privilege and thus involves normative questions. Rules establish stability in social institutions by privileging certain people (122). We usually call this phenomenon order. Stability ensues precisely because those who made the order benefit from it (158). Order is a fiction we believe in. "It is constituted by performative speech and constitutes propositional content for such speech" (155). The problem of order, conceived in this way, is therefore just the other side of the problem of privilege.

Onuf perceives the world as being made up of a material and a social realm, which are distinct but nevertheless closely related. Onuf believes in the materiality of the world "out there" (Onuf 1989, 29–30, 46; 1997a, 9). The constructivism that Onuf (1989, 40) wants to propose "does not draw a sharp distinction between material and social realities—the material and the social contaminate each other, but variably—and it does not grant sovereignty to either the material or the social by defining the other out of existence. It does find socially made content dominant in and for the individual without denying the independent, natural reality of individuals as materially situated biological beings."

If one grants the possibility of separating social and material reality, at least for analytic purposes, the concept of deed is a powerful basis for Onuf's constructivism precisely because he sees it as situated at the border between social and material reality. "A 'deed' is intelligible only as jointly a social construction and natural event, produced by mind and yet phenomenal in its own right" (1989, 43). Deeds therefore provide the link between the social and the natural world. As social phenomena, they are based on intentions and meanings. For them to function properly, however, they have to be addressed to the natural world. Deeds transport meaning, but they have to be related to both the social and the natural world correctly in order to produce the desired outcomes (Austin 1962). Deeds therefore make possible the linkage of the social to the material, the two realms construed as separate by Onuf. Another way of establishing the connection between the social and the material is through the notion of language or speech. This is, of course, only another way of looking at the same thing since the "point of a speech act is to have an effect on some state of affairs" (Onuf 1989,

98). A speech act is a form of deed. Thus Onuf argues that a "constructivist view denies that world and words are independent; it sees them as mutually constitutive. If categories of being are linguistically constituted, then they may be said to have social origins" (Onuf 1994, 94).

World of Our Making focuses on ontological claims (Onuf 1989, 43). However, Onuf's epistemological position is crucial. Onuf wants his book to contribute to postpositivist social theory (235 fn. 12). Therefore, he contests not only disciplinary boundaries, but also the epistemological assumptions IR has been operating on. He disagrees with positivist and empiricist but also realist leanings in the discipline. To him there is no single truth. Rather "[t]ruths as we take them to be are inextricable from the arguments offered for them" (35). This notion is supported by the realization that observers cannot detach themselves from the matter investigated. The "world science knows is *in degree* a social construction" (39, emphasis in original).

It is crucial for Onuf's conception of knowledge to understand that we can never leave the world of constructions: "We are always within our constructions, even as we choose to stand apart from them, condemn them, reconstruct them" (43). Accordingly, we can never occupy the position of a neutral observer. Ideas and events are not independent phenomena; rather, they necessarily interact (Onuf 1991, 426, 429). According to Giddens, "the point is that reflection on social processes (theories, and observations about them) continually enter into . . . the universe of events that they describe" (quoted in Onuf 1991, 426). Thus, we can only know from within. In other words, the knowers are part of the known. Knowledge only becomes possible through creating "an appropriate vocabulary," which assigns occurrences to "conceptual homes" (439). By giving certain concepts meaning, we create a starting point in relation to which other aspects of social reality gain meaning and become intelligible. Knowledge thus exists only in relation to a specific context (Onuf 1997a, 7). Therefore, it is crucial to know the make up of this context.

A socially constituted reality "is not just a collection of rules, but a variety of practices, all of which sort into three categories" (Onuf 1989, 112), those of speech act, rules, and reasoning. Actions become possible and gain meaning in the context of rules. Two closely related conclusions follow from this conception of reality. Firstly, knowledge is based on the phenomenon that rules make shared knowledge possible. Knowledge is intrinsically linked to the context of rules. Secondly, the context of rules provides the basis for the distribution of benefits, for answering the question of who gets what, when, and how. It is therefore closely linked to normative problems. As a result, knowledge cannot be separated from political and normative questions. Statements about the world—also or maybe especially scientific ones—are part of the process of the construction of reality and therefore of the allocation of benefits.

Kratochwil

While Wendt and Onuf are always identified as constructivists, this label does not readily come to mind for Kratochwil. Nevertheless commentators have started referring to him as a constructivist (Wendt 1995, 71; Waever 1997, 24; Wind 1997, 243; Smith 1997, 183). It is only in his recent work that Kratochwil explicitly develops a constructivist outlook, especially in an article coauthored with Rey Koslowski; but the inclination was arguably there earlier. Kratochwil claims to use the term "constructivist" in the way developed by Onuf (Koslowski and Kratochwil 1995, 159, fn. 3). Like Onuf, Kratochwil sees constructivism as centering on practices that are based on rules and norms (128). Political systems are remade or changed through actors' practices. Therefore, "[f]undamental change of the international system occurs when actors, through their practices, change the rules and norms constitutive of international interaction" (128). This happens "when beliefs and identities of domestic actors are altered, thereby also altering rules and norms that are constitutive of their political practices" (128). This formulation of constructivism is the result of a complex argument.

There seem to be two related, but nevertheless distinct, strands in Kratochwil's work that converge into constructivism. On the one hand, there is his dissatisfaction with the epistemological stance in traditional international relations theory. On the other hand, and flowing from it, is his preoccupation with the role of rules and norms for political life and its analysis. Kratochwil criticizes mainstream international relations theory for having an exceedingly narrow conception of politics and human behavior. Having adopted a notion of rationality as instrumental, interesting questions about the ends sought are excluded from the analysis (Kratochwil 1984a, 306, 316–317; 1987, 308). Furthermore, the obsession with method induced by an adherence to positivism limits the realm of permissible objects of analysis (Kratochwil 1993a, 66–69). The normative character of the political must be denied in the name of "science" (Kratochwil 1987, 308; 1988, 212, 218–22). To counter these detrimental effects of positivist theorizing Kratochwil suggests focusing on the dimension of everyday language and on the norms guiding human behavior (Kratochwil 1989, 28–30). Thus, his analysis is indebted to linguistic philosophy, especially speech act theory and practical philosophy, but also jurisprudential theories. His key claim lies in the assertion that international politics must be analyzed in the context of norms properly understood (10–12). The notion of norms guiding all human conduct is turned into a more clearly constructivist approach when Kratochwil uses the metaphor of Wittgensteinian games as a starting point for analysis (Kratochwil 1993a, 75).

Kratochwil complains about the "poverty of epistemology" in IR (Kratochwil 1984a, 305). His claim is that the positivist approach employed by much of international relations scholarship is simply inadequate to the problem of politics.   Referring to practical philosophy, he argues that "intentionality and goal-directedness" need to be considered in analyses of human action (Kratochwil 1984a, 306). Positivist explanations proceed in terms of antecedent conditions, rather than by reference to an aim towards which an act is meant to contribute. This, Kratochwil argues, makes it difficult to understand human action. To grasp the meaning of an action, we have to locate it in an intersubjective context. "To have explained an action often means to have made intelligible the goals for the purpose of which it was undertaken" (Kratochwil 1984a, 317; 1989, 24). Explaining an action is also "significantly shaped by the moral discourse and by our pragmatic interest" (Kratochwil 1989, 100). Eliminating the elements of appraisal and interpretation to make our analysis "objective" leads to a misconception of the problem of praxis (Kratochwil 1988b, 206). It is important to take into account the actual political discourse (Kratochwil 1982, 9) and the employment of moral criteria. "Precisely because human beings are 'self-interpreting' animals, the appraisals they engage in are more than guesses or predictions about future conduct" (Kratochwil 1988, 207) They also concern the normative aspect of social institutions and questions of morality (214). A moral point of view necessarily emerges, and it is based on the reasoning process related to obligations and on our emotions regarding ourselves and our way of life (207). By misrepresenting human action in the positivist way, we are likely to misunderstand ourselves and our role in the world (Kratochwil 1984a, 319). In other words, apart from making social life unintelligible, we define away the normative dimension and thus the problem of responsibility.

Kratochwil recognizes that imputing the meaning of behavior by searching for its purpose is problematic since we may commit errors of interpretation. However, the shared interpretation of a situation by the actors can serve as a starting point, even if it is disputed in parts. The "shared understanding of the situation illuminates these interactions and help us in our analysis" (Koslowski and Kratochwil 1995, 136). The interpretative nature of the analysis is inherent in human action itself. It is important to recognize that understanding action in terms of its meaning is always an interpretation; it is not an act of empathy (Kratochwil 1996, 217–218). It is not a question of getting into an actor's head. Since interpretation concerns the intersubjective context based on norms and rules, there is nothing idiosyncratic about this dimension of behavior. This aspect is shaped, in other words, precisely by what is shared by the actors. Therefore, imputing the context of rules and norms is distinct from imputing intentions or mental states (Kratochwil 1989, 100–101). This has implications for Kratochwil's conception of how knowledge is possible. He remains committed to such notions as the "unprejudiced assessment of the empirical evidence" (Kratochwil 1993c, 462) and the empirical testability of explanations (1984b, 347).[7]

The epistemological problems Kratochwil identifies are fundamentally important because our understanding of human action depends on our view of knowledge (1989, 21). The goal is, then, to provide a more adequate understanding of human behavior that takes into account its intersubjective and therefore normative dimension. He aims to develop an approach that "is sensitive to the social conditioning of our actions" (Kratochwil 1987, 304). Accordingly, he wants to move away from a conception of rationality that aims to define it as a property that can be specified *a priori,* to one that relates to common sense understandings of the term "rational." "Rational" refers to "a structure of communication in which validity claims can be examined intersubjectively" (304). Thus, the appropriate theoretical model for understanding rationality can be found in Jürgen Habermas's theory of communicative action rather than in some notion based on positivism (304). The meaning of rationality should be seen "to be constituted by the *use* of the term" (310, emphasis in original). An action or belief is commonly called "rational" when it "makes sense" to act in that way (310). At the same time, rationality is bound up with normative discourse because to "call something rational means then to *endorse it* in terms of some norm or moral feeling that permits it" (311, emphasis in original). Utilitarian calculation in the sense depicted by an instrumental notion of rationality only becomes possible after an actor has already taken an attitude towards a situation. This attitude will be influenced by values (318).

Kratochwil starts his discussion of political action with three assumptions. Firstly, he supposes "that it is useful to study the role of norms in shaping decisions from the baseline of an abstract initial situation which is defined, more or less, in public choice terms" (Kratochwil 1989, 10). In other words, rules and norms serve to reduce the complexity of situations and impose a certain rationality on actors, which forms the basis for decisions. He also assumes that human action is rule-governed. Rules give action meaning by providing the basis for an intersubjective context (10–11). In understanding "political action in terms of meaningful, rather than purely instrumental, action" (Kratochwil 1993a, 65), Kratochwil takes his cue from Max Weber. Action is meaningful if it can be placed in an intersubjectively shared context (Kratochwil 1989, 24). He sees this intersubjective context as based on and mediated by rules and norms. They are "the means which allow people to pursue goals, share meanings, communicate with each other, criticize assertions, and justify actions" (11). Nevertheless, rules and norms do not determine human behavior. Accordingly, Kratochwil's third assumption is that processes of deliberation and interpretation are important and need to be analyzed (11).

Norms are speech acts, and they depend upon successful communication (Kratochwil 1989, 34). Thus, they only function properly if the speech act produces the desired effect with the addressee. They are not independent of the surrounding situation. If they do produce the wanted outcome, they "link individual autonomy to sociality" (70) by providing guidance and acting as a problem-solving device. They do so in three ways. They may rule out certain forms of behavior. They may create schemes or schedules for coordinating the enjoyment of scarce resources. And they may provide the basis for a discourse in which the parties discuss grievances, negotiate solutions, and ask for third-party mediation (70). "Rules . . . are a type of directive that simplify choice-situations by drawing attention to factors which an actor has to take into account" (72). It is therefore crucial to understand that it is a gross distortion to view norms as merely constraining. They also provide a basis for justification, enable actions otherwise not possible, and serve to communicate (Kratochwil 1984b, 344, 366). There are regulative and constitutive rules, and the latter cannot be reduced to the former. Thus, we are unable to understand the role of norms in social life if we take regulative rules as paradigmatic (28; Kratochwil 1993c, 460). Kratochwil is most interested in what he calls "practice-type" or "institution-type" rules (Kratochwil 1989, 91–93). For this rule type the institutions of promising and contracting are paradigmatic. Following J.L. Austin's reasoning about speech acts, Kratochwil argues that these rules usually relate to performances and specify the conditions under which an act will be considered valid (91–92). Crucially, "it is only the rules of the institution which circumscribe the conditions by which we as moral agents can choose, and incur and limit responsibility for our actions" (152).

If we take into account that rules and norms are the key factors shaping human behavior, but that they do so in an indeterminate way, we have now come full circle to Kratochwil's criticism of positivism. Questions of "truth" or "consistency" are central as long as we believe that the social world functions much the same way the natural world does. If, however, there are no logically necessary solutions to social problems, if social situations are inherently indeterminate, our analyses should rather focus on how questions concerning validity claims are decided through discourse (Kratochwil 1989, 33). The question, then, is "how a decision based on rules and norms, though *not logically compelling*, can marshal support" (36, emphasis in original). Instrumental explanations fail as rules are often related to "what interest of *others* we have to take into account while making our choices" (95, emphasis in original). According to Kratochwil, the key to this puzzle lies in realizing that rule following does not involve blind habit but argumentation. Therefore, "it is through *analyzing the reasons which are specific to different rule-types that the intersubjective validity of norms and thus their "deontic status" can be established*" (97, emphasis in original). Kratochwil's solution is linked to the emergence of a "moral point of view" (123). The normative discourse classifies some violations of rules as acceptable but not others. Norms provide the basis for a process of reasoning in which the decision to take a certain course of action, rather than another, is justified. For this process the identification of *relevant premises* is significant (37). Whether an action can marshal support will depend on the definition of the situation. Therefore, the justifications given for a particular course of action will provide an important indication for its appraisal, as human action always must be interpreted (63), and justifications point to a fruitful basis of interpretation.

Kratochwil takes the reasoning process in legal discourse as a starting point as it is, in several ways, similar to the one in moral discourse. Both display a process of principled argumentation leading to an equally principled application of the respective norms. They also involve an element of regard for the other. The problem is that processes of reasoning do not lead to single best solutions, even if it may be agreed that some arguments are more persuasive than others. Thus authoritative decisions are necessary (Kratochwil 1989, 142, 208). This does not, however, mitigate the influence of norms and intersubjective context, as an authoritative decision that can be shown to be based on good reasons is very different from an arbitrary one (184). It is, in any case, necessary to put forward good reasons for one's acts and decisions. In this context the choice of a narrative becomes necessary and crucial (213). Such narratives usually start from a commonplace. "Topoi, or commonplaces . . . establish 'starting-points' for arguments but locate the issues of a debate in a substantive set of common understandings that provide for the crucial connections within the structure of the argument" (219). It is important to realize that we cannot talk about human acts in a neutral way. The "characterization of actions, whether in the legal or in the practical discourse, is not a description at all, but rather an *appraisal*; it is an evaluation of 'facts' in terms of some normative considerations" (229, emphasis in original). Thus, "what acquires here the status of an 'objective' fact is not the thing described but rather the inter-subjective *validity* of a characterization upon which reasonable persons can agree" (229, emphasis in original).

Kratochwil thus argues that the role of rules and norms in social life needs to be "radically reconceptualized." The notion of game in the Witt-gensteinian sense, which relates to rule governed action (Wittgenstein 1958), serves as a starting point for this project. In summary, one can say that "rules and norms are not simply the distillation of individual utility calculations but rather the *antecedent conditions* for strategies and for the specification of criteria of rationality. Norms not only establish certain games and enable the players to pursue their goals within them, they also establish inter-subjective meanings that allow the actors to direct their actions towards each other, communicate with each other, appraise the quality of their actions, criticize claims and justify choices." (Kratochwil 1993a, 75–76, emphasis in original)

Starting with the notion of game "fundamentally change[s] our conception of action and communication" because we realize that "language *does not mirror* action by sticking a descriptive label on the activity: it *is* action" (Kratochwil 1993a, 76, emphasis in original). International relations is to be conceived of as lying somewhere between a game well defined by its rules and the simple exchange of communicative moves. Thus, there is a margin for interpretation concerning the permissibility of behavior. As international politics lacks an organ empowered to take authoritative decisions, interpretations form a part of the shared existence. Contestations, and consequently noncompliance, are frequent (76).

Human behavior can therefore only be understood in the context of meaning, interpretation and judgment, that is, embedded in an intersubjective context. The intersubjective context is based on the existence of rules and norms, which fulfill all three functions above: They establish the rationality of the situation, give actions meaning, and provide the framework for processes of deliberation, interpretation, and argumentation. The analysis of the latter leads to an intensive examination of speech and the insight that language does not reflect action. Rather it *is* action.

The Creation of Meaning

All of the constructivist approaches under discussion agree that the *meaning* of human behavior and of social reality is crucial for the analysis of international relations. This meaning is neither awaiting discovery in the world "out there," nor does it merely exist in the mind of the single individual. The meaning of human behavior lies precisely in the fact that it can be understood by other human beings. Meaning can never be uncovered completely because several interpretations may be possible and legitimate. However, to a degree it is accessible to both observer and other actors. Meaning that is not communicated to others is in that sense no meaning (Wittgenstein 1958, paras. 262–275). Differences between the approaches become apparent when we focus on *how* meaning is created, on what is meant by the intersubjective context in which it is embedded. While for Wendt, intersubjective context arises from a "conversation of gestures," for Onuf and Kratochwil, it is created by speech acts and institutionalized by norms. The main difference is the theoretical position of language. While Wendt's actors are mute and his approach therefore open to the same criticism as Realism (Müller 1994a, 24–30),[8] language is central for Onuf and Kratochwil.

Wendt's actors do not speak. They signal to each other. A social act consists in sending a signal, interpreting it and responding on the basis of the interpretation (Wendt 1992a, 405). A "conversation of gestures" develops (Mead 1965, 77). According to Mead, whom Wendt refers to, actors must possess reflective intelligence and consciousness for this process (Mead 1965, 77–81). In order to be able to reflect and interpret, however, actors presumably have to be capable of using language. Wendt does not investigate the role of language in this context. He does not even mention it (but see Jepperson, Wendt, and Katzenstein 1996, 64, fn. 98). In the literature used by Wendt, the significance of language is mentioned time and again, but its role is never systematically conceptualized. Thus, Mead understands language as part of the creation of the situation (1965, 78). Berger and Luckmann point out that language "objectivates" shared experiences (1966, 36–40), which is crucial for making shared conceptions of reality possible.

We might assume that when Wendt refers to signaling and interpreting, he implies the actors' capacity to speak. This reading of his argument is not convincing, though. In his description, the development of relations between actors relies on gestures. In his story about *ego* and *alter*, *ego's* first communicative action may consist of different activities such as "an advance, a retreat, a brandishing of arms, a laying down of arms, or an attack" (Wendt 1992a, 404). If it may also consist of a declaration, a threat or an assertion, he fails to say so. I think in his story it may not since it is about a "first encounter." *Ego* and *alter* meet in a state of nature; Wendt is careful not to attribute characteristics to these agents, which they could only acquire by participating in a society (402). *Ego* and *alter* are unlikely to share a language; this is particularly obvious when we think of the example of aliens landing on earth.

Wendt's notion of communication is thus similar to an exchange of moves in game theory. Reaching an interpretation of a situation consists in an exchange of moves where *ego* classifies *alter's* gestures and responds to them on the basis of his—*ego's*—experiences. The interpretation is unrelated to the meaning *alter* attributes to his gesture; it is, therefore, as Jonathan Mercer (1995, 248) points out, "nothing but supposition, analogy or projection." A linguistic exchange, in which these judgments and interpretations, and the experiences on which they are based, could be at issue does not take place. Reaching a shared interpretation of the situation, if this is possible, is based on trial and error. Using this approach, it seems impossible to analyze more far-reaching communication, such as communication about the meaning of certain situations or actions (Müller 1994a, 25; 1995, 375). Wendt's actors cannot communicate about their behavior; they communicate *through* their behavior (also see Kratochwil and Ruggie 1986, 765).

The missing theoretical role for language is disappointing because it limits the scope of Wendt's constructivism. Linguistic exchange changes the situation. Thereby reality is constructed (Müller 1994, 28). From recognizing language as medium of communication, it is therefore only a small step to conceptualizing it as medium of the construction of reality. According to Onuf, language is an integral part of a constructivist theory. Not only does he explicitly include "words spoken" in his conception of deed, which he portrays as the starting point of his approach (Onuf 1989, 36). This goes back to the claim of speech act theory that speech can be an act in itself (82; also see Austin 1962; Searle 1969; Kratochwil 1989). He also emphasizes that world and words constitute each other (Onuf 1989, 94). Kratochwil points out that language also "frees us from the here and now and thus makes remembrance and planning possible" (Kratochwil 1989, 6; also see Berger and Luckmann 1966, 40–41, and Kratochwil's contribution to this volume). This is crucial for constructivism, as it must be possible to institutionalize and communicate constructions of reality. Accordingly, Kratochwil argues that language is significant precisely because it opens up the possibility of transcending the current situation. Therefore, it must not be conceptualized as just a "signaling system," as Wendt seems to do.

Moreover, language is the medium that makes the influence of the intersubjective context of rules on human behavior possible. In other words, the interpretations and processes of reasoning, which translate the underlying context of norms into social acts, are based on the use of language. Language makes shared interpretations of a situation and intersubjectivity possible. The argumentative production of a shared view of the situation, as

Kratochwil portrays it, points to human behavior taking place in a normative context. Therefore, normativity is not something that may be mentioned in passing as a special addition to an objective, "scientific" treatise on international politics, but an integral part of politics and thus of its analysis.

Moving language to the center of an analysis of politics has significant implications. Ontologically speaking, according to Onuf and Kratochwil, our social reality is at least to a degree a linguistic construction, although the existence of a material world is not disputed. The role of language in relation to the construction of reality, however, also leads to an epistemological problem. Knowledge, based on the perspective of a neutral observer, is not possible if the medium we use to gain, discuss, and transmit knowledge is part of the creation of the object of knowledge. If language influences the construction of reality, this implicates us, not only as scholars but also in the creation of that reality (Onuf 1989, 15). On the other hand, it reminds us yet again that the normativity of international relations is an unavoidable aspect of the discipline rather than a voluntary and basically unnecessary bonus (Smith 1992, 490). If rules lead to an asymmetrical distribution of power and if language is a system of rules, then language must support privilege. This means further that our theories support certain conceptions of reality and therefore certain groups of people (Onuf 1989, 21–22). As Robert Cox correctly remarks, theories are always "*for* someone and *for* some purpose" (1986, 207, emphasis in original). The question of the normativity of our theories therefore always arises, not just when ethical problems are addressed explicitly. It is especially important to take this into account because politics, and therefore the object of our investigations, as Kratochwil argues convincingly, permanently involves normative decisions. It is crucial to remember that politics is not just about who gets what when and how but especially *why* (Hoffman 1987, 234). Thus both the ontological and the epistemological claims of constructivism as presented by Onuf and Kratochwil point towards the problem of normativity, whereas this does not seem to be central to Wendt's approach (but see Shapiro and Wendt 1992, 218–219; and Wendt 1995, 74).

Constructivism in IR is therefore hardly a homogeneous approach. While Wendt focuses on the question of identity in his analysis, and otherwise closely follows neorealist and rationalist theories,[9] Onuf and Kratochwil focus on norms and rules, and therefore a linguistically created intersubjective context. The compatibility of these three approaches is not frequently questioned in constructivist analyses. Constructivism is seen to be that framework that deals with norms *and* identities (Jepperson, Wendt, and Katzenstein 1996; Risse-Kappen 1995, 502). Two of the theorists discussed here recently seem to be engaged in a mutual *rapprochement* in relation to this problematic. Wendt discusses the role of norms, which he had previously mentioned only in passing (Wendt 1992a, 399, 410, 413, 417), and recognizes the significance of language (Jepperson, Wendt, and Katzenstein 1996). Kratochwil (1994b, 1996) deals with the question of identity. This, however, should not obscure the fact that the fundamental differences between their theoretical assumptions are not easy to overcome. The same terminology does not imply agreement or compatibility.

In Wendt's approach norms are apparently defined as collective expectations about behavior (Jepperson, Wendt, and Katzenstein 1996, 54; also see Klotz 1995a, 14; 1995b, 451; Finnemore 1996a, 22). This is clearly different from Onuf's and Kratochwil's conception of norms. It remains unclear how norms are to be integrated into Wendt's approach without making language an important issue. Kratochwil makes the connection between norms and identity via the notion of culture, which leads him to a conceptualization of identities that is in its historicist focus different from Wendt's emphasis on expectations of behavior (Kratochwil 1996, 206–210). In any case, in spite of this terminological *rapprochement*, the fundamental difference in relation to the scope of constructivist claims remains. While Wendt only discusses the construction of the realm of "reality," Onuf extends the claim to the world of science, the realm of knowledge.

Conclusion

Having made an extended argument about the claims of three constructivists and the different status accorded to language in the approaches, it seems reasonable to conclude with a few brief remarks on what this means in terms of research in international relations. In general terms, it seems to me that both Kratochwil's and Onuf's line of reasoning demand a more intensive analysis of the linguistic element of politics. This means that discourse itself and its relationship to the context of norms needs to be analyzed. Yet the political discourse in that which we consider to be the empirical reality of international relations, or whether it also refers to the academic discourse, is possibly where Kratochwil and Onuf part company.

Both Kratochwil and Onuf focus on the role of speech acts in the construction of reality. From this perspective the analysis of real existing discourses in international relations seems to be the obvious starting point. Such analysis would have to investigate the function of the context of rules and norms as a medium of communication. It would also, however—and this is one way to set itself apart from other studies, thought to be constructivist but based on a different understanding of norms (see Onuf 1998b)—analyze the role of metaphors or "commonplaces" in political discourse. This necessarily leads to an investigation of *how* actors say what they say, that is, with the linguistic expression of claims to knowledge. After all, norms are not only interesting because they reflect collective expectations of behavior, but also   because they may be used in discourse to make certain positions intelligible and justifiable because they create reality. What is at stake in such a constructivist analysis is an adequate investigation of the intersubjective dimension.[10] Speech acts only function properly if they are "accepted" by the addressees of the communication. Therefore, those engaged in constructivist research must aim to address shared frames of reference rather than individual conceptions of reality.

Moreover, Onuf's arguments suggest that the position of the knower needs to be problematized far more than has been done; for they lead to a radical rejection of the possibility of the knowledge of a neutral observer. In other words, our knowledge and claims to validity are socially constructed. Accordingly, the question is not only who profits from which construction of reality, but who gets privileged by which grounds for legitimate knowledge. The mutual relationship between that which we hold to be the empirical reality of international relations, and that which we hold to be theoretical debates in IR, would then be a legitimate object of analysis. This throws up another crucial question, namely what constitutes acceptable empirical work if constructivist insights are taken seriously. Answering this question seems to me to be more difficult than has been acknowledged. If one wants to work with constructivist insights, one needs to ask first what constitutes "relevant facts," how they become such facts, and what our role is with respect to them as those who know or who want to know. After all, our relationship to that which we call empirical reality cannot, from a constructivist perspective, be a one-way street. Even if we do not intervene in the reality that we are investigating by moving material resources or making claims to knowledge within it, constructivist arguments suggest that academic discourse and social reality influence each other.

The challenge consists in thinking through the implications of constructivist approaches. To accept this challenge means to acknowledge the necessity of an intensive and different analysis of political discourse. I am not convinced that either Onuf or Kratochwil have been able to demonstrate how exactly this could be done. Kratochwil has a tendency to select issues for what he may consider a practical application of his thinking, which I think we may be forgiven for categorizing as rather abstract themes (see, e.g., Kratochwil 1994). When he engages "empirical" issues in international relations, Onuf seems to alternatively reduce his complex approach to the relatively banal insight that social life is based on meaning related to rules (Onuf 1991, 1995) *or* to discuss them in a way that is clearly indebted to his constructivism but again remains highly abstract (1997a). This, however, need not mean that their thinking does not point towards more challenging and promising ways of studying international relations than is reflected in a lot of what passes as constructivist analysis these days. After all, Onuf's and Kratochwil's apparent reluctance to directly address the blood and sweat flowing in international relations every day need not deter those wishing to do so from using their insights.

Engaging with what we hold to be empirical reality should involve questioning how it is related to "theoretical" problems and the other way around. The claim that our world is constructed throws a new light on the question of knowledge and the problem of privilege. It seems to me that it not only makes the recognition (as Kratochwil demands) of the genuinely political and normative dimension of human action inescapable, but it must lead constructivists to ask further questions about the function of "knowledge" in the world of our making. It is therefore crucially important not to merely domesticate constructivist approaches for the sake of "acceptable" empirical analysis.

Notes

1. A different version of this chapter has been published as Majs Zehfuss, "Sprachlosigkeit schränkt ein. Zur Bedeutung von Sprache in konstruktivistischen Theorien," *Zeitschrift für Internationale Beziehungen*, 5 (1998), 109–137. For their insightful comments on the various versions of this paper, I am grateful to K.M. Fierke, Knud Erik Jørgensen, Friedrich Kratochwil, Steve Smith, Roger Tooze, Christoph Weller, and Nick Wheeler.

2. Wendt's Social Theory of International Politics was published after this chapter had been completed. As the book does nothing to change the thrust of my assessment, or indeed my argument about the role of language in different constructivisms, I have chosen not to take it into account.

3. Wendt (1987) and Shapiro and Wendt (1992). In this chapter, "realism" is used as it is in the philosophy of science, and "Realism" as it used in International Relations.

4. This claim does not conflict with the justified criticisms which have been made of Wendt's concept of identity. See, for example, Heikka (1996); Neumann (1996, 163–166); Pasic (1996, 86–90).

5. For a short statement of his position, see Onuf (1997a).

6. Constructivism cannot be grounded. See Onuf (1989, 46). Yet elsewhere Onuf (1994, 4) defends the possibility of grounds.

7. On this point, see also Kratochwil's contribution to this volume.

8. Interestingly Müller (1994a, 28) does not oppose Wendt's approach in this context. See however his critique in Müller (1995, 384).

9. For instance in Lapid and Kratochwil (1996), Wendt's chapter appears in the section "Culturing Neorealism?" His assumptions also show his affinity with Neorealism. See Wendt (1995, 72).

10. The notion of intersubjectivity, which is crucial to constructivist approaches, is in itself problematic as it presupposes the possibility and accessibility of shared knowledge. That, however, is an argument for another paper.

4

Feminism: Constructivism's Other Pedigree

Birgit Locher and Elisabeth Prügl

It is not the birth of new ideas that changes world views and disciplines, but their deployment and evoking by those in a position of influence. Their social practices give ideas authority in historical contexts that favor new thinking. Thus it is with constructivism. The end of the Cold War, the failure and delegitimization of structural realism, together with the framing of constructivism as the new middle ground or the alternative to rationalist positions, have come together to valorize the approach in contemporary International Relations (IR). Clearly, constructivist ideas are not new and constructivists have traced their ancestries differentially to philosophical realism, the sociological classics (Durkheim and Weber, often via Anthony Giddens), Wittgenstein, speech act theory, and French poststructuralists. But scholars in IR have not considered feminism a distinct research tradition that is part of the constructivist pedigree and have instead subsumed (some) feminists under other traditions of constructivist thinking (e.g., Ruggie 1998b). In this chapter we argue that feminism constitutes a rich research tradition that adds a distinct body of ideas to the manifold ancestry of constructivism.

Feminist scholarship in IR is diverse in range and orientation. Plurality is in fact an inherent characteristic and a strength of feminism. Despite the diversity of approaches, the contention that gender, and indeed woman, is a social construct lies at the heart of feminist theorizing. Liberal ideas of women's equality, socialist ideas of a sexual division of labor, the Freudian suggestion that identities are produced, and functionalist ideas of sex roles all had come together by the middle of the twentieth century to thoroughly undermine any suggestion that gender was a biological or natural given (Connell 1987). The second wave of the feminist movement linked these insights to an analysis of women's subordination, suggesting that gender was not only a social construct, but also created women's oppression. Simone de Beauvoir's *The Second Sex*, published in France in 1949, was a landmark demonstrating this relationship by drawing on structuralist thinking. In the 1970s feminist writers developed the idea in the context of other research traditions as well. They linked women's subordination to unequal rights, sexuality, and the imperatives of social reproduction.

Feminists, including those in IR, have employed the notion of social construction in different ways. Cynthia Enloe (1990, 1993), for example, claims in her writings that relationships between governments depend on the construction and reconstruction of gender and that such relations produce certain understandings of femininity and masculinity. Gender constructions here are constitutive of international relations and global processes. Spike Peterson (1992a, 194) refers to gender as a "systematic social construction that dichotomizes identities, behaviors, and expectations as masculine and feminine." According to her, it is not "simply a trait of individuals but an institutionalized feature of social life." The structuralist notion of a deep dichotomy between genders merges here with an understanding that people are socialized into their genders while social expectations and ideologies reproduce notions of masculinity and femininity (see also Peterson and Runyan 1999, 5–7). This understanding bears strong resemblance to Ann Tickner's (1992, 6) notion of "hegemonic masculinity." In a slightly different form, social construction appears as an interaction of the triad of material conditions, institutions, and ideas in the works of Sandra Whitworth (1994) and Deborah Stienstra (1994). In this perspective, which shows the influence of Robert Cox, social construction designates an opposition to the material and is characterized by malleability and context dependency. Christine Sylvester (1994, 1998) draws on discourse theories to develop a somewhat more radical understanding of social construction that privileges "temporary homesteads" over stable identities. For her, socially constructed means "that men and women are the stories that have been told about 'men' and 'women' and the constraints and opportunities that have hereby arisen as we take to our proper places" (1994, 4). Taken together, feminist notions of social construction in IR express different though related issues: they signal a concern with "the social" as opposed to material capabilities, static structures, unquestioned positivities, or pregiven identities. The social becomes real in discourses, stories, practices, and ideas, and the term itself is meant to indicate impermanence, historicity, and malleability.

One aspect that distinguishes feminists from other constructivists in IR is their overarching concern with power. Constructivists have dealt with power to some extent, but few have done so systematically. And when they have talked about power, they have often treated it as a capability outside social construction. In contrast, feminists consider power as imbricated in the social fabric. It operates through discourses, meanings, and practices. It reflects the historically and socially contingent production of masculinities and femininities that encode messages of super- and subordination (compare Scott 1986, 1067). If the international world is a social world, as constructivists suggest, it must be a world that encodes gender. Indeed, feminists in IR have pointed to the lengths that policymakers, militaries, multinational corporations, tourists, and other international agents go to produce and reproduce certain meanings of femininity and masculinity in international politics, and to the way in which profoundly gendered practices sustain, for example, the global economy and the militarized security system (e.g., Enloe 1989; Moon 1997; Chin 1998; Steans 1998; Zalewski and Parpart 1998).

Just as feminists draw on different traditions in their understanding of social construction, so they take different approaches to conceptualizing the micropowers of gender. In what follows, we introduce feminist approaches to power by focusing on two concepts: identities and institutions. Both have garnered considerable interest and moved to the center of attention in IR after its constructivist turn. We probe the different understandings that feminists and constructivists bring to these concepts. As much as we suggest that relating back to a feminist pedigree could help constructivists to theorize power in novel ways, we also explore what feminists could learn from constructivist thinking in IR. We argue that constructivism can help the feminist identity literature incorporate the notion of an agential self and help the feminist literature on institutions theorize struggle and resistance. Based on our discussion, we identify avenues for empirical research that the juxtaposition of feminist and constructivist research points to.

Identity

The instabilities of the post-Cold War world have revived interest in culture and identity among scholars of world politics (Lapid and Kratochwil 1996). Taken for granted in realist, neorealist, and neoliberal depictions of an existing world, questions of state identity, sovereignty, and national and ethnic identification have found new resonance, in particular among authors who subscribe to a constructivist ontology of becoming (e.g., Wendt 1992a, 1994, Katzenstein 1996; Biersteker and Weber 1996; Risse 1998). In addition to reacting to global political developments, these constructivist treatments of identity also reflect a theoretical agenda: they challenge the utilitarian assumption of exogenously given interests and preferences.

Constructivists differ significantly in the way they use the term *identity*. These differences arise primarily from different concepts of the self. While seeking to correct the seemingly unproblematic approach to the self in utilitarian accounts, most constructivists remain wedded to a modern understanding of the self as the source of change. These authors describe identity as a changing set of beliefs, ideas, or norms that reflexive selves—mostly states—follow (see, e.g., various contributions in Katzenstein 1996). They tend to treat identities as causal, and (often mediated by interests) explaining changes in behavior. On the other hand are those (often with postmodern sympathies) who see the self as an ongoing accomplishment and emphasize the exclusionary and homogenizing tendencies of identity formation (e.g., Neumann 1999).

Feminists have navigated these extremes ever since de Beauvoir asked in the late 1940s: "Are there women, really?" ([1952]1989, xix). Her constructivist answer, suggesting that women were not born but created, triggered an extensive debate on the meaning of the identity woman. The discovery of the "otherness" of women led de Beauvoir and many of her contemporaries to conclude that women's inferior position could be overcome only through the denial and refusal of "female" attributes and characteristics (Tickner 1996, 150). Feminists of the second women's movement in the 1970s engaged in a new evaluation of women's otherness by insisting on the specificity of female characteristics and values and their potentially positive influence on politics and society (Daly 1978; Ruddick 1989a, 1989b; Gilligan 1982). Radical feminists interpreted phenomena such as the arms race, war, and environmental pollution as outcomes of a male defined and male dominated policy and argued that female values—such as peacefulness, empathy, solidarity—would change politics for the better. Yet, these feminists often assumed that women could speak from a unified standpoint since they supposedly shared a common identity. Women of color and women from countries in the South criticized the essentialist and homogenizing character of the category "woman" which, they argued, had been largely defined out of the experiences of Western white middle-class women. Women at the margins pointed to the complex intersections of gender with other identities such as race, ethnicity, class, or sexual orientation (Hooks 1981; Spelman 1988; Mohanty 1991). Postmodern and postcolonial feminists gave further weight to these critiques by emphasizing difference and especially differences among women as a new key concept (Butler 1990; Brown 1995; Scott 1988; Young 1990).

Not surprisingly, feminists in IR have pointed to the central importance of identity questions for the study of international politics long before the recent interest in identity. They have identified states as gendered, encoding unequal divisions of labor and exclusionary forms of citizenship; they have criticized the realist metaphor of state sovereignty for reifying the modernist image of "rational man" as autonomous and unconnected; they have probed the languages of nationalism and critiqued the profoundly gendered identities they propound (Tickner 1992, 1996; Peterson 1993, 1995; Zalewski and Enloe 1995; Pettman 1996; Steans 1998). In addition to questioning (and seeking to destabilize) state and national identities, feminists have argued that non-state identities, such as for example those based on gender, class, and religion, play a crucial role in world politics and should be probed (Krause 1996). Their investigations have steered a course between modern and postmodern theories. On the one hand, they have drawn on postmodern theories of identity for their theorization of power. On the other hand, they have groped for a way to combine postmodern theorizations of a "subjected" self with the modern theories of an agential self that most IR constructivists hold onto.

Central to feminist investigations of identity in IR has been the suggestion that identities do not only create interests and meanings (as constructivists with modern inclinations argue), but also relationships of superiority and inferiority. In their treatments of power, feminists have drawn extensively on the writings of Michel Foucault which, in locating power in discourses, suggests that power is pervasive. Feminists add that such micro-power often expresses itself in the language of gender. Identity then is a discursive effect of "subjection," that is, the parallel formation of subjects and their subjugation (Butler 1997). Feminists have often combined this theory of power with the understanding that there is a deep structure of dichotomies that underlies processes of modern identity formation, so that the construction of identity always also entails the construction of a subjugated other: "Any move to define an identity, a closed totality, always depends on excluding some elements, separating the pure from the impure" (Young 1990, 303). Thus, the duality of self and other effects power whenever it is invoked, and a systemized actualization of identities produces social hierarchies. Bifurcations, dichotomies, and dualisms are both sources and effects of power and point to the "regulatory practice of identity" (Butler 1990, 32).

In foregrounding the connection between power and identity, feminist approaches shed light on aspects of identity formation that most constructivist treatments obscure. First, feminists stress that identity formation entails the creation of differences between and within social collectives. Few other constructivist thinkers have addressed the need for difference and differentiation in the process of identity formation and investigated the role of the "other" (Ruggie 1998a, 873). But, as Wendy Brown (1995, 239) has pointed out, "identity requires difference—who we are is partly determined by who we are not, and the controlling of borders, literal and metaphorical, has been an important feature of determining who we are and who we are not."

"Othering" implies making the other lower or less important than the self, and this is often accomplished by feminizing the other. In the area of foreign policy, for example, Michael Hunt (1987) describes how gender and race stereotypes served as justifications for U.S. interventions in the nineteenth century. Latin America, and especially Cuba, were portrayed as "in need of macho Uncle Sam that would rush in and sweep the Latin lady off her feet" (Hunt 1987, 58). Hunt also argues that "Americans saw themselves acting benevolently, they liked to picture the Latino as a white maiden passively awaiting salvation or seduction" (58). In a similar vein, Doty (1996b) describes the othering of the Philippines during its time as a U.S. colony. Racial as well as gender stereotypes led to the image of the Filipinos as children or animals in need of care. The United States as a masculine actor was called to "take the Philippines" but in a specific colonial way, as "U.S. rule would be based upon love and sympathy" (Doty, 1996b, 334–335). As Tickner (1996, 151) concludes from such evidence, "just as sovereign man depended on the female other for his identity, so the state secures its identity through its relationship to identities of devalued and dangerous others, both inside and outside its boundaries."

Whereas the dramatization of differences *between* collectives "turns the merely different into the absolutely other" (Young 1990, 99), discourses of identity also forcefully diminish differences *within* collectives. The focus among many constructivists on territorially defined identities, in particular nation-states, serves not only to exclude others, but also to homogenize difference.[1] In contrast feminists have explored, for example, nationalist discourses to argue that collective identities often hide differences within. Nationalist discourses are highly gendered and sexualized in their symbolisms as well as in the ways in which they depict the proper identities of men and women. Nira Yuval-Davis and Floya Anthias (1989) have pointed to a Janus-faced quality in nationalist discourse: On the one hand, it presents itself as a modern project for all that allows women to move beyond traditional gender roles. On the other hand, the search for a national identity imagines a sedimented common past of gender difference that frames women as the guardians of a traditional national culture and the guarantors of community survival (Mosse 1985, 16; Kandiyoti 1992, 435). National discourses thus construct identity on the basis of female difference.

In addition to foregrounding and indeed speaking from the position of difference, feminist treatments have radicalized the suggestion that identities are socially constructed. Feminists agree with other constructivists that identities are not exogenously given (as utilitarians assume) but socially made and therefore culturally and historically contingent as well as potentially malleable. But, because feminists critically engage with identity, they reach beyond this understanding to question whether identities can ever be stable. In feminist debates over the essence of a feminine self, the constructivist argument has converged on the understanding that the meaning of woman is fundamentally dependent on political, cultural, and social contexts and has to be continually renegotiated in discourse. Constructivists in IR are quite divided on the matter of stability. For example, Iver Neumann (1996, 1998) argues that European identities, because they are context-bound and contested, are fluid and subject to frequent change. Alexander Wendt suggests that "social identities and interests are always in process during interaction" (1994, 386), but that change is nevertheless slow. Thomas Risse (1998, 5) also argues on the basis of cognitive and social psychological theories that national identities, because they are institutionally and culturally embedded, are usually rather sticky and only subject to gradual change.

Different understandings about the stability of identities result from different theoretical underpinnings. Neumann (1996) builds on what he calls "dialogical literatures," including poststructuralist writings, that theorize identity as accomplished through language, and that see a profoundly unstable, contradictory self that is not clearly separate from the other and is in constant need of tending.[2] In contrast, other writers draw on symbolic interactionism (Wendt 1994), on social psychological and other sociological literatures (Risse 1998; Kowert 1998) that retain the notion of a distinctively modern core self. This is not just a constructed self but one that actively participates in the process of construction. Whereas for Neumann identities are mere effects of discourses, Wendt and Risse conceive of collective identities as emerging from intersubjective (including discursive) exchanges located in complex agency-structure settings. For the former identity is an unstable performance, for the latter a subject that remakes itself.[3]

For feminists, much is at stake in sorting out this contradiction. On the one hand, describing identities as unstable counteracts the homogenizing, exclusionary, and regulative tendencies that feminists have come to associate with solid identifications. Thus, some postmodern feminists have refused identity as a useful analytical and political category. Instead, they consider identities to be sedimented power structures that forcefully categorize people along socially erected boundaries as they exist for example be-

tween men and women, blacks, Hispanics and whites, immigrants and natives, heterosexuals and homosexuals. On the other hand, the depiction of
identities as fluid risks the loss of agency, and thereby the categories of responsibility and autonomy that appear at the base of feminist struggle, and
indeed any emancipatory practice. Thus, a second group of feminists,
equally critical of essentialist notions of identity, has insisted that it is pre-
mature to jettison the notion of identity. At least the identity woman should
be retained, if only for strategic use in the sense of a "temporary home-
stead," as Sylvester (1994) has advocated. Collective identity, these feminists argue, is a necessary base for political action.

Within feminist political theory the debates over essentialism and constructivism of the early 1990s (Benhabib et al. 1995) have given way to
probing new approaches that combine the theorization of an agential self
with an acknowledgment of unstable identities and of difference. Seyla
Benhabib's (1999) narrative model of identity constitution is one example
that resonates with the efforts of constructivists in IR emphasizing the linguistic basis of social construction (e.g., Onuf 1989; Kratochwil 1996;
Weldes 1996). Benhabib combines Habermasian speech act theory with
Charles Taylor's understanding that identities emerge in "webs of interlocution." An agential self for her is one that has communicative competence.
She argues that to be and to become such a self "is to insert oneself into
webs of interlocution; it is to know how to answer when one is addressed;
in turn, it is learning how to address others" (1999, 344). This learning occurs within existing webs of interlocution that a newborn is thrown into,
from narratives about gender and family, to narratives of the nation. We
weave a narrative of the self out of these narratives, "a life story that makes
sense for us, as unique individual selves" (344).

The narrative constitution of the self theorizes a core self emerging out
of the intersection of discourses. But this self is also stable to the extent that
it has communicative competence. This perspective allows Benhabib to
view the self as an agent while at the same time allowing for a regard of the
other in the process of the constitution of identity. Because she views collective identities "as woven out of tales and fragments belonging both to
oneself and to others" (Benhabib 1999, 351), she retains a focus on otherness, and the focus on power that this entails, without giving up the notion
of an agential self. While her narrative self is coherent, it is not self-same in
two senses. First, it is not the same over time, indicating rather "the capacity to generate meaning over time so as to hold past, present, and future together" (353). Second, it has not rigid boundaries that separate it from the
other. This opens up the (perhaps utopian) path for a treatment of others as
different without seeking to assimilate the other to the self.

Benhabib's is just one of a number of recent feminist efforts to find a middle way between modern and postmodern understandings of the self, between "essentialist woman" and "deconstructed woman" (Zalewski 1998, 862).[4] It is one that incorporates constructivist principles without overlooking the violence and injustice that modern processes of identification have authored. Whether or not her proposals are tenable, they outline a promising terrain of dialogue between feminists and constructivists in IR, pointing the way for constructivists who, like Benhabib, consider speech acts a basic building block of social construction. Because speech act theory shares with discourse theories a focus on language, it may be particularly hospitable to incorporating poststructuralist notions of power, allowing for the theorization of an agential self in conjunction with a theorization of women's subordination. We believe that this is an area where constructivism can enrich feminist debates in IR, contributing a more systematic theorization of agency than is currently available in the subfield.

Institutions

When Friedrich Kratochwil and John Ruggie suggested in 1986 that research on intersubjective phenomena required an interpretivist methodology, their focus was the study of international institutions, that is, international regimes. When Robert Keohane developed the distinction between rationalist and reflective approaches in 1988, his focus was again institutions. Soon after, David Dessler (1989) suggested that research on international institutions constituted an established research area where his constructivist "transformational model" could be applied immediately. Indeed, institutions have held considerable theoretical and empirical interest among constructivists (Wendt and Duvall 1989; Onuf 1998b; Ruggie 1993). Keohane has furthermore suggested that there is a resemblance between institutionalism and feminist emphases on intersubjective relations. In this sense, feminism could be useful in founding an institutionalist alternative to realism and rationalism. Because (at least some) feminists share with neoliberal institutionalists an appreciation of "diffuse reciprocity" and cooperation, feminist theory can help articulate "an institutional vision of international relations—a network view, emphasizing how institutions could promote lateral cooperation among organized entities, states or otherwise" (Keohane 1991, 44). While feminists have legitimately criticized Keohane's text as a disciplining exercise (Zalewski 1993; Weber 1994), they have not taken seriously his invitation to help articulate an institutional vision of international relations. We attempt a response to his invitation in this section, albeit on the terrain of constructivism.

If social construction entails the construction of power, as feminists have argued, it is not tenable to conceptualize institutionalism as the feminine counterpart to masculine realism or rationalism: as an approach explaining cooperation (as opposed to conflict) in Keohane's liberal institutionalist framework; or as dealing with morality, emotion, social purpose, and ideas (as opposed to power and material phenomena) in a peculiar (neoliberal) version of constructivism (Finnemore and Sikkink 1998, 889–890). Femininity and masculinity, institutions, ideas, social purpose, as well as power politics and instrumental agency are all part of a constructed world. From a feminist perspective, conflict, power, and material phenomena are thoroughly enmeshed in institutions, and institutions implicated in the exercise of power. We would argue again that institutionalists, including most constructivists, have paid too little attention to power, and when they have done so, they have described power as outside social construction. Feminist treatments show how power operates through institutions. At the same time, feminist research has raised theoretical problems that, we believe, can benefit from a more thorough constructivist theorizing.

IR feminists have drawn on Robert Cox and writings in the Gramscian tradition to understand how gender operates in international institutions. Exemplary is the work of Canadian "feminist critical theorists" (the term is Stienstra's, 1994, 27; see also Whitworth 1994). Their writings constitute an effort to incorporate notions of gender, race, and other status distinctions into a Gramscian conception of hegemony that Cox has adapted to the international level. According to this conception, hegemony means not just the dominance of a state based on physical and material capabilities, but "a coherent conjunction or fit between a configuration of material power, the prevalent collective image of world order (including certain norms), and a set of institutions that administer the order with a certain semblance of universality" (Cox and Sinclair 1996, 103). Feminist critical theorists see gender as an element of this "image of world order" and have investigated how international institutions—a term which they often use interchangeably with international organizations—are implicated in the perpetuation of certain hegemonic notions of gender. They start from the assumption that "institutions reflect power relations, including gender relations, within society and usually maintain and stabilize dominant relations" (Stienstra 1994, 35).

For example, Whitworth has explored the International Labor Organization (ILO) as a "[site] of struggle, around which actors mobilize to both promote and oppose particular interests" (1994, 73–74), including gender interests. Such politics have led to a shift in the way ILO policies construct gender: while international labor standards tended to frame women as mothers in the first half of the century, this has given way to an understanding of women as workers equal to men. Whitworth analyzes the power implications of these understandings: Protective legislation kept women (defined as mothers) out of industries where men dominated while at the same time it failed to protect men. Contemporary proclamations on women's equality may reject unequal protections but often render invisible the family obligations of both women and men. Thus, contestations at the ILO may have changed understandings of gender, but also have perpetuated gender subordination.

In her survey of international women's movements in the twentieth century, Stienstra (1994) similarly approaches international institutions as sites of struggle. She argues that the interactions of movement actors, representatives of states and of international organizations, have contributed to shaping gender relations and identifies a shift in discourse (a term she favors over the Coxian notion of "ideas") from a marginal inclusion of women in international affairs (to deal with social issues), to recognizing women's place in international affairs based on the principle of equal rights, to emphasizing the need to incorporate women in the development process. Women working for peace in the first two decades of the century challenged the stereotype that women had no role in the public sphere; yet their public role was accepted only regarding social issues, presumably an extension of their caring work in the family. The acceptance of equal rights discourse marked a step forward for First World and middle-class women but did not attend to the needs of Third World women. Finally, talk about incorporating women in development does not signal a fundamental change in power relations but constitutes a taming of counter-hegemonic forces.

The basic message of feminist critical theorists is that institutions are implicated in the construction of power relations. In other words, power matters not only in creating institutions (the neoliberal institutionalists' view) or in maintaining institutions (the view of hegemonic stability theorists). Rather, power is a social construct reproduced through institutions along codes of gender, race, class, etc. This is a profoundly different understanding of power than that offered by neoliberals and neorealists. It is an understanding of power as social and contested, not a quantifiable property that actors possess, but a force that is produced. And it is produced on the terrain of institutions—whether international organizations, states, militaries, or families. Here hegemony encounters counter-hegemony.

There is, however, a weakness in this neo-Gramscian understanding of power: Feminist critical theorists have difficulty relating power to agency, and this difficulty is reflected in their ambiguous treatment of institutions. Whitworth's theoretical discussion of gender in international organizations provides an illustration (1994, ch. 3). Seeking to overcome the tension be-

tween structure and agency, she starts from a feminist constructivist understanding that defines gender as a "social relation" reproduced in social practices. Similarly, she conceptualizes international institutions not only as a
structure, but also a process. Yet her reliance on Coxian methods leads her
to shift focus from practices and processes to structures. In the Coxian
model, institutions, ideas, and material conditions together form a historical
structure that circumscribes agency. They constitute a "framework of action
or historical structure" that "does not determine actions in any direct, me-
chanical way but imposes pressures and constraints" (Whitworth 1994, 68,
citing Cox 1981). Structure is theorized in this model but not agency.
Whitworth seeks to overcome this shortcoming by conceptualizing institutions not only as structures, but also as an arena of struggle. But invoking
struggle does not amount to a theory of agency. Theorizing institutions as
arenas cannot account for the constitution of interests and identities of those
engaged in the struggle. Furthermore, the dual understanding of institutions
as structures and arenas reproduces the gap between structure and agency
that Whitworth's invoking of social practice had sought to overcome.

An important theme in the constructivist literature on institutions has
been to demonstrate the inadequacy of rationalistic accounts of agency,
such as that favored by Keohane, particularly in the study of international
regimes. Constructivists have criticized such accounts for treating states as
the primitive individuals of the international system and considering their
identities, powers, and interests as externally given. Rationalists investigate
the way in which states constitute regimes but fail to show how regimes and
structures are constitutive of states (Wendt and Duvall 1989, 55). Furthermore, although rationalist microtheory presumes institutions, it does not
show how institutions are formed; they are exogenous to the theory (Kratochwil 1993c, 445).

Ironically, the same critique can be applied to some versions of constructivism, especially those drawing on "sociological institutionalism"
(e.g., Finnemore 1996a; Katzenstein 1996). Like neoliberal institutionalists,
they have treated institutions (and culture) as outside social construction, as
part of an "environment" that shapes state interests (Jepperson et al. 1996).
Thus, the empirical cases in Katzenstein (1996) treat norms, defined as
"collective expectations about proper behavior for a given identity" (Jepperson et al. 1996, 54), this way. In doing so, the authors fail to move beyond what Dessler has called the positional model. While norms are not
fixed, they do logically exist outside behavior—constraining and disposing,
shaping and shoving (compare Dessler 1989, 466)—and raising the awk-
ward question of where norms come from (see Kowert and Legro 1996).

Because they insist that institutions reproduce through practice, feminist critical theorists should be able to avoid these problems. Practices are neither the rational choices of neoliberal institutionalists, nor the determined behavior of structuralists. Practice means agency in the context of institutions, where institutions are conceived as neither structure, arena, or environment. Nicholas Onuf's definition may show a way out. According to him, institutions are "families of rules," where "rules and related practices are almost impossible to separate in practice, because every time agents respond to rules . . . they have an effect on those rules and on their places in the families of rules" (1998b, 70). Institutions in this definition are practices—they do not exist outside them. As responses to rules, these practices realize both agency and structure, together with the messages of gender and power encoded in rules.

A structuralist approach has allowed feminist critical theorists to introduce gender to the study of international institutions by theorizing power in novel ways. Other constructivist approaches can add a theory of agency but are useful for feminists only if they are equally good at conceptualizing power. Constructivists have dealt with power in various ways—not all of them helpful. First are those that have not put power at the center of their analysis but have implied two conventional understandings: Domestically, power means legitimate authority; internationally, power is a material resource. In both cases, power is treated as a quantity that actors (states, militaries, interest groups) have and that they use differently depending on political cultures or identities (e.g., various articles in Katzenstein 1996; also see Wendt 1994, 1999). Understanding power as a quantity takes feminists no further than to say: Women don't have it. It says little about how power is constructed and reproduced. A second way in which constructivists have talked about power is by suggesting that institutions both create the world and delimit possibilities (e.g., Wendt and Duvall 1989). The suggestion that institutions delimit the world is familiar to critical feminist theorists; constructivism contributes an understanding of power as enabling as well. In this understanding, empowerment and constraint collapse into each other, adding agency to feminist critical theory, while theorizing power as part of the enactment of rules, norms, or discourses. A third constructivist understanding of power pushes the issue further: All rules and institutions always entail rule, that is, they systematically distribute privilege to create patterns of subordination (Onuf 1998b, 75). In this understanding institutions realize power not only in providing guides to practice, but these guides are always tainted, promoting formations of rule such as hierarchy, hegemony, or heteronomy (Onuf 1989). Feminist constructivists and feminist critical theorists need just such a strong conceptualization of power that lends itself to showing systematic forces of subordination aligned along the axes of gender, race, and other statuses.

Neoliberal institutionalism may resemble the relational ontology that has emerged in some theories of feminist psychology, as Keohane has suggested. However, our discussion makes clear that the explanatory value of neoliberal institutionalism (together with certain liberal versions of constructivism) is severely hampered because it offers no theory of gender subordination. Neoliberal institutionalism does provide a theory of rational agency. Whether the images of a caring self and a utility maximizing self are compatible is open to debate and needs further consideration. But a robust feminist theory of institutions needs to account for both the ways in which agents reproduce or challenge institutions, as well as for the patterns of rule that are constructed through such agency.

Directions

The recovery of constructivism's feminist pedigree has brought into focus strengths and weaknesses of various constructivist approaches and points towards new areas of productive research. These can be found where emphases differ between feminists and other constructivists. We have identified them in the analysis of institutions as gendered, in the focus on power as a social construct, in the intersection of agency and identity, and in an investigation of identity in global spaces. We develop these areas in more detail.

Research on institutions is a major meeting ground for feminists and constructivists, and we see considerable potential for a cross-fertilization of the two literatures. In particular, applying gender analysis to institutionalist approaches probing global governance and international organization can correct silences and yield useful insights to the way micropower plays itself out in processes of institutionalization. The absence of any feminist research on regimes is striking (Prügl 1996). Clearly, the state-centric and rationalist focus of most of this literature has discouraged such interventions, but constructivist approaches open up the regimes literature to feminist analysis. For example, Ruggie's (1993, 1996) theorization of multilateralism as a historically specific order associated with American hegemony and incorporating principles of conduct based on collective security, nondiscrimination in trade, and the observance of human rights calls out for an incorporation of feminist research. Such research has shown that these principles encode gender: The notion of human rights has systematically excluded women's rights (Bunch 1990), and liberalizing trade has often disproportionately hurt women (Sparr 1994). Similarly, Ruggie's (1983) theorization of the postwar economic order as "embedded liberalism" begs the feminist question of how states, with their new legitimate authority to intervene in the market, were gendered. The vast feminist literature on the welfare state provides ample materials for such an analysis.

A feminist constructivist approach may also point towards a new way of theorizing and empirically investigating patriarchy as a constellation of rules that make up international institutions. It would avoid the universalistic tendencies that have discredited such earlier efforts, and instead locate gender rules in the interactions of specific agents (states, NGOs, movements) that participate in processes of international organization. Such an approach would not need to postulate a link of gender rules to particular material conditions (as implied in critical feminist theory), or a feminine essence. Furthermore, it makes no prediction about the effects that "hegemonic" gender rules constructed in international institutions have in other arenas. Indeed, a theorization that links global constructions to specific agents limits and circumscribes the reach of such constructions. This makes it impossible to think of gender constructions emerging from international organizations as representing gender constructions around the world. Rather, they are situated constructions tied to the particular context of multilateral politics and interacting with constructions in other sites. Feminists have barely begun to investigate constructions of gender in international sites (Meyer and Prügl 1998; Prügl 1999), and there have been few efforts to relate them to national, regional, and local constructions (important exceptions are Elshtain 1995; Baines 1999).

Another productive area of further research concerns the intersection of power and agency and the theorization of power as a social construct. In particular, there is room for more extensive theoretical and empirical work that relates the power of brute military and economic capabilities to the micropowers that operate in institutional politics and in the politics of identity formation. An important first step is to explore how the framing of certain entities as "material" (as opposed to social) moves these entities beyond critical investigation. Materiality has been accorded to phenomena as different as human bodies, sexuality, weaponry, and economic resources. Framed this way, they appear as matters upon which cultural construction operates. Feminists have sought to unhinge the fixity of such "things" suggesting that they result from processes of materialization, from a ritualized repetition of norms that creates certain matters as "constitutive constraints" outside of which we would not be able to operate (especially Butler 1993). In this sense, neither bodies, nor sex, weapons, or economic resources are outside construction, as Carol Cohn (1987) has shown in analyzing the language of defense intellectuals, or as J.K. Gibson-Graham (1996) has illustrated in challenging the idea that capitalism is inevitable and natural. Such writings denaturalize and dematerialize seemingly natural and material forces. Feminist approaches are uniquely poised to push this type of inquiry further, adding important insight on the construction of power, a central analytic category in IR, and an area that other constructivists have virtually ignored.

We also see points of contact between feminists and constructivists in the study of identities, although they are less easy to capture. Constructivist treatments that dissociate power and identity are problematic for feminist projects. Feminists are also likely to be suspicious of approaches that depict the other as a reflection of the self who can be engaged on the terms of sameness. Furthermore, feminists critically look at theories of identity that fail to offer an alternative to the exclusionary and often violent vision of self and community that has informed statist IR. A feminist approach to identity needs to center around the challenging and creative tension of combining an agential self with an acknowledgment of unstable identities. This notion of destabilized identities refusing to remain within the clearly divided divisions of self and other is a central part of an emancipatory project. Furthermore, reaching out to the other without denying difference is central to developing a feminist ethics of world politics.

Feminists stress that non-state identities increasingly matter in global politics—as expressed for example in transnational networks or social movements based on race, gender, religion etc.—and we join here other constructivists who have moved beyond a state-centric paradigm (e.g., Risse-Kappen 1995c; Fierke 1996; Lynch 1999). We do not deny that states are important. However, even investigations of interstate politics need to connect to social phenomena at other levels. Suggestions that female bodies figure in global politics—symbolically, ideologically, and as stand-ins for government—accomplish a reconfiguration of the social space of international relations, no longer neatly divided into hierarchical levels of analysis, but collapsing levels into a fused landscape of the social. Here the power of power politics encounters the micropowers of gender, race, ethnicity, etc. Here also is space for a rethinking of international authority, one that accounts for the constitution of powerful agents, the distribution of privilege along socially constructed statuses, the creation of abject others, and the materialization of military and economic forces. It could be a distinctly feminist space for a constructivist research program that probes oppressions, injustices, and a lack of care.

We have benefitted enormously from the comments of friends and colleagues. In particular, we would like to thank Nicholas Onuf, Patricia Price,

Francois Debrix, Sandra Whitworth, and the editors of this collection for their critical but sympathetic reading of the manuscript.

Notes

1. For a recent interesting treatment that avoids this trap, see Kratochwil (1996).

2. Whether he lives up to this promise in his discussion of the "East" in European identity formation (Neumann 1999) is questionable, but beyond the scope of this article.

3. Risse (1998) focuses on party discourses in order to study empirically the Europeanization of nation state identities. For him, however, identities are more than textual constructions.

4. Other efforts include Ferguson (1993), Chodorow (1995), Weir (1995).

5

What Systems Theory Can Tell Us About Constructivism

Mathias Albert

The constructivist debate in International Relations (IR) fits the tradition of theorizing in this discipline rather well. Although a term is widely shared, disagreement—if not outright confusion—reigns regarding the overall meaning, its possible uses, let alone its philosophical underpinnings. Constructivism has been variously labeled as "mood," "method," "turn," "ontology," "epistemology," "nonsense," "potential banality."[1]

This chapter will not raise the many "what" and "how" questions that are being asked about constructivism. It will instead address a question that, up to now, has attracted little attention, namely that of "why."[2] It will take up this question from an angle that will not be familiar to most IR theorists, that is, modern systems theory (MST). In light of the variety of the contributions to this volume, it seems a worthwhile exercise to engage with the subject in this way. Constructivism should not be addressed from a narrow IR perspective alone precisely because, unlike other theoretical approaches to IR, constructivism draws on a greater range of—often seemingly incompatible—philosophical traditions.

Constructivism is a form of investigation that is found not only in the social sciences, but also in the humanities and indeed in the natural sciences. Thus, in a way, the increased attention to constructivism in IR reflects a development endemic to all sciences. Although this may appear to be a coincidence, it cannot be accounted for only in terms of a development within science or its various disciplines. Science does form a part of society, and its evolution is firmly embedded within it. Nonetheless, societal

93

evolution should not be treated as merely external to scientific developments. Science, like the society of which it is part, is in constant flux. What is thus needed is a conceptually rich account that traces the spread of constructivism and links it to the development of society.

To be sure, where it has been received and discussed, MST has been disputed, sometimes very hotly. Nonetheless, MST is one of the very few approaches that can rightfully claim the ability to offer a fully developed theory of modern society. More specifically, MST not only contributes an answer to the "why" of constructivism in general, and in IR in particular, but can also account for the great diversity of constructivisms. This alone should provide reason enough to take a closer and fresh look at constructivism from the perspective of MST; it should be mentioned at the outset that such an approach is, in a way, as I will explain later, self-referential. I will argue, however, that MST employed here to understand constructivism is as constructivist as constructivist can be. However, unlike most other constructivisms:

1. MST does not prioritize constructivism as the outstanding element of its own theorizing, let alone as a label (or self-advertisement). Constructedness is invested in the very constitution of modern society, and thus it is an elementary building block of advanced social theory rather than its result.
2. MST is both more radical and comprehensive, as well as more modest, than the other constructivisms on offer in the marketplace. It is more radical and comprehensive since it breaks with some of the fundamental assumptions of modern social theory and claims instead to offer an alternative, fully developed theory of society. It is more modest, however, since, for theoretical reasons, it is very self-aware of its position within that communicative system called science, as well as the contingencies in terms of its truth claims that result therefrom.

This chapter begins with a brief introduction to some aspects of MST. Even a lengthy introduction would not do justice to such a complex and elaborate body of theory; the most that can be done here is to provide some snapshots. The selection of these snapshots will be guided by the goal of explaining the "why" of constructivism by situating it in a wider context of social change. The reading provided is thus one of constructivism as more or less a result; or better, as a reflection of change rather than simply a method of analysis. I attempt to show that, from the perspective of a systems theoretical understanding of (social) science, any effort to bring about change cannot but be radically constructivist because the engagement itself in bringing about such a change is always an inseparable part of that change.

Since to some readers the arguments that follow may bear some resemblance with postmodern thought, a special effort is made to elucidate the relationship to postmodern approaches. It is not my intention to provide the reader with another route up the mountains of constructivism, let alone to add another summit to what is already a most formidable range. Instead, I propose a new way of undertaking the climb. Of course, it is up to every single aspirant to negotiate his or her way through, based on a comprehensive tour guide, which other contributions within and outside of this volume offer. At the end, some warnings will be issued as to paths better avoided and one or two recommendations for particularly "scenic" routes.

On the (Modest) Uses of Modern Systems Theory

In his article on the "social constructivist challenge," John Ruggie asserts that for IR "[n]o general theory of the social construction of reality is available to be borrowed from other fields" (Ruggie 1998a, 857). Of course, Ruggie is correct when he frames social constructivism as a critique of neoutilitarianism and observes that social constructivism must not be understood as providing a theory that could claim explanatory superiority when judged from some metatheoretical point of view. Nonetheless, with respect to the above quote, it is unclear how Ruggie reconciles this observation with his own argument. In his discussion of the "classical" sociologists—in particular Emile Durkheim and Max Weber—he does refer to at least two general theories of the social construction of reality.[3] Thus, Ruggie's observation would have been more accurate if he had asserted that some general theories of social construction are in fact available to be borrowed, particularly from sociology, but that for the most part they remain on the library shelves and indeed are not being borrowed. In this respect, it speaks volumes that Ruggie's article is among the few attempts to systematically explore classical sociology for potential uses in IR theory.[4]

Yet, Ruggie's article also highlights the problem that even "general theories" are in need of a theoretical overhaul from time to time, and in some cases actually are substantially improved (if not superseded) by new developments in various fields. Thus, Ruggie (1998a, 862) refers to John Searle to note that Durkheim and Weber—comprehensive though their theories were—"through no fault" of their own . . . lacked an adequate theory of speech acts, or performatives, of intentionality, of collective intentionality, or rule governed behavior." Given the prominence of these concepts the situation in the social sciences has obviously dramatically changed.[5]

Read in this way, it is less the case that "general theories" are in short supply—general theories abound in social thought—and more that IR constructivists need to become more aware of them. This is not, of course, to claim that some general theory would be preferable to other general theories, for which a neutral metatheoretical reason could be given. Thus, some people would argue that the "progress" identified by Ruggie is not that progressive at all; for example, Weber would be quite sufficient for understanding society even if it lacks a theory of performativity.

This chapter proceeds from these assumptions and builds on the view that there are no neutral grounds for judging the value of a theory. The selection of theories to be received, applied, and discussed reflects a number of contingencies. It is, nonetheless, quite surprising that MST, as one of the most elaborate and comprehensive social theories in existence, has barely been read in IR theory at all. To put it differently, it is not that MST had been read and found unworthy of further consideration; it simply hasn't been read.[6]

One could speculate as to why this is the case. MST is difficult and complex. As a theory of society, it does not rely on human beings as the basic units of analysis. MST does not claim to provide practical or normative guidelines for action but is rather more narrowly confined to showing the limits of action in a systemic context.[7] MST is primarily about observation, and in this respect it is concerned with what theorizing first of all is about. Rather than delegitimizing efforts to link theorizing to guidelines for action, MST is a mode of observation by which other theories are observed from the point of view of whether they make sense and can be applied.[8]

Given its many facets, there are many ways to introduce MST. That said, there can be no "correct" way to introduce or use it, particularly given its size and complexity. In this chapter, I will, therefore, choose a rather straightforward ordering principle, which will not only guide the short presentation of some of the theory's main tenets, but also may inspire a fresh reading of constructivism. This ordering principle follows that of Niklas Luhmann, the founding father of MST, as developed in *Die Gesellschaft der Gesellschaft (The Society of Society)*. This two-volume work arguably constitutes the opus magnum of MST, summing up three decades of research. While it does not capture all the detail of Luhmann's more than four hundred publications,[9] it provides the most concise statement of his theory of society, which is only in the initial stages of being received and intellectually appraised.

Most participants in the heated debates surrounding MST would agree on one thing: the theory turns most previously existing theories of society on their heads.[10] MST does not start by asking why certain social structures exist as they are and how they change, but rather by asking the more fundamental question of why almost all possible social interactions, and structures emerging there from, fail to materialize.[11] "Why is it part of the meaning of the forms of social life that the gigantic surplus of the possible is left unnoticed as an unmarked space? It would be conceivable at least that societal structures do not emerge as aggregates of preferred action motives, but in a much more elementary fashion as the inclusion of this exclusion into the form" (Luhmann 1997, 39).[12]

Out of this meaningless "unmarked space," meaning can only emerge from the drawing of distinctions. This is the basic precondition of, as well as the "content" of, observation. Drawing on Spencer Brown's *Laws of Form* (1979), Luhmann argues that "forms are no longer to be seen as figures, but as boundary lines, as markers of a difference which force clarification of which side is signified . . .The other side of the boundary (the "form") is simultaneously given. Every side of the form is the other side of the other side. No side is something for itself" (Luhmann 1997, 60–61). What at first sounds trivial, in fact has tremendous consequences for the philosophical underpinnings of social theorizing; in contrast to the notion of "notion" (*Begriff*), it gives up on the idea of somehow achieving unity of meaning through something other than difference.[13]

These thoughts form the basis for a systems theory that utilizes the difference between system and environment as the basic form in order to observe and describe (cf. Luhmann 1997, 64). Most of the systems observed on this basis are autopoietic systems, which means they are operatively autonomous systems: not only their structures, but their elements are constituted within the systems themselves (by recursivity, that is, connecting to previous operations within the systems), and not by an input of elements into the systems.[14] However, it must be emphasized that this state of operative closure refers solely to the systemic modus operandi, the constitution of meaning (by basically drawing distinctions): "In this of course nothing is implied which could be understood as causal isolation, absences of contact or closure of the systems" (68). Based on these basic observations, MST can identify the particular characteristic of the societal system:

> Accordingly, the societal system is not characterized by a certain "essence," let alone a certain morality (diffusion of happiness, solidarity, equalization of living standards, rational-consensual integration etc.), but only by the operation which produces and reproduces society. That is communication. It follows that what is meant with communication (as with operation) is some-

> thing happening in a historically concrete, and thus context dependent fash-
> ion—and not the mere application of the rules of correct speech. (Luhmann
> 1997, 70)

The difference between the *"Gesellschaftssystem"* (the "system of society"
or "societal system") and a *"soziales System"* (a "social system") seems to
get lost in the English translation (both could well be translated into English
as "social system"). Whereas the number of social systems (*soziale Systeme*) is infinitely high, there is only one societal system (*Gesellschaftssystem*). If social systems are constituted by communication, then a single
instance of communication forms a simple social system (in this case an
interaction system with a very low degree of complexity); more interesting
for a theory of society are the more complex, autopoietic social systems,
such as organizations and the great functional subsystems of society (e.g.,
economy, law, art, etc.). However, if communication is constitutive of
sociality and social systems (e.g., psychic systems do not utilize communication, but bear a strong affinity to social systems in that they form meaning
based systems), then there can be no communication that is "a-social" and
thus somewhere outside of society. Society thus includes all communication
and everything social. This also means that there cannot be more than one
society (since all parts of the globe have been discovered); thus, it seems
more than appropriate to call that society "world society."

It is important to highlight what is not meant by world society in this
context and what differentiates it from most earlier theories of society. As
the highest order social system possible, that is the social system that includes all communication, world society cannot be understood as something
that is integrated; rather, its unity can only be seen to lie in its difference,
particularly since it is characterized by a high degree of functional differentiation. The boundaries and limits of society can thus only be defined in an
operative fashion. Territorial boundaries, for example, are meaningless for
defining the external limits of society if there is only one society; they may,
however, define an internal mode of differentiation within society or of one
or more of its subsystems. Another point that cannot be overemphasized is
that human beings, that is individuals, do not form parts of society. Not
everything that is usually taken to be associated with the individual is fully
included in society; thus, psychic systems—which do not as such communicate and thus do not form part of society—are usually ascribed to "individuals." Conversely, most communication cannot usually be reduced to
individuals and thus society is "more" than an aggregate of individuals.
Seen in this way, MST as a theory of society is "a-human." It is not "inhu-
man," however; on the contrary, it refuses to make any assumption about

who and what human beings are or what makes an individual an individual. This is not to say that human beings are seen as irrelevant; it is only to say that some important aspects of human beings cannot be reduced to or be seen to be based on communication. Therefore, they do not fall into a theory of society.

Again, this "closure" of the societal system must not be seen as something that is differentiated from other systems in a naturally given manner: "The societal system's unity lies solely in its demarcations towards outside, in the system's form, in the operatively constantly reproduced difference" (Luhmann 1997, 90). If one does describe society as a system, then it seems worthwhile to follow through on some important insights of systems theory (i.e., the theory of autopoietic systems) in general. It then becomes important to realize that operatively closed observing systems have no contact with their environment on the level of their operation: "All observation of the environment must be conducted within the system itself as an internal activity, using its own differentiations" (92). This is a central point and one needs to be very clear and specific about it. It is not the case that there are no contacts or causal relations between various (social) systems. But if we are talking about operatively closed observation systems, it means that things only "enter" the system's operations by being observed and "operatively processed" by the system itself. This can only be asserted on the basis of a radical constructivist epistemology: "Anything which is experienced as reality results from a resistance of communication to communication" (95). And further on: "The system reproduces itself in the imaginary space of its references; it does this by renewing the difference between self-reference and other-reference as the form of its autopoiesis in every communicative operation" (98).

Against—philosophically banal—assertions that such a radical constructivist epistemology would logically lead to a denial of materiality, one can only assert that "instituting and keeping system boundaries ... presumes a continuum of materiality which does neither know nor respect these boundaries" (Luhmann 1997, 100). This observation leads Luhmann to identify the main task and difficulty of a theory of society: to explain the relation between society and its environment if society itself cannot "contact" its environment in its own mode of operation. Luhmann finds the "solution" to this problem in Humberto Maturana's idea of "structural couplings":

> Structural couplings limit the range of possible structures with which a system can conduct its autopoiesis. They presuppose that every autopoietic system operates as a structurally determined system, that is, that it can determine its own operations through its own structures only. Structural coupling

> thus excludes that givens in the environment can according to their structures determine what is happening within the system . . . [S]tructural coupling . . . does not determine what is happening within the system but it must be assumed [within the system; MA] since otherwise autopoiesis would come to a standstill and the system would cease to exist. (Luhmann 1997, 100)

Communicative systems are constituted by differentiating "medium" and "form," where a medium will couple elements loosely and a form will do so more strictly. The constant coupling and decoupling thus underlies the operation and structuring of a communicative system. This "undermines the classic distinction between structure and process" (Luhmann, 1997, 199). A form that is kept over a longer time, because it assumes an important function, Luhmann calls a "semantic." It is on this basis that one can distinguish between "dissipative media"—media that determine and, over time, increase the possible range of recipients of communication—and "success media"—media that assures that communication is received in a meaningful way, given the infinite complexity of communication enabled by the evolution of dissipative media. Dissipative media are first and foremost language "secrets," which provide interruptions and channel communication, and which are usually instituted via religion or morals (that is, for example, a moral code regulates what can be communicated and what must not), writing, printing and electronic media. "Success media" take the form of symbolically generalized communicative media, which regulate the probabilities of an acceptance or rejection of communication. Those identified by Luhmann (and it remains an open question whether this is a closed list for the time being) are truth, values, love, property/money, art, power/law.

Each of these media utilizes a basal code (e.g., lawful/unlawful being the basal code of the legal system; true/false the basal code of the scientific system). In this short introduction, it is impossible to further elucidate the details of MST; however, it is important to realize that the emergence and evolution of symbolically generalized communication media are a response to and a condition of the evolution of society. They allow the acceptance or rejection of communication in specific ways, reacting to the fact that this requires specialized media and cannot be achieved by a homogenized structuring device such as morality. It is on this rather fundamental level—and quite often not in the ensuing observation of society—that a theory of society based on MST parts company with theorizing about society in the extended tradition of the Frankfurt School, given that language is not accorded an operative mode of its own, but seen as only thinking or communication (cf. Luhmann 1997, 112).

If one does not let oneself be too distracted by the dense agglomeration of unfamiliar terms and concepts, the significance of such a theory of society to constructivism should be clear. From this perspective it hardly makes sense to question whether constructivism constitutes a fruitful approach. Rather, within such a theory, a radical constructivism is all there is. There are no neutral grounds of observation: "All orientation is construction, is differentiation reactualized from one moment to the next" (Luhmann 1997, 45). And to sum it up succinctly:

> Such a program inevitably leads to a "constructivist" understanding of science. A science that understands itself to be second order observation avoids statements of an external world given independently of observations. It finds the ultimate guarantee of the observer's relation to reality only in the facticity of its own operation and the insight that this would not be possible at all without highly complex presuppositions (we were talking of structural couplings). (1120)

The preceding brief presentation of some central tenets of MST relies on a distinct concept of society as the basis for social inquiry, which has a number of philosophical implications. This introduction cannot explore in what way MST can be useful for the study of more specific questions of international relations. Its primary purpose has been to show that one of the most powerful and elaborate, yet also the most disputed and misunderstood theories of society—and of the "social construction of reality," in Ruggie's words—in the academic marketplace has gone unnoticed in IR theory in general and constructivism in particular. This is particularly surprising if one considers that, from the perspective of MST, social theory is only possible on the basis of a radical epistemological constructivism.

To reiterate, this is not to argue for the adoption of MST, nor for examination of its possible uses for specific research questions in IR (but see Albert, forthcoming). It is to argue that the perspectives on the social world, that is society in general, offered by MST necessitate a fresh look at "constructivism" at a time when current debates on constructivism, in IR and elsewhere, seem more in danger of obstructing than facilitating understanding. If one is prepared to follow MST one simple step and concede that science is a second order observation of the world, then it is hardly possible to deny that a radically constructivist epistemology is at work. A functionally differentiated and specific subsystem of (world) society, science is inconceivable unless it is based on the basis of such a constructivist epistemology. The interesting question about the constructivist debate or turn in IR then becomes less one about adopting a constructivism and choosing its particular form, but rather why constructivism suddenly abounds in various scholarly discussions, clearly stimulating and thus regulating communication, albeit not in an always clearly structured fashion.

Why Does IR Theory Increasingly Describe Itself as "Constructivist"?

The frequent rationale for adopting a constructivist approach to IR—or for dealing with the different versions of constructivism in the field—is that it seeks to explain developments and puzzles in IR for which the standard or "mainstream" approaches are unable to provide sufficient answers. The "Third Debate" is usually credited with having paved the way for constructivism.[15] From thereon, however, opinions vary strongly as to how different constructivisms relate to (the equally unspecific field of) "postpositivism," in general, and to the more radical representatives of postpositivist thought, that is, postmodern approaches, in particular. While some would include "constructivism" and postmodern scholarship under a common constructivist umbrella (Hopf 1998), others (who want to avoid being put in one basket with the postmodern writers) are trying to construct constructivism as a kind of "middle ground" between postpositivist and mainstream approaches (Adler 1997). Still others would see constructivism as on its way to, if not firmly established as, the discipline's new mainstream. This constructivism does not in fact break with the old mainstream in any substantial fashion.[16]

The various forms of constructivism share the idea that it represents a reaction to what they perceive to be flawed mainstream theories, much as postpositivism or critical IR theory derive their identities as movements in opposition to or beyond established disciplinary forms of exploration. However, some proponents of constructivism share the idea that postpositivist and critical approaches remain less successful at delivering substantive theories, which could guide empirical research, than in providing a fundamental critique of long established elements of IR theory.[17] One can, rightfully, argue that the demand that postpositivist contributions deliver testable theories reduces them to the very nomological-deductive model of scientific inquiry, which they sought to dismantle in the first place. Such a demand does not seem to be a very compelling one in intellectual terms. However, most constructivists would presumably assert that there is basically nothing wrong with the dominant nomological-deductive model of doing science and that constructivism is, in essence, no more than a method within this model (see Checkel 1998).

To a degree, these constructivists accept the criticisms of postpositivists or critical theorists. However, they argue, against the latter, that theirs is not an "epistemological constructivism," but rather an "ontological constructivism." The main reason for proposing a version of "ontological constructivism" is to criticize a mode of inquiry that has regularly taken (the identity of) various units of analysis and their identity for granted. By contrast, "ontological constructivists" do pose questions about the identity of a unit of analysis at a given time and how it came about. They ask how, in the first place, the interests that guide action were shaped by various ideas, norms, socialization, and adaptation processes, as well as what are the relevant "units" of analysis, for example, agent or structure.[18]

Any exploration of why constructivism has gained so much prominence in IR theory has to take this variation—and sometimes opposed and mutually exclusive relation between various constructivisms—into account. A more or less "classical" and empirically dense sociology of science approach provides a basis for tracing, not only the emergence of constructivist approaches, but also their substantial variation; thus, for example, tracing certain theoretical developments to substantive changes, in various "intellectual styles" and discussion contexts ("discourses") etc. However, the observation that what is observed here is open to such a sociology of science approach shows how the question at hand can be addressed in a quite different yet potentially rich way. Formally conceived, sociology of science explanations first of all, provide scientific observations of scientific observations.[19] They illustrate that scientific observation can first and foremost be conceived to be an observation by the scientific system (which utilizes the basal code of true/false). Sociology of science approaches, thus understood, form self-references within the scientific system (and can thus be accorded an important role in upholding the latter's autopoiesis). Scientific observations, including constructivist ones, also utilize other-references of the scientific system (and thus form a part of the self-description of society in a scientific mode). However, these seemingly banal observations have important consequences for the way scientific observations are made in the first place.

The observation that science constitutes an operatively closed communicative subsystem of society leads to the conclusion that all scientific observation is coded according to the true/false code.[20] In relation to society as a whole, the emergence of science as an autopoietic system must be seen as a result of the differentiation of symbolically generalized communicative media, which allow communicative connectivity under the condition of an exponentially increasing communicative complexity.[21] Thus, the evolution of science as an operatively closed communicative system is, of course, the result of the evolution of society as a communicative system. This communicative system no longer described itself through a more or less "integrative" semantic but evolved through the functional differentiation of operatively autonomous subsystems. For science, this means, for example, that the true/false code operates autonomously from some reference to an external grounding of that code. There is no external guarantee that codes on the "true" side of the true/false distinction are true except in the relation to the false (that is, for example, true because it conforms to the will of God). Science—like every other communicative system—constantly produces new forms and thus partakes in offering new semantics. These semantics are kept for a longer time and thus form "stable" parts in the self-description of society. Such a semantic cannot be equated with singular theories or even "vocabularies"; rather, in providing a stable background for the self-description of society(ies), it could be equated with "cosmographies."

MST largely limits itself to "the description of society's self-description in the old European tradition, that is Greco-Roman-Christian thought, because it is the only tradition which accompanied modern society in its emergence and the only one which up to the present influences the expectations directed towards it" (Luhmann 1997, 893). This limitation is thus not to be understood as resulting from a normative predisposition or disregard for other semantics (Chinese cosmography, Judaism, etc.), but simply reflects an observation of the semantic that came to be predominant in (the worldwide evolution of) modern society. The transformation of such a "semantic" of modern society does not occur in the form of a sharp, "epochal" shift. In this respect, the description of society as postmodern is a description, not of a semantic, but rather of a reflexivity of society's self-descriptions in which it is realized that a transformation in its semantic is taking place. In this respect, it is hardly surprising that postmodern observations point to ruptures in the old semantic rather than provide an outline of a new one—they cannot since new forms of self-description only emerge in and through the self-description of society. Whether a form of self-description crystallizes into a semantic can only be observed *post factum*. The transformation of a semantic can thus primarily be observed in how an old semantic works to order and structure communication by providing points for communicative connectivity. Only then is it possible to identify how a semantic gradually loses this structuring potential.

Postmodern approaches to IR theory, as well as in social theory in general, have—to varying degrees—been successful in establishing the argument that there is a link between the way society describes itself (and science describes society) and the semantics of society. Various distinctions, such as order/anarchy, man/woman, etc., not only imply a hierarchy, but derive much of their power from the assumption of more or less "natural" hierarchical distinctions.[22] Extending the argument further, these hierarchical distinctions supplement an important part of the "semantic of Old Europe," namely, the distinction between the whole and its parts. In its basic form this has remained unchanged since Aristotle: hierarchical distinctions make it possible to process the paradox inherent in the distinction between a whole and its part (the paradox that something is at the same time one and many):

> With the distinction of a whole from its parts, the unity of an object, be it the world or be it society, is merely duplicated, that is, it is described twice. On the one hand, the unity is the whole and, on the other hand, it is the sum of parts whose interaction produces the supplementary value through which it becomes a whole. At the same time, it is a double description of the same phenomenon. This has to remain invisible, since otherwise the paradox would emerge openly. In the history of societal evolution, only the mythology of the "invisible hand" addresses this problem directly, but then with a metaphor that is paradoxical itself. (Luhmann 1997, 918)

Not only do postmodern approaches expose the paradox of whole and parts (and the associated processing of this paradox through naturalized hierarchizations) as increasingly thrown open and destabilized. One could indeed read the entire "processual turn" in various disciplines in much the same way.[23] However, what is, in contrast to the "processual turn," highlighted by various postmodern approaches—though barely put that way—is that the whole/part scheme is not replaced by an equally comprehensive one, but rather by a "multiplicity" of forms ("narratives," in postmodern jargon). The only aspect that frequently gets lost in postmodern accounts of incommensurability, however, is that the incommensurabilities—which do arise as a result of the breakdown of the unifying scheme of whole/parts—are not only incommensurabilities between narratives/forms which cover particularities (i.e., the former parts), but also between those and narratives/forms which cover the universal (i.e., the former whole):

> The cosmologically founded scheme of whole and parts was only definitively abandoned (which does not exclude the existence of semantic "survivals") in the context of world society and world wide modern culture, that is, perhaps in the nineteenth but certainly in the twentieth century. World society does not have enough visible harmony to be understood in this way. The scheme of tradition is, therefore, replaced by the less demanding distinction between particular (religious, ethnic, cultural) and universal forms of meaning [Sinnformen], which can be used everywhere. It thus becomes possible to develop particularity in opposition to universal structures of the modern world (for esample, religious fundamentalisms) and to participate in the technical conditions of modernity (for example, mass media, travel, monetary exchange). World-societal universality can then become the possibility for contrasting local particularities. But this constitutive playing off against each other requires that society either dispenses with "total" framework conditions or leaves them to disputable ideologies. (Luhmann 1997, 930–931)

The scheme of whole/parts, which forms an important part of the semantic of Old Europe, is unstable in a variety of ways. In the narrow context of IR theory, postmodern approaches have made the most visible contribution in this respect. Of course, the continuing importance of the scheme is even visible in advanced theoretical deliberations, such as the agent-structure debate which featured prominently in the discipline in the late 1980s and early 1990s.[24] Here a last attempt to process the paradox of whole and parts can be witnessed in the idea of a co-constitution of agents and structures. That it has contributed to the destabilization of yet another important aspect of the semantic of Old Europe—at least for the part of IR theory—reinforces my thesis that the constructivist mood in IR theory is but a reaction to the increasing inadequacy of the semantics of old Europe. Insofar as this is the case, it seems perfectly legitimate to subsume all constructivism in IR under the postpositivist badge of IR theorizing. This requires that postpositivism be read not only as a critique of positivism, but as a manifestation of the old semantic.

What distinguishes some of these constructivisms from, say, postmodern approaches,[25] is not, for reasons mentioned above, primarily an epistemological difference (i.e., even the most positivist approach cannot escape the radically constructivist epistemology of contemporary science). What distinguishes them—and it is not clear whether this is an epistemological difference as such—is the degree of reflexivity regarding scientific observations. The pretension that a constructivist method can respond to substantial problems is unraveling before our eyes (an unraveling which is, however, expressed in the flowering of those constructivist observations that postmodern writers would describe as mainstream), not the observation of the way this substance is constructed. Even mainstream constructivism, which is usually distanced from the more "radical" constructivisms, expresses a transformation of the semantics of Old Europe, aptly articulated in the idea that it is merely developing an ontological constructivism.

I take "ontological constructivism" to be the constructivism espoused by, among others, Emanuel Adler, Jeffrey Checkel, Peter Katzenstein, Thomas Risse, and others. This approach is primarily constructivist in the sense that it does not accept the relevant units and units of analysis, nor their properties, as given, but rather seeks to illuminate how it is that certain units and their properties emerge out of (discursive, learning, normative, and idea-driven) processes. Most proponents of this variant of constructivism would probably agree with the proposition that social facts are social facts not "because they are there," but because they are products of processes of social construction. The relevant "facts" may exhibit a high degree of stability over time, but if they are socially constructed facts, then they are contingent. Such a stance is indeed constructivist. However, it is not quite clear what is meant by ontology. Most who claim to advance an ontological constructivism have failed to notice that ontology itself has evaporated with this constructivist turn.

This is not the place to advance a particular philosophical understanding of ontology. This has not been done in the many places that ontological constructivists inhabit in IR (nor, for that matter, most other theoretical contributions to the field; IR theorists employing the term "ontology" seem to rarely bother with its meaning), although a minimalist understanding is implied in its more or less unreflected use. The category of ontology has historically and almost irreducibly been about the metaphysical distinction between being and nothingness (cf. Luhmann 1997, 911). It is the core of social constructivism, however, that what "is" (at least as a social fact) is entirely contingent upon processes of social construction, in which the constructivist observer inescapably takes part. One does not have to fully buy into the ideas of modern systems theory to admit that the social construction of social facts, that is, what constitutes the facticity of the facts, involves a number of social/communicative operations, such as drawing distinctions in observations and in processes of signification, etc. What and how relevant distinctions are drawn seems to be entirely non-ontological; very few social constructivists would be willing to concede ontological status to their ontologies, that is, see the facticity of the facts resting in their "existence," their "being there" (*Dasein*), their "presence" (*Anwesenheit* in a Husserlian sense) and so on. According to the distinction between being and nothingness, which was an integral part of the semantic of Old Europe, observation and the drawing of distinctions precede an ordering of the world. Without the primacy of these distinctions, the very concept of ontology begins to unravel, except perhaps as a historical marker. As Luhmann states:

> According to the new version, an observer must be generated first, before he or she can apply the being/nothingness distinction. But there is no metaphysical or logical rule for the choice of an initial distinction, only societal-historical plausibilities including, in modern times, an interest in the world's de-ontologization. (Luhmann 1997, 911)

Seen in this light—and to return to the point raised above—the outstanding difference between the various social constructivisms in IR theory is not one of kind, but of degree of reflexivity, for example, the extent to which they realize they form part of the aforementioned de-ontologization.

Three points warrant clarification in this respect. First, the movement away from the semantics of Old Europe, witnessed in the proliferation of social constructivisms in IR, does constitute a fundamental break with mainstream IR theories. As is well known, "classical" realism, in particular, and explicitly Niebuhr's, but also—in a more implicit and hidden fashion—neorealism, are based on very strong ontologies in a metaphysical sense, particularly in their conceptions of man (see Albert 1996, part I). In this respect, neoliberalism is also part of the break with the ontological expression of the semantic (this would arguably be less the case in relation to the whole/parts form).

Second, to observe that various versions of social constructivism in IR theory can be distinguished from one another in terms of a "degree of reflexivity" does not entail a normative valuation. Mainstream and radical constructivists employ different modes of observation. Since we want to trace why constructivisms flourish in the context of societal evolution, the aim is not to judge the superiority of one approach over another in whatever respect. To note various degrees of reflexivity is only to note a certain and quite expected variation in the way that the old semantic unravels.

Third, it is necessary to avoid reading any normative judgment into this description. The proliferation and prominence of social constructivism is not a move toward something "better" (at least not in the perspective applied here), but a result of the way that IR as a scientific enterprise makes sense of things, that is, its "normal" mode of observation and operation within one of world society's autopoietic functional subsystems.

Concluding Remarks on a Fresh Look: Which Ground to Seize?

The argument so far may seem unusual for two reasons. First, the question of whether constructivism, or which kind of constructivism, should be employed in IR theorizing has not been explored. I have rather asked why constructivisms proliferate and also why, despite their seemingly vast variation, they all share the same denomination. The question was answered by situating the scientific evolution of constructivism in the evolution of society. The link was provided by a reading of MST's theory of society. That such a theory of society has not been widely received in IR theory (nor, for that matter, in the English speaking world, in general) is the second reason why such a perspective may seem to be unusual.[26] At first, such a perspective would seem to provide no guidance at all as to how to conduct constructivist research. It does propose a theoretically grounded account for the variety of constructivist approaches, which is one of the main puzzles inspiring this volume.[27] However, in so doing, it relies on a number of implicit arguments about worthwhile routes to explore in the context of IR theory. As mentioned in the first section, and following from the self-understanding of the description provided, these arguments do not point to the best route, nor themes possible, but merely to suggested routes. By way of conclusion, two of these implicit arguments will be mentioned.

First, I have argued that the difference between the various constructivisms is largely one of varying degrees of reflexivity. A higher degree of reflexivity is not meant to denote any kind of superiority (reflexivity only refers to modes of observation and must not be read as implying any kind of critical attitude). However, a failure to conceive of the differences between the various constructivisms in this fashion leads to considerable inefficiency in the self-descriptions of constructivisms. If constructivisms are distinguished according to modes and degrees, then efforts to identify and establish kinds and positions (e.g., "middle ground") may not be so worthwhile after all. Efforts to seize ground thus may in the end work against some kind of cross-constructivist understanding and engagement, which it may be desirable to foster or enable.

Second, if one accepts that the semantic of Old Europe is unraveling, as reflected in the proliferation of constructivisms, a number of additional lines of exploration open up. One of these explorations would lead to an increased self-understanding in the discipline as a whole rather than an increased self-understanding of constructivism. The foremost question to be asked of constructivisms in IR would then presumably not be "why?" but "why so late?" A systems theoretical engagement with this question would systematically explore the structural couplings that exist between IR theory and other systems in modern society.[28] Another exploration would ask which parts of the semantic remain unassailed in IR, despite the proliferation of constructivisms. From this one could conclude that an engagement with them would provide a significant stimulus for theoretical evolution.

This chapter has attempted to open up a fresh perspective on constructivism through insights from MST's theory of society. It has shown that the evolution of constructivisms, and the way that constructivisms observe various forms in society, is part of or coupled with the way that society describes itself. By the same token, it applauds the transgression of IR's disciplinary boundaries due to the proliferation of constructivisms.

Notes

1. These terms are taken from publications as much as from discussions on the subject at which the author was present. It would take a bibliographical effort of its own to record the many uses of the term "constructivism" that have accumulated in IR theory alone. Even the almost simultaneous appearance of efforts to provide overviews on the subject is remarkable enough; see Checkel 1998; Hopf 1998; Ruggie 1998; Zehfuss 1998.

2. See the highly illuminating attempt by Ole Waever (1998) to use the sociology of science to map disciplinary developments in IR.

3. That is, if one accepts that a "general theory" is constituted by a reasonably well developed and comprehensive body of theory about society or the world, without any claim to analytical superiority necessarily attached to its generality.

4. This is not to argue that sociology has had no influence at all (on the contrary, it seems to be rather intensively received recently. That which systematically applies classical sociology's theory of society (rather than a more piecemeal fashion) to IR theorizing has been a rather rare exercise. Unfortunately, in one of the most influential books on IR theory, Kenneth Waltz (1979, 115 fn.) presents a highly contentious reading of Durkheim (also see Barkdull 1995); on the link between classical sociology and IR, see also the introductory chapter in Albert, Brock, and Wolf (2000).

5. It seems that speech act and discourse theories have been applied more intensively to IR than has classical sociology; for an overview, see the chapter by Milliken in this volume.

6. In English language IR, I am aware of only one PhD thesis (Noguera i Hancock 1998) that has dealt with MST systematically. Three people—F. Kratochwil, S. Rossbach and O. Waever—have read Luhmann's work and, over time, have made more than passing remarks on MST.

7. The latter point in this phrase seems to be rather peculiar to my reading of MST.

8. When systems theory talks of "first" and "second order" "modes of observation," it situates all kinds of observation and the ensuing communication in relation to each other in a more or less open space. This is not to be confused with the arbitrary and always disciplining distinction between "theory" and "metatheory."

9. Let alone the vast body of work by other prominent systems theorists, like Helmut Willke, Rudolf Stichweh, and others.

10. Which is also the reason for the heated debate that is similar to the often less than polite discussions surrounding the postmodern movement.

11. If my understanding is correct, this way of approaching things has recently also become very popular in cosmology/astrophysics (i.e., "Big Bang" theorizing).

12. All translations are my own.

13. Although offering a comprehensive system of thought that is often said to be as closed as Hegel's, this is probably the fundamental formal difference from Hegel. For Luhmann the unity of unity only consists in its difference and not in some final unity such as the Weltgeist.

14. This is, in a nutshell, Luhmann's critique of Habermas, regarding the recent applications of the latter's work in IR; Müller (in this volume) seems to be much closer to Luhmann than to Habermas, since he chooses to completely ignore the philosophical aspect of universal pragmatics, which underlies Habermas's programmatic. He is most concerned with working out what to do with a theory of communicative action in a historically concrete, context dependent circumstances (which is what Apel and Habermas have struggled with ever since). For the original positions in the debate between the Frankfurt form of critical theory and the Bielefeld's form of "systems theory," which has influenced intellectual debate in Germany over the past three decades, see Habermas and Luhmann 1971).

15. This refers to the stream of postpositivist scholarship heralded in the 1989 special issue of International Studies Quarterly, and the sometimes fundamental conceptual critique of basic concepts of IR theory that went along with it. For an overview of the central themes in the "Third Debate," see Lapid (1989).

16. I take this to be R.B.J. Walker's position, which he has taken in a number of discussions but not, to my knowledge, published yet.

17. See Hopf (1998). This view, which seems to be fairly common, follows the argumentative form put succinctly by Robert Keohane (1988).

18. The most concise statement of this program of constructivism can be found in Jepperson, Wendt, and Katzenstein (1996).

19. For the purpose of this chapter's argument, I advance a systems theoretical type of argument and more or less charge ahead where Friedrich Kratochwil, in his chapter, follows a curve through the more traditional vocabularies of political philosophy, however only to arrive at what I read to be a rather similar description/criticism of constructivisms in IR. Although I engage in a systems theoretical mode of observation, other system theorists would not necessarily come to the same conclusions.

20. To reiterate, it is the scientific system that observes, not, for example, people (and it seems to be commonsense that merchants and politicians can observe in a scientific mode while scientists do not always).

21. This is not to be misread as an argument that complexity is quantifiable (which seems to be one of the main ideas that distinguishes this concept of complexity from the most prominent in theories of complexity in IR).

22. Good examples of this work are to be found in Der Derian and Shapiro (1989) and Shapiro and Alker (1996).

23. A good statement of the rationale underlying and the promise following from this processual turn can be found in Lapid (forthcoming).

24. Having been sparked off by Wendt (1987).

25. This is not, of course, to suggest that any kind of uniformity could be bestowed on postmodern approaches.

26. On the basis of casual observation, it seems to me that MST and its theory of society has been received most widely in German speaking and Scandinavian countries, as well as in Italy and Spain.

27. See the editor's introduction.

28. Again, although not formulated in systems theoretical language, Ole Waever (1998) has made a good start in this direction.

Part II

Practicing Constructivism

6

Critical Methodology and Constructivism

K.M. Fierke

When constructivism first entered the lexicon of International Relations (IR) in the late 1980s, the term was applied to a range of modern and postmodern approaches, which shared an assumption that the political world is a social and constructed phenomenon as opposed to given and objective. The interest in constructivism emerged against the background of structural realism's hegemony within the discipline as well as the dramatic changes that were beginning to occur in the international system.

The hegemony of realism, and its positivist underpinnings,[1] was already being called into question within the context of a larger "Third Debate." Within this debate, postpositivists raised two broad concerns. First, the realist hegemony was unable to deal with change and historical contingency (Ashley 1986; Walker 1987; Wendt 1992a), a criticism that was later dramatized by events in the real world. Scholars in the discipline largely failed to predict, and its aftermath were having trouble explaining, the end of the Cold War, which was one of the most dramatic and significant changes of the century.[2] In this respect, the empirical concern about change is related to a larger metatheoretical question about the potential for positivist methodologies to say much of significance about a changing world.

The second broad concern implicated positivist social science in the ractice of power. The assumption and articulation of a world of timeless laws was said to reinforce the necessity of certain realist practices and therefore reproduce dominant structures of power (Ashley 1981; Cox 1981; Shapiro 1988). Scientists assumed themselves to be neutral observers of the political world. They assumed rigor in practices of fixing definitions and variables and testing them against the world. However, argued the critics, these practices of fixing hold the world in place and thereby reinforce the status quo.

Questions about the nature of the world we analyze and the importance of critical practice were interwoven in the "Third Debate." In contrast to the orthodoxy of the "unitary method of science," some early constructivists argued the need to "celebrate difference" (George and Campbell 1990; Lapid 1989), opening up spaces to learn from a range of theoretical, disciplinary, and methodological traditions. This celebration of difference has since given way to attempts by representatives of different schools of thought to draw clear boundaries distinguishing, in particular, constructivists from poststructuralists.

The process of boundary construction has come from both sides. The first part of this chapter is an analysis of how this boundary has been constructed, using two examples: Emmanuel Adler's article "Seizing the Middle Ground" (1997), which articulates the meaning of constructivism vis-à-vis the postmodern alternative; and David Campbell's epilogue to the revised version of *Writing Security* (1998a), which distinguishes his poststructural approach from a range of constructivisms.[3] I briefly summarize the difference between the two positions—in part by comparing their criticism of the other. I argue that this process of boundary construction has led to a separation between the empirical and the critical and that, given agreement about the importance of intersubjectivity and practice, a more consistent constructivism would be located between the two. The second half of the chapter explores a position at this boundary, which goes back to the later Wittgenstein (1958). This tradition is a jumping off point for arguing the importance of taking methodology seriously if we are to make critical claims about a changing world.

Constructivist Inconsistencies

As the selections in this book demonstrate, constructivism is a broad and rich tradition. However, within IR and particularly in the American context, constructivism has come to be identified with the thought of scholars influenced by Alexander Wendt and Peter Katzenstein. Generally, this school of thought has emphasized the intersubjective construction of identity and interests and, subsequently, the possibility of change. There has been a tendency, however, to cling to certain assumptions reminiscent of the "positivist orthodoxy." The first is a distinction between idea and material world. The second is the search for causal relationships. The third is an avoidance of the role of language in analysis. In this section, I examine one attempt, by Emmanuel Adler, to define a constructivist position toward these issues and a critical response.

Both constructivists and poststructuralists claim to be intersubjective and concerned first and foremost with practice. Adler's article contains a number of inconsistencies in this regard. First, Adler posits a causal relationship between ideas and material factors, which suggests a separation between the two. Ideas "are the medium and propellant of social action." Reasons are, for constructivists, "causes" (Adler 1997, 325, 329). For instance, a constructivist approach can "show that changing collective understandings of technology and national and global economies may have direct material effects on the wealth of nations" (Adler 1997, 342). Campbell argues that in this type of argument, the materialist causal logic of the mainstream orthodoxy is simply supplanted by a new causal logic that begins with ideas (Campbell 1998a, 217–218). This causal logic is inconsistent with the intersubjective underpinnings of constructivism. Intersubjectivity is a dialogical relationship in so far as meaning and practices arise out of interaction; the language of causality, by contrast, suggests a monological relationship by which one element clearly impacts on another.

Second, the articulation of this relationship in causal terms also gives rise to a distorted view of agency. Campbell points out that in constructivist accounts, state officials draw on an array of already available cultural and linguistic resources to create representations that are instrumentally applied (Campbell 1998a, 224).[4] Often, as is particularly evident in Wendt (1992a), the state is treated as an unproblematic given which acts with volition (Campbell 1998a, 219–220). This is overly agentic in so far as it does not sufficiently embed these state actors in a historical context and raise questions about how their agency became possible.

Third, the emphasis on instrumental agency is reinforced by Adler's reliance on a *verstehen* approach, which may begin with the importance of cultural rules and norms, but seeks first and foremost to "get inside heads" and understand the intentions or motives of individual actors.[5] This may make sense in a murder investigation, but how often are we really looking for "individual" motives at the international level that do not have some kind of intersubjective expression? The rationale for deploying missiles or an interventionary force is necessarily argued and justified in an intersubjective space, whether that be a bureaucratic forum, an alliance, or to public opinion. Possibilities and power are intersubjectively constituted and made meaningful through language.

One can point to examples where the choice of an individual leader was key, for instance, where they acted against an existing consensus. But consensus is not the point; rather, it is the boundaries of possibility within any given context and how particular acts, including how material resources will be put to use, are constituted as meaningful and therefore reasonable. For instance, Milosevic, in the context of the negotiations prior to the Dayton Accord, argued that he could not agree to anything for which he could not provide a convincing rationale to the Serb nationalists in Bosnia (Bildt 1998, 44). Whatever Milosevic's intentions, he had to place any decision in a framework within which it could be justified to others.

Finally, constructivists in this genre do not sufficiently theorize about the role of language in constituting practices. While emphasizing the importance of meaning and intersubjective understanding, constructivists seem to be primarily distinguished from poststructuralists by the greater importance that the latter attach to language.[6] In the dominant version of constructivism, including Wendt and Katzenstein, there is an implicit assumption that constructivists can somehow get at meanings, interpretations, or assumptions without thinking too explicitly about the nature and role of language.[7]

Given the centrality of meaning and interpretation to the constructivist enterprise, the relationship between word and world cannot be ignored, however. Questions of meaning and interpretation are fundamentally questions about language. One can accept the existence of a material reality independent of language, but one cannot say anything meaningful about it, one cannot SAY anything about it, without language. There are two ways to understand the relationship between word and world, which are not easily combined. Either the *meaning* of both the material and social world and our interactions with it are constituted in language, or one is back to the positivist claim that we can compare our statements about reality with the world to see whether they correspond. A consistent constructivist position, I would argue, has to begin with the assumption that we cannot get behind our language to compare it with that which it describes. As I argue in the second section, this argument about language has implications for how one approaches empirical research and suggests the importance of formulating distinctly constructivist criteria, which necessarily diverge from the falsificationist criteria of positivism.

These criticisms of Adler's constructivism suggest that a more consistent intersubjective position would move closer to the constitutive arguments of poststructuralists, emphasizing explicitly the role of language. But, from a constructivist perspective, the solution is not simply to go home and get on with reading Foucault and Derrida.

Poststructural Problematics

There are several poststructuralist assumptions that are problematic from a constructivist perspective. First, poststructuralists, in Campbell's argument, focus on the theorization of identity, rather than assuming an a priori agency or pre-given subjects, as many constructivists do. However, the poststructuralist emphasis on theorizing identity often leads to a practice that is not qualitatively different than the "positivist orthodoxy" they criticize, that is, the reification of a set of assumptions prior to detailed analysis.[8] In this case, the theoretical maxim is that identity is constituted in difference, and—this has been modified since the end of the Cold War— this is an antagonistic relationship. As Ole Waever (1996a, 122) notes, there is reason to question this assumption:

> Many critical and/or poststructuralist authors enjoy remonstrating against the alleged "other" that is at present taking place in relation to Russia, North Africa, or Asia. Many authors—including Campbell—balance between, on the one hand, (formally) saying that identity does not demand an Other, does not demand antagonism, only difference(s) that can be non-antagonistic and, on the other, actually assuming that identity is always based on an antagonistic relationship to an other, is always constituted as absolute difference. In the current situation, because of this unfortunate habit, when one notices that there are efforts in identity creation for Europe, one immediately looks around and asks, "who can it be directed against?" and then one discovers some more or less well-founded examples of, for example, Russia being castigated as other. I am not convinced. The dominant aspiration is rather to constitute Europe as a pole of attraction with graduated membership so that Europe fades out but is not constituted against an external enemy. Some of Europe's mechanisms for stabilizing or disciplining eastern Europe rely exactly on this non-definition of an eastern border, on the image of an open but heterogeneous polity of which some are more members than others, but none are defined as total outsiders or opponents.

The context of post Cold War Europe raises questions about the assumption that identity requires an Other. In contrast to the emphasis on theorizing identity, Adler argues that constructivists want to know in detail how identities and interests are constituted in particular cases. If one takes the practices of actors in the world seriously, then a more fruitful analysis would, to cite Wittgenstein (1958, 66–67), "look and see" how identities are constituted in specific contexts. As Onuf (1998b, 1) emphasizes, constructivism is not a theory; it is a "way of studying social relations."

Second, from Campbell's perspective, constructivists are too easily drawn into the "protocols of 'empirical social science' rule, to the detriment of a politicized account of important practices" (Campbell 1998a, 225).

This sounds very similar to Ashley's claim that poststructuralists are "not especially interested in the meticulous examination of particular cases or sites for purposes of understanding them in their own terms" (Ashley, 1989, 278). In fact, one can argue that the critical endeavor of the poststructuralists suffers precisely because their own, often very abstract, theoretical assumptions are not sufficiently related to the analysis of actual practices. While claiming a desire to open up spaces for marginalized voices to speak, there is often a closing down of that possibility precisely because of another assumption, which shares a family resemblance with realist accounts, that is, states do reproduce realist practices. Campbell, and other poststructuralists (Doty, 1993),[9] ask how *state* action becomes possible; they emphasize processes of marginalization rather than how alternatives, which had been considered unrealistic, become possible. Subsequently, Campbell (1998, 7–8) suggests that the practices of states remain largely unchanged since the end of the Cold War. [10] By contrast, constructivists such as Koslowski and Kratochwil (1995) and Fierke (1998) have taken dissident practice in the context of the ending Cold War seriously. As a result, there is an increasing awareness of the role of these actors in constituting the possibility of a change (Adler 1997, 342). When a detailed analysis of the practices of these actors is taken seriously, a different and more nuanced reading of both the end of the Cold War and the post Cold War practices of states is in order.

Third, Adler accuses poststructuralists of celebrating "semantic instability and interpretive multiplicity." Poststructuralists privilege deconstruction over the reconstruction of positive politics; the critical task is one of destabilizing and denaturalizing existing categories. Campbell implies, however, that the two are not mutually exclusive: "the deconstruction of identity widens the domain of the political to include the ways in which identity is constituted and contains an affirmative moment through which existing identity formations are denaturalized and alternative articulations of identity and the political are made possible" (Campbell 1998, 223). How are these made possible without some form of positive construction? The fear is that positive construction will once again reify a new political program or identity; but for politics to be possible, positive construction is unavoidable. The use of language, as opposed to its deconstruction, necessarily relies on rules, which are a positive construction. To be critical, whether as a theorist or a political actor, one necessarily relies on rules to speak meaningfully. This is precisely why the theoretical claims of poststructuralists often do end up being reified. The question is not positive construction or its absence but, rather, what kind of construction, which is precisely what is at stake in most political contests.[11] One way to avoid the reification of theoretical categories is to privilege the analysis of meaning in use in actual contexts of political contestation over the creation of theoretical languages.

Finally, Campbell, and other poststructuralists, to their credit, emphasize the importance of context for constituting agency and political possibility. But they do not sufficiently account for how critical action becomes possible against the background of a disciplining power that primarily reproduces state power and marginalizes alternatives. At the same time, the ability of the critical theorist to engage in performative acts is not problematized. Poststructuralists argue that the constructivist approach to agency is overly agentic and that the role of context in constituting possibilities must be taken into account. The solution to the shortcomings of both the overly structural account of poststructuralists and the overly agentic approach of the constructivists is to analyze the relationship between dominant actors and their critical challengers and how new possibilities are constituted out of the contest between conflicting language games.

In summary, I have argued that within international relations "constructivism" has come to be associated with an approach that identifies a causal relationship between ideas and material relations. This position is criticized by poststructuralists because it is overly agentic, in so far as ideas are understood to be instrumentally employed by individual actors, with insufficient attention to how these actors are constrained by a social and historical context of interaction. In addition, constructivists do not sufficiently theorize about the role of language in constituting practices. Poststructuralists, on the other hand, tend to be overly structural, failing to account for how critical action or—given the emphasis on deconstruction—any kind of politics becomes possible. The focus on how states reproduce practice and on the theorization of identity, accompanied by an avoidance of methodological issues, tends to reinforce—rather than resolve—an issue at the heart of the poststructural critique, that is, the reification of categories.

This process of boundary construction between the two has constituted the empirical and the critical as distinct enterprises. The political rationale for doing so is not far to see. Adler is trying to distance constructivism from the negative connotations attached to poststructuralism, in order to enhance its legitimacy to the larger community of international relations scholars, particularly in the United States. Campbell is critical of constructivism for precisely this reason, that is, because it reinforces the predominance of an empirical social scientific research agenda to the detriment of a politicized account of practice. The process of boundary construction contributes to a separation between the empirical and the critical. Questions of methodology have not been sufficiently addressed from either side.

By contrast, a more consistent constructivism would be located at the boundary between these two positions. It would assume that actors are embedded in structures of meaning but capable, within these, of a degree of agency. Further, to make credible claims about actual cases, we have to take methodology seriously, but this does not have to happen at the expense of critique and may in fact strengthen critique. This neither involves specifying causal relationships nor theoretical maxims in advance but, rather, that we "look and see" how actors bring meaning to their identities, practices, and interactions. Such an approach requires the analysis of language but not necessarily or exclusively its deconstruction.

At the Boundary

At the boundary between these two positions is another constructivism—a third way, if you will. Within IR theory this is represented by the work of Onuf (1989), who was the first to introduce constructivism to international relations, Fierke (1996, 1998), Kratochwil (1989) and Pin-Fat (1997). Its philosophical roots lie with the later Wittgenstein (1958).

Given the desire to bridge the critical and the empirical, it is not self-evident that we should turn to Wittgenstein. Indeed, not all of the constructivists mentioned above would consider themselves critical; and critical theorists of other traditions have argued that post-Wittgensteinian scholarship, given the emphasis on meaning in use, takes the world as it is, failing to deal with issues of power, history, and social change (Thompson, 1981; George and Campbell, 1990). While it is true that Wittgenstein's philosophy of language is not particularly useful for *theorizing* about power or change, I would argue that it does provide a point of departure for rethinking how we *describe* an historical context of power and change. Description, while not inherently critical, becomes so if it makes us look again, in a fresh way, at that which we assume about the world because it has become overly familiar. Taking seriously the criteria for describing contexts, such as the end of the Cold War, or the conflict in Bosnia, opens up the prospect of challenging realist accounts of these changes. In this way, new spaces are opened for thinking about the past and the present and, therefore, how we construct the future.

Use of the word "empirical" in this context is also not without problems. In the empirical tradition data is derived from experience or observation. Data is defined in contrast to theory but provides the necessary foundation for testing theory. As such, the word "empirical," and the data/theory dichotomy, presuppose a correspondence theory of truth. Wittgenstein criticized this way of "knowing," and indeed his own earlier work in the *Tractatus* (1961), which was a source of inspiration for the logical positivists of the

Vienna Circle. In his later work, *Philosophical Investigation* (1958), he presented an alternative approach to the relationship between language and the world. Analysis from this angle is thus not properly empirical as this word has traditionally been used. However, for lack of a better word to refer to the analysis of international relations, I have used it.

The final section of this article will address three issues, raised by the earlier comparison, from the boundary: agents and structures, methodology, and critical description.

Agents and Structures

The agent-structure problem in international relations was first articulated by Wendt (1987). The problem, like many problems in international relations, was adopted from another discipline, in this case sociology, and particularly the work of Anthony Giddens. The central issue regards the relationship between structures "out there" that constrain human and social action and the freedom of the individual agent, that is, whether structures determine individual behavior, or individuals are capable of acting as agents to change structures.

Within this debate, constructivists and poststructuralists are distinguished by an emphasis on, respectively, a priori rationality as opposed to a priori meanings. For instance, Wendt's (1992a) constructivist story about alter and ego presents two aliens meeting for the first time. In this story, their rational interest in survival is prior to any communicative ability or common language. Poststructuralists, by contrast, have argued that a priori meanings, rather than a priori rationality, provide the backdrop of action (Doty 1997; Campbell 1998; see also Zehfuss's chapter in this volume).

The concept of a game provides another way to think about the relationship between rationality and structures of meaning. I am not referring here to the games of game theory, which share more in common with Adler or Wendt's emphasis on a priori rationality.[12] Game theory focuses on the rationality of moves within the structure of a given game. The emphasis is on instrumental rationality, and the rules of the game are largely ignored. By contrast, our everyday concept of a game is much broader. It is a structure of rules within which identities and practices are given meaning. A game is a relational context within which—with the exception of solitaire—we interact with others. Confronted with knowledge of the multiple possible games we might play—from monopoly to cribbage to poker to chess—it makes no sense to ask whether a move is rational until we have identified the game itself or the structure of rules within which a move has *this meaning*, is undertaken with *this object*, and is rational or irrational *given a posi-*

tion within a game in process. In short, if one speaks in terms of games, a priori meanings circumscribe the rationality of specific moves; rationality must be embedded in a context.

How, if actors are constrained by the rules of a given game, would agency be possible? An example—Gorbachev's agency in bringing about the end of the Cold War—illustrates the distinction between the three positions. Poststructuralists would have difficulty getting beyond the power exerted over actors by the dominant discourse of the Cold War. Gorbachev may have tried to act on the basis of an alternative to the realist discourse, but we would have expected his voice to be marginalized. Constructivists, such as Wendt (1992a), show Gorbachev, as an individual, going through a cost-benefit calculation and coming to the conclusion that a change of games was necessary. Although Wendt's theoretical argument is one about the role of intersubjective understandings, in the empirical example, the Soviet leader's rational calculations are prior to a larger process of meaning construction.[13]

From the boundary, the key question is how was it possible for Gorbachev, embedded in the structure of the Cold War, to engage in a qualitatively different game? Within the Cold War and the New Thinking games, the identity of the players, and the types of moves available to them are quite different, as are the ways in which actors would reason about possible action. For instance, disarmament would be clearly irrational within a Cold War game, while, as a form of "besting," it would be quite rational within the framework of the New Thinking.[14]

To understand how a change from one game to another became possible, it is necessary to shift emphasis away from the a priori rationality of Gorbachev to the wider context within which Gorbachev could *meaningfully* introduce the new thinking. The agent-structure problem would contrast Gorbachev, as an *individual* introducing change, with the *structural* constraints of the Cold War.[15] But, given the emphasis on the *intersubjective* constitution of identity and interest, we want to place Gorbachev in a larger political *context*—both domestic and international—where the reasons for his action are not purely a matter of individual calculation but must be justified to others, where Gorbachev may have been the grandmaster but did not himself construct the possibility of a new game.

In this respect, Gorbachev, much like Milosevic later—in a different context and involving a different kind of thinking—moved into the position of key player and catalyst within a structure of rules that had already taken root in a larger intersubjective space. Neither was determined in their action, but the context had changed such that a choice was possible.[16] That either may have had economic or political motivations for a change of games is beside the point; the key issue is how their move to change games would be *possible* within a larger political and intersubjective space in a way that it had not been at an earlier point in time. Earlier Soviet leaders, who also had economic motives for introducing a change of games, had no more success, given the structural constraints of the Cold War, than would a Milosevic mobilizing along nationalist lines within Tito's Yugoslavia.

To summarize, beginning with an alternative concept of games, the key issue is to identify the larger intersubjective context within which moves of one kind or another would be seen to be reasonable and therefore justifiable. Individual leaders, as the central players, are likely to be trapped within the constraints of a dominant game; we therefore have to look at the larger context itself to identify the impetus for shifts toward an alternative.

Methodology

Constructivists, as defined by Adler, often use the language of causality and explanation in much the same way as positivists; they have also been criticized for claiming to identify causal relations or test hypotheses but doing so poorly (Moravcsik 1999; see also the response by Risse and Wiener 1999). Poststructuralists tend to view the adoption of more traditional methods as evidence of being hostage to the "protocols of empirical social science" at the expense of critical practice. In what follows, I draw a distinction between two practices, that is, providing criteria for claims about the world and the positivist criterion of hypothesis testing and falsification. I argue that the former is of crucial importance for constructing a critical account of practice, but the criteria of constructivism necessarily differ from those of positivism.

Despite claims to the contrary by some, we are all, as scholars—postpositivist or positivist—engaged in attempts to disconfirm other approaches and provide a better account of international politics. Critique involves pointing out either a metatheoretical, empirical, or a normative mismatch between theories and reality. For instance, the argument, which emerged during the Third Debate, that realists cannot adequately account for processes of change, is an act of disconfirmation. In this respect, to disconfirm is to raise questions about the validity or accuracy of a set of theoretical assumptions.

The more formal name for an act of disconfirmation in the positivist framework is falsification, which finds practical expression in hypothesis testing. The underlying logic of this Popperian proposition is that, while we can never prove theories or hypotheses to be ultimately "true," we can do our best to demonstrate that a statement is false.[17] In so doing, one draws on the assumptions of a theory, for instance, realism, to formulate statements regarding specific cases. This statement is then compared with the world to see whether they correspond.

There are several problems with this way of proceeding. From the perspective of a Wittgensteinian constructivism, falsification assumes a correspondence theory of language and truth; that is, we can compare our statements about the world with the world to see whether they correspond. Language is a set of labels that either correspond or don't with a real world. Wittgenstein, by contrast, argues that we can't get behind our language to compare it with that which it describes. Rather, language is constitutive of the world. Language use is a form of action in itself that is bound up with other kinds of practices.

The more subtle problem—which is not unrelated—is that this way of proceeding makes any actual falsification highly unlikely. The world is a complex place and the massive amount of detail has to be simplified in some way. The Popperian solution is to reduce complexity by drawing on the assumptions of an a priori theory, which defines the meaning of terms, defines which actors are most relevant and which questions are of potential importance. This means that the criteria for description, and subsequently explanation—the patterns to be identified—are external to the particular context of examination. In a stable context this might prove to be less of a problem in one respect; for instance, where the practices of states are guided by a realist logic, there might be a correspondence between the practices of states and the assumptions of theory.[18] However, this observation would not contribute to *falsification* but would rather reinforce the theory. One concern of poststructuralists and other critical theorists is that realist theories serve to reproduce realist practices because they reinforce that certain acts are *necessary* for survival in an objective world.

The falsification problem is different; that is, when one's selection from the detail is guided by the assumptions of an a priori theory, one tends to see what one sets out to see. Thus, realists and liberals look at the end of the Cold War and come up with competing descriptions and explanations, each of which coincide with the assumptions of their respective theories (see Kegley 1994; Fierke 1998). Or, in the context of the debate over the democratic peace, realists and liberals select different details related to the same cases and thereby substantiate their own theoretical argument (See Layne 1994; Owen 1994). In either case, the pattern of causal inference or the criterion for constructing a description are imposed from outside, on the basis of an a priori theory; they are not discovered in the context itself. From a constructivist position, it is crucial to make one's point of departure the meaningful practices of the actors themselves and how these led to the construction of one outcome rather than another.

This begs the question of what uniquely constructivist criteria would consist of. I argue the need to return to a logic of discovery. This is not the same logic of discovery as promoted by positivists, who assumed that we could collect "facts" and from these facts identify patterns. Rather, because actions and practices are dependent on rules, embedded in the context of a game, we can discover the structure of these meanings in the context itself.

Critical Description

It is impossible in so short a space to demonstrate the application of a method in any meaningful way.[19] In this section I would, however, like to think through what constructivist criteria might consist of, by reference to a specific case, the end of the Cold War.

The conventional wisdom about the end of the Cold War is that it was a case of the West "winning," which suggests intentional agency by the United States or NATO in bringing about a victorious end. Based on this realist account of the past—an account constructed in the present—we draw conclusions about how "states" should act in the future; for instance, if we remain steady in the threat or use of force, the other will eventually back down—a lesson that was implemented once again in Iraq and Kosovo.

A positivist might want to falsify a proposition related to the victory argument by formulating a hypothesis and testing it. The proposition might be drawn from either realist or liberal theoretical assumptions, thereby emphasizing, respectively, Western military and economic power or the power of democratic ideals. Either *could* identify factual evidence to bolster their case. The United States was clearly more powerful militarily and economically, as it had been throughout the Cold War. One can point to several examples of the power of Western democratic ideals, and particularly human rights concerns, in central and eastern Europe. We do not, however, have any criteria—other than the assumptions of either theory—for determining which account is better. The argument that Western material power was fundamental rests on an assumption that states only understand the language of force; this assumption would be denied within a liberal framework where domestic politics and ideas play a clear role in the constitution of power. The outcome is an endless debate between realists and liberals, a debate that has been underway for decades.

Both accounts begin with a proposition constructed in the context of the present and look back for confirming evidence. An alternative approach to disconfirmation—or a puzzle to guide our analysis—might begin with the discontinuity between the *current* dominant explanation of this change, which assumes intentionality on the part of Western states, and the meaning states brought to their practices *within the Cold War and as it was ending*. In the early stages of the conflict, there was some talk of rolling back communism; however, the status quo of the Cold War, represented by the détente of the 1970s, rested on an acceptance of the division of Europe and the nuclear arms race between the superpowers. NATO, and the United States within NATO, understood themselves to be imprisoned within the structure of a security dilemma that could not be escaped. Given the "objective" nature of this security dilemma, their practices had to conform with the requirements of this structure or they would not survive.[20] As a result, the central act of the United States and NATO was one of *maintaining* a balance, and therefore maintaining a structure of interaction (Fierke 1998, Chapter 5). While disarmament might have been the preferable option, as in a prisoner's dilemma, it was not the rational one. Stability was prized above all else, and stability took the form of a continued arms race, complemented by forms of arms control that would limit destabilizing developments; as a result, ABM systems were considered taboo.

It is interesting that fifteen years later newspapers and scholarly conversations assume the language of Western victory. We have forgotten how enduring, at the time, the Cold War seemed to be, how reluctant most politicians were to consider change, and how social scientists failed miserably to predict the end of the Cold War, which was, not incidentally, declared well before the collapse of the Soviet Union.

We have come to assume this change was brought about by the deliberate agency of the West—how does one have a victory without the intention to win? Yet, at the time, winning was not the central point of the Cold War game of states in either West or East. Even if winning was, for some, an end, *practices* were structured by a shared understanding that stability was prized above all else and that the Cold War would be an enduring phenomenon.

Poststructuralists, such as Campbell, would probably argue that the powerful have once again succeeded in reproducing their interpretation of what happened and therefore their power. They have once again succeeded in marginalizing and silencing voices who would provide an alternative account of these changes. This is a powerful argument; however, it is limited in two respects. First, it suggests the game is over. In this respect, it shares a family resemblance with the realist argument that the West won, if in a slightly different way; in this case, success in reproducing the Western version of events has constructed triumph. Second, there is little critical about this account except to demonstrate that we are all victims of the propaganda apparatus of the powerful. It does not tell us *how* the marginalized would be given more space to speak. More importantly, it does not give us any criteria for coming up with a *better* account of what happened.[21] The argument is that multiple stories can always be told, although the story of the dominant tends to prevail. By contrast, we want to think through the criteria for constructing a better account of the past.

The point of departure for constructivism is that the world is changeable, that the past, present, and future are constructed through our practices and interactions with others. This means there are no ultimate end points. The game continues to unfold. If the current victory argument, based on a realist story of the past, is constituting the meaning of current practice, then a different—and better—account of this past would also presumably open up spaces for rethinking action in the present and the future.

The surface description of the end of the Cold War as a victory leads to conclusions about the legitimacy of the United States, as the last remaining superpower, and NATO, as the most successful alliance in history, a legitimacy which extends to the use of force, with or without the consent of the UN Security Council. A thicker and more critical description of these changes would make us look again at what has become overly familiar, and to raise question about the meaning of this change, how it came it about, given our assumptions about the Cold War as an enduring phenomenon, and how this makes us think differently about future practice.

Since it is impossible to illustrate a method of critical description here, I want to conclude by highlighting several lessons, both methodological and empirical, that grew out of a larger analysis of this case (see Fierke 1998).

First, the discussion above of games suggests that it is necessary to look outside the motives of individual actors, such as Gorbachev—or Reagan—to changes in the larger political context, which would have made a change of games thinkable for these leaders. The importance of this move is reinforced by the further observation that states at the time understood themselves to be acting within the framework of a structure that was inescapable. If states were trapped in the logic of the Cold War game, then it is necessary to look at other actors, in addition to states, who may have been in a position to challenge the public parameters within which states acted. Subsequently, the point of departure *cannot* be an assumption that certain actors are more relevant than others, a practice which often leads to the exclusion of non-state actors from the start. The important thing is to look for *relationships*; who is interacting with whom or who is a source of concern for whom, and begin to piece together a map of identities and practices.

Second, in the last section I referred to a logic of discovery that involves the identification of patterns within the context itself. These patterns do not exist in an objective world "out there," as assumed by the behavioralists; they are to be identified in the shared *meanings* that structure the space for maneuver within a particular context. A brief example may clarify the difference. A behavioralist might argue that balance of power is a law-like pattern. The emphasis is on the sameness of balance of power across time, and the hope is to generate a theory, based on this law, which would provide a point of departure for predicting and explaining.

By contrast, we might similarly look for patterns of balance of power, but the emphasis would lie with the *family resemblance* between historically distinct contexts. For instance, in the Cold War, the balance of power was given *meaning* as a conflict between two stable and permanent nuclear "families" (alliances) within which it was largely unthinkable that a member would leave to join the other family (Fierke 1997b, 1998). Compare this with the classical European balance of power, which even Waltz captured in the entailments of a "courtship" metaphor, within which states were trying to remain attractive to new suitors in a context of ever changing affairs (Waltz 1979, 165–166). While there is a family resemblance between the two—both are balances of power and both rely on language games related to intimate relations—the practices by which balance is maintained in each case *are diametrically opposed*. In the one case, it is irrational to change alliances; in the other, changing alliances is part of playing the game. If we were going to explain or predict outcomes within either of these two historical structures, these language games would be a far more useful guide than the single picture of a balance of power transcending time and space. There are multiple overlapping games of balance of power, which share a family resemblance rather than an essence. For this reason, the formulation of a priori definitions is problematic; instead, it is necessary to "look and see" the pattern of rules that structure the language games of a particular context.

Third, while the patterns are to be identified in language, and are therefore dependent on language, we are not here dealing "merely" with language. Wittgenstein discusses the use of language as analogous to making moves in a game. The analogy reveals several features of language. First, it is dependent on rule following. Second, these rules must be known and shared by the participants in a game to be comprehensible. Third, these rules constitute the meaning of objects and actions within the patterned activity of a game. From this perspective, language use cannot, as is often supposed, be neatly separated from the material world. By contrast, our everyday use of the worlds "idea" and "discourse," as used, respectively, by (Adler's) constructivists and poststructuralists, carries a connotation of being detached from the material. This perceived separation makes possible an argument from more traditional quarters that analyses of this kind are dealing "merely" with language (see Wallace 1996, 316).

The chess example is useful for thinking about the relationship between the three. Chess as an "idea" suggests a concept or a blueprint, prior to the development of the game itself or adoption of its rules. In this respect, our idea of chess might cause, that is, might provide the reason for, developing the game in practice. To say we have a "discourse" of chess, on the other hand, suggests a way of thinking, writing, or speaking about chess. Given the emphasis on multiplicity, we might have multiple alternative discourses of chess. If chess is approached as a *language game*, the language and rules of chess are inseparable from the objects with which the game is played, the practices attached to the objects, or the reasoning by which one makes decisions about how to move within a match. All of these are constituted and made meaningful on the basis of a language and rules of that particular game.[22] This is the difference between a bunch of wooden objects randomly bumping around on a level surface and an orderly game of chess. A knight is a knight rather than a piece of wood by virtue of its role within a game. The moves that can be made and the rationality of doing so, likewise, only have meaning within a context of rules. We can try to look inside Kasparov's head to identify his next move, but the possibilities will be defined by his position within an unfolding game.

I do not mean to suggest that it is wrong to examine ideas or discourse, only that the analysis of language games involves a different cut into political language. The central question becomes how *practices* at the international are given meaning within a context of rules, "a whole consisting of the language and actions into which it is woven" (Wittgenstein 1958, par. 7). For instance, the meaning of a nuclear missile and how one reasons about what to do with it is very different within the context of a Cold War or New Thinking game.

Finally, the key question is how this provides the criteria for constructing a "better" description. Poststructuralists would argue that storytelling or narrative construction is a way of bringing order to an otherwise messy reality. Consequently, we may have any number of stories about any one set of events or historical context, each of which provides the structure of a particular story. Likewise, in the political world, actors in different positions are likely to tell very different stories about the past, about what they and the other are doing, about the reasons for their action, about what is possible in the future. The outcome, in this case, is multiple narratives about the end of the Cold War, for instance, from Western leaders, from former Soviet leaders, from peace activists, or from Eastern human rights initiatives. The Western leaders, as the most powerful, were successful in imposing their narrative and marginalizing the others.

By contrast, the construction of a "better" description does not involve preferencing one narrative over another but rather constructing a single narrative structured by the shared language of this context. The actors mentioned above were engaged in a political contest; one of the areas of contestation was the meaning of the Cold War and their respective practices within it. Despite the existence of political contestation, patterns could be identified across texts that point to a *shared* language by which the conflict was given meaning; it was within this shared language that dissident actors maneuvered to change the rules of the dominant Cold War game. For instance, I stated above that the Cold War conflict constituted two permanent alliance *families*; within this context, peace movements engaged in acts to *emancipate* Europe from these families. Or, as stated above, states, in both East and West, were engaged in acts of *maintaining* the structures of the Cold War and the cohesion of their respective families; peace and human rights activists in East and West began to *dismantle* and *breakdown* the structures of the Cold War. The shared grammar of structure and family created the boundaries within which the meaning of practices by both actors was constituted and the space within which those trying to change the game maneuvered. They were engaged in a political conflict over the meaning of Europe, the Cold War, human rights and nuclear weapons; but the space of this contest was defined by an intersubjective language.

Why should this relationship between the language of actors engaged in political contestation interest us? It interests us because it provides the criteria for identifying a systematic relationship between the *practices* of the different actors and the *outcome*. Earlier, I stated there was a dissonance between acts by leaders in both East and West to "maintain" the structure of the Cold War and claims, after the fact, that this was a case of the West "winning," which suggests some kind of intentional agency. Also, if one looks at the changing relationships over time, given consistent use of a grammar of structure—again, by *all* parties—a similar dissonance is evident. NATO was consistently maintaining the status quo until the inevitable could no longer be ignored. Independent peace and human rights initiatives in both East and West were engaged in dismantling and breaking down the structures of the Cold War from the early 1980s on. Around 1985 to 1986 Gorbachev and Reagan, in quite different ways, began to change games, no longer maintaining, but undermining the foundations of deterrence thinking and stating the need to build bridges across the division of Europe. The final outcome by 1989 to 1991 was a series of *collapses* as the Cold War structures began to dissolve. There is a positive correlation between dismantling or breaking down and collapse; there is a negative correlation between acts of maintenance and restoration—what Reagan was doing during his early years—and collapse.

The important issue is not ultimately whether independent peace or human rights initiatives in East or West were important. The important issue is how we understand the meaning of the Cold War's end and how this constitutes our understanding of what is possible or necessary in the future. The victory argument assumes two competitors and one who won; it assumes that power is primarily military and economic and that threats are effective. Victories are endings. The game is over. By contrast, on the basis of this critical description, the end of the Cold War was not about winning or losing; it was about the conflict between two different games of security. The one game was about the necessity and inevitability of deterrence or balance of power thinking and the necessity of the threat or use of force; the other was about the possibility of change, the possibility of dialogue and resolving conflicts in a different way. NATO was the advocate of the former Cold War game. Gorbachev was the advocate of the latter, that is, the New Thinking, which was made possible—but not determined—by the existence of a larger process of public questioning. States leaders in both blocs, trapped by the logic of the Cold War, began to maneuver toward alternatives as others, outside the established structures of power in both blocs, politicized the dominant rules of the game.

The two games do not represent merely two different interpretations of the end of the Cold War. The victory argument is an interpretation, imposed after the fact. The conflicting games argument is a "better" description because it embeds the moves of any one actor in a larger intersubjective space and traces, over time, the transition from one game to another. In contrast to the disjuncture between the Cold War and post Cold War meaning structures of NATO elites, we see the gradual unfolding of a context over a twenty-year period, a gradual unfolding that can be systematically traced based on the meanings actors brought to their practices and interactions. The distinction is ultimately important because in rethinking a received wisdom about the past, we re-open the possibility of being agents in constructing the future.

Notes

1. Positivism is a word that is as misused as postmodernism. In a strict sense it refers to the logical positivism of the Vienna Circle in the 1930s. Its use in discussions of the debate between positivists and postpositivists implies a broader category of positions that prioritize the search for causal laws and generalization, a correspondence theory of

truth and language, and the division between an objective external world and subjective mental acts. I use the word in reference to these debates.

2. From one angle, this failure is not surprising. Positivists search for patterns of recurrence, not change. Identities and interests are assumed to be given and the hope is to discover timeless laws rather than how identities and political realities are transformed. Studies that have theorized change, such as Gilpin's (1981) book, which is a part of a genre on hegemonic change, all assume the centrality of war and were therefore of little use for explaining the end of the Cold War.

3. I am not denying the existence of diversity within either camp, and I hope to minimize the inevitable over-simplification by focusing on specific arguments; it is the process of boundary construction between the two that is my focus, and these two pieces are examples of it. While some will argue that a poststructural approach is not constructivist, the imperative to deconstruct is inseparable from demonstrating that a subject or discourse is a social construction; thus the earlier reference to modern and postmodern constructivisms.

4. Campbell attributes this particular claim to Weldes (1996, 279, 281), whom he distinguishes as a "critical" constructivist who nonetheless shares a starting point with Wendt and the contributors to Katzenstein (1996).

5. Weber's concept of *verstehen* begins with the importance of intersubjective rules but then posits that action must be understood from within (Hollis and Smith, 1990). Meaning is equivalent to studying "what is in people's heads" (Adler, 1997: 326).

6. Adler's boundary line relies on a distinction between a constitutivist approach, which he associates with the poststructuralists, and a mediativist approach characteristic of constructivists. The constitutivists, while not denying the existence of material reality, believe that it cannot be known outside human language. In Adler's account of the constructivist view, reality exists independently of our accounts, but does not fully determine them. Social reality emerges from the attachment of meaning and functions to physical objects. What is the main distinction? While both accept the existence of a material reality, the constitutivist account more explicitly articulates our dependence on language for making sense of the world. Adler (1997, 332) says "constitutivists concede too much to ideas; unless they are willing to deny the existence of the material world, they should recognize, as constructivists do, that 'a socially constructed reality presupposes a nonsocially constructed reality as well and that, consequently, the question of how the material world affects and is affected by the conceptual world is crucial for social science.'"

7. Maja Zehfuss' contribution to this volume makes a very succinct argument in this regard about Wendt's work.

8. Thomas McCarthy (Hoy and McCarthy, 1994, 218) notes that: "despite the repeated denunciation of all 'binary oppositions' and every 'critical tribunal,' postmodernist discourse actually relies quite heavily on a series of stark 'either/or's' to justify a stringent list of 'do's' and 'don'ts': thou shalt not spin grand historical metanarratives, construct big societal pictures, entertain high utopian ideals, or think deep philosophical thoughts. The supreme opposition, which structures all the rest, is that between Reason—that is, foundationalist and absolutist conceptions of reasons—and whatever in a given context is identified as The Other of Reason—sensibility, imagination, desire, the body, women, nature, history, the non-Western world, language, culture, art, rhetoric and so on. [...] It is only when one accepts an extreme diagnosis of modernity as everywhere corrupted by 'ontotheology' or the like, that the extreme remedy of deconstruction seems necessary."

9. Weldes (1996, 1999), although categorized by Campbell as a critical constructivist, is also concerned with this problem.

10. In a brief discussion of the "end" of the Cold War, Campbell claims that post Cold War developments "have been represented in ways that do not depart dramatically from those dominant during the Cold War." The main concern is the function that difference, danger, and otherness play in constituting the identity of the United States as a major actor in world politics.

11. Campbell's book on Bosnia (1998b) is a case in point. One of his central theoretical arguments is the ultimate "undecidability" of politics, yet he, at the same time, provides very decided ethical criteria for judging narratives of war.

12. For an analysis of the differences between formal and a constructivist approach to games, see Fierke and Nicholson (Forthcoming).

13. This is consistent with the constructivist theme that individual elites manipulate meaning. In so far as Gorbachev was the key promoter of the "New Thinking," this may be partially accurate. But to formulate the explanation in this way is to fail to ask a prior questions: how did Gorbachev become possible within the structure of the Cold War.

14. For a discussion of besting as a strategy, see Fierke 1999b.

15. As Doty (1997) notes, the agent-structure problem defines structures and agents as two distinct and opposed entities each with essential properties. Further, there is a contradiction at the heart of Wendt's notion of structure. On the one hand, he relies on scientific realism, within which structures operate according to natural necessity; on the other hand, he takes from structuration the idea that structures are relational and agents and structures are mutually constituted. The approach to games as structures, by contrast, is explicitly intersubjective.

16. The precondition for this choice is one's location at the intersection of two language games, in this case, Cold War and the New Thinking. This element of choice is key to the constructivist notion that agents could have acted otherwise. Either choice served to reinforce the dominance of one or the other or constitute this future possibility.

17. In this framework, falsification occurs on two levels, that is, one tries to falsify hypotheses related to specific cases, but this contributes to the larger project of attempting to falsify a larger theory. My concern is primarily with the falsification of statements regarding specific cases.

18. As Nicholson (1996) argues, we can, in a stable context, treat rules as if they were objective laws.

19. For concrete applications of this methodology, see Fierke (1996, 1997, 1998, 1999a, 1999b, 2000).

20. There has been an on-going theoretical debate about whether security dilemmas are objective or subjective. My emphasis is on an intersubjective context where certain acts were understood to be necessary because of the existence of an "objective" security dilemma.

21. Except, as mentioned earlier, ethical criteria. See Campbell (1998b).

22. This emphasis on material objects is slightly different than Wittgenstein's in his discussion of language games; my use addresses concerns in International Relations in a way, I believe, that is consistent with his thought.

7

Discourse Study: Bringing Rigor to Critical Theory

Jennifer Milliken

Studies involving discourse as a key theoretical concept are now being regularly undertaken by poststructuralists, postmodernists, and some feminists and social constructivists, an exciting development in critical International Relations (IR). But what makes good research concerning discourse? A now standard answer to this question is (in David Campbell's words) that discourse research should embrace "a logic of interpretation that acknowledges the improbability of cataloguing, calculating, and specifying 'real causes' and so should elucidate the "manifest political consequences of adopting one mode of representation over another" (Campbell 1993, 7-8). However, beyond the important idea of studying the politics of representation, there has been strikingly little examination to date of appropriate methods and criteria for discourse study.

The inattention to such issues is not without its reasons. Based upon the postmodern critique of foundationalism, leading figures in the discourse community have rejected the establishment of methodological and research design criteria as attempts to silence alternative experiences and perspectives (Ashley and Walker 1990a; Campbell 1996). They have also opposed efforts to categorize this scholarship, or to assess its accomplishments (Ashley 1996). All of these things, desiderata for those working within other approaches, are said to render scholarship complicit with structures of domination, which become normal partly via "sovereign" social scientific projects claiming foundations and setting "rules for thinking and research" (George 1994, 196).

This stance against "scientism" has drawn people—myself included—to discourse analysis as a project that is self-aware of the closures imposed by research programs and the modes of analysis which scholars routinely use in their work. The stance has also worked strategically in that it has given to the discourse community one of the means by which scholarship can be included and excluded,[1] as well as one of its enduring narratives for claiming "cognitive authority" vis à vis other disciplinary approaches (Fuller 1988, 196). But it is time to question the position which entailed rejecting as "paradigmatic conceits" the elaboration of methods and the setting of research standards, debate about research design, or evaluation of substantive research (Ashley and Walker 1990a, 398).

The first problem with this position is that it puts discourse analysts and their critics essentially on the same side with respect to social science standards (what these are, and what it means to meet them), in the sense that both conclude that discourse study is not fundamentally about doing rigorous empirical research or developing better theories. Discourse analysis as (good) abnormal science is one inversion away from the definition of (bad) abnormal science used by other scholars to discount this sort of work. Second, closure on these topics involves "the imposition of unnecessary limitations upon the work of thought," contradicting the spirit of critical praxis that is supposed to be at the center of discourse analysis (Ashley and Walker 1990a, 402; on this point, see also Waever 1996b; Ó Tuathail 1996; Price and Reus-Smit 1998). Third, this position is at odds with other aspects of recent discourse scholarship, including the elaboration of different analytic approaches and of methods of analysis and, via a growing number of substantive empirical analyses, the development of both theoretical concepts for and critical readings of international relations.

This chapter draws upon this emerging body of literature to examine discourse study as a research program whose community shares certain basic commitments. After elucidating some of these commitments, I take them as presuppositions of discourse studies. I will therefore not discuss whether the commitments are reasonable or justified, nor answer common objections to them such as "language isn't everything," "events are not constructed, they are caused," or "where is the space for agency." Nor will I weigh the strengths and weaknesses of alternative frameworks to the discourse approach given some extra-paradigmatic explanatory goal (e.g., the goal of explaining the role of ideas in foreign policy, or of improving explanations of international norms). These are important and necessary intellectual issues, but they are generally not intended, nor do they generally help, to develop discourse research in IR.

Instead, my approach in this chapter is to use the commitments I elucidate as an *internally established basis* for critically evaluating discourse research. Separating "discourse analysis" into different, albeit related types of research and methods, I also offer exemplars of good work and suggest ways that discourse studies could be improved both conceptually and in terms of their research design. My aim in this is to demonstrate that, in order to advance its critical agenda, discourse scholars need to reflect more seriously on how to do discourse studies well.

Towards a Normal Science of Discourse Study

Discourse study, as some claim, may be different from other research programs in its commitment to studying the politics of representation (although see Price and Reus-Smit 1998, 268–270). But discourse research is not otherwise so exotic or foreign a mode of collective intellectual labor. Like other paradigms, the adherents of this one attend to, cite, and follow up on the work of knowledge producers socially acknowledged as important for the research program.[2] As part of a shared "argumentation format" demarcating the program, scholars in this area also build their research upon a set of theoretical commitments that organize discourse studies and implicitly restrict appropriate contexts of discovery and justification (e.g., some claims may be grounded on empirical facts determined through study of data of some sort; others may be grounded on reason and reflection alone) (Fuller 1988, 191–192). Among the most important of these commitments are the following three analytically distinguishable bundles of theoretical claims.

Discourses as systems of signification: this first commitment is to a concept of discourse as structures of signification which construct social realities. Underlying this commitment is a constructivist understanding of meaning: things do not mean (the material world does not convey meaning); rather, people construct the meaning of things, using sign systems (predominately, but not exclusively, linguistic). However, discourse theorists understand significative construction in a way not shared by all constructivists. First, drawing on de Saussure, emphasis is given to the *relationships* in which things are placed in a sign system and, more precisely, in relations by which one object is *distinguished* from another in the system (De Saussure, 1974). Second, drawing on Derrida's philosophical work, discourses are expected to be structured largely in terms of *binary oppositions*–educated/ignorant, modern/traditional, Western/third world—that, far from being neutral, establish a relation of power such that one element in the binary is privileged (Derrida 1981).

Discourse productivity: the second theoretical commitment is to discourses as being productive (or reproductive) of things defined by the discourse. The point here is that beyond giving a language for speaking about (analyzing, classifying) phenomena, discourses make intelligible some ways of being in, and acting towards, the world and of operationalizing a particular "regime of truth," while excluding other possible modes of identity and action. More specifically, discourses define *subjects authorized to speak and to act* (e.g., foreign policy officials, defense intellectuals, development experts) and "the relations within which they see and are seen by each other and in terms of which they conduct the . . . business with respect to that issue-area" (Keeley 1990, 92). Discourses also define *knowledgeable practices* by these subjects towards the objects which the discourse defines, rendering logical and proper interventions of different kinds, disciplining techniques and practices, and other modes of implementing a discursively constructed analysis. In the process, people may be destroyed as well as disciplined, and social space comes to be organized and controlled, that is, *places and groups are produced as those objects*. Finally, it is of significance for the legitimacy of international practices that discourses produce as subjects *publics (audiences) for authorized actors*, and their *common sense* of the existence and qualities of different phenomena and of how public officials should act for them and in their name (e.g., to secure the state, to aid others). Throughout, discourses are understood to work to define and to enable, and also to silence and to exclude, for example, by limiting and restricting authorities and experts to some groups, but not others, endorsing a certain common sense, but making other modes of categorizing and judging meaningless, impracticable, inadequate or otherwise disqualified.

The play of practice: the theoretical commitment of discourse productivity directs us towards studying dominating or hegemonic discourses and their structuring of meaning as connected to implementing practices and ways of making these intelligible and legitimate. However, even if dominant discourses are "grids of intelligibility" for large numbers of people, the third theoretical commitment is to all discourses as being unstable grids, requiring work to "articulate" and "rearticulate" their knowledges and identities (to fix the regime of truth) and open-ended meshes, making discourses changeable and in fact historically contingent. As Roxanne Doty explains:

> Its [a discourse's] exterior limits are constituted by other discourses that are themselves also open, inherently unstable, and always in the process of being articulated. This understanding of discourse implies an overlapping quality to different discourses. Any fixing of a discourse and the identities that are constructed by it can only be of a partial nature. It is the overflowing and incomplete nature of discourses that opens up spaces for change, discontinuity, and variation. (Doty 1996a, 6)

Following from this commitment to "the play of practice," as Ashley (1989) and Doty (1997), among others, have called it, is a concern in the discourse literature for drawing out the efforts made to stabilize and fix dominant meanings, as well as for studying "subjugated knowledges," alternative discourses excluded or silenced by a hegemonic discourse.[3] At least in theory, this latter aspect of discourse study differentiates discourse studies from other approaches, such as the study of norms in IR, which generally considers only norms as articulated by Western elites, other knowledges apparently being presumed to be inconsequential. This commitment also entails a critique of conventional IR theory as providing "ahistorical accounts of continuity and structural form" that ignore historical transformations and a concern for "genealogies" that explore historical discontinuities and ruptures in international relations that conventional theories have erased (Walker 1993, 110).

These three theoretical commitments can be taken as an interrelated set of starting points for discourse analysis to be a *normal science* for its practitioners. The question to which I now turn is how, given this definition of normal science, discourse studies can be evaluated and improved.

Studying Discourses as Systems of Signification

The study of structures of signification is basic to all discursive approaches. If discourses are differential systems of signification, however, how do these systems operate to construct things and give people knowledge about social reality? One answer at least loosely shared in the IR literature is that discourses operate as background capacities for persons to differentiate and identify things, giving them qualities and attributes that are taken for granted, and relating them to other objects. As background capacities, though, discourses do not exist "out there" in the world; rather, they are *structures* that are actualized in their regular use by people of discursively ordered relationships in "ready-to-hand language practices" or other modes of signification (Shapiro 1989, 11). This view of a discourse as "a structure of meaning-in-use" implies that discursive studies must empirically analyze language practices (or their equivalents) in order to draw out a more general structure of relational distinctions and hierarchies that orders persons' knowledge about the things defined by the discourse (Weldes and Saco 1996, 373).

There is no single method for analysis and abstraction along these lines, but rather a number of ways that scholars can identify key aspects of significative practices and, based on their study, establish a discourse. Nonetheless, in light of the relative lack of explicit discussion of methods for analyzing systems of signification, it may help to give a brief sketch of one particular method. This method, *predicate analysis*, is suitable for the study of language practices in texts (e.g., diplomatic documents, theory articles, transcripts of interviews), the main research materials for discourse analysts in IR.[4] I will illustrate the method using the example of how one might analyze the discursive constitution of international relations subjects, which is also a key issue for many working in this area. Note, however, that predicate analysis is not in principle limited to the study of subjects and can therefore also be an aid in, for example, analyzing the social construction of space and of geopolitical reasoning.

Predicate analysis focuses on the language practices of predication: the verbs, adverbs, and adjectives that attach to nouns. Predications of a noun construct the thing(s) named as a particular sort of thing, with particular features and capacities. Among the objects so constituted may be subjects, defined through being assigned capacities for and modes of acting and interacting. For example, suppose a diplomatic document stated:

> If the United States does not take any action in Korea, this would produce a marked psychological reaction in the public mind and in the minds of Asian leaders. U.S. prestige would be damaged throughout the region. Japan, the linchpin of our policy in Asia, would lose morale and experience a strengthening of the widespread desire for neutrality, with the result that not even a commitment of significant U.S. military strength would keep Japan in the West.

Among the predications of *Japan* in this statement are:

- linchpin of U.S. policy in Asia;
- would lose morale;
- would experience a strengthening of the widespread desire for neutrality;
- would not be kept in the West [Western alliance];
- [as with other Asian countries] Japanese leaders and the Japanese public would have a marked psychological reaction.

The language practice of these predications constructs Japan (its leaders and public) as a subject that experiences emotions (a desire for neutrality) and reacts psychically (loses morale) but that does not generally act in a positive sense. Even the possibility of Japan leaving the Western alliance is presented in quite passive terms. Thus these predications construct Japan as an independent but subordinate state that is key to U.S. policy, but one that is acted upon, especially psychologically, rather than one that makes decisions of its own and rationally chooses a course of action.

As the references to Korea and the United States in our example already suggest, a text never constructs only one thing. Instead, in implicit or explicit parallels and contrasts, other things (other subjects) will also be labeled and given meaningful attributes by their predicates. A set of predicate constructs defines *a space of objects* differentiated from, while being related to, one another. For example, suppose that our diplomatic document also stated that "if the US were to give rapid and unhesitating support for the Republic of Korea, this would reassure the Japanese as to their own fate. Soviet aggressive intentions in the Far East would be underlined, enhancing Japanese willingness to accept US protection." That predication constructs the *United States* as a subject that, in contrast to Japan, makes choices and takes material action that affects the psychic conditions of other states (e.g., to reassure those states). Implicitly, in assigning to it "intentions," the *Soviet Union* is also constructed as being like the United States in this respect. But the Soviet Union is also constituted as an aggressor state ("Soviet aggressive intentions"), in opposition to the United States, a protector state for Japan ("U.S. protection").

I have referred to a text in the singular in my illustration, and research based on predicate analysis would certainly entail systematic analysis of a text's object space, drawing up lists of predications attaching to the subjects the text constructs and clarifying how these subjects are distinguished from and related to one another. Discourses, though, are background capabilities that are used socially, at least by a small group of officials if not more broadly in a society or among different elites and societies. Also, the concern in discursive analysis is not only with particular distinctions (that made in a text between Japan and the United States), but also with the structuring of relational distinctions, posited to be a "center that organizes and makes them [particular distinctions] coherent" (Doty 1997, 378). Since discourses are social systems of signification, it will not do (as sometimes appears to be the case) to base a discursive analysis only on one text, even some "key" document (e.g., NSC 68, the Caribbean Basin Report). A single text cannot be claimed to support empirically arguments about discourse as a social background, used regularly by different individuals and groups. Instead, if the analysis is to be about social signification, a discourse analysis should be based upon a set of texts by different people presumed (according to the research focus) to be authorized speakers and writers of a dominant discourse or to think and act within alternative discourses. In order to address issues of selection bias—and to enable better theorizing—one might also more narrowly select texts by whether they take different positions on a relevant issue (e.g., whether or not NATO should intervene in Kosovo), and so could provide evidence of a discourse as a social background for meaningful disputes among speakers of the discourse.

Assuming an appropriate initial set of texts, how is a researcher to undertake an examination of the structuring of relational distinctions? The import of this concern is that beyond identifying the object spaces of different texts, a discourse analysis should compare these object spaces to uncover the relational distinctions that arguably order the ensemble, serving as a frame (most often hierarchical) for defining certain subject identities. So, to continue our example above, a researcher might find that in different texts Japan was repeatedly represented via emotion predicates (e.g., "fear," "desire") in contrast to the United States, represented via judgment predicates (e.g., "weigh options"). She might also find that in the object spaces of the texts she was studying, Japan was represented via immaturity predicates (e.g., politically immature), in opposition to the United States, represented via predicates suggestive of maturity (e.g., "firm and courageous leadership"). In this step of the analysis, the researcher would abstract from these two particular oppositions to a core opposition underlying both, for example, a core opposition of *reason/passion*.

Three points may help to clarify this sketch of a predicate analysis. First, the method is useful not just for establishing a particular discourse, but also for elucidating both how discourses overlap, as well as the structures of meaning that they share. For example, "Western security discourse" has often been analyzed mainly on the basis of representations by U.S. officials or defense intellectuals. However, the "security imaginary" of the United States is not congruent with that of the elites of other Western countries, and (following the theoretical commitment of the play of practice) it would therefore be appropriate to examine how different Western discourses do and do not overlap. This question can be addressed concretely through a comparison of the object definitions and core distinctions used systematically by members of different groups (see Milliken 1999, for Western discourse analyzed in this fashion). Alternative discourses involve for their study more than an initial empirical differentiation. But whether one is seeking to establish the nature of subjugated knowledges, or to study empirically historical continuity and change in discourses, a predicate analysis can help a researcher to better justify and refine an interpretation.

Second, what is being proposed for predicate analysis is a process of empirical study and abstraction which goes hand in hand, in the sense that theoretical categories are drawn from and answer to the empirical data upon which a study is based. This approach has long been advocated by qualitative sociologists under the rubric of "grounded theory" (Glaser and Strauss 1967). In the sociological formulation, a grounded theory is one that, rather than selectively choosing data according to *a priori* theoretical categories, formulates the theory from the data by developing provisional categorizations via empirical study and abstraction, comparing on the basis of new data whether these categories fit and, if necessary, reformulating the categories so that they are empirically valid. Thus, the theory emerges from empirical research, about which it generalizes in a grounded fashion.[5]

Predicate analysis as grounded theory offers an answer to a problem that researchers necessarily encounter in studying discourse, namely when to stop analyzing texts. An analysis can be said to be complete (validated) when upon adding new texts and comparing their object spaces, the researcher finds consistently that the theoretical categories she has generated work for those texts. This is also a partial response to the issue of the reliability of discourse analyses. The interpretation offered has been checked and reworked until it fits with and explains consistently texts that were not originally part of its empirical base. It is worth highlighting that the reliability of any interpretation ought also to be a matter of external checks. Thus, a researcher could usefully compare her theorization to others' studies (discursive or not) of the same issue, again to test her categories and to ascertain whether in this light her interpretation continues to work well; and she could also discuss her findings with others who know the empirical materials with which she is working.

Third, in presenting predicate analysis here, I am not advocating it as the only appropriate method for studying systems of signification. Other methods also exist and could be used instead of or together with predicate analysis. One such method is *metaphorical analysis* as developed by the linguists Mark Johnson and George Lakoff (Lakoff and Johnson 1980; Lakoff 1987; see also Lincoln 1989 for a third method of narrative analysis). A metaphorical analysis focuses upon metaphors (conventional ways of conceptualizing one domain in terms of another) as structuring possibilities for human reasoning and action. From empirical study, the researcher establishes metaphors used regularly in the language practices of a group or society to make sense of the world (e.g., governments as overindulgent mothers using money they don't have, and citizens as children begging for handouts). Abstracting from these particular metaphors, a theory of metaphorical categorization is then developed to account for particular metaphors as variations of a central model or models. The potential for this approach to discourse analysis is evident in Lakoff's (1996) study of liberal and conservative metaphorical common sense in contemporary American politics, and Paul Chilton's (1996) examination of Cold War security discourses in the United

States, western and eastern Europe from 1945 to 1990 (see also Milliken 1996; Mutimer 1999).

In giving attention to certain linguistic elements and their combination, predicate and metaphorical analyses are more formal approaches for studying language practices than is typical of IR work in this area. Some may find them (or similar methods focusing on specific signification mechanisms) too close to "methodologism, of which there is already a surfeit in international relations theory" (Der Derian 1989, 7). I demur. In other disciplines, treatments of significative practices are considered entirely appropriate, in part because they make abstract theory about signification researchable in the actual products of a sign system. In any case, and separately from the value of this particular method, the importance of a method as such deserves to be highlighted. Using a method for "reading" or "seeing" can make research better organized and, therefore, easier to carry through. Through its control over interpretive procedures, it can also bring greater insight into how a discourse is ordered, and into how discourses differ in their construction of social reality. Not insignificantly, it can also be shared to facilitate communication and debate among scholars.

Incorporating Issues of Productivity

Although discourse analysis is concerned with significative practices and the knowledge systems underlying them, it is insufficient to study only the way a discourse constitutes background capabilities for people to understand their social world. The theoretical commitment of discourse productivity makes it important to explain how a discourse *produces* this world: how it selectively constitutes some and not others as "privileged storytellers . . . to whom narrative authority . . . is granted," how it renders logical and proper certain policies by authorities and in the implementation of those policies shapes and changes people's modes and conditions of living, and how it comes to be dispersed beyond authorized subjects to make up common sense for many in everyday society (Campbell 1993, 7). Examining discourse productivity differentiates discourse study from other approaches that do not examine "how foundations and boundaries are drawn—how states [or other entities] are written . . . with particular capacities and legitimacies at particular times and places" (Weber 1995, 29). This aspect of discourse analysis also has clear political and ethical significance: in explaining discourse productivity, scholars can potentially denaturalize dominant forms of knowledge and expose to critical questioning the practices that they enable.

No individual study, even a monograph, can deal with all aspects of discursive productivity, however, and there are foci that follow from choices that scholars make about whose system of signification they will principally study. Surveying the literature in IR, three types of studies can be distinguished on this basis: foreign policy, IR theory, and international diplomacy and organization. Extending significative analyses of foreign policy elites, *foreign policy studies* address discursive productivity by analyzing how an elite's regime of truth made possible certain courses of action by a state (e.g., intervening militarily in the Gulf War) while excluding other policies as unintelligible or unworkable or improper (e.g., doing nothing, seeking a diplomatic settlement) (Campbell 1993; Weldes and Saco 1996). Arguments may also be made for how a particular case or cases illuminate the more general and long term production of the state as a sovereign entity (Campbell 1992) and of international relationships and hierarchies (Shapiro 1988; Doty 1996a). *IR theory studies* usually extend analyses of theoretical representations via arguments that knowledge produced in the academy is fused with that of policy makers to make up a "dominant intellectual/policy perspective" (George 1994, 34). Theoretical representations (as scientific truth) are then presented as helping to legitimize particular policies taken by states and international organizations (Milliken and Sylvan 1996), as well as helping to reproduce a common sense among different populations more generally supportive of state-centrism, the Cold War, the liberal economic order, and post-Cold War reassertion of Western dominance over postcolonial states (Ashley 1989; Klein 1994). Finally, *international diplomacy and organization studies* extend analyses of diplomatic interchanges and organizational knowledges to the discursive production of authorities and experts and their networks (Litfin 1994). They also seek to demonstrate how the coordination of policies is made possible between different state elites and how policies that might seem *a priori* plausible are excluded from the international agenda and from state practices (Price 1997; Mutimer 1999).

These different types of studies are viewed within the discourse community as sharing the same context of discovery and justification for explaining discursive productivity, namely scholarly reasoning and reflection (and not primarily empirical study or theory building). Explanations of policy productivity in both foreign policy and diplomacy/organization studies, for instance, are based mostly on counterfactual reasoning about how, if the significative system and its objects had been different, a different policy or agreement might have been possible (Mutimer 1999). Some bolster this explanation via comparisons to rival or complementary explanations (Price 1997). As Price and Reus-Smit (1998, 277–278) rightly observe, this strategy can add strength to explanations of discursive productivity, but it, too, is essentially justification via scholarly reasoning. More can and should be done in this area in terms of conceptual development and empirical research. Two aspects of discourse productivity that deserve further refinement (and individual study) are the production of common sense and the production of policy practices.

Common Sense

A recurrent theme in the discourse literature is that discourses (re)produce the common sense(s) of societies, limiting possible resistance among a broader public to a given course of action, legitimating the state as a political unit, and creating reasonable and warranted relations of domination (Waever 1995; Huysmans 1998). This thematic is tied closely to a critical goal of discourse analysis, namely, that the readers of discourse studies would reflect upon and change their common sense. With most readers being university students and colleagues, the challenge to common sense is directed at discursive authorities (scientific experts and would be policy makers and international affairs workers), but especially at the educated audience for these authorities.[6]

Despite its critical significance, exploration of the production of common sense has been relatively limited, with most work being done in IR theory, but some also in foreign policy analysis. With regard to such theory, scholars have argued that theoretical practice "is . . . implicated in the production of particular discourses," as in the case of the United States in the Cold War era (Doty 1997, 386). More broadly, IR theory has been presented as a specifically modern form of representation, contributing to the common sense acceptance of the paradigm of sovereignty with its core opposition between international relations (as a domain of ever repeated violence and anarchy) and domestic politics (as a realm of order and progress) (Ashley 1989; see also Walker 1993; George 1994). It is argued that IR theorists therefore have "complicity in the practices of statecraft," which they should reexamine, as should readers of their texts (Ashley 1996, 246).

Those presenting these arguments acknowledge that IR theory is one of many sites of the production of common sense. The overwhelming concentration on the theory site nonetheless works to belie this acknowledgement. Without questioning that IR theory does contribute to the creation of common sense, it is time to rethink this concentration. IR theory is limited as an *academic knowledge site* for the production of common sense. Economics, law, and history are at least as important, yet they are rarely reflected on, much less studied in our discipline (a notable exception is Edkins 1996a). The study of theory is also limited as an *expert knowledge site*. Most expert knowledge of international relations is created and circulated not as the "pure science" of (mainly U.S. neoliberal and neorealist) IR theorists, but as the "applied science" of scholars advising governments and international organizations, working for think tanks and nongovernmental organizations, and speaking publicly on issues of the day in institutional publications, magazine articles, editorials, television interviews, and trade books.

A second issue for theory and foreign policy arguments alike is a lack of concepts for explaining processes of this production. Put differently, writing (security, for example) also implicates processes of reading in which people come in some fashion to take up discursive constructions as representing reality for them. One way that this "uptake" can be usefully theorized is via concepts of articulation and interpellation that Jutta Weldes (1999), building upon Stuart Hall's work, has developed for foreign policy study (for another approach, see Edkins 1996b).

Articulation in Weldes's usage means the construction of discursive objects and relationships out of "cultural raw materials" and "linguistic resources" that already make sense within a particular society (1999, 154). In combining and recombining extant cultural materials, and in repeating successful combinations, "contingent and contextually specific representations of the world" can be forged that "come to seem as though they are inherently or necessarily connected and the meanings they produce come to seem natural, to be an accurate description of reality" (154–155). *Interpellation* refers to how these representations work to "hail" individuals so that they come to accept the representations as natural and accurate. The basic idea is that foreign policy representations by governments and other authorized speakers do not only define an object space for international relations, but also create subject positions or identities for individuals to identify with and to "speak from" (163). As Weldes writes of this construction of common sense during the Cuban Missile Crisis:

> They [the representations used by US officials during and after the Cuban Missile Crisis] invited members of their audience ... to imagine themselves as a powerful yet concerned family member who—because they were committed to the solidarity of the Western hemisphere, to the integrity and virtue of the "American family" and its common values, to democracy and diversity, and to the disavowal of secrecy and treachery—was in a uniquely responsible position that both enabled and obliged them to challenge the global threat posed by totalitarianism and the hemispheric threat posed by the Soviet "Trojan horse" and by "Communist infiltration" of Cuba. In so doing ... [t]he audience was interpellated as a democratic subject which ... defended the free way of life around the world ... as open and honest people ... [who] wished to preserve peace and order, freedom and the independence of nations. (343–344)

Concepts of articulation and interpellation take us some distance in thinking through the issue of the production of common sense. But they—or similar efforts to theorize this issue—must also face the question of what works as "cultural raw materials" and "linguistic resources" for different societies or, indeed, within a society. Weldes notes in passing that the use of "we" to mean the United States and actions taken by the U.S. government, a powerful and highly common mode of interpellation in U.S. culture, is not so prevalent in other cultures (1999, 184 fn. 9). Similarly, neoliberalism—an apparently successful set of articulations in Reagan's America and Thatcher's Britain—did not work equally so well to interpellate publics in France, Germany, or Switzerland, among others. Thus explaining the production of common sense appears best served by empirical study that examines "mundane" cultural knowledge in specific contexts and asks what resources it actually provides.

I would suggest two approaches to what would largely be a new domain of inquiry for discourse scholarship in IR. The first is a popular culture approach, analyzing the everyday cultural conditions of novels, comic books, television, and film and how they render sensible and legitimate particular state actions. Although it too easily translates U.S. popular culture into modern culture in general, Michael Shapiro's (1997) study is one exemplar of work of this sort. The second approach is anthropological, analyzing the everyday culture of people in their work and family lives. Here, IR scholars could learn from Joseph Masco's (1999) investigation of "national security" as meaningful to Native Americans, Nuevomexicanos, and U.S. military industrial workers living near and employed by New Mexico's Sandia and Los Alamos National Laboratories.

Policy Practices

In contrast to IR theory studies, foreign policy studies and diplomacy and organization studies are directly concerned with explaining how a discourse articulated by elites produces policy practices (individual or joint). These types of discourse analysis also share an understanding of what it means to explain the production of policy practices, namely to take the significative system which they have analyzed, and to argue for that system as structuring and limiting the policy options (joint policies, norms of state practice) that policy makers find reasonable.[7] This approach is an appropriate one, and one which I too have followed. But like the treatment of common sense, it also deserves to be reexamined and refined as a way to explain policy production. The current approach's main weakness (or puzzle, in another idiom) is that it leaves out what happens after a policy is promulgated among high level officials, that is, the implementation of policy as actions directed towards those objectified as targets of international practices.

Analyzing how policies are implemented (and not just formulated) means studying the operationalization of discursive categories in the activities of governments and international organizations, and the "regular effects" on their targets of interventions taken on this basis (Ferguson 1994, xiv). The operationalization practices of these entities is a subject rarely taken up in mainstream IR, as attested to by the general lack of discussion of implementation in most theories and studies of foreign policy or of international regimes. When implementation is considered, the discussion is usually couched in very general terms, outlined as a stylized type of act or policy (e.g., "land redistribution," "intervention," "foreign aid") but not as explanation of how the actions putatively covered by the term were organized and enacted in particular circumstances. Governments and international organizations do document and record implementation practices and take measures of their effects, but in an arcane language that, for public consumption, usually involves the use of vague and general labels (e.g., "measures taken to improve debt servicing" to describe IMF demands to Indonesia). Discourse studies which include the implementation of policy practices can potentially problematize such labels and expose readers to the "micro-physics of power" in international relations (Foucault, 1977, 26). This exposure might in turn give readers a basis with which to "question" and "enquire about" the workings of states and international organizations, a critical goal that discourse studies share (Edkins 1996a, 575).

Foucault's (1977) work on the development of criminality and the prison system demonstrates the need for the study of policy implementation. In Foucault's analysis, a significative process of definition was necessary— but not by itself sufficient—in order to create a disciplinary society. Rather, the meaning of categories for "the criminal" and "the delinquent" also had to be operationalized through measures organizing space in prisons and practices of surveillance developed to regulate the lives of prison inmates. It was the two processes together, and not just or mainly fixing objectives and naming things, that produced a discourse of criminality that could discipline subjects, shaping their activities down to the smallest detail.

In the concepts of disciplinary technologies, surveillance, and governmentality, Foucault's studies (1977, 1980, 1991) provide IR scholars with a means to theorize the production of foreign policy and international practices. This type of thinking—basically in terms of examination of how corporate actors order, control, and shape bodies and spaces—has perhaps been most fruitfully pursued outside of our discipline in development anthropology (Ferguson 1994; Escobar 1995) and geography (Ò Tuaithail,

1996). Exemplars in IR can also be found, though, including Milliken and Sylvan's (1996) examination of the implementation of U.S. intervention in Vietnam, Bigo's (1996) work on procedures for police cooperation in Europe, and Doty's (1996a) study of British colonial policy towards Kenya.

Doty's examination of the British colonial practices of land ordinances and tribal reserves illustrates what such research can provide that a study of policy formulation alone cannot accomplish. Her study shows, first of all, how British policy became comprehensible via the construction of Kenyans as "natives" needing to be controlled and mastered, and of the British as civilized subjects capable of handling the power and authority necessary for this. Looking at the operationalization of policy, Doty then examines Britain's governance of Kenya, tracing how, in its organization of space and the controls it established for persons' movements, employment, etc., the British administration put into action the "truths" it was constructing for Kenyan "natives." The latter aspect of her study is essential, for it enables Doty to explain how this discourse produced Kenyan "natives," literally by disciplining their bodies and by reforming and regulating the social, economic, and political spaces in which they lived and worked.

Not every analysis of foreign policy or international organization can or should address in depth how the policies being analyzed are operationalized. It would be a "progressive problem shift," however, for this to become a type of study regularly undertaken by discourse scholars in IR. For scholars considering such an undertaking, a comment on data sources is also appropriate. Most studies of foreign policy or international organization, focusing on policy formulation and not on implementation, will have limited utility for a research project of this kind. The same applies to diplomatic or policy histories, if written (as is usually the case) with a focus on the decision makers and not on the "action in the field." Researchers interested in historical studies are likely to be better served by field histories (e.g., military histories) and, especially by archival research and writings by firsthand observers. Similarly, scholars engaged in contemporary studies should use firsthand media reports, Internet network resources, and even fieldwork and interviews.

Addressing the Play of Practice

Explanations of the production of discourse have largely been explanations of how a dominating discourse of international relations produces the social reality that it defines. However, discourses require effort on the part of authorized speakers in order to (re)produce them, and such efforts are not always successful. This open-endedness and instability of discourses means that they are liable to slip and slide into new relationships via resistances that their articulation and operationalization may engender. To be considered well done, any type of discourse study thus needs to address not just the orderly constitution of international society, but how this order is inherently contingent, entailing that its orderliness needs to be worked for it to be reproduced.

IR scholars use or propose four main methods for addressing the play of practice in their work, all based on empirical analysis and evidence. In the *deconstructive method*, the contingent nature of a discourse is revealed through textual analyses that show how internally to a text, the poles of oppositions which it privileges and the realities it thereby makes basic or original can be reversed and displaced, thereby producing other truths. The orthodox meanings of a discourse in such cases are shown to lack the stable foundations claimed for them, indicating that these are imposed readings which could have been different.

The *juxtapositional method* works similarly to deconstruction, but does so by juxtaposing the truth about a situation constructed within a particular discourse to events and issues that this truth fails to acknowledge or address, and also by pairing dominant representations with contemporaneous accounts that do not use the same definitions of what has happened and that articulate subjects and their relationships in different ways. The point of this method is not to establish the right story, but to render ambiguous predominant interpretations of state practices and to demonstrate the inherently political nature of official discourses.

The next method, focusing on *subjugated knowledges,* is essentially an extension of the juxtapositional method, with the difference that alternative accounts are not just pointed out but are explored in some depth, showing that they are enabled by a discourse that does not overlap substantially with a dominating discourse. This may also involve an examination of how the subjugated knowledge itself works to create conditions for resistance to a dominating discourse, and also perhaps an exploration of how the dominating discourse excludes or silences its alternative.

Finally, in the *genealogical method*, the contingency of contemporary discursive practices is examined through historical studies of past discursive practices that "record the singularity of events outside of any monotonous finality" (Foucault 1977, 139). That is, in a genealogical study history is not interpreted as a progression leading to the present, but as a series of discursive formations that are discontinuous, breaking with one another in terms of discursive objects, relations, and their operationalization. Genealogical studies thereby emphasize that dominating discourses, including contemporary ones, involve relations of power in which unity with the past is artificially conserved, and order is created from conditions of disorder.

These methods for studying the play of practice are often combined, which is a good triaging strategy in qualitative research terms, as well as a good way to help convince the skeptical reader. However, it can be questioned whether some of these methods do not work better than others to achieve the critical aims of discourse study. My own view is that the approaches of subjugated knowledges and genealogy have the most potential to lead readers to question orientations and actions that they ordinarily take for granted. These approaches do not only show that the world could in principle be interpreted differently (deconstruction) or that on some instances it has been interpreted differently (juxtaposition). They also have the potential of showing that the world has been and is being interpreted (judged, enacted) in different ways in a routine and regular fashion by various groups and cultures as part of their everyday being-in-the-world. Concretizing other possibilities is surely the best way to enable people to imagine how their being-in-the-world is not only changeable but, perhaps, ought to be changed.

But if studies of subjugated knowledges or of past alternatives have this potential, this has not been fully realized in the discourse program in IR. Current research on genealogical and, in particular, subjugated knowledges is not especially extensive. As I next discuss, there is also a need to improve upon their research design.

Studying the Politics of Hegemony

In oft repeated figurations of "dissent" and "marginality," the less orthodox part of the IR literature has given considerable metatheoretical space to the study of subjugated knowledges and to resistance to dominating discourses (Ashley and Walker 1990b; George 1994; Ashley 1996). However, little systematic research on the politics of hegemony has been undertaken. Only a handful of studies actually study subjugated discourses, as opposed to pointing at putative examples of these, and fewer still enquire directly into how dissent is made and unmade (see, among this limited group, Manzo 1992; Sylvester 1994; Hansen 1997; Fierke 1998).

Undoubtedly, part of the problem lies with the potential difficulties of such research. Unlike studying U.S. foreign policy towards Vietnam or Western diplomatic discourse on chemical weapons, subjugated knowledges are often not articulated in English or in other languages commonly spoken by North Americans and West Europeans. These discourses may also be local (e.g., the culture of farmers in northern India) and therefore not be recorded, thus requiring fieldwork for their investigation. Even if they are recorded, they are still likely to present to a researcher "another world" whose referents take time to learn (e.g., the cyberculture community, and development discourse in Chad). However, these research issues are not the only reason for the relative inattention given to the politics of hegemony. A contributing factor is the truncated understanding of discursive productivity which has been typical of work in our field. If people's common sense of the world is taken as already made (and in one form only), there does not appear to be any point in studying the politics of hegemony. If international practice is treated as an issue of formulation and choice by elites, and not as policy definitions that in their operationalization have regular effects on their targets, resistance becomes difficult to imagine, and, even more so, to trace out.

The top-down view of discourse implicit in these orientations has not been as prevalent in other fields, and IR scholars can find in disciplines such as cultural studies and anthropology concepts and approaches to help them in theorizing the politics of hegemony in international relations (another source within IR is work being done in Gramscian political economy). Bruce Lincoln's work provides an illustration of one possible approach. Lincoln uses narrative analysis to identify the cultural myths (i.e., narratives that in a culture have "the status of *paradigmatic* truth") by which elites can articulate an official version of a course of action and of a social order likely to be persuasive in their society (1989, 24). As he points out, though, societies are syntheses of constituent subgroups "only imperfectly and precariously bound together by the officially sanctioned sentiments of affinity" (10). Elite discourse may therefore fail in its hailings, opening a space for those marginalized under the existing social order to agitate for change. To construct new social formations, these people make use as well of myths, albeit in different ways. They can contest the authority of an official myth, so as to "deprive it of the capacity to continually reconstruct accustomed social forms" (25). Drawing on other available cultural myths, they can seek to counter the persuasiveness of an official myth with a different paradigm. They can also reinterpret the official myth in a different variation that is supportive of social change.

In his studies of (among other events) the Spanish civil war, the Iranian revolution, and the St. Bartholomew's Day massacre, Lincoln shows how myths as cultural resources have been articulated in different ways by subgroups in societies so as to produce the conditions for resistance and, indeed, for social change. This general approach (with its clear connections to Weldes's work on societal common sense) is by no means limited to a particular state and to resistance within that state. It can also be applied to global processes and international discourses, as Akhil Gupta does in his ethnographic examination of indigenous discourses of agronomy and ecology in the Uttar Pradesh state of India, and of how these "mingle and jostle with one another to interrupt the teleological narratives" of post-1945 development discourse (1998, 13). Gupta's analysis does not valorize indigenous discourses for their antimodernism or their authenticity, which are definite risks in this sort of study. Rather, he highlights how they are "hybridised discourses"—blending "scientific" theories, "humoral" accounts of the lands and its capacities and strengths, and prevailing development discourses, and how this hybridization gives farmers a way to make sense of and to organize against the emerging regulation of biodiversity (159, 5).

Constructing Genealogies

The clear message of Gupta's study, echoed also in Diana Saco's (1999) work on the politics of cyberspace, is that new modes of governmentality that are being instituted to regulate the relationship between people and things are not processes of complete closure. They operate by fits and starts, often creating the conditions for unintended consequences. This type of analysis is one which we might expect to see developed also in IR genealogies. However, what one learns from reading many (although not all) of the genealogical investigations is not so much about how discourses of international relations have been discontinuous, with heterogeneous conditions of emergence and spaces for dissent, but how dominating discourses have been largely *continuous*.

Following in part on Derrida's deconstructions of Western philosophy, many discourse scholars have given a strong reading to modernity and its binary oppositions as constitutive of IR theories, both past and present. Shapiro (1992), for example, presents geopolitical thinking as a discourse that helped constitute and has gone on constituting international relations throughout the modern era; and Jens Bartelson (1995) traces the contemporary discourse of sovereignty in international political theory as a formation intact since the Renaissance. The result is to bind a rather long history (at least from Kant to the present) to a continuation of the same discursive structure and logic of difference, with the effect that despite surface changes, IR becomes a quasi-eternal recurrence. Discourses constitutive of state practices have also been cast as modernist, and analyzed as being basically continuous for several centuries or more in their oppositional structures and modes of productivity. David Campbell, for example, argues that U.S. identity constructions from the seventeenth and eighteenth centuries are "oddly similar" in "structural logic and modes of representation to the

Cold War, indeed, that the Cold War is "another episode in the ongoing production and reproduction of American identity" (Campbell 1992, 145). Similarly, Iver Neumann's (1998) study of Russia as an object in European identity formation illustrates that although the qualities and attributes given Russia in European discourse have varied somewhat, such variation is secondary to enduring core oppositions rendering Russia an enemy "other" of Europe.

Perhaps these quasi-structuralist readings are correct, and that only contrasts like, for instance, that between a Greek versus a modern era can draw out a discursive formation different from that of the present era. The conclusion is troubling, though, not least of all for its political prospects. If the United States has always drawn upon similar identity oppositions in its foreign policy practices, it seems unlikely that this discourse can develop any time soon "an orientation to the inherently plural world that is not predicated upon the desire to contain, master, and normalize threatening contingencies through violence" (Campbell 1992, 252). If Russia has been Europe's enemy "other" for several centuries, this would seem an historical lesson also valid today for European policy makers. Even if one argues that this is not so, there would still be the issue of how such a longstanding feature of European culture and political practice can ever be changed.

As an historical thesis, the continuity reading is, however, questionable. Gearóid Ó Tuathail's work on the emergence of geopolitics in the late nineteenth century demonstrates this problem. As he argues (1996, 16–17), in a remark on the modernist reading of geopolitics by critical theorists in IR as well as geography:

> [T]he difficulty with such generalized inflations of the concept of geopolitics . . . is that they can efface the historical and geographical particularity of geopolitics as a way of envisioning and writing space-as-global from the turn of the century. The term "geopolitics" was first coined in 1899. As a consequence of the imagined significance of a German school of geopolitics in explaining Nazi foreign policy during World War II, geopolitics became the name of a tradition with a canon of classical texts and a parade of prophetic men . . . The inflation of the term in recent critical intellectual discourse . . . is understandable and not new.

State practices and international relationships have also changed historically rather more than the thesis suggests. To list some of these changes, marriage has stopped being a typical mode of alliance formation, just as alliances themselves have changed. Slavery has disappeared as a form of international commerce. Vassal states, suzerain states, and imperial states, all possible international statuses/state identities in the late eighteenth and early nineteenth centuries, became impossible entities by the mid-twentieth century. So too did practices of colonialism. Exterminism was once practiced in U.S. foreign policy (as well as by certain other Western states), but it has now become unthinkable. Techno-war, on the other hand, has emerged in this century as a new type of U.S. policy practice. So has foreign aid, as well as other technologies of power of the development discourse.

Examining the work of those like Saco (1997), Richard Price (1997) or others who are able to genealogize international relations in a more differentiated way, two things appear to contribute to breaking with "generalized inflations." The first is that the researcher foregoes her conceptualizations in favor of studying how others have constituted their meanings. As David Sylvan, Corinne Graff, and Elisabetta Pugliese note (1998, 5), a fixed meaning for the concept of sovereignty often continues to be used by genealogists despite claims to the contrary. Bartelson, for example, fixes a meaning for the concept of sovereignty as a frame separating the inside of political units from their outside; the frame is said to vary, but from the Renaissance to today, the frame-meaning is treated by Bartelson as remaining the same. A discourse study adopting a grounded theory approach, in contrast, can attend to how sovereignty might have been defined rather differently by others in the past.

Second, genealogies that reveal discontinuities do not treat the past as a series of interpretations (series of representations of Russia, series of U.S. identity constructions), they instead focus on state practices and how these are and are not produced by significative systems. In this vein, they ask about practices that could be pursued in earlier periods, but that are not possible now (e.g., chemical weapons). They also look at the way that relationships were previously regularly constituted, but not practiced today (e.g., alliance through marriage). In other words, they use the study of *impossibilities in practices* as a means for comparing discursive formations and differentiating them historically.

The answer that some give to the issue of genealogizing continuities is that it is a matter of emphasis (stressing historical similarities rather than difference) and of political strategy: against the chorus of a New World Order, for example, it may be critically useful and important to point out continuities between the Cold War and today's international relations. However, as historians of the present, discourse scholars presumably seek to help people to find potentialities for contemporary change. A person's ability to do this is unlikely to be encouraged by repeated demonstrations of structural quasi-permanence which (in a rather utopian fashion) locate "real difference" only in premodern social realities.

Conclusion

The study of discourse in IR is not just a project of metatheoretical critique, it has also become a vibrant research program that deserves to be further advanced. Building upon theoretical commitments of the discourse community, I have sought in this chapter to lay out some potential areas for advancement, including improving the analysis of significative systems, furthering the study of common sense and policy practices, and developing research into the politics of hegemony and historical change in discourses. Research in these areas can contribute to progress in discourse scholarship, both as a social science and as political and ethical criticism.

Acknowledgment

In an earlier form this chapter was published in *European Journal of International Relations* 5, vol. 2 (1999): 257–286. The author thanks Sage Publishers for permission to republish the work here.

Notes

1. See, for example, Jim George's examination of "alternative" scholarship that due to its "commitment to a positivist ontology of real meaning" and its "closure of . . . behavioralist training rituals" ends up by reinforcing the "discursive limitations of the orthodoxy" (1994, 15).

2. There is actually a tripartite ascription of value: to "canonical" social theory and philosophical texts (e.g., de Saussure, Foucault, Derrida), to "credible" contemporary works in social theory (e.g., Judith Butler, Henri Lefebvre, Emanuel Levinas) and IR (e.g., Richard Ashley, David Campbell, James Der Derian, Michael Shapiro), and to IR work "discredited" by its rationalism, positivism, etc. (e.g., Robert Keohane, John Ruggie, Kenneth Waltz, Alexander Wendt). Perhaps the most valued of all are the credible works in social theory.

3. The term "subjugated knowledges" comes from Foucault (1980, 82), who defined them as "a whole set of knowledges that have been disqualified as inadequate to their task or insufficiently elaborated: naive knowledges, located low down on the hierarchy, beneath the required level of cognition or scientificity."

4. For the linguistics background to this method, see Lecomte (1986) and Lecomte and Marandin (1986). I owe my familiarity to it to David Sylvan's work (see Alker and Sylvan, 1994); the method is also used in Doty (1996a); Milliken and Sylvan (1996) and Milliken (1999).

5. To counter a possible confusion here, the idea is not that the researcher starts with a blank slate conceptually but that, in contrast to a hypothesis-testing model, she deliberately seeks to develop and challenge her concepts in response to the research process.

6. Some have sought to reach other readerships through media appearances (e.g., Ole Waever), teaching and publishing outside a university context (e.g., Der Derian), in Britain's Open University (e.g., Jenny Edkins), or through engaging directly with policy makers and military officials (e.g., Andrew Latham, Sandra Whitworth). These projects

can involve compromise and risk cooptation, but they also pose perhaps the greatest challenge to contemporary practice that discourse scholarship can offer.

7. An additional important part of such studies is to show the prior historical "naturalization" of the discourse (in an alteration of or, more often, a reproduction of the discourse's structures of meaning).

8

International Relations as Communicative Action

Harald Müller

This chapter is the result of an increasing dissatisfaction with the dominant utilitarian theories of action as I have encountered them and sought to apply them within the discipline of International Relations (IR).[1] Work in the area of regime analysis, as well as its theoretical premises (Müller 1989, 1993a, 1993b), has made me increasingly aware that many significant elements of political reality cannot be systematically accounted for within the framework of these utilitarian theories, for example, the importance of implicit or explicit conceptions of justice on the part of the actors, the meaning of trust, or the phenomenon of "learning through negotiation." Of course, utilitarian theory recognizes these phenomena, but it attempts to account for them with the help of ad hoc assumptions, without being able to integrate them into the theory as such. The present chapter is an attempt to deal with these difficulties.[2]

All rational choice models have one remarkable feature in common: the players are mute. They do not speak to each other, and in three of the most important of the game theoretical models—Cherry Hunt, Prisoner's Dilemma and Coward—this muteness is constitutive of the decision-making dilemma.[3] This becomes particularly noticeable in the full version of Bueno de Mesquita's "International Interaction Game," which we can treat as a prototypical model of the utilitarian theory of action. The modes of communication available to the governments ("Demand—Counter-Demand—Concession—Capitulation—War") reduce their communicative competence to the level of three-year-old children. It is indicative that the game ends when the players choose the "Negotiation" alternative (Bueno de Mesquita 1981; Bueno de Mesquita and Lalman 1992, ch. 2).

When game theory is applied to the modeling of actual conflicts, as frequently happens in the analysis of ongoing negotiations, game theorists try to make use of two tricks (Keck 1993). Either they simply presuppose language as the "play material" of their players, or they describe a series of games as "communication." This, however, is misleading, for it means that communication takes place between partners who do nothing more than exchange moves in the game. Each partner makes a move, observes the opponent's move, works out its effects on his own preferences, recalculates these, adjusts his strategy in order to make the next move, and so on. What does not take place is communication in the sense of an exchange of meaning through the medium of language, our normal understanding of the term. In neither of these variants is language given any theoretical weight of its own; it remains external to the game theoretical model.[4]

It is an undeniable fact that international politics consists predominantly of actions that take the form of language. Diplomacy is largely a matter of language. Even where nonlinguistic transactions take place, as in the cases of monetary payments or military actions, this always happens in a context of action in the form of language. Indeed, all utilitarian theories can quite well describe discursive exchanges between governments when they get involved in the empirical analysis of international politics. But language is given no theoretical weight of its own here; rather, it is treated rather naively as a premise. In view of the significance that language has acquired in speech act theory, the philosophy of language and the theory of knowledge, this approach can no longer be defended.[5] What is required is a theory of action that gives due weight to the importance of language as action. Such a theory is available in Jürgen Habermas's theory of communicative action.[6]

Habermas does not remove utilitarianism from the theory; rather, he places it in a subordinate position within a more comprehensive concept of action. He gives "strategic action," the pursuit of goals in the world, that is, of goals related to other subjects who are themselves acting, an important position in the overall spectrum of human actions. Strategic action, which is to a considerable degree identical with the utilitarian concept of action, concerns itself with the realization of self-interest by means of influence on objects, be these things or persons. Habermas makes it clear that this kind of action has its limits. Many objectives are only realizable through the coordination of action with others; up to this point, the parallels with utilitarian arguments are very clear.

Now Habermas introduces a second concept of action which by its nature differs from strategic action: action oriented to reaching understanding, or communicative action.[7] This form of action involves the attempt to reach agreement between the actors through reciprocal argumentation, within and by means of the medium of language. A speaker makes a claim to validity in three respects, each of which demands recognition from the listener: in relation to the truth of what he has said, that is, its correspondence to the facts; in relation to the rightness or validity of the normative claims made; and in relation to the speaker's sincerity, that is, a demand that the listener should accept that he means what he says. If the listener has doubts about any of these validity claims, the speaker must defend them with acceptable arguments which can be elucidated in rational discourse.

Habermas assumes that in an ideal speech situation there is agreement about what counts as good reasons in each dimension of validity. This is to say that each of the three dimensions—the factual, the normative, and the internal (accessible to the speaker only)—are open to rational testing through argument. In this connection, it is important that the speakers share what Habermas refers to as a *lifeworld* (*Lebenswelt*). The lifeworld is understood as the sum of shared and inherited experience, a culturally inherited store of models of interpretation that is organized through language. For each participant, a part of this world provides the material for the question under debate, while the lifeworld as a whole serves as an unquestioned background and provides the shared assumptions for the principles accepted as validity grounds. The lifeworld reproduces itself by means of countless daily interactions between the social actors, in which historical traditions, culture, value and so on are simultaneously transmitted and transformed.

Communicative action has its own premises. First of all, it requires mutual recognition by the communicating partners. No rational discourse can come into being between parties who are in dispute over the question of entitlement to participate. Secondly, the parties must have equal access to the discourse; if not, the application of power, rather than rational understanding, decides the argument. Thirdly, the partners must be capable of changing their positions, of shifting from the speaker's role to that of listener or observer, and of taking up the opposite side's point of view. In this way action oriented towards agreement requires the capacity to empathize.

Strategic and communicative actions are ideal types. In everyday action they cannot be sharply distinguished from one another and occur simultaneously. Strategic actors reach understanding with one another because they cannot achieve satisfactory coordination by means of strategic action alone. Communicative actors do not abandon their own strategic goals (see Habermas 1988). What is decisive is the fact that both types of action are present from the start. "Utilitarian egoists" grow up as members of a language community in which understanding-oriented action is as universal as strategic action. This is the reason why it is possible for states to break out of the blind and mutual application of their power resources and to seek solutions for their conflicts and problems of coordination through argument.[8]

Habermas contrasts the ideal type of understanding reached through language and argument with strategic compromises achieved via the weighing up of conflict potential on both sides, which becomes necessary when the sides are pursuing particular interests that cannot be universalized (Habermas 1992). In my view this is too much of a concession to utilitarianism. Habermas overlooks the fact that a significant element of understanding must also be involved in reaching compromises. The conflicting parties must have a clear idea of the object of their dispute, and especially of which interests are legitimate and which are not. They must have reached some kind of understanding regarding how to measure power potentials. They must have at their disposal some kind of shared concept of justice in the form of a view to the "appropriateness" of the results achieved; if not, even the weaker party could be tempted "out of desperation" to use its combat resources to bring the jointly built house down (Bueno de Mesquita and Lalman 1992, 164-166; Lebow 1981, 61-80). And, last but not least, the parties must have developed sufficient trust in the honest intentions of the other side to be able to put the result into practice. To put it another way, they must reach agreement about the validity of the results achieved even in circumstances when the constellations of interest are changing.

All this presupposes the achievement of a high level of understanding so that the particular interests can be fitted into a generalizable framework. Only when this level of understanding is reached can the "negotiation poker" of compromise building unfold.[9] It may be that Habermas has underestimated the importance of understanding as a vital precondition of compromise because his main concern is with processes taking place within societies, that is, processes that are to a considerable extent restricted by frameworks of law. Whether or not this is the reason, the researcher specializing in international affairs notices this gap in Habermas's analysis immediately.

When states, as collective actors, come up against the boundaries of purely strategic action in their international dealings, they know intuitively and on the basis of experience that the repertoire of action of all actors—their own and that of their opponents—contains this alternative. Here lies the decisive distinction between this approach and the utilitarian paradigm, which cannot turn to this alternative. States also know that this type of alternative action makes lasting coexistence and cooperation with the communication partner possible. In the same way states are able to make use of indicators showing whether and when the partner is willing and able to make a shift from one kind of action to another. Discourse makes it possible to test these criteria. Only knowledge of the availability of another type of action, understanding-oriented action, justifies the risk of turning off the path of pure utilitarian action while still making it possible to keep one's own interests in view.

In this way the theory of communicative action is able to dissolve the static initial conditions presupposed by utilitarian theory. It is not simply a question of changing the utilitarian repertoire of action by adding an additional option. Rather, the assumptions of utilitarianism must be fundamentally corrected on the basis of the internal logic of communicative action. Communicative action creates and develops a social relationship between the actors. The assumption of static preferences is abandoned, as is the presumed "state of nature" in which the strategic actors first meet. The "situation structure" becomes a dependent variable which changes along with the verbal exchanges between the parties. This applies not only to the mutual recognition of sincerity, but also to normative attitudes and even to the jointly undertaken construction of the "world of facts." It is precisely in this sense that Alexander Wendt is correct when he says that anarchy is what the actors make of it (Wendt 1992a).

Use of this communicative action approach also gives us a plausible explanation of why, contrary to the assumptions of utilitarianism, regimes are able to bring about major changes in dispositions to action. States that embark upon an attempt to reach understanding must, according to the assumptions of Habermas's theory, come to three kinds of agreement. Firstly, they must agree on the nature of the segment of the world in which they wish to act. This corresponds to the first element of the classical regime definition of 1982 (Krasner 1983a, 2), according to which the principles of the regime contain a shared definition of the relevant facts and causal connections in the policy area in question. Secondly, there is the question of understanding in the normative dimension, which is promoted by the establishment of the most general goals of action or principles. In his own further development of the theory of communicative action in the field of legal theory, Habermas himself has put forward the idea that a successful discourse must rest on more specific behavioral regulations (norms or rules) and on more general ethical standards or principles on which understanding has already been reached.[10] Regime structures provide a perfect example of this. Thirdly, the discourse must make it possible for both partners to assure themselves of the other's sincerity—more on this below. Here it should suffice to say that in the regime structures precautions are taken in the form of precise standards for the assessment of compliant or deviant behavior (rules), or of the setting up of testing procedures (especially verification) which are essentially there to provide a way of redeeming the authenticity of the respective contributions to understanding (Müller 1993a). In this sense it is quite true that, as is frequently said, verification is above all a measure of "trust building."

The regime analysis reveals that numerous well-established procedures within a regime serve the purpose of making further communication between the partners easier (Aggarwal 1985, 28). While the utilitarian approach has placed the greatest emphasis on the increased flow of information and the reduced transaction costs (Keohane 1984, 89–95), what is more important here is the fact that as the procedure is repeated, so the store of shared interpretations is gradually enriched and the thesaurus of understanding grows.[11] This is how the Standing Consultative Commission set up under the SALT treaties has made it possible for the partners gradually to give a precise content to the deliberately ambiguous language of the treaties (Buchheim and Farley 1988).

State leaders are involved in two types of discourse.[12] As has already been said, the first of these is conducted with the governments of other states. The other serves the purpose of determining national goals of action and the justification of international agreements in domestic politics.[13] The model of a two-level game (Putnam 1988) captures only the part of this process in which the actors really do act strategically. But there is also a two-level discourse being conducted here, in which the governments are confronted by the problem that they may have to deal with divergent or even irreconcilable truth, normative or sincerity systems against a background of different lifeworlds.[14] One thinks, for example, of the great difficulties encountered on both sides by the communist leaderships of Eastern Europe in their attempts to find the appropriate balance between detente and distance (Abgrenzung).

My essential point is that the theory of communicative action helps us to build a bridge between the motivations for cooperation as it is accounted for in utilitarian theory, and the actual realization of that cooperation. My argument is as follows. Cooperation between states arises in dilemma situations, in which the actors (states) can only reach their goals through cooperation and only under conditions where:

1) they develop mutual trust in the authenticity of their partners' speech acts;

2) they reach understanding on the definition of the situation;

3) they reach understanding on the normative framework;

4) they are able to negotiate a distributive compromise (strategic action).

Six Tests of Plausibility

In this section I explore a number of specific problems in order to show that the communicative action approach makes it possible to ask questions which cannot be posed within the terms of the utilitarian theory of action, but which are demonstrably of great significance for international negotiations. I then go on to discuss some further cases where utilitarianism cannot help, but where the theory of communicative action possesses superior explanatory power. I rely heavily here on findings from empirical research on negotiations, which, in contrast to the formal and often sterile field of negotiation theory, has dealt extensively with the discursive dimension of international negotiations.

(1) The theory of communicative action would predict that successful cooperation can only be established, and indeed that conversations can only begin at all, when the preconditions of communication are fulfilled; namely, that the partners recognize each other as equals in discourse independently of existing power imbalances. There is indeed a good deal of empirical support for this supposition: Konrad Adenauer's famous steps on the proverbial red carpet symbolized the achievement by the representatives of the new, democratic Germany of equal status with the victorious powers of 1945; decades of refusal to recognize the GDR delayed attempts to bring about detente in the East-West conflict; the bitter dispute over the shape of the table during the Vietnam negotiations in Paris was about nothing less than the legitimacy of the negotiating parties; Sadat's spectacular flight to Jerusalem was a breakthrough in Egyptian-Israeli relations because it symbolized a recognition in principle of Egypt's right to exist; and after apparently interminable arguments about the composition of the Arab delegation, that is, the way in which the Palestinians were to participate, it was the actual mutual recognition in the secret negotiations in Oslo which for the first time gave rise to realistic hopes that peace in Palestine might be possible. William Zartman has described the central object of the prenegotiation phase, that is, the period before the opening of the "genuine" official dialogue, as "questions of mutual recognition and dignity" (Zartman and Berman 1982, 48–49, 58–59, 68–69, 84, 138–139; see also, Fisher and Brown 1989).

(2) Prenegotiations themselves are a further important indicator of the fruitfulness of the theory of communicative action. From the utilitarian point of view, there is no need for such experimental, often secret exchanges. The interests of the parties and the structure of the situation are clear, and those parties must apply their power resources and pursue the negotiations until compromise is reached. In view of the clarity of the situation, there is no reason why they should see any need to put out feelers be-

forehand. From the viewpoint of the theory of communicative action, however, we can see that the parties are preparing for change in the type of action and that this change involves a risk. There is initially a need to test whether one can afford to take this risk. This test must remain as nonbinding as possible in order to keep open the option of a retreat into strategic action. Prenegotiations serve this purpose (Zartman 1989, 8–9).

In order to reduce the risks involved in negotiations oriented towards cooperation, and to create conditions in which further exchanges seem worthwhile, such prenegotiations must perform three main tasks:

(a) The partners must be able to convince each other that the problem confronting them is in principle solvable. An analysis of interests based on a calculation of the "game situation," carried out by either party on its own behalf, is insufficient. It is more important to develop the respective factual and normative points of view through discourse and to assess possible ways of moving these positions closer to one another.

(b) The partners must establish a minimum of trust, which can be initially tested in small, relatively risk free steps in the context of prenegotiations. I shall return to this point in a moment. It is, however, important to note that the problem of sincerity arises even at this early stage, where one might think that predominantly formal questions are involved.

(c) The prenegotiations must give the partners a "belief in the reciprocity of concessions." In other words, they must be able to furnish a sketch of an initial normative framework for a shared concept of justice (Stein 1989; see also Zartman 1989, 9).

In the case of arms control negotiations, the transition from strategic to communicative action can frequently be observed at the point where the parties move from exchanges of purely propagandistic moves to genuine negotiations. By virtue of their high degree of emotional appeal, the fields of disarmament and arms control lend themselves well to the strategy of making attractive sounding but insincere proposals over the negotiation partner's head, as a way of appealing to the partner's public opinion or even to world public opinion, and thereby of damaging his reputation. When these attempts come to an end and serious proposals begin to be presented, a change in types of action has occurred.[15]

(3) In discourses within societies, the authenticity of the speakers is not usually the most serious problem. Parties in communication with one another have an abundance of criteria from their own lifeworld at their disposal, with the help of which they are able to assess the sincerity of others' speech acts. Moreover, the legal system, which exists above discourse, provides insurance against breaches of agreements. Neither of these preconditions is present in international relations. Here, therefore, we must expect

that the actors, in order to reach understanding, will make particular efforts to test their partner's authenticity, and will also have to take great care to establish their own sincerity. This presents no great *theoretical* problem for utilitarian approaches (although their *empirical* analyses certainly take note of the problem of trust). Realists assume that competitors can only be kept in check by their own interest in the symmetrical distribution of gains; no one expects to receive an advance donation of trust from his opponent, and no one is prepared to make such an advance himself. Nor is there a problem here for utilitarians, for they assume that the partners in cooperation know their opponents' preferences from the game matrix, which means that cooperation is secured through knowledge of the other side's orientation towards its own advantage.

We can sum up this point by saying that all empirical analyses of negotiations emphasize the cardinal significance of winning trust through empathy. The ideal negotiator is not seen as a diplomat who, with a great display of strategic cunning, and without consideration for his partner, achieves as many of his own goals as possible. Rather, successful negotiators distinguish themselves by the fact that they are able to win the other side's trust and to keep it throughout the negotiation process. Trust is produced by means of a number of communicative techniques: by helping the other side to achieve its initial goals; by making small offers calculated to appeal to the other side's interests, and offered without an expectation of reciprocation; and above all by dispensing with threats, which play such a central role in strategic action.[16]

Trust does not arise through abstraction from the subjectivity of those negotiating in an objectified procedure (Luhmann 1968); this is simply not possible in international negotiations where improvisation and contingency are bound to play a role. It must be built up gradually in the course of the discursive exchange between the actors. Christer Jönsson has made a particularly intriguing comment on the role of language as a trust building bridge between partners. He points out that the development of a joint language of negotiation, which could be called a "regime language" shared by the partners, helps them to achieve greater certainty with regard to the intentions behind the statements made on both sides.[17]

There is no dispute about the importance of verification for arms control agreements.[18] From a utilitarian perspective, one can certainly ask why so many in the United States have held the reasonable criterion of the "strategic significance" of treaty violations to be inadequate, and why—well into the political center—every infringement, however insignificant, has met with denunciation and with relentless insistence that the treaty should be observed to the letter. The Reagan Administration's noncompliance reports dealing with real or alleged Soviet violations provided the decisive legitimation for the arms control blockade of the early 1980s. Here, too, the answer lies in the element of trust that is needed between partners on communicative action. When there are doubts about sincerity, communicative action becomes impossible. From this point of view every breach of a promise, however strategically trivial, places in question the kind of action that has been chosen. The Gorbachev leadership's decision to provide for transparency through on-site inspection and so to create trust opened the door to a degree of progress that had up until then been considered impossible (Krass 1985, ch. 3).

(4) Within language communities, the experience of a shared lifeworld provides the background against which common criteria for evaluating validity claims can in principle be found. Habermas stresses the importance of the lifeworld for understanding:

> Unless we were able to make reference to the enormous pre-understanding achieved by the communicating partners in the culturally familiar and self-evidently socialized environment of a life-form that is intuitively present, pre-reflexively known and seen as unproblematic, we would be unable to explain how the daily process of consensus building is time and again able to cross the threshold of the risk of dissent, which is built into the praxis of understanding along with the criticizable validity claims. (Habermas 1988, 369, my translation)

How, then, does understanding come into being in an international environment in which a shared lifeworld cannot be assumed? In view of the unmistakable fragmentation of the world, it is hard not to be skeptical about claims that a world culture is already developing and can be seen in globally shared truth criteria (derived from the concept of truth as used in the natural sciences) and in rational efficiency standards for assessing the performances of governments.[19] In fact, in research on "global culture" the existence of such a world culture is for the most part disputed (Smith 1986; Archer 1988).

For both the realist and the institutionalist variants of utilitarianism, the structure of cooperation itself is unproblematic as long as the structure of the situation can be clearly seen. For realism, international anarchy and the shared experience of the power struggle that arises out of it furnish the natural background against which the rivals are able to agree, if need be and under conditions of strictly symmetrical distribution of gains. The uniform evaluation of the situation structure as existence-threatening makes the states' behavior mutually understandable and unproblematic. For institutionalism, the game structure provides the shared point of reference from which cooperation can start. The theory of understanding-oriented action, on the other hand, must expect that actors struggling to reach understanding must first create a substitute for the missing lifeworld. There is no problem involved in admitting that international relations are not simply an empty space waiting to be filled by the actors' preferences. One can certainly see the justice of the English School's argument that the general tradition and rules of international intercourse, above all international law, fill this space and weave a kind of web of connections, creating a weak "sense of community" between the actors (Bull 1977; Wendt and Duvall 1989; Franck 1990; Wolf 1991, 39–40). But this web is too fragile to serve as a substitute for the existing intra-societal lifeworld, which is much richer and denser.

One point in favor of the communicative approach is the fact that, as a number of studies have shown, cultural differences can sometimes make negotiations and understanding considerably more difficult.[20] Different views of justice have proved to be especially problematic, because they make it all the more difficult to create a shared normative framework for problem resolution (Zartman and Berman 1982, 102–109). The considerable culturally—and historically—conditioned differences between U.S. and Soviet strategic thought placed obstacles in the path of arms control in the 1970s that in the end proved insurmountable: the relationship between offense and defense, the weighting of stability as against damage limitation as central objectives of arms control, and other disputed issues (Weber 1991b; Gray 1986).

When differences between lifeworlds have the predictable effect of making understanding more difficult, it is evident that substitutes or assistance must be found, in order to fulfill the important function of the lifeworld in processes of understanding where the fragile web of international law and tradition is inadequate.

(a) The argument so far accounts for the fact that international regimes frequently come into existence immediately after such dramatic events as crises, economic collapses, and wars.[21] These "dramas" are specific, intense, shared experiences. The founders of the world economic regime after World War II derived the ideology of "embedded liberalism" from their experience of the depression after 1929 (Ruggie 1993); the Cuba Missile Crisis brought both superpowers face to face with the consequences of strategic instability and political tensions, and thereby gave birth to arms control (Bundy 1988, ch. IX).

(b) When this experience of having just passed through a crisis is missing, negotiators are able to fall back upon the invocation of earlier shared experience or suffering. One striking example is the exchange of memories of war in high level U.S.–Soviet negotiations, which could still be observed during the negotiation of the German unification settlement (see Bundy 1988, passim; Garthoff 1985; Shevardnadze 1991). The same technique was used in the Israeli-Egyptian peace negotiations at the end of the 1970s, and most recently in the Israeli-Palestinian dialogue. A particularly vivid example of how an "artificial lifeworld" can be created to encourage negotiations has been reported from the secret negotiations in Oslo. Whenever the dialogue threatened to break down, the negotiating partners got down on the floor and played with the four-year-old-son of the Norwegian foreign minister, thereby giving symbolic expression to elements of a shared lifeworld (parenthood, caring for children, the threat to the private world if the negotiations should fail).[22]

(c) In addition to the examples mentioned up to this point, of the selective compression of experience into an "artificial lifeworld," there is also the possibility that in individual areas of policy, "epistemic communities"— (see especially Adler 1992) or "third [expert] cultures" (Useem et al. 1963; Rehbein (1985) can emerge, which can reach a high level of agreement in the practical and normative fields, and within which complete trust in the sincerity of the other side can be developed on the basis of long years of familiarity. This common ground helps to create a firm foundation of knowledge and norms for negotiations in the relevant areas of policy. Such developments can be shown to have occurred in numerous fields, from environmental to security policy.

(d) Finally, the communicative action approach also helps us to better understand Czempiel's model of the "broken bars" (Czempiel 1981). In regions of the world where transactions create a denser network of ties than elsewhere, where a background of similar historical and cultural experience may perhaps be available, political cooperation can also develop on a much higher level and over a much broader area. Here we have a significant contribution to an explanation of the high level of cooperation in the OECD world, and an additional argument in favor of Senghaas's call for a stronger "contextualization" of research on international cooperation (Senghaas 1992b; Müller 1993c). The same line of thought helps us to refine our arguments in favor of regional peace processes, where it is precisely longstanding opponents who can at least use their common experience of enmity as something like a shared lifeworld. In this way a virtue can be made out of necessity, as long as one can get the communication process off the ground (Brock 1991).

These remarks serve once more to emphasize the central role of discursive interaction in theory. Without the overlap between everyday language and more artificial diplomatic discourse, which share certain common features even when there is a significant cultural distance between them, the communicative approach would also be open to the *petitio principii* objection, since the gap between the two lifeworlds would be unbridgeable. On the basis of these minimal common features, however, the communicative interaction process is able to create new lifeworlds, whose diplomatic artificiality is no obstacle to their providing a basis on which understanding can gradually establish itself more firmly.

(5) Utilitarianism treats the results of cooperation as nothing more than the distribution of gains. The theory of communicative action, by contrast, anticipates an agreement which contains factual, normative and authenticity directed elements and which comes into being through a process in which arguments about these elements are exchanged.

The importance of verification for this last aspect has already been demonstrated. Fisher and Ury (1988, 119–138) conclude, on the basis of years of analysis of negotiations, that results must be derivable from "objective criteria," which must be understood as independent of the particular interests of the parties involved. Zartman has discovered that the first phase of negotiations is without exception devoted to the effort to find a "formula" for the solution to the problem (Zartman and Berman 1982, ch. 4). This formula generally contains strong normative elements and questions about the negotiators' authenticity, and most important of all, a shared understanding of fair distribution (Zartman and Berman 1982, 102–109). Alexander George, on the basis of his study of U.S.-Soviet security cooperation, has concluded that such cooperation only becomes possible through a basic, preliminary conception which establishes the normative framework for the overall relationship between the two parties (George 1988, 667–670). Only within this framework can the proper "haggling" begin, which is frequently misunderstood as the actual negotiations. We know from international environmental negotiations that scholarly work and the suggestive moral force of an undamaged environment can play a major role in convincing stubborn negotiating parties (Benedick 1992). The conclusion Zartman draws from the 1978 Sinai negotiations could be taken from a textbook on communicative action: "Details must be justifiable within a framework of defensible criteria" (Zartman and Berman 1982, 176).

Distributive results thus retain a certain connection with the distribution of power, but they cannot be derived from the existing power balance within a negotiation situation. Rather, they must be seen in the light of the shared factual understanding of the respective segments of the world created in the discourse of the negotiations, and on the basis of the criteria worked out for a fair distribution of gains (see Bunn 1992, ch.10). Even negotiation theorists more oriented towards formal strategic models occasionally admit that the participants measure the course and results of negotiations against standards of fairness (Bartos 1977). Arms control negotiations have often broken down because the parties were unable to agree on a shared interpretation of "parity" (Carter 1989, 269–270). Daniel Druckman and Terrence Hopmann have shown that in real life situations (as distinct from laboratory experiments), the strategy of absolute reciprocity (tit for tat) leads nowhere unless it is supplemented by understanding.[23]

(6) Two processes are always entangled with one another in negotiations: the shared "creation of values," which is a communicative act, and the distribution of goods, which represents a strategic competition. The question of whether the communicative action prevails over the competitive elements depends on whether the communicative process succeeds; it cannot be answered on the basis of knowledge of the structure of the original situation (Lax and Sebenius 1986, 29–45; also Ikle 1964, 215). The theory of communicative action has a procedural understanding of cooperation. In particular, it assumes that the partners change as they participate in discourse. These changes can be observed in all three areas of validity: they are, after all, the objective of the process of understanding. As far as the utilitarian approach is concerned, "learning" is restricted to improving one's ability to use appropriate means to achieve the desired ends. Representatives of the utilitarian school claim to have shown that other lessons are also learned, for example, that changes occur in the ordering of preferences, but these effects cannot be appended to the premises of the theory.[24] Once again, the examination of negotiations and of actual cooperative relationships corroborates the more comprehensive concept of communicative learning.[25] Negotiations are not just a matter of choosing between unalterable alternatives, but of creating new values and options (Sebenius 1992; Zartman and Berman 1982, 70–74). And this happens via the central instrument of understanding, of putting forward well-grounded arguments. This insight is taken as self-evident even by so tough minded a realist as Henry Kissinger.[26] Recent developments in negotiation theory, which move away from modeling negotiations after the prisoner's dilemma and treat them as a kind of participatory problem solving, fall back implicitly on communicative action as the central medium of negotiation (see Kremenyuk 1991; Dupont and Faure 1991, 47–49). In the negotiations on the Law of the Sea Convention, two seemingly irreconcilable normative concepts collided with one another: the sea floor as "common heritage" of mankind and as an object of private enterprise. Contrary to initial expectations, the participants succeeded in establishing that the two concepts were normatively compatible and in putting them both into practice. It was only the re-ideologization of U.S. policy under Reagan that led to the failure of this integrated normative concept (Wolf 1991, 121–176).

Methodologically speaking, therefore, it is not entirely satisfactory to infer the outcome of negotiations from a reconstructed matrix of preferences (Zürn 1992, 238). There is always a degree of contingency involved where the effects of arguments are concerned. One can never quite predict whether a given argument will prove to be convincing, what effect it will have on the views of two or more negotiating partners, and so what a final understanding (or, to make it even more complicated, a mixture of understanding and compromise) will look like.[27] All that can be said for certain is that the result cannot be reliably deduced either from the initial preferences, or from the analysis of the power relations between the negotiators, without an interpretation of the process of argumentative exchange between those actors. It is therefore quite correct to say, in the words of Druckman and Hopmann, that "the final results can only be understood through the process of negotiation itself."[28]

Conclusion

The theory of communicative action is a more complete theory of action than the various versions of utilitarianism, and therefore has greater explanatory power. It does what other theories fail to do and offers an explanation of language, the fundamental medium of international politics. It provides a way of dealing with the considerable theoretical implications of the fact that politics must for the most part be produced through understanding via the medium of language. The theory identifies the process of discursive understanding as the decisive bridge leading from the initial motivation to work together to actual long-term cooperation. In this way it allows for the possibility that political actors may do things we expect of ourselves and of others in everyday life: allow ourselves to be convinced by a good argument, change our opinions, be able where appropriate to reconsider our goals, and not remain prisoners of established objectives and priorities.

Even so, the theory of communicative action is not blind in relation to interests, advantages, and power. It should be clear that the question of which interests dictate action does not disappear in a fog of harmonious discursive understanding. Rational choice analysis can still claim to be able to explain a good deal of the behavioral variations within international relations, wherever strategic action is brought into play. The rational choice approach, as long as it is conscious of its own limitations, remains an indispensable component of theory and of empirical analysis even within the framework of a theory of communicative action.

The theory of communicative action's distinction between two types of action serves as a corrective to the purely utilitarian approach which considers the egoistic pursuit of one's own interests to constitute the normal condition in international relations and any suggestion of "idealism" to be a pathological deviation. This theory not only provides space for the alternative type of understanding-oriented action, but also goes on to postulate that the actors cannot avoid shifting from strategic to communicative action if they want to realize their interdependent objectives. What might at first glance look like irrational idealism appears in the light of this theory as an aspect of rational action under which the parties enjoy equal rights. The theory is therefore able to track down strategic pathologies in the negotiation and cooperation process which can emerge when actors are either unable or unwilling to make the jump from one type of action to another.

The theory of communicative action is also able, with its triad of validity claims, to generate a richer range of questions and hypotheses. Authenticity and normative compatibility, that is, the capacity to develop shared standards of justice, are questions that take us far beyond the excessively simple mechanism of balancing interests. Furthermore, we can pose the important question of the background provided by the lifeworld.

There are three questions which the theory of communicative action can help to answer:

(1) what is the breakdown between the strategic and communicative actions in foreign policy and international politics as a whole? This chapter has by no means been able to solve the major methodological problems raised by this question. However, there exists a large number of empirical analyses of negotiations, which can be further analyzed with the use of this approach. Unlike the rational choice analysis, which is limited to only the analysis of the initial situation and the final results the communicative action approach, focuses on the entire interactive process of negotiation.

(2) can the obstacles encountered in intercultural negotiation processes be overcome with the help of this approach? It is obvious that this question is of enormous practical political significance, and not only for international relations. Here, too, we could use material already available from the study of negotiations. The methodologically logical way to proceed would be via a comparison of negotiations between parties sharing the same or a broadly similar lifeworld with negotiations between partners from markedly different cultures.

(3) how do international agreements and regimes influence domestic political discourse in the relevant fields? Can they bring about changes in the ways in which the most important facts, the normative aspects of the situation, or the credibility of the cooperation partner are seen? The communicative action approach reformulates the fundamental question of regime analysis ("Do regimes matter?") and alters the angle of investigation: the

most important question now is not the "hardware outcome" (e.g., does the United Nations Framework Convention on Climate Change help to reduce emissions of harmful substances?), but rather the question of changes in political discourse.

These three questions would by no means exhaust all future research. However, in all three areas the theory of communicative action would be able to make a significant contribution. The theory of communicative action creates a coherent theoretical framework for research findings, derived over a long period with the help of the rational choice perspective, but which have up until now simply been attached without any theoretical grounding to the prevailing utilitarian paradigm. The new theory does away with the naive anthropological dogma permeating the utilitarian approach that human beings and their social units are nothing more than individual or collective gain maximizers. The new approach also places human language, without which there would be no society and no politics, in its rightful place at the center of our attention.

Notes

1. I shall not deal here with the arguments for studying international relations with the help of theories of action rather than systems theory, but see Zürn (1992, ch. 1), von Beyme (1991, 19–34, for a general treatment), and Scharpf (1988).

2. Editors' Note: When published earlier, this paper included an extended critique of neo-utilitarian theories of international relations. Given the focus of this text on constructivist approaches to IR, and in the interest of space, the section detailing the critique has been cut out.

3. This insight is also familiar, but it has apparently been forgotten. It led Anatol Rapoport more than thirty years ago to distinguish between "fights," "games" and "debates" (Rapoport 1960). Fights and games on the one hand, and debates on the other, correspond in the context of international relations fairly precisely to Habermas's distinction between strategic and communicative actions. Rapoport subsequently developed this line of research further, but did not extend it into a full fledged theory of action.

4. Lewis (1969) is a partial exception, but even he does not give language as a form of action the theoretical weight it deserves.

5. See the valuable collection edited by Opp de Hipt and Latniak (1991), also Edelmann (1985) and Emig, Huttig, and Raphael (1992). Karl Deutsch (1957) and Ernst Haas (1982) both came close to developing theories of international relations that would have placed language in an appropriately central position, but both were diverted in other directions—Deutsch by his purely information-theoretical treatment of communication (1966) and Haas by his interest in organizational learning (1990).

6. Habermas 1981; the most concise presentation is Habermas's own (1992). Otto Keck (1993) has confusingly given a purely utilitarian work the subtitle "The dilemma of rational communicative action: an international comparison of atomic energy policies—(my translation); this study makes not the slightest theoretical reference to Habermas, who could after all lay claim to a copyright on the concept. An interesting

examination of the political implications of Habermas's theory can be found in Greven (1987, 1991).

7. Habermas (1988, 361–366) distinguishes the two types of action very clearly from one another. There is in my view no substance to Frank Nullmeier's (1993, 188) claim that drawing a distinction between the two ideal types of action renders Habermas's approach worthless for purposes of empirical political analysis. On the contrary, this approach enables us to pose, for each specific political process, the question (a) of the concrete relationship between the two, and (b) of the shift within a given interaction from the dominance of one type of action to that of the other. Research on the transition from strategic to communicative action promises new insights into the process of international cooperation; it is this very distinction that promises not sterility, but considerable heuristic returns.

8. On the role of argument in politics and law, see Majone (1989) and Kratochwil (1989).

9. Habermas himself suggests this at one point (1988, 357–358).

10. Habermas (1992, 97ff). Kratochwil and Ruggie (1986, 764) remarked that regime building is only conceivable as the creation of an "intersubjective quality."

11. The qualitative distinction between information and understanding has been most convincingly analyzed by Brock (1994, 29–31).

12. Habermas (1988, 376) considers it quite possible to apply the theory of communicative action to collective actors.

13. See Czempiel (1981, 119–136), and (1986, 110–143); on the political process in democracies considered as discourse, see Habermas (1992, 349–398 and 600–631).

14. A very clear account of this can be found in Bunn (1992); see also Müller (1993b, 361– 388).

15. See Bourantonis's (1993) instructive study. The history of the INF negotiations provides a particularly good illustration of this process, as can be seen in Risse-Kappen (1988) and Talbott (1988).

16. Zartman and Berman (1982, 17–18, 27–41); Fisher and Ury (1988, 17–32); Fisher and Brown (1989); Pruitt (1981); on the empathy requirement, see also Senghaas (1992, 69–71, 128).

17. Jönsson (1993, 213). Jönsson (1993, 206–207) also emphasizes the, centrality of trust. It is worth mentioning in this context the story of the U.S. Navy's lively protests against Defense Secretary Weinberger's politically motivated decision to stop the annual discussion with the Soviet Navy within the framework of the Incidents at Sea Agreement. The U.S. naval leadership considered these discussions vital to the successful continuation of this highly regarded agreement; see Lynn-Jones (1988, 499). On the development of a "language of negotiation," see also, Zartman and Berman (1982, 154, 157).

18. See the outstanding dissertation by Manfred Efinger (1991, 40–63).

19. See Rosenau (1986); the concept of "trans-societal relations," as used in Ellen Dorsey (1993), is also relevant here.

20. Zartman and Berman (1982, 224–229); Jensen (1988, 14–18); see also Unger (1986) for an informative case study of an Asian negotiating culture.

21. Müller (1993a, 159); on crises as "learning processes" see Lebow (1981, ch. 9).

22. The pop song released during the second cold war, "The Russians love their children, too," followed the same strategy.

23. Druckman and Hopmann (1990); Rittberger and Zürn (1990, 45–46), also take a critical view of "tit for tat."

24. This has been shown with great clarity in Steve Weber's outstanding game theoretical work (Weber 1991a). Weber shows that the development of arms control depends on path dependency, since learning takes place on both sides, but he is unable to move beyond his paradigm of two monadic players who "exchange moves." The convergence of convictions comes about, according to Weber, as an "unintended side-effect," a clear indication that this theory cannot explain the real effects of communication (see Weber's ch. 7, especially p. 309). One can draw a nice contrast here with the view expressed by a hardliner like Max Kampelman (1986, 102–103), that negotiations consist of "speaking and listening," and his description of the substance of a dialogue with his counterpart during the worst phase of the second cold war, or with Joseph Nye's description (1986, 88) of how he was able, using reasoned argument, to convince the French government not to export a reprocessing plant to Pakistan. Jönsson (1991) has also commented on the inadequacies of a purely game theoretical analysis of negotiations.

25. Beate Kohler-Koch (1989) voiced this criticism as early as 1989, and applied it to my own instrumentalist concept of learning on a number of occasions. It was a long time before I was able to grasp the validity of this criticism and to recognize its implications.

26. The art of diplomacy is not to trick the other side, but to convince them in the event of deadlock of the existence either of joint interests or of disadvantages" (Kissinger, 1982, 214).

27. See the remarks on learning in Thomas Bernauer's (1993, 348–363) excellent analysis of the Convention against Chemical Weapons.

28. Druckman and Hopmann (1990); see also Tracy (1978). "One of the constant paradoxes of negotiations is the fact that they allow the weaker party to confront the stronger and still to achieve a result that would not be possible if it were only a matter of weakness and strength" (Zartman and Berman 1982, 204).

9

Communicative Action and the World of Diplomacy

Lars G. Lose

> In the simulated world, actors cannot communicate and engage in behavior; they are condemned to communicate through behavior. In the real world, the situation of course differs fundamentally. (Kratochwil and Ruggie 1986, 765)

When trying to understand and explain international politics, International Relations (IR) scholars often limit themselves—in the name of parsimony and generalized theory building—to a focus on state behavior. But, as Kratochwil and Ruggie emphasize in their path breaking 1986 article, in the real world communication and behavior are two entangled and equally important elements of the understanding of what states do and do not do. This captures the essence of the general argument that I put forward in this chapter; namely that working with behavior and communication focuses attention on more reflective international action that is constitutive and transformative (Müller 1994a, 26; 1995, 384; Jachtenfuchs 1995, 425–31).

A constructivist perspective is more conducive to an approach that deals with reflectiveness, constitutive and transforming behavior. As a metatheoretical position, social constructivism assumes a mutually constitutive relationship between actors and structures as mediated in social interaction (Berger and Luckmann 1966). Social interaction, the heart of the matter, embodies the dynamics of collective self-interpretations and self-definitions through which actors create the intersubjective understandings that in turn constitute the actor and her actions as meaningful (Taylor 1978).

The purpose of this chapter is to argue that the combination of a focus on communicative behavior and social constructivism is important to two debates: On the one hand, the debate over how to take social constructivism one step further from a metatheoretical position, which deals with ontological and epistemological questions, to an explicit first order theory dealing with the understanding and explanation of specific issues in international politics (Wendt 1991); on the other hand, the debate over how to understand and explain interstate coordination of behavior in general and international cooperation in particular.

Concerning the first debate, I argue that social constructivism can be converted into a substantive IR theory, through a focus on social practice conceptualized as diplomatic communicative interaction. This substantive theory of practice will build on Jürgen Habermas's theory of communicative action (TCA) (Habermas 1981, 1985, 1990).[1] To justify this claim in an IR context, I turn to the second debate, arguing that the focus on communicative behavior is important for explaining international cooperative efforts. Cooperation is conceptualized as a social relationship conducted inside a complex web of intersubjective social structures of principles, norms, and rules produced and reproduced in the communicative interaction between states.

This chapter will not deal with the pros and cons of TCA in relation to other theories of international cooperation.[2] Instead, I take the argument one step further and investigate the extent to which TCA and its preconditions can be related to the realities of international politics. I will argue that the core elements of TCA can be identified in international life, and that they offer an interesting account of how states coordinate behavior through the continuous communicative production and reproduction of collective understandings of reality, legitimate social norms, and socio-political identities.

Following the discussion of the two debates, the chapter is divided into two main parts. The first and smaller part deals with TCA as a social constructivist approach to social dynamics. This includes a brief theoretical discussion of some of the elements in Habermas's theory that are controversial from an IR perspective. The second larger part will be a discussion of the extent to which elements of Habermas's theory can be related to the reality of international relations, and enhance an understanding of the construction and importance of coordinated state behavior. Here the focus will be on diplomatic interaction conceptualized as the element of practice where the dynamics of the continuous interplay between actors and structures are located. When discussing whether it is possible to associate TCA with diplomatic practice, I will focus on the analyses of different scholars who have investigated the realities of diplomatic interaction.

Social Constructivism and the Theory of Communicative Action

During the last ten years social constructivism has been established as a prominent, and not least, a legitimate, metatheoretical point of departure for IR scholars. This is reflected in Wendt's path breaking articles on the social construction of the nature of interstate relations (1987, 1992a, 1994, 1995), Kratochwil's writings on rules, norms and decisions in state interaction (1989, 1993c, 1997) and Onuf's (1989) attempt to reconstruct IR theory from a constructivist point of departure. Nevertheless, there is no such thing as a unified school of social constructivism in IR. Confusion prevails as to what social constructivism actually is. Social constructivism cannot in itself be said to be a substantive theory about international politics (Andersen, 1998). Social constructivism is nothing more and nothing less than a metatheoretical point of departure. Its worth must therefore be proven by conversion into a first order theory that explicitly conceptualizes the social dynamics of international politics (Risse 1997).

As I have argued elsewhere (Lose 1997, 51–78), this has presented a massive challenge to the social constructivists in IR theory. The main problem is to conceptualize the actual constitutive dynamic between actors and the collective structures of meaning so important to the understanding of interstate behavior and especially cooperative efforts. A possible solution to this problem can be found in combining social constructivism with a focus on communicative behavior, conceptualized in accordance with Jürgen Habermas's theory of communicative action. In making this argument I build on the ideas of a German speaking IR community which stresses the potential of TCA for explaining and understanding the emergence and persistence of international cooperation and institutions (Müller 1994a, 1995; Risse-Kappen 1995b; Risse, 1997; Schmalz-Bruns 1995; Gehring 1995a, 1995b). Hence, I argue that TCA is not only important to the debate concerning international coordinated behavior, but also to the debate on social constructivism. This claim is founded on three arguments.

First, TCA introduces a valuable perspective to the theoretical debate on social constructivism, in general, and its conversion into first order theory, in particular. TCA offers a much needed microfoundation of social constructivism, in so far as it stresses the collective communicative process of interpretation through which intersubjective structures of meaning are produced and reproduced, and the process through which the agents themselves—their identities, interests, and shared understandings of meaningful behavior—are continuously produced and reproduced (Risse 1997). Stressing communication and behavior offers a theoretical opportunity to conceptualize collective processes of interpretation, and accordingly social practice, defined as the crux of the mutual constitutive relationship between agents and structures.

Second, TCA introduces a valuable approach to the understanding of how states can coordinate behavior. TCA focuses directly on the molding of cooperative norms and rules, as it offers an explicit theory of intentional interaction, that is, intentional efforts aimed at achieving a collective understanding of the rules and norms that can serve as a foundation of cooperation. Gehring (1995a, 1995b) has pointed to the importance of isolating how states consciously transform a dilemma, such that cooperation becomes possible and is manifested in collectively formulated norms and rules (see also Rosenau 1992, 3–8). As Gehring (1995a, 12) argues:

> Norms do not constitute suitable instruments of governance unless they are moulded purposely and unless their moulding takes place independently from the action which they are designed to influence. For this reason governance requires the establishment of a second sphere of interaction at which the actors concerned do not immediately act but merely communicate about norms. Negotiations constitute the most familiar form of communication for this purpose.

Governance—defined as order plus intentionality—develops as a product of a collective process of negotiation. This collective process is oriented towards an understanding of desirable coordinating structures, which again can be conceptualized as an integrative learning process.

Third, TCA gives impetus to the crucial discussion of how to conceptualize the "international actor." It forces us to look for actors made of flesh and blood, so to speak, rather than short circuiting social constructivism by working with the state-unit as a constituted actor. Hence, in order to conceptualize the behavior of states, through a focus on the internalization of identities and interests, one has to open up the state and search for constitutive and constituted actors (see also Weldes 1996, 280). The state, conceptualized as a black box, cannot be part of a social constructivist theory since its presence there would prevent the development of a micro theory of collective interpretations. Conceptualizing the state as a black box makes it impossible to say anything about either how the state is constituted as an actor, or how the state plays an active role as actor in the collective process of interpretation. Jaeger (1996, 317, my translation) has pointed this out in a critique of Wendt:

> A collective actor like the state only exists when it is reproduced by means of an institutionalised practice by bureaucrats, politicians and societal actors. To treat the state as an actor reifies the state, instead of problematizing its mechanisms of reproduction.

This does not necessarily mean that one has to treat the state as a structure in itself (Katzenstein 1990, 9–14). I do think that it is possible to conceptualize the state as an actor that constitutes and is constituted in certain international structures of meaning. But focus must shift to the foreign policy decision makers, that is, decision makers who act as agents in the international system and represent the state as an actor. As Weldes (1996, 280) puts it: "The meanings which objects, events and actions have for 'states' are necessarily the meanings they have for those individuals who act in the name of the state." Thus, by focusing on foreign policy decision makers, it is possible to conceptualize the foreign policy part of a state's mechanism of reproduction, that is, the part that is constituted in the interaction with those structures of meaning that constitute the international system.

Having stressed these benefits associated with TCA, there are, of course, problems comparing the theory with the reality of international politics. The main concerns can be summarized in two questions:

1. In the international realm, which is normally perceived to be defined by power politics and self-maximizing behavior, can we expect to find behavior oriented towards mutual understanding, the ideal speech situation, and the achievement of consensus?
2. In a system normally perceived to be defined by pluralism, can we expect to find the existence and development of a collective *life-world*?

Before addressing these questions from an IR perspective, some theoretical elaboration of two important elements in Habermas's theory is needed: the *ideal speech situation* and the concept of *communicative rationality*.

Habermas stresses that, in a situation of nonstrategic social action, validity claims regarding social behavior can be established and evaluated critically. Communicative action is an independent and distinct type of social action in which the intention of actors is less to influence others than to reach agreement about something in the world (Habermas 1981, I, 199). This concept of "*verständigungsorientierte Sprechhandlungen*," that is, social action oriented towards mutual understanding, implies that whenever some person invokes a norm to influence another person's behavior, the first person implicitly recognizes the other as a partner in a dialogue. In this dialogue, claims are substantiated with reference to rational arguments about the objective world, legitimate social norms, and subjective intentions (Habermas 1981, II, 97–117; Nørager 1993, 85–133).[3] If a claim is recognized as being valid on the basis of a common understanding of the situation, it will also be socially binding, hence, ensuring that interactions can be coordinated consensually. Interaction is thus coordinated through collectively constructed intersubjective structures. These structures define understandings of reality, legitimate social norms and sincere subjective intentions. The intersubjective character of these structures is, therefore, a product of their validity plus the impartiality they are assigned in the process of communicative action.

Validity and impartiality require that communication be freed from any form of compulsion. This basic assumption is embodied in the concept of an ideal speech situation within which discourse is based on openness, equality, and the absence of internal as well as external coercion (Habermas 1990, 88–89). This concept can be translated into two principles: (1) The principle of universal respect, that is, recognition of all interested parties as participants in the collective process of interpretation, and (2) the principle of egalitarian reciprocity, that is, acknowledgement of the symmetrical rights of all participants with regard to the conduct of speech acts and demands for validity (Benhabib 1992, 29).

This concept of an ideal speech situation is normally considered to be the weak spot of TCA, given its focus on communicative behavior oriented towards mutual understanding, rather than the second mode of social action, that is, strategic behavior. However, Habermas continuously stresses that the ideal speech situation is a counterfactual hypothesis that does not have to be fulfilled in detail. The important thing is that it is embedded in the very nature of discourse. Insofar as participants understand themselves to be engaged in a cooperative search for common ground solely on the basis of good reasons, then they must—as a condition of the intelligibility of their activity—assume that the conditions of the ideal speech situation are satisfied to a sufficient degree, that is, they accord to each other the principles of universal respect and egalitarian reciprocity (Habermas 1990, 43–115).

In the same vein, it is important not to deny TCA any relevance with reference to implicit actor assumptions. Habermas does not expect agents to empathize 100 percent, thereby ignoring their own interests and preferences in the search for consensus. Impartiality should be understood to be what Habermas (1990, 29, 74–75) calls "negotiated impartiality." In Habermas's writings, impartiality is the core of an orientation to mutual understanding, which is crucial to the collective process of interpretation. It can only be obtained by participation in practical discourses, and cannot be ascribed to the individual reflection of agents. This implies that the demand for impartiality is not contrary to individual needs and interests. The communicative demand for impartiality only requires a reflective attitude toward the interpretation of one's own needs and interests and the ability to convey those needs and interests linguistically. Impartiality does not, therefore, demand self-suppression; it demands a communicative interpretation and eventual transformation of needs and interests during a discourse. As Habermas (1993, 58) puts it, negotiated impartiality "calls for the extension and reversibility of interpretative perspectives so that alternative viewpoints, interest structures and differences in individual self-understandings and worldviews are not effaced but are given full play in discourse."

Therefore, Habermas's social constructivist theory does not build on a utopian understanding of the agent as an altruistic person who suppresses all needs and interests in the name of the common good. Habermas's social constructivist dynamic rests on the assumption of an agent who has the ability to critically reflect on her own understandings of reality, interests, preferences, and maxims of behavior; to estimate the consequences for other actors should she decide to pursue her own interests; and to participate in a discourse with others regarding the interpretation of interests and norms for the coordination of behavior and interaction (Benhabib 1992, 71–72; Baynes 1992, 5–6). This also implies that agents can never be reduced to "structural dopes." They will always have the reflective capacity to change intersubjective structures of understandings through a discourse in which validity claims can be raised.

The Lifeworld and Social Integration

With the theory of communicative rationality and communicative action, Habermas introduces an argument regarding the coordinating effect of linguistic communication. Our relations are not the result of a random interplay between impenetrable circumstances. Social relations are coordinated communicatively, which means we are able to implicitly adopt mutual obligations when we interact. Our understandings of reality and desirable behavior are coordinated without the use of threats, but through the aim of obtaining a collective understanding—a condition of intersubjectivity (Habermas 1985, 151–177). The main virtue of this line of thought is that it gives an explicit account of the complementary relationship between communicative interaction among actors and produced and reproduced intersubjectiveness. The latter, in Habermas's writings, is termed "lifeworld."

The one side of this complementarity is that the lifeworld constitutes communicative action. It comprises the linguistically acquired and organized stock of patterns of understanding and, hence, constitutes an intersubjective structure of collective understandings that enables meaningful communication (Habermas 1981, II, 206). Inspired by John Searle's linguistic philosophy, Habermas attributes to the lifeworld a contextual as well as a constitutive function. Contextually, the lifeworld functions as an implicit horizon, that is, a stock of understandings of the elements of reality. Constitutively, an acting agent is constituted by the structures of meaning embedded in the lifeworld, that is, in the acquired understandings that are the resource that one has to apply in order to conduct meaningful action, including speech acts (Habermas 1981, II, 182–192, 205–223).

In order to engage in communicative action and hence coordination of social behavior, some degree of overlap in the lifeworlds of the different actors needs to exist. Otherwise communication would not be possible as there would be no common understandings, or in Searle's words, no common horizons, to build upon.

While assuming that a basic overlap facilitates the initiation of communicative interaction, it is through communicative action that social relations can be further developed. By building on a basic overlap in lifeworlds, actors can secure additional social integration through communicative action. They do so (1) by obtaining new collective understandings of reality and thus meaning, (2) by agreeing on just and legitimate norms and rules, and (3) by securing social affiliation (Habermas 1981, II, 182–208; Nørager 1993, 31). Hereby the overlap in lifeworlds is extended and deepened, allowing for meaningful coordinated social behavior.

As an intersubjective structure, the lifeworld itself depends on communicative action as it is reproduced through this form of social interaction. This constitutes the other side of the complementary relationship between the lifeworld and communicative action. Thus, it is in communicative action that the lifeworlds of the participants are subjected to the claims of validity inherent in discourse, and the collective understanding of meaning, normativity, and identity necessary for social integration is created and coordinated (Habermas 1981, II, 208–228). Claims about the objective world, the social world, and the subjective world, therefore, only become intersubjectively shared, and thus socially obligating, when they have been subjected to the claim for validity inherent in communicative action. In the reciprocal interaction between communicative actions, oriented towards mutual understanding and the structural components of the lifeworld, there is a continuous test of the acquired and collected knowledge, which is taken out of the lifeworld, discussed, and put back into it. It is through this symbolic reproduction that the social-integrative force is created, cementing groups as communities defined by a collective understanding of goals, action plans, and mutual expectations of rights and duties (Andersen 1988, 156–157).

This understanding of social integration distinguishes itself from a communitarian approach as it does not rely on pregiven common values, but is embedded in the dialectical relationship between agents and the structures of the lifeworld as mediated by communicative interaction (Warnke

1995). What is interesting about this concept of social integration is that it conceptualizes social integration in a modern pluralistic world where a multitude of different lifeworlds exist. In such societies agents cannot coordinate their behavior with reference to pregiven collective values (Moon 1995).

Thus TCA is built on a basic sociological argument: social integration in plural modern societies can only be achieved when social relations are organized "according to the principle that the validity of every norm of political consequence be made dependent on a consensus arrived at in communication" (Habermas quoted in White 1995, 6). This is the core of Habermas's theory of social constructivism. It is founded on the fact that modern societies possess a normativity that is modern in the sense that it is self-referring and self-reflecting, and therefore can be subjected to the demand for consensus and collective interpretation (Habermas 1981, I, 72–113; 1992, 37–45, 55–57; Nørager 1993, 128–34). In these post conventional societies, agents are integrated through collective communicative procedures of interpretation, where the intersubjective structures of meaning, and thus the intersubjective structures of norms and rules, are continuously produced and reproduced and eventually transformed.

This element of TCA is of value to IR scholars in so far as pluralism is often claimed to be the defining characteristic of the international realm. This defining characteristic normally diverts attention away from social integration in IR, as it is claimed that states cannot be truly integrated in coordinating structures. TCA nevertheless offers a much needed middle ground inasmuch as it conceptualizes genuine social integration positioned between two extremes: on the one hand, pure interest driven contractual integration and, on the other hand, full fledged communitarian integration.

Diplomacy and the Dialogue Between States: Communicative Action and the Social Construction of Diplomatic Communities

In discussing diplomacy I draw on insights of the so-called English School and, in particular, on the focus on international society and the role of diplomacy within it.[4] The English School directly links the societal element in international relations—and hence the intentional effort to coordinate interstate behavior through collective rules and norms—to diplomacy. Hedley Bull argues that international society is constituted when foreign policy decision makers internalize generalized—intersubjective—principles, norms, and rules that define the element of society in the international system (Bull 1969, 28; 1977, 40–41; Dunne 1995). In this sense, diplomacy is accorded a crucial role; it is through diplomatic interaction that foreign policy decision makers participate in the social construction of a coordinated international reality. Thus I agree with Raymond Cohen (1981,105) when he argues that "[i]n the making of the rules of the game . . . negotiation performs an indispensable function." It is through diplomacy that governance without government becomes possible. Diplomacy enables an international society to exist in a position between chaotic anarchy and world government (Watson 1982, 22–32).

Bull (1977, 162) defines diplomacy as "[t]he conduct of relations between states . . . by official agents and by peaceful means." Diplomatic actors are defined as "persons authorized to act in the name of a particular state or other recognized political entity" (163). Diplomats are hence accorded the role of state agent; they speak for the state, negotiate treaties on behalf of the state, define the goals, and determine what means should be applied in the pursuit of these goals. The essence of diplomacy can be described as a continuous process of dialogue and negotiation, that is, as a process of communication, explanation, and persuasion, through which the foreign policy of different states is coordinated (Watson 1982,11). According to Bull, this coordination is ensured by the four functions of diplomacy: First, diplomacy ensures continuous communication between the agents of foreign policy, without which the societal element could not exist. Second, diplomatic interaction makes it possible to define those areas where the interests of states overlap. It is on this basis that negotiations are conducted and agreements are reached. This is a crucial function, as "without the negotiation of agreements, international relations would . . . consist only of fleeting hostile encounters between one political community and another" (Bull 1977, 170). Third, it is through diplomatic channels that necessary information is collected and given. Fourth, it is through diplomacy that states try to minimize the friction that is an inevitable product of states' togetherness and interdependence, and which would create an unnecessary amount of conflict were it not addressed through diplomatic interaction.

This process of negotiation—and related functions—provides much more than just functional and pragmatic solutions to a technical problem. It signifies in itself a fundamental constructive and constitutive dynamic affecting the involved actors as well as the outcome; it is foreign policy decision makers who construct and in turn are constituted by international social reality. This reality is conceptualized as an intersubjective structure of collective understandings, and hence norms and rules for social behavior. I relate this understanding of diplomacy, and its role in establishing coordinated state behavior, to the above reading of Habermas. I argue that the general interest is uncovered as a collective understanding through diplomatic communicative interaction. This is constructed on the basis of discussion, information gathering, and the desire to coordinate behavior in order to minimize interstate friction. In making this argument, I stress that TCA builds on the most basic precondition in the anarchic system of states: the absence of a formal hierarchy of authority. This absence implies that agents are forced to, and have opportunities to coordinate their actions through, communication oriented towards mutual understanding (Andersen 1988, 156). Adam Watson, who has explicitly pointed this out, argued that diplomatic practice only develops because "a group of independent states are obliged to manage the consequences of their independence, not absolutely and in isolation but in a setting of interdependence" (1982, 14). For this reason, "states are not content merely to observe one another at a distance. They feel a need to enter into dialogue with one another" (14). Thus one can say that "diplomacy answers an imperative need in any system of independent states" (93; also see 213). Because states feel the need to communicate in order to handle their interdependence, they are forced to recognize each other as partners in a dialogue, where the regulation of behavior is sought.

Moreover, in order to justify the claim that one can ascribe a social constructivist dynamic to diplomatic interaction, one must analyze whether the remaining preconditions of TCA have been fulfilled. In order to do this, I will examine, from an IR perspective, the above mentioned questions concerning the existence of (1) behavior oriented towards mutual understanding and (2) an international lifeworld.

The Ideal Speech Situation in International Politics

In his discussion of diplomatic interaction, Bull identifies important elements of behavior oriented towards mutual understanding. Thus he argues that "[d]iplomacy can play no role where foreign policy is conceived as the enforcement of a claim to universal authority, the promotion of true faith against heretics, *or as the pursuit of self-regarding interests that take no account of the interests of others*" (Bull 1977, 170–171, emphasis added). Bull furthermore argues that "[a]greements are possible only if the interests of the parties, while they may be different, overlap at some point, and if the parties are *able to perceive that they overlap*" (170, emphasis added). Diplomatic interaction is by its nature oriented towards achieving a collective understanding of the interests and goals that states wish to translate into norms and rules guiding interstate behavior. This collective understanding can only be achieved through negotiations where confidence, reason, empathy, understanding, reciprocity, knowledge, and judgment are assigned high priority.

Building on TCA, I argue that diplomatic interaction is characterized by behavior oriented towards mutual understanding, where perceptions of reality, interests, preferences, and desirable behavior are subjected to a collective process of interpretation guided by argumentative rationality and the claim of validity. The following quotation illustrates the relationship between this line of thought and Bull's understanding of diplomatic actors and their interactions:

> The diplomatist, or at all events the "ideal diplomatist," helps to minimize friction through the conventions he observes in dealing with foreign officials, and also through his influence upon his own state's policy. In dealing with the representatives of other states, he observes conventions of language. In advancing or defending his own state's interests he seeks always to keep his objective in view, and use only those arguments that will promote the end in view, avoiding arguments that are intended to give vent to feelings or to satisfy his own or his country's pride or vanity. He seeks always to reason or persuade rather than to bully or threaten. He tries to show that the objectives he seeks are consistent with the other party's interests, as well as with his own. He prefers to speak of "rights" rather than "demands," and to show that these rights flow from rules or principles, which both states hold in common, and which the other state has already conceded. He tries to find the objective which he seeks in a framework of shared interest and agreed principles that is common ground between the parties concerned. (1977, 172)

Bull points to elements that constitute the very essence of communicative action: behavior oriented towards mutual understanding, argumentative rationality, and the appeal to collective interest, rules, and principles. Following this interpretation, the diplomatic speech act can be said to be structured according to negotiated impartiality and the claim of validity, bringing about collective understandings of reality, legitimate social norms, and sincerity with regard to subjective intentions. Watson puts forward an argument that supports the essence of this reading when claiming that communication and sincerity are promoted by the fact that ruthless behavior will undermine the state itself, "because a state which is careless about what credence is placed in the word of its diplomats on individual occasions will soon find that its word is not believed in any context. When that happens and its credibility is debased, a state finds it difficult to make agreements with any but equally fickle partners. There is no substitute for trust in diplomacy." (Watson 1982, 66; see also Lipson 1991, 508–514)

The above observations are reinforced by scholars specializing in interstate negotiations—theoretically as well as empirically. Christer Jönsson (1983, 1993) convincingly argues that confidence, an orientation towards mutual understanding and the construction of collective understandings, are crucial elements in interstate negotiations. He continually stresses that the normal perception of diplomatic interaction as strategic rational engagement is not supported by the wealth of empirical studies that emphasize the importance of flexibility and mutual understanding in the process of negotiation (1983, 141). This argument is integrated with a focus on the process of knowledge building brought about by the collection of information which is a crucial part of negotiations, and which has a heavy influence on the decisions made (142). One has to perceive international negotiations as a process of learning, where diplomats, through communicative interactions, try to confirm or adjust their mutual expectations. This results in a process of interpretation where the different agents coordinate their belief systems—defined as the understanding of one self, others, and the situation. A collective decision is made possible on the basis of a positive mutual identification (142–148; also see Müller 1993b). The parallel to Habermas is obvious; the communicatively created coordination of belief systems corresponds well to the theory of how an intersubjective overlap in lifeworlds is socially constructed. This parallel is even more obvious in Jönsson's later elaboration on his studies of international negotiations. Here he focuses on the importance of linguistic communication, whereby a collective language is constructed—representing a collective understanding—and provides a bridge between the different agents so that the trust and understanding, as a precondition for cooperative behavior, can be constructed (Jönsson 1993; Midgaard 1983, 159–165).

In this connection, one can argue that the preconditions for the ideal speech situation are fulfilled as part of the diplomatic practice itself. The argument corresponds to Habermas's counterfactual hypothesis: As one is trying to coordinate behavior communicatively, one has to acknowledge other implicated agents as partners in dialogue, and thus assign to them the rights that are necessary in order to conduct a speech act and raise a claim to validity. Precisely these elements are highlighted by Knut Midgaard (1983, 160), another theorist of negotiation, as crucial elements in any negotiation: "In giving a thorough and nuanced justification of a proposal which I submit on behalf of my delegation, I commit myself in a double way: I commit myself, and my delegation, quite strongly to the proposal in question, but at the same time also to listening to possible counterarguments." In negotiations this can be translated into five rules for communication: "There has to be a meaning to what one says; one has to be sincere; the argument must be relevant; one must listen to counterarguments; and one has to respect other agents as participants in the negotiation" (161). Like Habermas's ideal speech situation, these expectations of meaning, sincerity, relevance, attentiveness, and respect represent an ideal that cannot be fulfilled in detail. Nevertheless, it has to be the point of departure, as "any negotiation ceases to be negotiation if any of the above rules is officially violated beyond a certain degree. The acts of submitting, accepting or rejecting a proposal require a minimal official respect for any of them" (162).[5]

This understanding of mutual rights in discourse can be given a more formal content. In the same way that national recognition of communicative rights gave rise to civil and political rights, expressing the general principles of universal respect and egalitarian reciprocity, one can argue that these rights are also accorded in international society. Hence, one can say that state actors are recognized as participants in communicative diplomatic practice by virtue of the right to sovereignty. When sovereignty is defined as the equal right of states to self-determination, it is less nonintervention and exclusive jurisdiction that are crucial. What is crucial is that states are recognized as equal sovereign actors. This represents a recognition of the principle of universal respect, that is, the recognition of the right of all affected actors to participate in the collective process of interpretation—and the recognition of egalitarian reciprocity, that is, the principle that all participants in the discourse are accorded symmetrical rights to conduct speech acts and raise claims to validity. Watson touches on the same understanding of sovereignty when he claims that "the ability to deal with other states, and therefore to conduct a dialogue with them . . . [is] the very heart of sovereignty" (1982, 15). The recognition of sovereignty as a communicative right thus springs from the fact that "a state must recognize other states as able and entitled to take their own decisions if it is to communicate and negotiate with them effectively about how they will act" (37; also see Bull 1977, 172).

All these arguments are reinforced by the changes—in form as well as substance—that diplomatic practice itself has undergone over time. Concerning form, one can point to a decline in importance of professional diplomats. Instead there is a rapid increase in high level meetings between heads of state, ministers, and other key figures enhancing the importance of negotiating multilateral diplomacy at the expense of traditional bilateral contacts (Bull 1977, 173–177). This should be seen in relation to the explosive development in the number of meetings, visits, negotiations, treaty engagements, etc., which can be ascribed to the increasing demand for multilateral coordination. The latter arises especially from increasing economic interdependence (Barston 1988, 6–7; Watson 1982, 176–194).

This development in the multilateral forms of interaction has been paralleled by crucial developments in the nature of diplomatic interaction. The end of the Second World War marked the end of "traditional diplomacy," where diplomats with cunning, hidden alliances and, in the last instance, war, sought to promote the national interest. In its place, we have seen the development of "modern diplomacy," defined by more open negotiations oriented towards mutual understanding (Butterfield 1966). It is no longer power alone that determines the outcome, but, to a larger extent the arguments put forward, which are accepted on the basis of a mutually acknowledged system of rights, defined as the principle of sovereignty. Cornelia Navari (1982, 16) characterizes modern diplomacy with reference to "its concern for parliamentary forms and war-avoidance, without speaking nonsense." Modern diplomacy is labeled "parliamentary diplomacy," defined as "the application of the principle of one-man-one-vote, the first principle of legal equality, to the society of states" (25). Diplomatic interaction can be said to have been democratized. Multilateral forms of cooperation in particular are largely based on consensus seeking negotiations, where small states also participate and have influence by virtue of their sovereign status (Barston 1988, 6, 116–119; Watson 1982, 28–30; Rittberger 1983).

Watson nicely describes this understanding of modern diplomatic practice and sums up the arguments above:

> [Diplomacy] is an organized pattern of communication and negotiation, nowadays continuous, which enables each independent government to learn what other governments want and what they object to. In a developed international society it becomes more than an instrument of communication and bargaining. It also affects its practitioners. It is an activity which even if often abused has a bias towards the resolution of conflicts. It is a function of the diplomatic dialogue to mitigate and civilize the differences between states, and if possible reconcile them, without suppressing or ignoring them. Conflicts of interest are a major subject of diplomacy, which can function effectively only when the necessary level of understanding exists between the parties to the dialogue about the maintenance of the system as a whole and about the rules for the promotion of their separate interests within the system. The diplomatic dialogue is thus the instrument of international society: a civilized process based on awareness and respect for other people's points of view; and a civilizing also, because the continuous exchange of ideas, and the attempts to find mutually acceptable solutions to conflicts of interest, increase that awareness and respect. This civilizing tendency visibly does not prevent diplomacy from being perverted and misused—its methods lend themselves to duplicity. But the bias towards understanding other points of view and other needs, towards a search for common ground and a resolution of differences, is unmistakably there. (1982, 20–21)

This description underlines the social constructivist dynamics inherent in behavior oriented towards mutual understanding and the argument that the preconditions of the theory of communicative action can be said to exist in modern international politics. Notice that this is not to say that diplomats empathize 100 percent and ignore the national interest in pursuit of international consensus. It is to say that a diplomat as an international actor is capable of negotiated impartiality and can be said to possess a reflective attitude towards the interpretation of national needs and interests. Diplomats are able to make these needs and interests linguistically transmittable by reference to shared understandings of reality, legitimate social norms, and social identity (see also Risse-Kappen 1995b, 181; Schmalz-Bruns 1995, 354–357).

This understanding can easily be associated with Watson's argument that diplomatic communication constitutes a "civilized" as well as a "civilizing process." An orientation towards mutual understanding can be identified and used to explain how behavior is coordinated through communicative coordination of collective understandings. In this sense it is possible to embed the social constructivist ontological understanding of the relationship between structures of meaning and actors in diplomatic communicative interaction. A discussion of the lifeworld and its reproduction further substantiates this argument.

The International Lifeworld and Its Reproduction

As discussed above, an orientation towards mutual understanding is not enough in itself. Communicative action can only be conducted on the basis of a shared stock of collective patterns of understanding, that is, an overlap in lifeworlds. The question is whether this overlap can be said to exist in the international realm.

Obviously one cannot expect an overlap in lifeworlds equivalent to that of national political communities, which are cemented by a common cultural history. Nevertheless, some overlap arguably exists. This overlap constitutes the basic structures of understanding that are necessary for starting up interstate communicative action. Harald Müller, who has dealt with this question (1994a, 34), emphasizes that one would expect an international lifeworld to be primarily constituted by common historical experiences. Not least would be experiences stemming from the problems associated with a lack of behavioral coordination, which constitutes the basic defining characteristic of the anarchical system. In more specific negotiations, the basic collective patterns of understanding are often sought in more universal values such as parenthood, care and duties towards children, etc. (1994, 34–35). A more extensive overlap in lifeworlds must be expected to exist in those regions of the world where not only common historical experiences go far back, but where there is also an overlap in traits of civilization.

In this sense, it seems reasonable to expect the existence of a basic collective lifeworld in the international realm, and therefore of a fundamental collectivity on which states can build more elaborate forms of cooperation. It is through communicative action that this foundation is discussed and thereby reproduced and eventually transformed in line with reconstructed collective understandings of reality, of legitimate social norms, and social identity. A common historical experience, perhaps combined with shared traits of civilization, can serve as the embryonic basis for a continuous development of intersubjective structures of meaning and coordinating norms and rules. Hence, as Watson (1982, 93) argues, "diplomacy, as an instituted way of ordering the affairs of the states system, tends to grow into something more than its machinery, and becomes an accumulation of experience and wisdom which transcends the mere mechanics of dialogue." It is through continued dialogue—conceptualized as a collective process of interpretation—that state actors collect and coordinate their understandings— their "experience" and "wisdom"—which is lifted to the intersubjective level as a collective overlap in lifeworlds, and is expressed in a given social practice. This overlap constitutes the basic understanding that facilitates cooperation around a collectively defined aim.

The English School has a tradition of working with the basic collective understandings of those goals, principles, and norms that constitute an international system as a society. It was this basic element that Bull was looking for in his studies of history when he discussed "what common assumptions are held about how things are done in international relations by those who speak and act in the name of states" (Suganami 1982, 2365). Martin Wight (1966, 97) was looking for the same thing when he focused on "an international consciousness, a world-wide community sentiment," and C.A.W. Manning (1962) when he studied diplomatic discourse in order to uncover the "shared diplomatic assumptions." These elements can all be read as a parallel to the overlap in lifeworlds, that is, the international lifeworld of which foreign policy decision makers are a part.

In contrast to the English School, which has problems grounding its position theoretically, I argue that this perspective can be embedded in a diplomatic social constructivist process of interaction. It is here that the fundamental interest in social order has been transformed from a common interest to a truly collective interest, given expression in an intersubjective complex of norms and rules. This complex not only regulates state behavior, but also constitutes the "selection" of meaningful ways of behavior that state actors can apply and define themselves in relation to (Wendt and Duvall 1989, 60–61). This social constructivist reading of the English School seems to be supported by Watson, who explicitly relates the development of international society to the diplomatic process of interaction. He argues that "[t]he rules and institutions which . . . [are] the requisites of an international society are established by diplomatic negotiations between the member states, and are constantly amended by the same means to meet pressures of change. . . . That is why it is legitimate to speak of diplomacy as shaping and organizing these rules and institutions, and of states so organized as forming a diplomatic society." (1982, 213)

From a social constructivist perspective, a multitude of interesting arguments can be deduced from English School studies of the creation and development of the fundamental societal element in the international system. Of special interest are Watson's analyses of the development of international society (1982, 82–120; 1992; Bull and Watson 1984). As discussed above, Watson's fundamental point is that in every international system where states interact sufficiently to make every state acknowledge other states' actions, there will be a need to communicate that initiates the diplomatic dialogue. At this embryonic starting point the shared understandings of the diplomatic community in question will be minimal. One expects only a limited overlap in lifeworlds constituted mainly by the collective historical experiences of the states. But this embryonic starting point has allowed for the development of different socially integrated diplomatic communities in different regions of the world. Hence, it is possible to identify different societies of states as defined by the diplomatic social construction of regional reality, as related to the specific history of a given region, traits of civilization, specific problems and interests, etc. Accordingly, in a discussion of diplomatic systems, Watson points towards communities in such different regions as the aborigines in southern Australia and the ancient civilizations in the Middle East, India, and China (Watson, 1982, 82–94; 1992, 21–94). In this sense, one can identify distinctive communities of communication, which are different due to the different lifeworlds constituted by their different regional histories. As Watson formulates it (1982, 16–17):

> In the past, sustained dialogues developed and flourished between groups of states in a circumscribed geographical area and with a history of close contacts. Such groups of states formed, so to speak, a single magnetic field of political forces. Their identity was determined by membership of, or close contact with, a common civilization. Their diplomatic dialogue was conducted, and the pursuit of their separate interests was mediated, in terms of the concepts of law, honor, morality and prudence which prevailed in that civilization.

Despite these differences, Watson (1982, 83) claims that the most remarkable result is that these diplomatic systems share "a family resemblance, because they were designed for the same purpose: the conduct of a dialogue between independent states. . . . We should be impressed by what seems permanent in diplomacy, by the continuities and recurrences in different systems, rather than by the individualities which were peculiar to each age and culture." What characterizes these different systems is highly developed interstate communication, which in all cases is built on argumentative rationality and persuasion (Watson 1982, 82–94). This underpins the argument that the preconditions for behavior oriented towards mutual understanding are embedded in the diplomatic practice itself, and therefore do not refer to the special history of given diplomatic communities of communication.

The substance of communication is different in the different systems, given a difference in regional lifeworlds. Collective understandings of meaningful behavior hence differ, which again explains why cooperation between different regions is often difficult to establish. Consistent with TCA, the necessary negotiations oriented towards mutual understanding cannot be established given the lack of overlap in lifeworlds. The collective structures of meaning that are a precondition for communicative action are often absent in such situations (Jönsson 1983, 147–148). This argument is supported by Cohen's studies of the problems of communication that arise when states negotiate across cultural differences. Cohen (1991, 153) concludes that "when interlocutors attempt to convey messages across linguistic and cultural barriers, meanings are lost or distorted in the process. What one culture takes to be self-evident, another may find bizarre . . . crosscultural dissonances may strongly affect the conduct and outcome of diplomatic talks."

Nevertheless, negotiations often do succeed despite cultural differences. This can be explained by reference to two arguments: (1) Diplomatic communicative interaction in all regions is designed for the achievement of behavioral coordination, given a need for rules and communication; (2) the highly developed European community of communication has become worldwide (Watson 1982, 95–119; 1984, 13–32; 1992, 265–276). The fundamental complex of principles, norms and rules, which Bull identified, has spread and become global, promoting an orientation towards mutual understanding across historical and cultural boundaries. As Bull states: "The remarkable willingness of states of all regions, cultures, persuasions and stages of development to embrace often strange and archaic diplomatic procedures that arose in Europe in another age is today one of the few visible indications of universal acceptance of the idea of international society" (1977, 183; also see 1984, 117–126). One would furthermore expect this tendency to have been amplified by globalization. But as Watson (1982, 158–175) points out, a substantial development in the behavioral coordinating potential of diplomatic discourse would demand a radical collective process of interpretation, where some of the old principles, which accompanied the expansion of the old European community of communication, would be subjected to a test of validity and adjusted in accordance with the needs and interests of other states.

Finally, when discussing the question of whether or not an international lifeworld exists, it is crucial to raise the question about the importance of language. It is obvious that a collective language, which can mediate the orientation towards mutual understanding, is the most fundamental overlap in lifeworlds that needs to exist if communicative coordination is to be established (Pleydell 1982). As indicated in the above discussion, this question has been touched on by Jönsson (1993), who emphasizes that a collective language is an important precondition for the coordination of the different belief systems. Such a language does seem to exist in the international system. Cohen (1981, 31–48) has outlined the special collective diplomatic language, which is crucial for the conduct of diplomatic negotiations, and which in this connection can be said to constitute the foundation of communicative action. Cohen himself formulates it as follows (1981, 31):

> [T]he diplomatic profession has evolved, over many years, a very subtle and variegated stock of words, phrases, euphemisms, gestures and maneuvers, each item having its own weight and shade of meaning. . . . That states of different culture, religion, ideology and language communicate intelligibly with each other is one of the remarkable aspects of international politics. Without this ability rules of the game facilitating international order could hardly be arrived at . . . . Notwithstanding the problems involved states somehow mostly succeed in communicating their intentions—transmitting encouragement, warning, approval or displeasure when required, negotiating understandings of subtlety and complexity. All this thanks to the possession of a common code or language of discourse.

In conclusion, an overlap in the lifeworlds of foreign policy decision makers in the different states is conceivable. This overlap is constituted by historical experiences and possible common traits of civilization. Through continuous diplomatic interaction, and collective processes of interpretation, this collective foundation has developed as an intersubjective structure of collective meanings, which among other things, has found expression in a common language.

Concluding Remarks

The purpose of this chapter was in part to contribute to the debate over whether social constructivism can be a first order theory, and in part to relate this to a second debate regarding the construction of interstate behavioral coordination. Concerning the first issue, I have argued that Habermas' theory of communicative action is a promising candidate for translating an ontological focus on the mutually constitutive relationship between actors and structures into a first order theory. This line of thought is especially valuable to IR theory in so far as it can be applied to the understanding and explanation of how states are able to coordinate behavior through the communicative construction of intersubjective understandings of reality, legitimate norms, and social identity. I suggest locating this constitutive dynamic in communicative interaction, that is, negotiations between diplomats who represent the state as an actor.

To substantiate these arguments, I turned to a discussion of diplomatic interaction in international relations and in particular to studies undertaken by the English School and scholars of international negotiation. This exercise served two purposes: Firstly, I provided evidence that the essential theoretical elements of TCA—including behavior oriented towards mutual understanding, the ideal speech situation, actor assumptions, and the lifeworld—can be identified in international politics. Secondly, the discussion shed new light on many of the arguments about how to understand and explain the intentional coordination of interstate behavior.

The point is not to argue that diplomatic interaction necessarily results in consensus and eternal harmony. Instrumental rationality, where the goal of action is to optimize individual interests and preferences, of course, plays an important role in international politics. But there is another mode of social practice, which Habermas refers to as communicative rationality. I argue that when states negotiate in order to coordinate behavior in accordance with a given objective, a social constructivist dynamic is initiated, a dynamic which enables states to construct a collective understanding of the situation at hand. State actors can only go so far in controlling international existence on the basis of isolated reflections and isolated political decisions. If state actors wish to proceed beyond this point, in order to coordinate interaction and engage in cooperative efforts, then this can only be accomplished on the basis of diplomatic negotiations. These negotiations involve actors who try to construct a collective understanding of the situation they seek to regulate, and a collective understanding of those norms that state actors obligate themselves to and internalize in the process of negotiation. Communicative action, therefore, enables actors to bridge the gap between the motivation to cooperate and the actual achievement of cooperation.

Due to the limited amount of space available, it was not possible to cover all of the relevant aspects of Habermas's theory. I have only touched on the preconditions for a social constructivist dynamic, building on the most basic elements of international communication. The next logical step would be to discuss how this dynamic is played out in more specific negotiations around more concrete interstate needs to coordinate behavior. This calls for a more detailed focus on the negotiation process and its different layers (e.g., Young 1994). In this respect Habermas's more recent process-model for political integration and social construction of the collective political will (1990, 1992, 1993) presents itself as an obvious approach that deserves further discussion from an IR perspective.

Notes

1. For a brief outline of the theory of communicative action, see Müller's article in this volume.

2. Besides Müller's chapter in this volume, this discussion may be found in Schneider (1994), Keck (1995), Lose (1997), Risse (1997).

3. This part of Habermas's theory is called the theory of formal pragmatics. For elaboration on this very complex notion of communication, see Baynes (1992, 88–108).

4. Although it can be disputed whether a distinct English School exists in IR, my use of the term comprises those approaches distinguished by their focus on the international society, and their focus on historical studies of different developments in the international system. I associate writers such as Hedley Bull, Martin Wight, C.A.W. Manning, and Adam Watson with the English School.

5. Much more could be said about the theories and empirical studies of Jönsson and Midgaard. There is no doubt that a more thorough investigation of the extent to which the theory of communicative action can be applied to interstate relations would benefit from a review of the somewhat neglected literature dealing with negotiations.

10

Constructing Globalization

Ben Rosamond[1]

Surprisingly perhaps, constructivists have said relatively little about global-ization. As a signifier of large scale social change and the imperatives of external context, "globalization" has few rivals. The term has become a commonplace, not only in the academy, but also in corporate, journalistic, and policymaking circles. Politicians across the world have learned to use this compelling buzzword. A conception of globalization is integral to both deregulatory neoliberalism and "third way" social democracy. As a social scientific concept, the term commands voluminous debate—to say the least.

This chapter attempts a reading of the literature on globalization through constructivist lenses. It suggests that such a reading has the potential to shift the emphasis of the globalization debate into interesting alternative direc-tions. Much of the debate across the social sciences focuses on the veracity of the "globalization thesis" or on the historical novelty of globalization. It is argued here that a constructivist inspired understanding of the concept di-rects attention to how knowledge about globalization is used by actors, the extent to which globalization discourse becomes a cognitive structure, and, therefore whether intersubjectivities about globalization shape patterns of behavior within the global political economy.

The argument commences with a discussion of the ways in which con-structivists have treated external context in the light of (a) the salience of globalization as a signifier of substantial and far reaching change to the fab-ric of the international system and (b) the nature of constructivism as a set of interventions in the academic discourse of International Relations (IR). It moves, via a critical review of the main strands in the literature on global-ization, to thinking about how constructivism might offer a useful gateway for the organization of discussions about the significance of discourses of globalization.

Constructivism in International Relations

The key task facing constructivists, as many see it, is to build a coherent alternative research program in the political sciences. Within IR, this task has
been translated into developing alternatives to the rationalist orthodoxies of
neorealism and neoliberalism, on the one hand, and the alleged "reflectivist" excesses of critical and postmodern theory on the other. Mainstream
constructivists have used a two-pronged strategy to meet this challenge.
First, they have tended to chip away at rationalist presumptions about the
international system. This maneuver consists first of the ontological claim
that the world is best construed in social rather than material terms and,
therefore, leads to the view that the norms of international relations (such as
anarchy and the national interest) are ongoing social constructions rather
than perennial givens. The second element of mainstream constructivist
strategy has been to make claims about the possibility of using rationalist
epistemologies in pursuit of these claims (Checkel 1998). Also, while there
are many constructivist exceptions to this basic pattern (Jørgensen 1998),
the fact remains that much work conducted beneath the banner of constructivism confronts conventional IR on its own terms insofar as it deals with
states and the relations between states. In this regard alone, the constructivist contribution can be seen to be valuable, perhaps because of the difficult
questions it forces us to confront about the way in which the international
system is reproduced. Through constructivist lenses this is clearly rather
more than the ongoing product of the interaction of self-regarding states.
Similarly, institutions are radically reconceptualized as considerably more
than low risk, functional vehicles for the exchange of state preferences.

The fact that constructivist contributions have sought to build better explanations of the games played between states needs to be properly contex-
tualized within the sociology of the discipline. For instance, it is noticeable
that constructivists for the most part have purposely *not* moved away from
the state-centric terrain of conventional IR. This is explicitly articulated in
the work of influential constructivists like Alexander Wendt: "I am a statist
and a realist. I have argued . . . that statism need not be bound up with realist ideas about what 'state' must mean" (1992a, 424). Constructivists have
not, by and large, embraced so-called "postinternational" understandings of
international politics. Yet it is perfectly clear that IR, broadly defined, contains many alternative readings of the nature of world politics. In addition
to the strategic interaction of states or national executives, world politics
can be treated as the domain of cross border transactions (that may be inter-
societal as well as interstate) or the development of world society in various
forms (Brown 1997). Add to these postpositivist, feminist, and ecological

critiques of IR orthodoxy, along with the conspicuous intrusion of debates from across the wider social sciences, and it becomes clear that there is something of a paradigm struggle within the discipline (Cerny 1996; see also Booth and Smith 1995; Smith, Booth, and Zalewski 1996; Gill and Mittelman 1997).

Many of the concerns raised by these critics of the standard Westphalian ontology (Strange 1996) connect to discussions about globalization. With globalization, goes the argument, the field of action within which world politics takes place is rendered more variegated and complex. Authority is found in new sites, more actors become significant players, traditional authoritative actors (notably states) lose their capacity to act or are transformed fundamentally. If globalization is transforming the world into a single social economic and political space, then the conventions of order based upon territorial divisions become largely redundant. State-centrism as an analytical premise is, therefore, deeply misconceived (Youngs 1996).

Globalization discourses tell particular stories about the world and the value added by constructivism derives from its concern with the relationship between knowledge about the world and the nature of the world. It helps us to ask questions about how ideas about the world—particularly ideas about the context within which actors operate—are gathered, disseminated, and accepted. Moreover, constructivists have developed interesting observations about the social construction of external contexts that carry interesting implications for questions of structure and agency. This may help us to move to a more sophisticated conception of structure as subjective rather than (purely) material. Finally, a constructivist account may direct thinking to ways in which the widespread diffusion of particular ideas about the properties that structure social and economic life give rise to distinct senses of the repertoire of constraints and opportunities that confront actors.

Constructivism and the Social Construction of External Context

While the constructivist turn in IR has had a lot to do with bringing agency back into the study of international politics (Kratochwil and Ruggie 1986), all of the keynote contributions to constructivist IR have drawn attention to the social construction of actors' external context. In *World of Our Making*, Nicholas Onuf (1989) draws on various currents in social theory to discuss the uses of language by human beings to invent the world they inhabit. Put another way, the first premise of constructivism is that the world is *social* rather than *material*, or to be more precise, "material structures, beyond certain biological necessities, are given meaning only by the social context through which they are interpreted" (Checkel 1998, 326). So alongside the obvious concerns with communicative action, language games, and the dynamics of discursive construction, constructivists are interested in cognitive structures—stocks of information about the world that actors carry around with them and which in turn help to structure behavioral patterns and influence understandings of others. As Wendt notes, "[i]t is collective meanings that constitute the structures which organize our actions" (1992a, 397). Thus in Wendt's state-centric constructivism, the systemic condition of anarchy does not emerge through a rationalist logic as the pure consequence of self-regarding actions by unitary states. Anarchy is rather an intersubjective condition. As Jutta Weldes remarks: "[T]his is the case because both the interests of states and the identities on which those interests depend rest not solely upon the structure of the system but also upon the collective meanings that constitute the structures which organize state action" (1996, 279).

Such arguments are clearly designed to thicken Waltzian conceptions of the relationship between system and unit. Neorealism deploys a rational choice logic to describe the interaction of self-regarding states in the context of a system without overarching authority. The project of Wendt and others has been to emphasize the fundamental contingency of the system by showing that actions cannot simply be "read off" from either structural location or endowments of power: "To go from structure to action, we need to add . . . the intersubjectively constituted structure of identities and interests in the system" (Wendt 1992a, 401). The key to understanding the constitution of interests is to comprehend the mechanisms of social construction that occur in moments of interaction and within institutions. From the constructivist standpoint, interests cannot be treated as exogenous. They are endogenous to (interstate) interaction and derive from complexes of relational identities. In other words our understandings of who "we" are become (inevitably) bound up with our notions of who "they" are. Also, the act of defining the situation in which we and they are situated helps to clarify interests and, therefore, the range of *possible* and *appropriate* action. The radical implication of constructivism is that the international system is only stable so long as ongoing processes of social construction take place. This recognizes that there is a space for agents to reshape and thereby transform their structural environment, reflecting the proximity of much constructivist argument to the premises of structurationism (Giddens 1984).

Onuf's emphasis on rules takes this line of thinking a little further. Rules occupy the "black box" between structures and agents. Not only do rules tell us what we should do; they also help to nominate who are the key agents in any given social situation. As Onuf puts it: "[A]gency is a social condition" (1998b, 60). States or, more accurately, national executives, know they are significant actors because there is a widespread intersubjective understanding that states are important. Moreover, these collective cognitive certainties contribute to the *material* importance of states. Onuf observes that structures—or "social arrangements" as he prefers to dub them—are made concrete by actors through the manufacture of congruent institutions. So power politics, self-help, diplomacy, and even the format of intergovernmental organizations can be read as attempts to institutionalize and make real the narrative of anarchy as a guiding structure:

> By calling international relations anarchic, scholars are not saying that there is an absence of rule. This would be chaos, not anarchy. Instead, they seem to be saying that structure—and especially a stable pattern of unintended consequences—rules the day. In the same sense, we might say that the market rules the behavior of sellers and buyers. (Onuf 1998b, 62)

Structures—via institutions—help to create the ongoing and immediate imperatives that shape interests and preferences. Yet, at the same time, constructivists—or those with constructivist persuasions—place emphasis on institutions as zones of intensive communicative action (Risse-Kappen 1996b). Structural imperatives are not simply read off by actors. Rather they are deduced and reinforced through processes of persuasion and advocacy that go well beyond the utilitarian exchange of preferences anticipated by rationalistic accounts. As Thomas Risse notes

> Ideas become consensual when actors start believing in their value and become convinced of their validity . . . communicative processes are a necessary condition for ideas to become consensual (or fall by the wayside for that matter). Instrumental use of ideas works because their value has been previously established in discursive processes of persuasion and deliberation. (Risse-Kappen 1996b, 69–70)

As this implies, constructivists owe significant debts to certain strands in critical social theory. The emphasis on intersubjectivities connects with an interest in knowledge and specifically the relationship between knowledge about the world and the nature of the world about which knowledge is gathered. Control over the production of knowledge about the nature of the world is a serious issue worthy of rather more detailed consideration than is possible here (but see, among others, Cox and Sinclair 1996; George 1994; Smith 1995). For the purposes of this chapter it is worth remembering that critical social theory raises all manner of questions concerning the relationship between academic discourses about the world and the knowledge held about that world by social actors. Without doubt, what Jan Aart Scholte (1996b) calls the "methodological nationalism" and "methodological territorialism" of conventional social thought bear a close resemblance to widely held views about the nature of the world, and thus about the context within which we—as social actors—operate. That said, the advent of globalization has brought with it a distinct challenge to the orthodoxies of social thought and to the presumptions of actors engaged in the day-to-day world of international exchange. A globalized world—at least in hyperbolic accounts of globalization—is one where the agency of states is chronically weakened and where territory ceases to be the primary organizing principle of human existence. Paradoxically, narratives about globalization have become significant to the deliberations of national executives but have not necessarily replaced the (apparently rival) discourse of a state-centered world. As the discussion below shows, much of the debate about globalization has pivoted on whether states remain significant. The suggestion here is that constructivist forms of analysis direct us away from searching for the "truth" about globalization. The fact that discourses of state-centrism and globalization coexist is interesting and the broadening of constructivism beyond "normal science" might have very useful consequences.

Globalization

Globalization commands such attention in the contemporary social sciences that it has become almost impossible to avoid both the term and the debates that it has spawned. Sociologists, anthropologists, geographers, psychologists, economists, political scientists, and political economists have all developed distinctive points of view on globalization, and debate has evolved in distinct ways within different disciplinary environments. Notwithstanding this diversity and considerable nuance, the debate in most disciplines has tended to revolve around the veracity of globalization: is the world globalized, or is it merely globalizing? Is the process or condition of globalization as novel or as significant as some claim? Is globalization (as either process or outcome) a mythology? Is the narrative of globalization simply a rhetorical device used to serve particular interests in the global political economy? Is it possible to show through careful empirical research that globalization is a "tall story" and, thus, that it should be treated as epiphenomenal? In short, debate tends to alight on the question of whether there are discernible, objective, material shifts that are genuinely changing the social, economic, and political fabric of the world.

Broadly speaking, the cases for and against globalization can be made both normatively and analytically. There are those who extol the alleged virtues of globalization. Take for example this communiqué from the 1996 G7 summit:

Economic growth and progress in today's interdependent world is bound up with the process of globalization. Globalization provides great opportunities for the future, not only for our countries, but for all others too. Its many positive aspects include an unprecedented expansion of investment and trade; the opening up to international trade of the world's most populous regions and opportunities for more developing countries to improve their standards of living; the increasingly rapid dissemination of information, technological innovation and the proliferation of skilled jobs. These characteristics of globalization have led to a considerable expansion of wealth and prosperity in the world. Hence, we are convinced that the process of globalization is a source of hope for the future. History shows that rising living standards depend crucially on reaping the gains from trade, international investment and technical progress. (European Commission 1996, 1)

Such depictions essentially resuscitate and modernize themes of the classical discourses of commercial liberalism. Globalization—defined crucially as an economic phenomenon—represents the universalization of market discipline. Economic openness, capital mobility, and free trade will have broadly utilitarian consequences provided that economies render themselves competitive. In the vocabulary of the G7, these processes should be promoted by governments, but they also pose serious challenges. Globalization heightens risk, and these risks can only be confronted with the implementation of sound economic policies. Former European Commissioner Leon Brittan argues in effect that the soundest response to the challenges posed by economic liberalization is in fact further economic liberalization (see Brittan 1997a, 1997b). These policy driven normative accounts push debate about globalization in the direction of a conversation about the virtues of market driven neoliberalism.

This conversation often crystallizes around the question of whether the retreat of the state is necessary or desirable. Thus for traditional social democrats, ecologists, and those concerned with the welfare of developing societies, globalization becomes an expression of the interests of the most powerful and mobile agents of capital or a signifier of materialist excess and the perpetration of asymmetries in the world system. Thus the argument against globalization is usually framed in terms of a critique of the logic of neoliberalism. This has produced, for example, strenuous efforts to refute the globalization thesis with the aim of reopening the space for social democratic forms of governance (Hirst and Thompson 1996). In a more philosophical guise, communitarian critics of globalization (or post nationalism or post territorialism in any form for that matter) maintain that nation states continue to be the ideal capsules for social interaction and for the social bonds that lie at the heart of efficient and democratic forms of human governance (Miller 1994).

The normative slant on globalization can alter quite drastically in cases where the concept assumes a broader more sociologically inclusive meaning. The compression of time and space, the deepening and widening of social relations, the liberation of human potential through technological change, and the capacity to communicate transnationally can all be read as conditions for human emancipation that do not necessarily carry the baggage of neoliberalism. To occupy the opposite side of this discussion could be perceived as apologism for autarchy and nationalist recidivism. Indeed the growth of antiglobalization movements espousing policies of economic nationalism was a distinctive feature of the closing years of the twentieth century. This has been especially prevalent in the United States—for some the hub of globalization—where politicians like Patrick Buchanan and Ross Perot have attempted to build coalitions against economic openness.

It is clear though that the bulk of academic discussion about globalization has come to treat globalization in economic terms—as the product of a series of interlocking trends of the past thirty years or so. These are usually identified as heightened capital mobility, the progressive multi- and transnationalization of production, and shifting and intensifying patterns of trade. Such transformative processes are often thought of as occurring simultaneously (or perhaps as a consequence of) revolutionary leaps in communications and information technology. They are said to generate serious pressures on nation states and national executives. Concurrently (or perhaps as a consequence), patterns of governance are thought to be undergoing radical transformation. Authority has become dispersed, semiprivatized, and multilayered, thereby residualizing the traditionally authoritative role of national governments (Strange 1996). As the world economy evolves into a singular entity, so distinctive national capitalisms wither away and the tools of traditional (Keynesian) economic analysis become obsolescent (Ohmae 1999). Faced with economic forces and market imperatives largely beyond their control, national governments (especially in OECD/European countries) are forced to concede the futility of pursuing Keynesian welfare statist strategies. Both the burgeoning paradigm of neoliberalism and the appearance of the regulatory state in developed countries (Majone 1994) can easily be connected to the rise of globalization. Moreover, the observable tendency of states to abdicate from their traditional functions of redistribution and stabilization (Majone 1996) can be read as a strategy of retrenchment, with welfare states becoming "competition states" geared to the imperatives of the global economy rather than to the demands of domestic publics (Cerny 1990; Cerny and Evans 1999).

This focus upon states and executive capacity reveals that globalization is often seen as amounting to significant structural change. In this context, the possibilities for agency—particularly that of states—are much altered. At the same time the processes of economic globalization may empower some actors at the expense of others. Financiers, bankers, bond rating agencies, and multinational firms, among others, become potential sites of powerful nonstate authority. In Kenichi Ohmae's terms, these alternative authoritative agents are better suited to the texture and rhythms of the new global economy than nation states precisely because the latter are designed for economic interaction based upon the conventions of territory (1995). Meanwhile, the growth of nonstate forms of authority spawns multiple nongovernmental organizations, creating a nascent polity at the global level that erodes the territorial limits of pluralism while not necessarily doing away with authentic processes of domestic politics (Higgott 1998, 11–4). The consequences of these processes are perhaps most manifest in the reconfiguration of authority suggested by the retreat of the (social democratic) state, but others notice connections between globalization and regionalization.

Regionalization—the intensification of economic integration among regionally adjacent economies—is sometimes identified as a collective attempt to contain the worst excesses of globalization. Alternatively, it may be identified as the mechanism through which ongoing globalization is facilitated (Rosamond 1999). The dynamics of regionalization processes also highlight debates about agency in the globalization process. For many, the growth of cross-border transactions (common, interestingly, to both globalization and regionalization) is embedded in the actions of private economic networks. For others, such activity is only possible with the deliberate sanction of states (Wallace 1990; Higgott 1998). In some accounts, states have been responsible for unleashing forces that they are no longer able to contain. For instance, Helen Milner's two-level game approach suggests that financial liberalization was undertaken by states largely at the behest of powerful domestic economic constituencies. Yet these actions have left states with severely circumscribed capacities in the macroeconomic sphere and governments vulnerable to the detrimental electoral effects of globally induced economic cycles. This leads states to seek collective solutions to these problems, often in the form of regional integration arrangements. Yet these collective interstate bargains are conducted under the gaze of those same powerful social forces in the domestic political economy (Milner 1998). States are far from irrelevant in this scenario; they are decisive shapers of globalization, but their capacity to act is structured by the imperatives of a two-level game.

Debates around these themes are well developed and ongoing (for discussions and lengthy surveys see Baylis and Smith 1997; Held et al. 1999;

Higgott 1998). The claim that globalization matters might be thought of in terms of a "world in itself" view of the phenomenon. That is to say, globalization amounts to a series of observable, material shifts in the way that economic life is structured. Critique thus becomes an exercise in adding nuance to or providing empirical refutation of the view that the world is globalizing/globalized. Such work has taken many forms (Held et al. 1999, ch. 1). One view is to cast doubt upon the novelty or significance of globalization. Argued historically, this view maintains that the interdependence of distant localities has been a feature of human life since at least the middle ages (Abu-Lughod 1989). A variation on this "nothing new" theme identifies the period roughly between 1914 and 1971 as an anomalous age of state power and unprecedented restrictions on international economic openness. Thus the appearance of an open international economy since the mid-1970s is a reversion to type rather than a dramatic change.

Moreover, economic historians like Jeffrey Williamson (1996a, 1996b) have developed the Polanyian argument that the growth of the Keynesian welfare state in industrialized countries represented a reaction to the socially destructive excesses of nineteenth century laissez faire. It follows that late twentieth century globalization might represent the first phase of a "similar double movement" (Higgott 1999a). This kind of analysis attacks head on the implicit teleology of much globalization discourse and opens a space for denials of the logic of no alternative that sit at the heart of much contemporary policy prescription (Hay and Watson 1999). Other historically inspired critiques seek to show that national governments have always been attentive to the potential dangers associated with circulating financial capital (Hont 1994), but that their ability to retain legitimate political authority has always followed from the successful exercise of statecraft (the shaping of public expectations) by national elites (Thompson 1997).

A second critical literature—while not totally separate from these historical accounts—develops a critique based upon the contemporary empirics of globalization. One of the most influential versions of this critique maintains that the world economy is characterized by *internationalization* rather than globalization (Weiss 1997). Paul Hirst and Grahame Thompson's (1996) well known rendition of this argument treats globalization as mythology. By and large, the world continues to be characterized by an international economy where the primary units are national economies and within which, therefore, national governments retain the potential for a significant degree of control. This thesis directs research to treating discourses of globalization as rhetorical embodiments of the interests of anti-interventionist political forces. If it can be shown that states still have significant executive capacities in the economic domain, then the array of policy portfolios available to national governments is rather more than globalizers might suggest. Social democratic concepts of control are far from ruled out, but buying into the mythology of globalization—in the manner of the "third way" politics of Blair, Clinton, and Schroeder—induces highly negative views about the prospects for established forms of progressive politics (Hay 1999; Hay and Watson 1999; Watson 1999). Paul Krugman describes "an odd sort of tacit agreement between the left and the right to pretend that exotic global forces are at work even when the real action is prosaically domestic" (1997, 2). This skeptical position—which has evident normative overtones—draws sustenance from many contributions seeking to question the idea that the national state has become redundant. Many have sought to cast doubt upon the idea that distinctive national economies and regimes of accumulation are being eroded (see Berger and Dore 1996; Boyer and Drache 1996). This creates a significant space for the specificities of national regulatory structures as mediators of the dynamics of global capitalism.

Alternatively, it is argued that the way in which global trends are mediated in national environments has much to do with politico-cultural factors. This sort of argument can branch out in at least three ways. First, it might be used to explain significant variance in national economic performance or policy programs. Second, it could be used to deny the importance of globalization as an explanatory variable. Governments might frequently blame exogenous imperatives for domestic policy decisions when the latter might be better explained with reference to endogenous variables. For Krugman the deployment of this type of rhetoric could have important political implications: "the public misguided into believing that international trade is the source of all our problems, might turn protectionist—undermining the real good that globalization has done for most people here and abroad" (1997, 3). The third way in which politics might be brought back into the discussion is via an analysis of the ways in which markets are (a) social constructions and (b) only legitimate insofar as they are embedded in domestic social contracts (Higgott 1999b). All told, these critiques attack the invisible hand logic of much of the "hyperglobalist" literature and in so doing seek to clear a space for political agency.

These skeptical positions are often confronted with a number of objections. The emphasis on internationalization (rather than globalization) is accused of devoting too much attention to the empirics of trading patterns and investment flows and not concentrating enough on how particular economic practices, habits, and ideas—such as those associated with the practical consequences of neoliberal political economy—are spread, implanted, and mediated within distinct local settings (Gill 1995). Moreover, the fact that states remain important does not necessarily rule out the possibility that the form and function of the state may be undergoing some radical alterations (Ruggie 1998a; Scholte 1997).

More seriously, the debates sketched above are often accused of over-emphasizing the economic dimensions of globalization at the expense of significant sociological contributions to the literature. It is certainly the case that globalization is normally used to signify profound economic change. But, in academic terms at least, the concept has been developed in quite different ways within sociologically inclined circles. Indeed, it can be argued that the concept's intellectual genealogy is best traced through a reading of debates in anthropology and sociology rather than the literatures of economics and business studies. This has persuaded some leading scholars to suggest that the most common understanding of globalization—as a phenomenon associated with the hypermobility of capital and the irrelevance of borders to corporate strategy—is founded on a corrupted reading of the concept (Robertson and Haque Khondker 1997). The main objection is that the obsession with economic globalization presumes that we are talking about a uniform, homogenizing process where dominant economic dynamics create common imperatives and necessitate similar kinds of responses from actors within domestic political economies.

The sociological literature has paid special attention to the relationship between globalization and difference or, in Roland Robertson's compelling vocabulary, "the universalization of particularism and the particularization of universalism" (1992, 100). Writers in this vein prefer more inclusive and less deterministic definitions of globalization such as "those spatio-temporal processes of change which underpin a transformation in the organization of human affairs by linking together and expanding human activity across regions and continents" (Held et al. 1999, 15). This deepening and widening of social relations (a) refuses to privilege the economic domain and (b) has no particular sense of what the impact of globalization might be—beyond a sense that it induces multiple flows of activity. This "global cultural economy" (Appadurai 1990, 1996) is a complex arena where multiple flows of people, finance, technology, images, and ideas that both coexist and intersect in an indeterminate way. The mediation of globalized artifacts can be radically different in distinct cultural environments. Globalization may rehabilitate difference, rather than sameness and may resuscitate old narratives, rather than create all-encompassing new ones (Albrow 1996; Axford 1995; Featherstone 1990; Laïdi 1998). Transformationist views from within this wing of the globalization literature argue that the key changes include the increasing velocity of human transactions, time-space compression, rapid technological change, the routinization of uncertainty, and the ubiquity of external context to everyday life.

There is not enough space in this chapter to do justice to these debates about the material dimensions of globalization. But it is worth remembering that they deal with the objective qualities of globalization—a world in itself. As Robertson has frequently noted, a further aspect to globalization is the widespread consciousness that profound change is occurring. Moreover, actors increasingly contextualize themselves within a global rather than a national or local environment. There is, in other words, a sense of a world *for* itself. The research questions that arise out of this observation seek to interrogate neither the longevity nor the empirical demonstrability of globalization, but rather the extent to which knowledge of globalization as *the* defining attribute of social life has become widespread.

Constructivism and Globalization

It is at this point, given their interest in the social construction of contexts of action, that constructivists would appear to have something to offer the globalization debate. At the same time, the analysis of discourses of globalization is not exclusive to constructivists. In many analyses, globalization is treated as a discourse of power or as a rhetorical strategy associated with particular material interests in the global political economy. As a discourse of (a) the benefits of widespread and extensive liberalization and (b) the inevitability and desirability of the withdrawal of the state, globalization becomes a convenient legitimizing narrative for the interests of transnational and circulating capital (Gill 1995). Globalization discourse, or "globaloney" as some would have it, is treated here in a quasi-Marxist way as superstructural—as an ideological expression of factors rooted in the material substructure. In many ways, this amounts to the dismissal of globalization discourse as mythic. The deployment of these ideologically charged expressions might be seen as masking the genuine possibilities for progressive political agency that lie immanent within the real fabric of the political economy.

Some scholars of discourse have been heavily influenced by skeptical views of globalization, as developed by writers such as Hirst and Thompson (1996). In the British context, Colin Hay and Matthew Watson (1999) have mapped the ways in which the New Labour government has legitimized continued recourse to welfare retrenchment through the systematic citation of the imperatives of globalization. Hay and Watson's strategy is to assemble the considerable academic evidence that casts doubt upon theses about globalization that sit at the heart of New Labour politicians' pronouncements. The discrepancy between the evidence and the discourse shows how progressive values can be sacrificed at the altar of globalization. A clear reading of the material realities, therefore, allows for the reconstruction of an alternative account to the platitudes of neoliberalism. This is a political act, given the strategic leaps necessary for the social democratic left to recapture its political imagination. Retheorizing economic context, or at least looking for alternative forms of knowledge about the economy, is an essential prerequisite for developing alternatives to neoliberal modes of governance. As Scholte suggests, "much is at stake in the formulation of knowledge about globalization" (1996b, 43).

The manufacture of knowledge(s) about the world is not a straightforward issue. Hay and Watson's work hints at the idea that globalization discourse is rather more than an epiphenomenal expression of material economic forces. The discourse has what we might call "truth effects." In Hay and Watson's terms, it "renders the contingent necessary" and thus creates a reality founded on the (false) premise. That said, there is still a powerful sense that the revelation of "reality" can demonstrate globalization discourse to be a matter of false consciousness. This way of thinking is not inconsistent with much constructivist reasoning. Many constructivists insist that rationalist epistemologies within a broad realist philosophy of science are compatible with a structurationist ontology. In short, it is possible to know the real world beyond its discursive construction. The worst excesses of both rationalism and reflectivism can be avoided (Adler 1997; Checkel 1998).

The debate here is complex and nuanced (see Jørgensen 1998). But it seems clear that there are a number of potential constructivist positions in relation to globalization. The posture taken will be related to how analysts understand the relationship between *socially constructed* and *social* reality. A soft constructivism might view discourses as relatively autonomous from the world they describe, whereas a harder version might employ a more authentically structurationist position such as that articulated by Philip Cerny:

> The spread of the discourse itself alters the a priori ideas and perceptions which people have of the empirical phenomena which they encounter; in so doing, it engenders strategies and tactics which in turn may restructure the game itself. With the erosion of old axioms, what follows might be called paradigmatic selection. And in this process, the concept of globalization increasingly shapes the terms of the debate. (1996, 620)

Constructivists will also differ according to the extent to which they see their project as a "critical" intervention. Many constructivists see their purpose as primarily analytical (Onuf 1998b). The goal of intellectual work is to deepen understanding of the international system by refusing to take for granted many of the axioms of utilitarian schools of IR theory. Alternatively, there is significant potential for constructivists to contribute to the development of critical theories of globalization (Scholte 1996b; Sjolander 1995) where the intention is to intervene normatively in pursuit of particular values (often those said to be attacked or marginalized by economic globalization). The constructivist contribution would not necessarily be to develop an alternative form of knowledge to the orthodoxies of economic liberalism, but to show how such an alternative could be discursively constructed and made meaningful through systems of rules.

Indeed in one of the few explicitly constructivist interventions in the globalization debate, Kathleen McNamara (1997) clearly positions herself as a critic of the globalization thesis. The premise of her argument is that a thoroughgoing assessment of the political economy of market integration is not possible without an honest assessment of the role of social beliefs and socialization. "Bond traders and foreign exchange dealers, and corporate strategizers certainly won't have an incentive to change their beliefs about putative correctness of neoliberal reforms if the discourse surrounding them completely supports it" (1997, 21). The problem is that, as McNamara implies, much powerful (economic) globalization discourse carries within it a particular sense of economic rationality. Not only are external imperatives constructed, but actors are also positioned as rational agents within that globalized structure. They are guided to conceptualize themselves as rational agents where the rationality supplied is that of global neoliberalism. It is not just a fuller understanding of market dynamics that is needed to engage critically with globalization. It is also a better appreciation of the understandings of structural constraints and the possibilities for agency held by actors themselves. As McNamara notes, these understandings are likely to be constitutive of interests, and actors will behave in accordance with their understandings of others' interests and in anticipation of others' reactions, rather than in response to exogenous stimuli.

This phenomenon of "anticipated reactions" amounts to genuine value added from constructivists. In terms of Hay and Watson's example, governments pursue fiscal rectitude and deregulatory policy making in anticipation of the reactions of certain key economic actors and "the market" more generally. This in turn is facilitated by the commonplace assumption that the economy is globalized.

It is clear also that the propagation of globalization discourse is a strategy pursued actively by certain groups. In the European Union (EU), for instance, analysis of the discursive strategies of elements within the European Commission reveals the powerful effects of the active social construction of market imperatives. This has the dual effect of helping to legitimize the pursuit of deregulatory neoliberal policy agendas, while at the same time assembling a persuasive case for the *Europeanization* of governance functions. What Europeanization might mean is another matter, for while the consensual economistic definition of globalization may prevail in such circles, the question of whether the EU is an agent or a recipient of globalization is a matter of some ambiguity (Rosamond 1999).

This is an ambiguity that constructivists should relish for two reasons. First it shows that the discursive construction of external context does not necessarily lead to consensus or to the creation of new norms. Second, it demonstrates the significance of the relationship between knowledge about the world and the way in which that world evolves.

Therefore, a key constructivist inspired task should be the development of a deeper understanding of the transmission of knowledge about globalization. At face value, there is a close fit between certain academic renditions of the concept and the views about globalization held by politicians, corporate chief executives, journalists and so on. At the same time, it is also clear that many academic reworkings of the concept do not appear in everyday discourse (Robertson and Haque Khondker 1997). One way into this is to suggest that public figures rely on relatively simplistic readings of the so-called "first wave" literature on globalization. Richard Higgott (1998) describes the debate unraveling in three phases. The first wave amounts to hyperbolic claims about the uprooting of established political and economic logics and the world wide spread of new technological and economic imperatives. The second wave is essentially backlash; a combination of empirical refutation and the reassertion of erstwhile statist certainties. The third wave literature steers a course between the first two schools by tempering the excesses of the first wave, acknowledging the residual capacities of states, but still contemplating the emergence of significant alternative nodes of authority. At the same time, the third wave adds rather more nuance with the acceptance that global economic liberalization is but one facet of globalization. One immediate qualification is that these waves of literature did not necessarily emerge chronologically. Indeed, some of the sociological descriptions of globalization could be said to have predated some of the first wave work. However, the important consideration remains the apparent resemblance between the sentiments of first wave literature and the conceptions of globalization uttered in the public sphere. The research task is extensive, but important. The question of whether there is a transmission belt of knowledge between globalizing elites and the academy can be set against the alternative hypothesis that the ideas that became associated with globalization arose among networks of private economic actors.

A further related argument becomes apparent in the work of Ronald Diebert (1997). Deibert provides an important account of the relationship between the material technologies of communication and the way in which the world is conceptualized. His sociology of knowledge approach asks why particular beliefs are held in particular contexts, but refuses to make a straightforward unidirectional causal connection between context and belief. Thus it is not enough to make a deterministic link between the material existence of globalization and the widespread use of the term to frame policy relevant discourses. Rather, Deibert is pointing to shifts in social epistemology, which he defined as

> the web of beliefs into which people are acculturated and through which they perceive the world around them. It encompasses an interwoven set of historically contingent intersubjective mental characteristics, ranging from spatial or temporal forms, to various group identities, or to "imagined communities," which are unique to a specific historical context, and differentiate one epoch from another. (Deibert 1997, 33)

In terms of globalization, Deibert points to the fit between the "hypermedia" environment and the ascendancy of a more variegated and decentered system of rule and the increasing density of transnational social movements. This argument contributes interestingly to the constructivist concern with communicative action since Deibert posits a mutually constitutive relationship between the means of communication and the discourses that describe the world emerging from that communicative infrastructure.

On the face of it, constructivism would seem to offer the ideal theoretical entry point for the discussion of discourses of globalization because globalization—like anarchy—can be thought of as an intersubjective structure. Yet in many ways state-centered constructivism has an easier job because it borrows from realism a notion of primary units (states) that discursively define the structure (anarchy) of unit interaction (international relations). It would seem to be a rather more difficult task to investigate the social construction of globalization as a defining component of actors' environments. It is persuasive, on the face of it, to agree with McNamara that "globalization is what we make of it" (1997). But who are "we" in this context? For Wendt and others, self-help, power politics, and the like are norms of unit interaction in situations *where the units themselves engage in the social construction of those norms*. The social identities that emerge do so in the context of intergovernmental exchange and in relation to the systemic property of anarchy. But globalization as a systemic property is rather different from anarchy, not least because most discourses of globalization tend to multiply significantly the number of relevant actors in the system. Also, notwithstanding the dominance of a particular conception of economic globalization, there are rival forms of knowledge about globalization. This means that there are a variety of ways of positioning identities and interests in relation to knowledge about globalization.

While globalization may initiate a new set of intersubjectivities about the nature of the world and the boundaries of the possible, it is also evidently a discourse of contingency, crisis, and the unbundling of erstwhile certainties (of territoriality, the possibilities of national governance and so on). Globalization is a discourse of *change* (and radical change at that), whereas anarchy (as illustrated by the transhistorical certainties propagated by realist and neorealist theory) is a discourse of continuity. To be blunt, the chief claim of constructivist IR may be that it provides a more solid account of continuity in the international system, in contrast to the realist/neorealist invocation of the "state of nature." The social construction of globalization entails the problematization of the status of certain actors, notably national governments. Consequently, the domain of globalization discourse is not necessarily likely to be characterized by the iteration and largely consensual reproduction of a particular external reality. Rather, it may be a deeply contested terrain involving the exchange of rival narratives about global context. It offers the opportunity to realign policy coalitions, engage in policy innovation, and advance particular claims at the expense of others.

Conclusions

It is important to stress that none of the foregoing is trying to argue that globalization is purely illusory. Many rationalist critics of constructivist thinking assume that talking about social constructions means that a kind of null hypothesis is being advanced. If a phenomenon like globalization is socially constructed, then presumably the constructivist is also suggesting that globalization is a myth. So if actors invoke global economic imperatives as the reason for their action, then the constructivist contention must be that these imperatives were not "real" (this line of reasoning is followed by Moravcsik 1999). But a constructivist analysis of globalization is trying to do something rather different. At one level it is an attempt to add significant value to rationalist accounts by investigating the ways in which material transformations are given meaning by actors. Delving deeper, the constructivist position enables us to think in more complex ways about the relationship between structures and action. The hegemonic conceptualization of globalization brings with it certain messages about opportunities for and constraints upon meaningful agency. It also tells stories about the relative significance of particular actors. Not only that. It also positions some actors as globalizers and some as globalized. So while the material transformations wrought by technological changes in the fields of production, finance, and trade are real enough, we need to think about how they represent a reflexive encounter between agents and structures. Exploration of how and why actors position themselves—in terms of interests and identities—in relation to globalization will facilitate discussions of discourse that connect the material and the ideational. In so doing we will be able to get to grips with some real issues of power and authority in the contemporary global political economy.

Notes

1. For their comments and input, I am indebted to Jane Booth, Thomas Christiansen, Charlie Dannreuther, K.M. Fierke, Knud Erik Jørgensen, Rey Koslowski, Rohit Lekhi, Nick Rengger, and Glenda Rosenthal.

Epilogue

11

Can We Speak a Common Constructivist Language?

Audie Klotz

Constructivists are developing increasingly sophisticated arguments about core themes in global politics.[1] As we articulate empirical answers to questions about structures, agency, and the processes that link them, we create an autonomous agenda, one that leaps beyond the interparadigm divide that characterizes our academic field of International Relations (IR). In light of this shift, as the editors and contributors to this book aptly recognize, constructivists would do well to focus more energy on intraparadigm debates.

Basic questions remain unresolved, such as whether "we" even accept the constructivist label. The term, coined in IR by Nicholas Onuf (1989) and popularized by Alexander Wendt (1992a, 1999), means different things to its diverse practitioners and critics alike. We should, therefore, explore convergences as much as divergences in our positions. While "we constructivists" disagree among ourselves about epistemology and methodology (variously categorized as modern versus postmodern or positivist versus postpositivist divides), we nevertheless accept a basic ontological position (which stresses intersubjectivity and the mutual constitution of structures and agents). But can we—should we even try to—develop a common constructivist identity?

The chapters in this book raise this question of labels, yet the volume as a whole, understandably, offers only hints at an answer. As much as each individual contribution suggests one (or a few) direction(s) for common research, the development of any collective research agenda calls for more guidance, or at least a more explicit demarcation of lines of consensus and abiding disputes. Many of us engaged in the first wave of constructivist empirical work, for example, recognize that we underplayed—at best left implicit, at worst ignored—agency. But a focus on language also doesn't adequately characterize identities, intentions, and behaviors of actors in world affairs. In other words, constructivists of all stripes would benefit from self-critique.

While not promising to save us from any or all potential perils—and certainly eschewing aspirations of hegemonic labeling—my goal in this epilogue is to highlight what I see as some similar research interests, which I consider worthy of more intensive exploration from all sides. Specifically, I think we need a better understanding of the processes of socialization and resistance that link ideational and material structures with agents. Returning then to epistemological issues, I question whether we can or should call constructivist claims "causal" and conclude with a few suggestions for ways to engage more productively with so-called mainstream IR.

Who Are "We"?

My perspective here, including my questions about research agendas, may too quickly lead me to be categorized as one of those "American positivists" who underestimates the role of language. I beg to differ on two counts, calling into question both the supposed geographical markers of division and the very notion of those differences. Thus I unabashedly part ways with K.M. Fierke and Knud Erik Jørgensen (Introduction), although I acknowledge that our personal experiences within the politics of academia unavoidably influence our perspectives.

I remain suspicious of geographically demarcated intellectual categories. While "ideas do not float freely" (Risse-Kappen 1994), they do traverse state borders, as do researchers. How would we define the boundaries of this American hegemony? Should we associate scholars with their country of birth, degree-granting institution, or locale of employment? Are Canadians (a few being particularly significant in the constructivist and postpositivist debates) complicit in U.S. dominance or do we associate them with the British, a legacy of colonial spheres of influence? By this logic, Australians become Europeans as well (assuming—problematically—that we count Britain as part of Europe), which may or may not amuse those in Germany, France, Italy, Sweden, Norway, and elsewhere.

Perhaps we should shift to scholars' favorite publishing outlets, which we all recognize have particular biases and agendas. But editorial boards, not to mention tenure review committees, generally seek international representation, once again blurring geographical boundaries. Using publishers' legal homes, furthermore, disregards the global nature of that industry, as well as their willingness to publish whatever they think will sell. Perhaps U.S. dominance reflects economic considerations, specifically the number of universities and thus size of the American consumer-student body. But constructivists shy away from such gross materialist arguments, so let me leave off with the suggestion that funding agencies might also play a role in creating (or dismissing) academic agendas. For example, if you check the acknowledgments in many of our books, the MacArthur Foundation, based in the United States, appears often. We could benefit from a good constructivist analysis of the political economy of scholarly identity; in other words, I hope someone will write one soon.

In the meantime, I agree with the assertion that "constructivism" means different things to different people. Genealogies of its origins (see, e.g., a number of contributions to this volume) do reveal multiple philosophical roots. Let's talk about those ideas, on their own merits, rather than creating a false dichotomy between "American" and "European" camps. After all, various secondary camps within Europe also exhibit their own professional pulls and fiefdoms. No one is innocent of playing some type of academic game.

Regardless of epistemological labels pinned on constructivist scholars because of our multiple philosophical roots, I see us all grappling, in one way or another, with questions of causality and culture. Certainly not everyone would be comfortable with those two particular words, and I do not claim that we should all unquestioningly embrace them. Yet our abiding concerns implicitly or explicitly make claims about how global relationships operate; we can debate whether seeking to understand constitutive processes should then be reconceived as an epistemologically separate endeavor from analyses of causality (more on that later).

Let us remember, in any case, that debates over history, epistemology, and method are hardly unique to constructivists in IR, nor to their American detractors (of the realist, behavioralist, choice theoretic, or any other ilk). Here I simply invoke disputes among realist followers of E. H. Carr, Hans Morgenthau, and Kenneth Waltz as one example of the tensions over how "scientific" our work should be. None of us offer journalistic, atheoretical "thick descriptions"—an accusation lodged by avowed positivists against those who take historical and social context seriously and doubt the utility of regression analyses. Indeed, some might say that this charge is based on a misreading of Geertz (1973), one of the (few) standard texts on interpretation found in U.S. political science graduate programs.

Thus my modest contribution here hopes to enable us to recognize a range of key issues that motivate our research and move us beyond unproductive divisions, geographical or linguistic, between conventional and critical, sociological and poststructuralist, modern and postmodern, or positivist and postpositivist constructivisms (see also Price and Reus-Smit 1998). Rather than sitting within categories each of us represents a point on a spectrum (Adler 1997; Christiansen, Jørgensen, and Wiener 1999). We all seek to make some kind of implicit or explicit general claims, often with prescriptive (rather than predictive) significance.

People Talk

Constructivists of various persuasions agree upon an intersubjective ontology—ideas, norms, rules constitute meanings which frame actors' identities, interests, and actions. Thus we reject notions of an objective reality that can be explained by universal law-like generalizations. Moving beyond this shared starting point, we confront, as numerous contributors to this volume note, a core dispute over the extent to which language necessarily becomes the center of our analyses. How profoundly do we disagree about how to explore intersubjectivity in IR?

Many if not most of the first wave of empirical constructivist studies in the 1990s demonstrate that "intersubjective understandings" matter in world politics. Regardless of whether they willingly accept the constructivist label, these scholars draw on interpretive philosophies and methodologies to reexamine the formation and operation of international regimes, organizations, and social institutions (e.g., Klotz 1995a; Doty 1996a; Finnemore 1996a; Price 1997; Lynch 1999), question the historical basis for sovereignty and the modern state system (e.g., Hall 1997; Reus-Smit 1999), explore the role of culture in foreign policies (e.g., Campbell 1992, 1998a; Johnston 1995; Weber 1995; Kier 1997; Weldes 1999), and reassess alliances and other regional institutions (e.g., Risse-Kappen 1995c; Adler and Barnett 1998; Barnett 1998).

Interparadigm battles reigned, as most of these scholars initially sought in diverse ways to debunk (neo)realist orthodoxy, which dismissed the importance of ideas. Richard Ashley, Friedrich Kratochwil, and John Ruggie in particular offered rallying calls to this generation of scholars unwilling to accept Cold War era orthodoxy (Ashley 1986; Kratochwil and Ruggie 1986; Ruggie 1986; Kratochwil 1989). A second dimension of these critiques targeted the rationalism of social choice theory, which agreed that ideas matter yet rejected intersubjectivity. Unlike constructivists, neoliberal institutionalists (including many game theorists) separated ideas from interests, rather than claiming that norms and rules shaped the identities and interests of actors. Following Wendt (1992a), many constructivists argue, at minimum, that constitutive questions of interest formation should be separated from behavioral outcomes based on those interests.

One consequence of such attempts to argue with and against mainstream realist and liberal theories, not surprisingly, has been a persistent state-centrism in the first wave of empirical constructivist research. In most cases, these studies also ultimately came back to questions of policy and behavior, leading many constructivists to present their claims in positivist sounding terminology, though rarely going so far as talking about variables and hypothesis testing. Hence, many see constructivism as a peculiarly American variant of interpretive critique. (Caution: we should avoid conflating state-centrism with positivism, even if both deserve critique.)

Various "European" scholars consequently accuse "Americans" of overlooking their historical and philosophical traditions, such as the so-called English School or approaches based on Wittgenstein, Habermas, Derrida, or any other theorist of choice. Yet these presumed divisions both underestimate the broad range of influences on so-called American constructivism and overestimate the commonalities of supposedly European approaches. My own experience illustrates this point. As someone especially influenced by Kratochwil and Ruggie, who in turn note intellectual debts to Wittgenstein, Durkheim, Weber, and others, I draw on Foucault (but not Nietzsche) and a broad reading in feminist theory. I find Derrida and Habermas less useful, and consider the English School problematic. But few of these works (or my critiques of them) appear in the notes of my published works, making it difficult for anyone else to surmise these influences. Rather than building camps and erecting fences, we should, as this volume seeks to do, explore these diverse philosophical schools and—of critical importance—draw out more systematically their implications for the study of international relations.

Furthermore, some postmodern scholars accuse "conventional" constructivists of parroting positivism by trying to translate the implications of our empirical work into a language comprehensible to our social science colleagues. This misjudges the disciplinary and disciplining roles of these debates. We should not underestimate the extent to which the constructivist empirical challenge opened up an intellectual space that would have remained closed to other postpositivist studies, self-characterized as marginal (also see Price and Reus-Smit 1998; Marcus 1999). In the academic context, we are "epistemic communities"; research designs are strategic plans in struggles of domination and resistance. Constructivism's successes in these disciplinary assaults now enable us to develop a more autonomous research agenda, one that can maintain a momentum of its own. Taking advantage of this new space requires us to consolidate our gains and to turn our attention to strengthening our own agenda. As this volume makes clear, that turns us to the question of language.

To say that conventional empirical constructivist work ignores language is, at a very basic level, unfair. How can one identify norms and rules without at least looking to the expression of these codes of conduct in diplomatic texts and policymakers' public pronouncements? But to claim that all of us use discourse in a deeper sense would indeed be disingenuous. Few scholars in this first wave seriously engaged Derrida (Weber 1995 and Doty 1996a being the most obvious exceptions), even as we adopted or adapted Foucaultian notions of pervasive power relationships.

To some extent, however, our reluctance to embrace semiotics or deconstruction flowed from the limitations of these approaches for our purposes, and not necessarily from ignorance of their existence or stereotypical American parochialism. For those of us interested in policy choices and their consequences, conceptualizations solely in the realm of linguistic oppositions fail to link in more than a vague way to people's conceptions of themselves, their goals, and the means available for satisfying them. In other words, certain formulations of discourse analysis lose sight of agency amidst pervasive "representations." That is not to say that these connections cannot be made, but as Birgit Locher and Elisabeth Prügl point out in their contribution, not enough have done so.

Can we reconcile these different notions of discourse, the one as methodology, the other as philosophical critique? One possibility, as Jennifer Milliken proposes in her chapter, would be to outline a more "rigorous" analysis that fosters self-conscious attention to types of texts and consistencies in interpretation that enable a degree of replicability. Moving discourse analysis from subjective interpretation to intersubjective acceptance of knowledge claims marks a considerable epistemological shift, potentially reconciling modern and postmodern constructivists. Does our adoption of these and other methodological "tweaks" necessarily indicate that we have "sold out" to the disciplining power of positivism? No. As Fierke observes in her chapter, and many others acknowledge as well, we cannot avoid implicit claims that one "description" is somehow more accurate or "better" than another.

These methodological debates are not new to the constructivist turn in IR. Historians, anthropologists, legal scholars, religious proselytizers, environmental activists, policymakers, and a host of other analysts and practitioners grapple with these issues on a daily basis. At the level of epistemology, yes, we need to recognize that dominant interpretations are not objective or neutral; knowledge is indeed power. But if we are, at minimum, going to describe what we think is the dominant narrative, at any given time or within a particular context, we still need techniques for identifying discursive patterns. Or posing the question from the other, conventional side, how do we know when a norm exists?

Traditional historical analysis encourages us to present more complete stories, presumably based on a wider range of documentation or by rereading existing materials in a different light. To the extent that many constructivists, conventional and postmodern alike, delve into archives and reconsider secondary sources, we offer nothing methodologically exceptional. Indeed, even game theorists now recognize the importance of historical narratives (Bates et al. 1998). Similarly, many constructivists concerned with policy outcomes adopt some version of "process tracing" methodologies, since such an approach acknowledges claims of contingency and context, and produces dynamic rather than static analyses.

Yet constructivist scholars also offer an explicitly epistemological critique that sets these narratives within the context of disciplinary knowledge and power. Historical interpretation, in other words, is not a process of creating an objectively more complete or better story. Rather it is a question of understanding metanarratives in the practices of both international relations and academic positioning, within which these traditional historical methods contribute to a more political understanding of the creation of truth claims (Lynch 1999; also see Barnett 1998; Fierke 1998).

Emphasizing discourse in the creation of historical narratives and process tracing analyses of policy choices (rather than, say, delving into the psychological motives of key decision makers) offers a route for reconciling different constructivisms. But while methodological measures certainly help us find a common ground, we cannot use them to evade questions of the relationship between language and agency.

Socialization Processes

Does language so profoundly frame consciousness, and hence behavior, that actors are reduced to the level of predictable automatons who mindlessly follow social dictates? Of course not. Since these norms and rules evolve over time, someone must challenge prevailing practices enough to transform that which is taken for granted. Our quest, therefore, leads us to the agent-structure debate.

To reconsider language seriously, we need to move beyond both the positivist tendency to reduce discourse to a methodological tool and the postpositivist fixation with representation. How can we reconcile our assumption that norms and rules constitute actors, and vice versa, and our commitment to resolving the role of language in constructivist research? What language do our agents speak, and with what effects?

Even if constructivists can agree that actors speak, we have not sufficiently conceptualized agency. Practice presumes behavior as well as language and has implications beyond speech acts. At least in principle, all variants of constructivist research recognize the role of agents in both reproducing and challenging the language (norms, rules, discourses) of the international system. We disagree, often adamantly, about the processes which characterize practice, that is, the links between agents and structures.

For constructivists seeking theories of agency, recent IR research offers a plethora of possibilities but few that clearly or distinctively follow from the intersubjective assumptions of the approach. In other words, we analysts have a choice to make, since none of the available options necessarily derive from our ontological starting point.

Take the debate about the state. Wendt (1992a, 1999) most frequently gets credited, or blamed, for advocating a state-centric constructivism. Rather than jump to discard the state, however, others make a case for modifying our conception of it. As Ben Rosamond points out in his contribution, theorists of globalization focus on the transformation—rather than the collapse or eclipse—of the state. Lars Lose proposes another tack, drawing on Habermasian communicative action: disaggregate the state (see also Weldes 1999). His chapter examines the specific cross-cultural language of agents of the state, rather than agents outside the state. If we want, we can keep the state, but if we're going to understand its role in world politics, we need to make additional conceptual and methodological choices to examine it empirically.

Those rejecting state-centrism can turn to a range of nonstate actors, from scientific elites (Adler 1997) to transnational activists (Keck and Sikkink 1998), as well as economic actors, often ignored or understated in constructivist analyses (Cutler, Haufler, and Porter 1999; Haufler forthcoming are notable exceptions). What shall we do with this embarrassment of riches? Must we resort to a supplementary theory of interest groups or bureaucratic politics, perhaps expanded to include epistemic communities and transnational networks? Or can we develop an understanding of agency that is ontologically consistent with basic constructivist tenets?

Locher and Prügl imply that merging feminist and constructivist analyses would enable us to develop such an understanding of agency. I agree on the need to theorize struggle and resistance (Klotz 1995a), as much as the persistence of institutionalized social understandings (such as gender hierarchies) but claim more generally that we ought to explore transnational social movements (feminist and otherwise). While social movement theory has its own limitations and disputes (for an overview, see Tarrow 1998), it leads us to look at the dynamics of mobilization against dominant norms or rules as well as the reasons for success or failure in attempts to institutionalize alternative discourses.

In other words, scholars of transnational movements, from both positivist (e.g., Thomas forthcoming) and postpositivist (e.g., Lynch 1999) directions, question how actors shape the language of power and protest. Furthermore, we can link concepts of framing and narratives to Gramscian notions of hegemony and conceptualizations of epistemic communities so as to understand learning as well. Those who are drawn to Habermas, such as Harald Müller and Lose in this volume, can stress negotiations within regimes without losing sight of the agents at the heart of communication processes. Similarly, approaches drawing on Wittgenstein, including Kratochwil and Fierke in their contributions, then have tools to answer questions about who constructs the dominant meanings that frame speech acts and underpin language games.

Rather than dispute which of these processes—learning, negotiation, communication, framing, mobilization, adaption, and such—offers "the" answer to the agent-structure conundrum, constructivists would be better served by exploring all of these as elements of an overarching socialization process. While discourse is crucial for defining meanings, we should not forget that international relations function within the context of multiple languages. Yes, we need to ask how a prevailing discourse gets established, but we cannot stop there. How do certain meanings get diffused into local practices? And how do local communities resist socialization into a dominant discourse? Language is dynamic, not static.

Neither conventional nor postmodern constructivisms adequately answer these questions which are at the heart of our research endeavors. To say that we need to take language more seriously, then, is only the first step in developing a common constructivism that escapes being driven by debates against realism and liberalism. As the contributors to this volume demonstrate, it remains a crucial path—perhaps the only route—if we hope to bridge the presumed positivist-postmodern divide.

Causality Revisited

The very existence of this volume demonstrates that constructivist practitioners with diverging epistemological commitments might reconcile. This assertion will raise objections from all sides. At the core of these disagreements is the question of causality (e.g., contrast Jørgensen's chapter with

Fierke's). In the eyes of postmodern scholars, any general claims tread dangerously close to assertions of universal laws, tainting research that even vaguely adopts the vocabulary of cause or effect with the tar of positivism. Meanwhile, those concerned particularly with policy decisions insist that we need to relate constructivist ontological claims to "real world" choices that go beyond texts or historical analyses of unique events. To what extent, then, do we implicitly or explicitly share a commitment to deriving broader lessons or discerning general patterns from their research?

Constructivists embrace a common core set of research concerns, even if these get articulated through different vocabulary. Regardless of whether one looks at norms, discourses, rules, representations, or other labels for intersubjective understandings, we all seek to understand how certain ideas get taken for granted or dominate while others remain unspoken or marginalized. We also try to discern the consequences of prevailing assumptions and the reasons why some get challenged but others do not. Some talk about the "production" of "representations;" others, the "functions" of "norms." In other words, we can—and should more often—translate questions (and answers) back and forth, in and out of causal and noncausal terminologies.

This translation exercise necessarily raises the question of epistemological commitments. Is this an unbridgeable divide? I think not, as Jørgensen and Fierke, each in their own way, illustrate. Postpositivists such as Fierke object to attempts at deriving universal knowledge claims. Yet more conventional constructivists such as Jørgensen hardly pursue such agendas either. All constructivists, in other words, stress that knowledge claims are context-bound and historically contingent. We all implicitly or explicitly engage in comparative and historical studies and make some general claims (at varying levels of abstraction). The terminology often used by postpositivists implies as much of a general claim as the more explicit statements of scholars with positivist leanings. We shouldn't let the discourse of causality overshadow our basic agreements; we shouldn't get sidetracked by epistemological posturing.

I do not mean that such a translation exercise is either simple or straightforward. If we shift our attention to common questions, such as the social construction of identities, we encounter important epistemological issues. For example, should we talk about "constitution" in terms comparable to "causality"? If we insist that constitutive processes are inherently different from causal processes, how do we characterize those forces? Here we must again revisit the agent-structure debate. Our conceptualizations of norms, rules and discourses, as discussed above, need to capture the interrelationship between agents and structures, thus eschewing linear arguments associated with positivist approaches to causality. Social context both constrains and enables action. The issue, then, is how to conceptualize and analyze "constraint" and "motivation."

These debates will never be resolved in the abstract. To further an agenda for all constructivists, we should explore whether our epistemological commitments make a difference in our empirical studies. Resolution requires a more precise discussion of the specific claims we implicitly or explicitly make. What do we mean when we say social structures enable or guide behavior, or that we should see reasoning as a noncausal explanation for action? Are we rejecting probabilistic predictions? Are all analyses of structures compatible with the terminology of enabling or framing conditions? To what extent do any of us, positivist and postpositivist alike, seek to understand intentions rather than (or in addition to) constraints? Let's debate the difference between norms (intersubjective phenomena) and attitudes (subjective phenomena), rather than simply proclaiming that these inherently require epistemologically distinct research approaches.

Since positivists hardly resolve questions of "true" causes for behavior, we shouldn't expect more from constructivists. We shouldn't get stuck in the debate over understanding versus explanation, but we should strive for a more precise articulation of our differences. Only then will we design research strategies that can explore the meaning of constitution versus causality and reason versus rationality. Let's compare the logics of psychological, sociological, and anthropological methods.

Constructivists disagree on a vast range of specific research questions but agree on an overarching agenda. If we lose sight of our commonalities amidst irresolvable—and misguided—proclamations of epistemological commitments, we will miss an opportunity to make substantial strides in understanding and explaining international relations. We will also undermine our potential for convincing scholars in the mainstream that social construction is an ontologically unavoidable approach to IR.

Do We Need an "Other"?

Most identity theorists claim that we define who we are in opposition to an "other." For postmodern scholars, everyone falling under a positivist label belongs in one camp, just as much of mainstream IR (either rationalist or materialist) throws all types of constructivism into a "relativist" category. Perhaps IR (either as a subfield of political science or a discipline of its own) needs such divisions to fuel debate and perpetuate academic fiefdoms.

I won't claim that we can avoid profound divisions—I don't think "normal science" is or should be our goal. Nor do I think disputes about cau-

causality and constitution should be the dividing line. Rather than perpetuating guilt-by-epistemology, I see a range of concepts and questions that offer the basis for engaged, if not friendly, dialogue across ontological divides. I   offer three examples here but plenty more abound.

Many of the contributors to this volume stress the importance of communication, but so have plenty of nonconstructivists. Signaling, for example, plays a major role in bargaining theories (including game theory). Constructivists rightly point out that these scholars presume the nature of the game, that is, the rules, the payoffs, and the identities of the participants. Should a constructivist approach, then, seek to offer an explanation for these assumptions, thus presenting a complementary approach? Or does constructivism posit a distinct, qualitatively different dynamic in a bargaining relationship, based perhaps on the Habermasian notion of communicative rationality? Kratochwil, Müller, Maja Zehfuss, Fierke, and Lose all touch on these concerns (and see Risse 2000), but much more could be said. Such an engaged debate would deepen what Fierke and Jørgensen characterize in their Introduction as the now predominant disciplinary dispute between rationalism and constructivism.

Of course, not everyone agrees that materialism has lost its field-defining role. Many constructivist studies target the realist emphasis on military might. We can and should push these debates further. For example, constructivists frequently refer to reputation in connection with community norms and processes of justification. Here again, other IR scholars already use this concept, sharing in our call to take social power seriously. To what extent is a psychological approach to reputation (e.g., Mercer 1996) consistent or compatible with a constructivist one (Klotz 1995a; Milliken 1996)? We may reject ontological individualism (of either the rationalist or psychological type) but can we ignore individuals in our conceptualization of agency? Or should we use social psychology, especially cognitive evolution and learning (Adler 1997), to debate more precisely these alternative approaches?

Nor can we ignore international political economy if we're serious about exploring ideational versus materialist and rationalist approaches. A whole new range of arguments, for example, are emerging under the label of globalization (see Rosamond's chapter). One strand of this writing focuses on the spread of capitalism; another emphasizes increased cultural connections (e.g., Appadurai 1996). For those constructivists claiming that we need to look more at communication, the computer revolution presents vast new pathways for research at the intersection of language and political economy, as well as global governing institutions (see Diebert 1997).

These three examples illustrate ways in which constructivists can explore the implications of our ontological assumptions, particularly in contrast to the materialism and rationalism that still dominate IR. I offer them in the hopes of provoking all of "us"—the broad IR community—to engage more directly, to identify common research questions with potentially profound implications for both the study and the conduct of international relations. By moving beyond the epistemological divide, however, I recognize that we risk losing our comfortable "other." I'm sure the professional practices of identity construction will push us to find a replacement. Hopefully, we can work together to overcome the pathologies of disciplinary power.

Notes

1. Cecelia Lynch improved this chapter by offering detailed reactions and suggestions. Although we develop many of these themes further in *Constructing Global Politics: Strategies for Research* (Cornell University Press, 2001), she remains absolved of any responsibility for the views I express here. I also thank Karin Fierke for her helpful comments and good humor in the face of critique.

12

The Politics of Constructivism

Nicholas G. Onuf

Politics are an inescapable feature of our social arrangements.[1] *Constructivism* is not simply a framework by which to investigate, at least in principle, all such arrangements. It is a social construction no less political than any other. Indeed, insofar as it functions as a social movement (and I think it does, at least for the contributors to this book and for quite a few of its readers), constructivism is markedly more political than most of the institutions and practices constituting our social realities.

By politics, I mean those practices in any society to which its members attach the most significance (cf. Onuf 1989, 2–5). Obviously, being political is a relative condition, and the ways that people can be said to be acting politically are highly contingent on the full range of institutions and practices that, as a complex of relations, constitute particular social arrangements (including academic disciplines and activist movements). Moreover, social arrangements are particular, as I put it, only in relation to the particulars of other, often more inclusive arrangements, or societies, all of which are therefore relative, highly contingent affairs. The only further generalization that I feel safe in making is that the members of societies tend to set apart political matters for special, or at least different, treatment.

If we look at constructivism *socially*, as an institutionalized set of practices (however contingent), we know that it must have some sort of political salience for those who actively engage in this practice, considered on its own and in relation to more inclusive social arrangements. Among the latter, the discipline of International Relations (IR), itself a highly contingent affair, stands out for its salience. The politics of constructivism play out in panel discussions at professional meetings, published manifestos, and reviews of the state of the discipline. Publishing this book is a political act.

As such, it would seem to be appropriate to consider the several ways in which its contributors put political matters on the table, so to speak—and sometimes keep them off.

For anyone at all to consider the politics of constructivism through the contents of this book would be a political act. I have been involved with constructivism from its beginnings in IR. I have definite ideas about what makes constructivism an effective and comprehensive framework for social inquiry. These considerations will no doubt prompt many readers to see me, and any considerations that I put forward, as partisan. Just so. Politics are always partisan.

For convenience, I divide the politics of constructivism five ways. There is nothing natural or necessary about this division, and the ensuing discussion will make it clear how much overlap there is. First, I discuss what I will be calling identity politics. Consideration of IR as a discipline points out the issue of identity for many scholars. Gender and generational considerations also play a part in identity politics.

Second, I give some consideration to what I will be calling status politics. Status ordering is as much a feature of academic life as it is of social life in general, and, of course, status ordering is preeminently a political matter. Third, I will discuss the politics of language. Constructivists differ on the importance that they ascribe to language in social construction. Even when they agree on its importance, they differ on the ways that language does the work of social construction. These differences are deep, and they are political.

Linked to the politics of language is the century long struggle over appropriate methods for scholarly inquiry in social contexts. Endemic, inordinately divisive, and frequently destructive, this struggle remains unchanged in its basic terms. Positivists claim to have a methodical interest in seeing how the world works, and their opponents claim that positivists see little and know less. Whether constructivists have something to offer beyond the usual claims for or against positivism—something *postpositivist* in any practical sense—is another, inevitably political, question. Its consideration is my fourth task.

Finally, I consider what, for lack of a better label, I will be calling personal politics. Of course, politics are always personal. I mean here, though, that all of the contributors participate politically in a wide variety of social arrangements. They are scholars, but not simply scholars. As people, they have generalized political stances affecting their political responses to constructivism as a particular social reality, and frequently motivating their choice of particular scholarly undertakings in the name of constructivism. Conversely, constructivism seems to imply a generalized political stance that confines its appeal to scholars who fall within a certain range of personal political proclivities.

Identity Politics

In the world of scholarship, disciplinary identities loom large. Most contributors to this volume are constructivists, describing themselves as such in accordance with a set of understandings specific to IR. That IR is a discipline is a "social fact" that several contributors assert and not one of them contests. That IR, as a discipline, is a source of identity is a related social fact that they all seem to take for granted. On the very first page of this book, the editors say that "constructivism occupies a central place in the discipline." The discipline is unnamed, because *we* know what it is and to whom it belongs. When we celebrate *our* importance to *our* discipline, both its existence and our scholarly identities are strengthened. This is, of course, co-constitution at work.

I suggest that this process of co-constitution depends, as is so often the case, on the presence of an unnamed, but hardly unknown "other," which (we have no doubt) denies a central place to constructivism, lowers the value of our scholarly labors, and diminishes our identities. More colloquially, I suggest that Political Science is the elephant in the living room. After all, IR is but one of several "fields" offered in Political Science departments in the United States, and scholars trained in these departments are strongly encouraged to identify themselves as political scientists in the first instance. It is how I identify myself. Indicatively, one of the most cited pieces of constructivist scholarship in IR (Wendt 1994) appeared in the *American Political Science Review*.

In a country the size of the United States, domestic politics give Political Science its iron core, and the state gives a magnetic, or perhaps I should say polarized, ordering to the discipline. As a consequence, those of us whose interests lie outside the state are left on the outer margins of the discipline. Proclaiming that relations among states are *prima facie* political fails to impress our colleagues, precisely because they are better disciplined than we are. As political scientists, we all know how the iron filings line up and where they point.

If this already seems like a grim picture, its status implications make it even worse (more on this in the next section). Nevertheless, North American scholars in the field of IR seem generally content to identify themselves as political scientists, however marginalized. That they do so confirms the power of both their disciplinary socialization and the extensive institutional benefits that fall to them even on the margins of Political Science. The movement to make IR into a discipline and to give constructivism a central place in the discipline—in my opinion, they are, at least at this juncture, substantially the same movement—has come largely from outside of North America. More than this, the movement's members are disposed to confirm their disciplinary identity by setting themselves apart from, and even in opposition to, Political Science and its all too evident infatuation with rational choice. As a thoroughly marginalized political scientist, I see some irony here, because constructivism pretty much got its start in North America.

I also think that this rather complicated constitutive process (and these processes always are complicated) brings significant costs with it. Disciplinary frontiers work the way all frontiers are supposed to. They limit trafficking, foster autonomy and some measure of self-reliance, protect infant industries with significant productive prospects (such as constructivism), give people a sense of common purpose and make them feel comfortable. Whether these are good things for whole societies, I do not think they are generally much good for scholars—especially those whose disciplinary domain is so lacking in "natural boundaries" and subject to poaching.

In short, the cost of independence from Political Science is keeping everything else out too. Trafficking among the disciplines stimulates novel lines of inquiry (even if some of them turn out to be empty fads) and limits the well known propensity to reinvent the wheel. Frontiers discourage visits to other disciplines, and smuggling anything back is hard and risky work. Protected industries never live up to their potential, common purpose gives way to conformity, and comfort yields complacency. Is this what *we* want?

Knud Erik Jørgensen remarks in passing that "Onuf wants to reconstruct the entire IR discipline" (p. 42). Lest it be thought that my aim is to fortify IR, let me repeat myself: "The reconstruction of International Relations requires that the discipline be stripped of its current pretensions. If this is taken as abandonment of International Relations (the discipline as it is) and the abandonment of international theory (theory peculiar to International Relations), then I agree" (Onuf 1989, p. 27). A decade later, I think it was a tactical mistake even to concede the premise that IR *is* a discipline. My hope then was to open IR to social theory, itself a "force field" transcending disciplines. This remains my hope, and I still think constructivism does the job. At least it *can* do the job if it is not commandeered for frontier defense. Far more importantly, constructivism can do the job if we think of it as a comprehensive framework joining many elements of social theory and covering social relations of every sort.

While the contributors to this volume seem generally to share the conviction that IR is a discipline and that constructivism has an important place in making it so, they are remarkably free from defensive tirades on this subject. With commendable self-assurance, several contributors pick up important strands of social theory and bring them to bear on issues and problems of international relations. Yet they do so, in the name of constructivism, without showing how any one strand of social theory might fit with other strands also put forward in the name of constructivism. The effect is to bring a variety of conceptual materials to IR and to suggest that anyone who does so is a constructivist. In this process, IR seems to go its own rather aimless way.

Though claiming to be centrally placed, constructivists in particular seem to lack any clear sense of direction. Issues of identity hardly suffice. Other issues and developments get short shrift. Consider Ben Rosamond's telling assessment (Chapter 10) of constructivist neglect in the instance of globalization. More generally, there seems to be an informal hands off policy towards anything that might be described as political economy. The distaste most constructivists feel for material considerations on the one hand and rational choice theory on the other is a poor excuse for ceding this territory to other scholars.

In short, constructivists exhibit an unbecoming insularity. Constructivism ends up being less than the sum of its parts. The reigning version of international theory—far too limiting to serve any longer as a disciplinary core—suffers ritual condemnation. Yet constructivists propose nothing as systematic, but less limiting, to replace it.

At least Mathias Albert (Chapter 5) wants to think about social theory as broadly and systematically as I believe circumstances require. For reasons that I investigate below, his invocation of modern systems theory is convincing, if at all, then only as an alternative to constructivism. Friedrich Kratochwil's contribution (Chapter 1) works from just the sort of framework I have in mind—one he introduced some years ago—and expressly seeks to dismantle disciplinary barriers, in this instance between IR and International Law. Simply by reviewing Kratochwil's early work, along with my own and Alexander Wendt's, Maja Zehfuss (Chapter 3) makes it all too clear that most constructivists have done little or nothing to address, much less resolve, the limitations and contradictions that she identifies in her sympathetic treatment of those early efforts.

There is one glaring limitation in constructivist scholarship from the beginning—one that Birgit Locher and Elisabeth Prügl have little sympathy for in Chapter 4. Constructivism emerged at a time of extraordinary intellectual ferment. During that time feminist scholarship came to the fore, defying disciplinary frontiers, challenging comfortable assumptions, and generally shaking things up as it did so. Furthermore, feminists made the social construction of gender a central concern. Even so, early constructivists drew little evident inspiration from feminist scholarship.

As one of those early constructivists, I should say that feminist concerns mattered to me personally, altered my own sense of identity, and reinforced my conviction that constitutive processes are central to social relations of every sort. I still feel this way, and yet there is little direct evidence of these convictions in my work. (Not using masculine pronouns counts for something perhaps, but not much.) It would be disingenuous for me to deny the relevance of status politics and its disciplining effects. Forging alliances with feminist scholars was sure to compound marginality, while bowing to the great social theorists (virtually all of them male and sexist) was a plausible source of legitimacy.

I think there was more—something more subtle and yet still political—involved in keeping feminist scholarship at arm's length. Angry and frustrated at the power of existing, masculinist social constructions, many feminist scholars decried patriarchy as an overarching system of rule. Much concerned with rule myself, I considered this claim to be overly general. Rule and domination are not to be confused; rendering the concept of domination in class terms only added to the confusion. Perhaps unfairly, I saw in this state of affairs a certain tendency among feminist scholars to avoid thinking in systematic terms. As a matter of politics, many of them believed that thinking systematically is a masculine conceit, or worse, a patriarchical ploy, and they scorned the existing stock of social theory because it was indispensable to the social construction of patriarchy. As Locher and Prügl make clear, feminist scholarly identity has come at a price that a fresh generation of feminist scholars no longer needs to pay.

The first generation of constructivists came out of a troubled time—a decade or so—in the world of scholarship. Great challenges from intellectual movements, including feminism, had swept through all the social sciences. Those of us who were not much satisfied to start with went back to basics. Some of us ended up repudiating even the basics, and others tried to think through the implications of new basics, no matter how tenuous we knew them to be. We shared a sense that all is basically provisional, and beyond that a certain improvisational sensibility.

The first generation tried to improvise systematically (the oxymoron suggests, if not the absurdity, then the abstruseness, of the undertaking), and we took social theory seriously in this perhaps naive and certainly daunting quest. The next generation of constructivists exhibit the same improvisational flair. As I said above, they do not seem to have the same systematic intentions. First generation frameworks are not so much insufficient as irrelevant to second generation needs. All that the second generation seems to think it needs is a few bare propositions about social construction and its consequences. Just as irrelevant to the second generation is the intellectual and social context of the 1980s, which helped give first generation frameworks their recondite character.

"By engaging ourselves in debates on constructivism and other matters, we inevitably run the risk of forgetting or neglecting what obviously should remain the substance of International Relations, namely international relations" (Jørgensen, p. 34). This admonition hardly applies to many constructivists of the second generation. For them, the fall of the Berlin wall and the demise of the Soviet Union are the relevant sources of inspiration, not scholarly debates preceding these events. Constructivism is shapeless and episodic because most constructivists see the post-1989 world that way. In this process of social construction, constructivist claims of being at the center of IR render the field incoherent.

Status Politics

Scholars occupy tight little worlds. Even more important than disciplinary frontiers are those that separate the vocation of scholarship from other walks of life. Scholars impose steep fees for admission to their worlds—years of doctoral training—and inculcate strict rules of conduct, including rules by which to evaluate performance. Any such system of rules constitutes a condition of rule by distributing resources preferentially. Some of these resources are materially important for larger social contexts—successful scholars live better than those whom the rules define as less successful. Nevertheless, small worlds always have one locally prized resource that its rules constitute from even the most meager materials. These same rules also distribute this resource internally (albeit with external effects), never equally, and always to great regulative effect.

That resource is, of course, status. Scholars are notoriously preoccupied with their scholarly reputations. As institutions, universities are marked internally by striking distinctions in status, and their importance in conferring status throughout society has grown immensely. In an allegedly egalitarian society such as the United States, higher education is a peerless status marker. As constructivists would expect, institutional status inevitably affects scholarly reputations, and the reverse is just as true. Disciplines have status orderings in which individual reputations and institutional affiliations are closely related.

Hegemony is the best name for the condition of rule in which status is the dominant consideration. Status decides who will speak about what, and whether others will listen. Since status is common knowledge, scholars use it as the first and most important clue to the quality of scholarship—their own and others. In this context, it is useful to speak of a "hegemonic discourse" without implying that the contents of any such discourse are perfectly homogeneous or that high status scholars scrupulously monitor what lower status scholars have to say. Hegemony works because all scholars in the discipline have internalized the rules and monitor themselves accordingly.

Among the contributors to this volume, only two actually speak of hegemonic discourse: Kratochwil and Jennifer Milliken. In Milliken's case, she does so as part of scholarly movement critically concerned with hegemony wherever it occurs. In Kratochwil's case, his concern with hegemonic discourse is intensely personal and very much bound up in his efforts to have his own scholarly voice heard. The context for this struggle was the turbulent decade of the 80s, when, to use Kratochwil's words, a "rather motley crew of researchers who got defined as the "outgroup" (p. 14) actively, self-consciously sought to outflank the hegemonic center. The members of this crew included Hayward Alker, Richard Ashley, Matthew Bonham, Robert Cox, James Der Derian, Raymond Duvall, Jean Elshtain, Cynthia Enloe, Yale Ferguson, Kratochwil, Richard Mansbach, James Rosenau, John Ruggie, Michael Shapiro, R. B. J. Walker, and Wendt. I too was among them, and I may well have neglected to mention others.

These scholars stood at different points in their career trajectories. Some of us had always straddled disciplinary frontiers. Some had impressive institutional affiliations. Being "outside" is a relative, highly subjective matter dependent on not being too far out to start with. All of us saw ourselves as relative outsiders in a specifically North American frame of reference. We struggled for our identity, day by day, in the hegemonic immediacy of Political Science departments whose members overwhelmingly spoke in a different voice. When Robert Keohane (1988) took the occasion of his ISA Presidential speech to divide IR into two camps, rationalist and reflectivist, he made public the "in" and "out"-dynamics that all of us knew all too well.

This motley crew took different routes in flanking the hegemonic center. By seeking to upset hegemonic assumptions about the subject matter of international relations, Ferguson and Mansbach (1988, 1996) and Rosenau (1990) went one way. Cox (1996 *passim*) went straight ahead with a withering critical assault. Quite a number of us sought inspiration and legitimacy by reaching across to other disciplines, especially those that accord a higher status to the postpositivist movement than Political Science ever has. Sharing little beyond a taste for philosophy and social theory, we sorted ourselves into two loose groups—postmoderns and constructivists—in even looser affiliation with feminist and post-Marxist critical scholars. In this struggle against hegemonic discourse, there was neither the possibility nor the disposition to speak in a single voice and thus to forge a hegemonic counter-hegemonic discourse.

In almost every respect, these challenges to hegemony failed. If anything, they put hegemonic leaders on alert as high status departments shifted toward rational choice theorizing (with unsettling implications for political theorists, many of whom took postpositivist premises seriously). As Kratochwil suggests, the motley crew is still just that, and discourse just as hegemonic as ever in North America. There is, however, one respect in which the ground shifted.

Ranking political scientists saw in Wendt's brand of constructivism an opportunity to widen the scope of acceptable discourse and make it somewhat more pluralist. This they accomplished without changing status ordering in the field of IR or indeed acknowledging the motley crew's ragged chorus of challenges. Once sanitized, constructivism's enshrinement as one of three ways to go about the study of international relations (Katzenstein, Keohane, and Krasner 1998) comes as no surprise. Nor is it any surprise that North American constructivism is a bland and featureless victim of its own success (but see Jørgensen, p. 43, for a somewhat more charitable assessment).

Outside of North America, constructivism has experienced a quite different fate. Europeans have by and large not been encumbered with IR's inclusion in Political Science or indeed the hegemonic tightening that the latter has undergone in North America. Europeans tend to view the dissident challenges to 1980s orthodoxy as so many menu choices, free for the sampling. Broadly conceived, constructivism has fared well in these circumstances.

On the evidence of this volume, European scholars are refreshingly indifferent to the rigors of status politics in North American universities. For them, IR is a discipline blessed by the absence of a hegemonic discourse. There is no disciplining, because North American rules do not hold. As I suggested above, there may not be quite enough discipline either. Constructivism offers more than the scholarly equivalent of a free lunch. The first generation of constructivists had good reasons to try to be as systematic as they could, and the next generation does not have to relive the political struggle of the first generation to build on their efforts and accomplish far more.

Nevertheless, taking constructivism seriously—I mean conceptually, as a framework for understanding social relations in general—does involve a risk. Many scholars will turn to that framework in the mistaken hope that it is, or leads to, a general, field defining theory—a proper successor to theory predicated on anarchy as a distinctive condition—that would permit IR to stand on its own as a discipline. Constructivism would have earned its central place, but it could also become a hegemonic discourse. Given enough time and resources, this process of reconstructing IR around a new orthodoxy is likely to take place whatever scholars do in the name of constructivism. I would like to think, however, that constructivists could speak for systematic thinking and against hegemony, and that doing so would make some sort of difference as IR globalizes.

The Politics of Language

The editors assert that they and the other contributors to this book "challenge the idea that constructivism is what IR scholars make of it" (p. 4). In my opinion, this assertion is wrong—it fails to represent the contents of the book accurately. Moreover, it would be wrongheaded in my opinion to make any such challenge, at least from (what I assert to be) a constructivist point of view. Constructivism is pretty much what a number of scholars *have* made it, first by identifying themselves as constructivists, then by setting out in their work an ensemble of propositions that they believe are necessary to constructivism, and finally by accepting, at least implicitly, the constitutive consequences of overlapping propositional structures. Insofar as professed constructivists issue incompatible propositions, they have made a mess of constructivism.

From the beginning, constructivists have differed on one fundamental proposition. Zehfuss locates the difference in the way Kratochwil, Wendt, and I conceptualize intersubjectivity, which all three of us, and constructivists in general, regard as the key to understanding social reality. For Kratochwil and me, but not for Wendt, "language is central for the analysis of politics" (p. 51; notice Zehfuss's assumption that intersubjectivity is a political affair). Zehfuss is entirely right to make as much as she does of this difference, because it is the fundamental fissure in constructivism and the deepest source of its incoherence. I see little reason to celebrate, and much reason to put language to work—the political work of persuading constructivist scholars that we must all make language central if we are to make more of constructivism than we have yet.

By leaving language out of consideration, Wendt confirmed the one way that it has always been central to modern social inquiry. Language allows its users to represent and communicate states of affairs more or less accurately. As a consequence, language makes the objective world intersubjectively available, and disciplined inquiry can make intersubjective understanding more reliable. I have no quarrel with these propositions *as far as they go*. Because the propositional structure of Wendt's constructivism goes no further, it could be absorbed into the hegemonic discourse of North America without undue discomfort on either side. It cannot be reconciled with claims that language does more for its users than represent the world as it or as they might want it to be.

Scholars making these sorts of claims are conventionally said to have taken the linguistic turn. Kratochwil and I self-consciously took this turn, but not as far as some of the other dissidents. They disputed the proposition that linguistic representations ever correspond to an objective world, at least insofar as we language users could ever know. The result was another fissure, perhaps as deep as the one dividing us from Wendt. On the one side are those constructivists who think that language is indispensable to social construction, and on the other side are postmodern scholars who think that there is nothing beyond language as social construction.

Insofar as linguistic phenomena cannot represent the world, they constitute a world of their own, a world true only to itself. Words are performative, but only in a theatrical sense. By enacting the propositional content of what is spoken, any such performance simultaneously objectivizes the world it creates and hides behind its representational success. Inevitably, bringing this performative trick into the limelight shifts attention to the self-representing propositional content of whatever is spoken, which the observer aspires to represent intelligibly, and thus more or less accurately. Therein lies the paradox of postmodern scholarship: Identifying an ensemble of spoken performances as hegemonic discourse depends on participating in a hegemonic discourse—it takes one to know one.

Of all the contributors, Milliken is perhaps the most in debt to postmodern scholarship. She is also acutely aware of the paradox that I just identified. To her credit, she refuses to escape it by rejecting the possibility of rigorous research. Her intention is rather to identify methods for the critical study of discourse that meet the *kind* of standards that positivists insist on when they claim at least some degree of success in representing the world as it is.

Since Milliken is critical of any such claim and its hegemonic consequences, her standards must be rigorous enough to survive positivist criticism and yet they must be critically transparent. They must also be elastic enough to suit a fully realized conception of discourse. She succeeds admirably in meeting the first of these requirements, and she does well enough in meeting the second. If she is less successful in meeting the third requirement, she is hardly alone in this respect. In my opinion, no one with critical intentions or postmodern sensibilities has represented *representation* appropriately and thus conceptualized discourse adequately.

Representations are the objects of Milliken's critical attention. She speculates, for example, that "a researcher might find that in different texts Japan was repeatedly represented by emotion predicates (e.g., "fear," "desire") in contrast to the United States, represented via judgment predicates ("weigh options")" (p. 130). As a matter of method, Milliken offers up a highly plausible empirical generalization—a representation of some general state of affairs—and proposes that a detailed examination of representative statements will bear out the accuracy of her general statement. Repeating the process in slightly different terms (say, by identifying "immaturity predicates") will enable the researcher to make yet more general statements meeting the same tests of credibility.

I do not wish to suggest that Milliken has carelessly slipped into just those practices that the "postmodern critique of foundationalism" (p. 124) would have her reject. Precisely because she is careful and methodical in just the way that we (hegemonically speaking) would want all scholars to be, she has no choice but to try to represent states of affairs as fairly and accurately as she can, and to try to persuade us that she has done so successfully. She wants us to think that her statements about hegemonic discourse are truths about the world—provisional, limited truths all too vulnerable to misrepresentation and misappropriation. No constructivist should have any difficulty with such a claim, because any world that we make by speaking is nevertheless an objective condition for us who make it.

From a constructivist point of view, the problem with the critical study of discourse is that it is too narrow in representing language as a means of social construction. If we look carefully at Milliken's method, we see that she gives the idea of representation two meanings. The propositional content of any sentence represents some state of affairs, and the sentence itself represents that state of affairs to be true about the world. This second sense of the term *represent* is somewhat archaic. We are more likely to *assert* the truth of some state of affairs. Any number of other verbs also do the job.

Recall the series of assertions that I made, with obvious rhetorical intentions, at the beginning of this section. Milliken's careful representation of predicate analysis (in the first sense of the term) took the form of a series of assertions about discourse (representations, in the second sense). To be socially meaningful, language must *have* propositional content (I think that everyone agrees with this assertion), and it must *do* something systematic with that content (here Milliken and quite a number of other contributors would seem to part company with Wendt, for example). Assertions *produce* social meaning by securing their acceptance. When they succeed in doing so, hegemony reigns, at least to the limits of the discourse that accepted assertions may be said to produce. Indeed Milliken wishes "to explain how a discourse *produces* this [any social] world" (p. 132, her emphasis).

Production is not just, or even chiefly, a material process. The term also suggests a theatrical event, all the more engrossing for not being deliberately staged. As a metaphor, it appeals to postmodern sensibilities about the properties of language, but it also is a metaphor that constructivists can favor when they assert that speech acts operate in different ways to bring about systematic social (and material) effects. Kratochwil made this point earlier in the book and drew several important conclusions, all of which are crucial to a fully developed constructivist position. Since I agree with him so emphatically, I will quote him at some length (p. 29).

> The discovery of speech acts has had revolutionary implications not only for linguistic theory but also for social science in general. Since it can be shown that speech acts are incredibly numerous, ranging from demanding, to appointing, to apologizing, to asserting, and threatening, etc., its relevance for the analysis of social life is hardly controversial. [The "etc." conspicuously includes promising, which Kratochwil turns to a little later.] The other point is that speech acts are constituted by norms [or rules, which speech acts in turn produce]. . . . Only within a practice governed by certain institutional rules will a certain utterance have any meaning. Finally, we can show that it is through such institutional arrangements that we, as members of society, constantly bridge the gap between the "is" and the "ought." . . .

Discourse does indeed—in *deed*—produce the social world. The speech acts constituting discourse consist of much more than assertions, and they produce much more than hegemony. That they do produce (the rules that constitute) hegemony is always important to remember but never sufficient for critical scholarship. There is more to language than representation, and more to the social world than "the politics of representation" (Milliken, p. 124).

Methodenstreit

Kratochwil's final point about the way that we bridge the gap between *is* and *ought* is a telling one, and I will return to it presently. While the gap itself may find its origins with David Hume, its importance to us as scholars is chiefly due to the great methodological struggle—*Methodenstreit*—that took place in German language scholarship a century ago. Dignified as a debate, it more closely resembles a civil war that never ends because neither side will accept defeat or offer peace. As a measure of its continuing importance, a large majority of the contributions to this volume dwell on one or more of the several issues that have set the terms of debate from the beginning. Several of these contributions suffer from the perceived need to take sides.

Karin Fierke's contribution (Chapter 6) points out the divisive power of competing hegemonic discourses, which, to her great credit, she has been seeking to dampen through an ongoing dialogue with Michael Nicholson (Fierke and Nicholson, Forthcoming). In Fierke's hands, the great struggle has its apotheosis in a single, compelling figure—Ludwig Wittgenstein. Her characterization is a useful one (p. 112).

> In the empirical tradition data is derived from experience or observation. Data is defined in contrast to theory, but provides the necessary foundation for testing theory. As such, the word "empirical," and the data/theory dichotomy, presuppose a correspondence theory of truth. Wittgenstein criticizes this way of "knowing," and indeed his own earlier work in the *Tractatus*, which was a source of inspiration for the logical positivists of the Vienna Circle. He presents an alternative approach to the relationship between language and the world. Analysis from this angle is not properly empirical as this word has traditionally been used.

Following convention, Fierke starts with a methodological point to expose an epistemological problem: Representations of the world do not correspond to the world as it is, because language conveys "meaning in use" (p. 111). Using language constitutes the world. For that world to have any sort of intersubjective meaning, it must be constituted, not just in our practices, but finally in our heads. Knowing what the world means to us is not to be confused with explaining how the world works. Fierke finally comes back to the methodological point. Explanation depends on observation and description, but these empirically oriented activities are too fraught with meaning to serve the purpose conventionally ascribed to them. Figuring out what we mean by what we say is an empirically oriented activity that produces, rather incidentally, a different understanding of what we mean when we say that something is empirical.

Despite her inclusive understanding of what it means to be empirical, Fierke's stance forces her to choose up. The conventional terms of choice are explanation versus understanding (and see Jørgensen, p. 41, for some current variations), the first a search for objective cause and the second for intersubjective meaning. At least for Fierke, the latter search does not prohibit discovery through "causal inference," but allows it only in the context of meanings ruled by language use (p. 115). When she says that "reasons or justifications are *not* causes; rather they constitute a framework for action" (p. 105, my emphasis), her choice is clear.

Her reasons are not so clear. My choices in life may have causes apart from the reasons that I offer for them, but in the process of reflecting on my choices, my reasons assume causal force—they contribute to an explanation of my actions. No less do they contribute to the framework for action, which, as a whole, gives meaning to my reflections and makes my choices understandable. Obviously, there is no simple correspondence between reasons and causes. Nevertheless, observing myself, for example, I can identify innumerable occasions in which it makes sense for me to say that my reasons are causes for my conduct. Unless I and others could assume as much, it is difficult for me to think why any of us should worry about reasons at all.

To the extent reasons function as causes, they are subject to empirical assessment (in the narrow sense) and explanation—*rational* assessment. After rational assessment, I make choices that I expect to have causal effects that I desire—that is my reason for making them. By supposing rational assessment, rational choice theory effectively explains quite a few of the choices that I routinely make. It is much less useful for understanding the context of my choices, since I do not rationally choose my framework for action. Instead it is constituted by the ongoing stream of choices that I and others make, reasons that we offer, and material constraints that we are obliged to take into account when we make choices.

Remember Kratochwil's amusing tale of the rational choice theorist (p. 13): With a hammer like this, the whole world is a nail. Indeed the whole world is not a nail. By insisting that it is, the rational choice theorist chooses a position, as uncompromising as it is untenable, on the other side of the great struggle. Constructivists for their part should always bear in mind how many nails—rational agents and their choices—it takes to hold a world together. Hammering away at them is hard to condemn, so long as it is not the only thing that scholars do. North American hegemony seems to leave little choice, but I do not find this a convincing reason for methodological chauvinism.

The rational choice theorist who talks about wholes is already in trouble. On the other side, Wittgenstein had good reason to treat context "as a whole consisting of the language and actions into which it is woven" (Fierke, p. 120, quoting Wittgenstein 1958). As Albert observes in his contribution, consideration of wholes and parts goes back to Aristotle, and so does "the paradox inherent in the distinction between a whole and its parts (the paradox that something is at the same time one and many)" (p. 96). Insofar as a whole is the sum of its parts and their relations, I see no paradox. As a constructivist, I see great value in describing social processes relating parts (agents, for example) to wholes (institutions, observed structures) as processes of co-constitution. Wrongly, in my opinion, Albert calls this sort of undertaking "a last attempt to process the paradox of the whole/parts scheme" (p. 97).

Nevertheless, the Aristotelian scheme is paradoxical if it is taken to mean that the whole is greater than the sum of its parts and their relations. Albert sees no paradox in this position, just a solution to the confusion over parts and whole. He would have us forget parts altogether, and think about systems exclusively. Parts in relation to the whole become "autopoietic functional subsystems" (p. 100; *cf.* p. 88). Albert's highly compressed exposition of one important version of modern systems theory—Niklas Luhmann's—is not very likely to persuade many native English speakers to turn to Luhmann's systematic work for guidance. Constructivists have no reason to do so.

Albert notes (p. 102, n. 14) that differences between Luhmann and Jürgen Habermas have shaped thirty years of German debate (a late episode in a hundred years of *Methodenstreit*). Constructivists have found much of value in Habermas's systematic efforts to develop a theory of social action, not least because it makes the uses of language its central feature. Two contributors—Harald Müller (Chapter 8) and Lars Lose (Chapter 9)—adopt Habermas's distinction between strategic and communicative action, the former aptly modeled by rational choice theory and the latter, oriented to understanding, modeled by the conditions under which the use of language makes understanding possible. Communicative success produces a shared lifeworld, to which both Müller and Lose attach much importance as social construction.

Müller gives fair warning. "Strategic and communicative action are ideal types. In everyday action they cannot be distinguished from one another and occur simultaneously" (p. 147). For political reasons, both contributors devote most of their attention to conditions that would enlarge understanding, and find themselves obliged to live by the methodological consequences. Conceived as a framework for action, lifeworld takes over as a frame of reference. As that frame of reference becomes more general, its contents become harder to specify in any useful or convincing way. For Müller, lifeworlds end up being indistinguishable from cultures (p. 159). According to Lose, diplomats make a lifeworld for themselves in which "confidence, reason, empathy, understanding, reciprocity, knowledge and judgment are assigned a high priority" (p. 172). Not found in most people's lives most of the time, these conditions are unlikely to describe diplomatic life in nearly the degree that Lose surmises (but see p. 182).

The problem comes from contriving two worlds in the abstract—a world of strategic action and a world of understanding—where there is but one social world, or the infinitely many worlds of everyday life. Müller quite properly points out that strategic considerations do "not disappear in a fog of discursive understanding," and that the "rational choice approach, as long as it is conscious of its own limitations, remains an indispensable component of theory and of empirical analysis even within the framework of a theory of communicative action" (p. 158). If there are indeed "two types of action," as he immediately goes on to say (p. 158), then they take place in one world, or infinitely many. They do so constantly, but in ever changing relation. In this process—a process to which language is central— they constitute each other as types of action.

The close relation between types of action parallels the close relation between fact and values. This gap exists because language enables us to think about actions two ways. There are actions that we may or will perform, and those that we should or must perform. Language and, as Kratochwil suggests, the institutional arrangements that come of language use also enable us to jump back and forth across the gap with such extraordinary ease and grace that we do it all the time.

A reason becomes a cause with a turn of phrase: "I should write Karin because . . ." "I will write her because . . . ." This ceaseless traffic between is and ought makes our world whole—seemingly seamless and pervasively normative. If we stop on either side and stand back, we can pick out parts, find causes, offer reasons and make judgments. As scholars, and as lifetime language users, we should be as competent in stopping and standing back on either side as we are in shuttling across the gap. As constructivists, we do well to accept the gap for what it is, and pay attention to all the traffic across it. This is postpositivism in practice.

Personal Politics

Scholars are taught to keep ourselves—our personal concerns and political commitments—out of our work. We hide behind passive constructions and the global "we." This is no doubt one deep consequence of *Methodenstreit*: we *should* stay on the *is* side of the gap between is and ought. Feminist and critical scholars self-consciously resist this mandate, and signs of resistance are easy to spot in Locher and Prügl's and Milliken's contributions to this volume. Jørgensen also has quite a bit to say about personal politics, but not his own. He deems it a "fact"—correctly in my opinion—that "for some reason liberals have been more active than realists and globalists in promoting the constructivist turn." But what *is* the reason?

As a matter of status politics, if realists hold the hegemonic high ground, then they need no help from constructivism. Lumped with globalists and tarred as idealists, liberal institutionalists found their deliverance in constructivism. Idealists to the end, globalists are happy to have liberals find a banner of their own. Yet this short story demands a second telling. Realists are, after all, on the right side of the general political spectrum. Their geopolitical antecedents, security concerns, and preoccupation with stability fit this profile. Adding concerns over human welfare and dignity to the agenda, liberal institutionalists stand to the left of realists. With transformational politics in mind, globalists stand even farther to the left.

This picture is more or less complete for the United States, where constructivism offset the neoliberal rapprochement with neorealism (a move to the right in general political terms, and in keeping with the times). Beleaguered liberal institutionalists found a fresh voice in constructivism and successfully used it to ask for hegemonic legitimation in a centrist alliance. Such alliances look good, undercut resistance and cost the dominant partners little enough. Those few scholars in the United States with critical sensibilities immediately saw the deal for what it was, and they have kept their distance from constructivism.

Events in Europe tell a different story. Larger, more vital and more leftward, the European left included social welfarists and Marxists in several hues. The great changes symbolized by 1989 forced the left to regroup, in the process redefining itself and its understanding of the world. Among European scholars on the left, one consequence was the surge of interest in IR, not as a relatively conservative field of North American Political Science, but as a discipline in its own right.

In this context, constructivism had an obvious appeal. Its dissident origins in North America made it more palatable than most imports, all the more because the dissidents had fashioned it from European social theory. Liberal institutionalists in Europe needed no accommodation because most of them already had International Law as a well furnished disciplinary home. European constructivists pushed realists aside by reconceptualizing security (Waever 1995; Buzan, Waever and de Wilde 1998), and settled themselves at the center of the discipline. North American constructivists are welcome sojourners so long as they keep their imperial tendencies under control, and quite a number have become permanent residents.

In this pleasant story, constructivism is more homogenous than a closer look shows it to be. Scholars from across the left turned to constructivism, finding in it renewed hope for social understanding, a framework for programs of social and political reconstruction, or a critical instrument for political emancipation. Others had the label pinned on them, whether they thought it suited their political outlook or conceptual needs. Personal political preferences this diverse are not always reconcilable. There will always be politically motivated calls to be constructivist in prescribed ways. Here Fierke is right: reasons and justifications loom large, not for what they say about causes, but for what they say about intentions—good intentions, as others judge them.

Under the broad mantle of constructivism, there is no justification in making emancipatory commitments a political test. As Jørgensen points out, I have made this complaint before (pp. 43–44). Nevertheless, because my personal sympathies are with the left, I do feel the need to justify my mandarin detachment (as I have had it described to me more than once). I offer two justifications, one negative and one positive.

First, the negative justification: Critical scholars have fooled themselves into thinking that their actions meaningfully challenge systems of rule. Yet these same scholars have an impoverished understanding of how rules in conjunction with speech acts yield systems of rule (international relations constituting one such system) and, in this process, distribute privilege. In my opinion, critical scholars share with liberals an aversion to questions of rule because they associate social theory focused on these questions with the rise of fascism. Systematically conceived, constructivism provides the requisite understanding without its unsavory political associations (also see Locher and Prügl, p. 191).

Underlying this negative justification is a positive one. As Zehfuss remarks, "constructivist arguments suggest that academic discourse and social reality influence each other" (p. 68). Scholarship *is* political. Zehfuss goes on to say that "Onuf's and Kratochwil's apparent reluctance to address the blood and sweat flowing in international relations every day need not deter those wishing to do so from using their insights" (p. 69). The large point is well taken. Yet there are two ways I would rephrase it.

What flows in international relations every day are blood, sweat and words, words, words. Zehfuss intimates that neither Kratochwil nor I deal sufficiently with the specific conditions—blood and sweat, and other words—in which words do their work. This is no doubt because we cannot escape the abstract thinking that governs our systematic constructions, and makes them more than "insights." What we have tried to do, necessarily at a high level of abstraction, "throws a new light on the question of knowledge and the problem of privilege" (p. 69)—or so I believe—without dictating a particular political stance to anyone who would put our words to work.

Note

1. I am grateful to Elizabeth Prügl and Maja Zehfuss for comments on the first draft of this paper, and to members of the Miami International Relations Group for their support.

Bibliography

Abu-Lughod, Janet L. 1989. *Before European Hegemony: The World System A.D. 1250–1350.* New York: Oxford University Press.

Adler, Emanuel. 1992. "The Emergence of Cooperation: National Epistemic Communities and the International Evolution of the Idea of Nuclear Arms Control." *International Organization* 46(1): 101–145.

———. 1997. "Seizing the Middle Ground: Constructivism in World Politics." *European Journal of International Relations* 3(3): 319–363.

——— and Michael N. Barnett. 1998. *Security Communities.* Cambridge: Cambridge University Press.

Aggarwal, Vinod K. 1985. *Liberal Protectionism: The International Politics of Organized Textile Trade.* Berkeley: University of California Press.

Albert, Mathias. 1996. *Fallen der (Welt-)Ordnung. Internationale Beziehungen und ihre Theorien zwischen Moderne und Postmoderne.* Opladen: Leske und Budrich.

———. (in preparation). *The Politics of World Society: Identity, Law and Security.*

———, Lothar Brock and Klaus D. Wolf, eds. 2000. *Civilizing World Politics: Society and Community Beyond the State.* Lanham: Rowman and Littlefield.

Albrow, Martin. 1996. *The Global Age: State and Society Beyond Modernity.* Cambridge: Polity Press.

Alker, Hayward R. and David Sylvan. 1994. "Some Contributions of Discourse Analysis to Political Science." *Kosmopolis* 24(3): 5–25.

Andersen, Heine. 1988. *Rationalitet, velfærd og retfærdighed: belyst ud fra nyere samfundsvidenskabelige teorier.* København: Nyt Nordisk Forlag.

Andersen, Kenneth G. 1998. *The (Re)Construction of a Common Foreign and Security Policy for the European Union.* MA thesis, University of Aarhus, Department of Political Science.

Anderson, Benedict. 1983. *Imagined Communities: Reflections on the Origin and Spread of Nationalism.* London: Verso.

Appadurai, Arjun. 1990. "Disjuncture and Difference in the Global Cultural Economy." In *Global Culture: Nationalism, Globalization and Modernity,* ed. Mike Featherstone. London: Sage.

———. 1996. *Modernity at Large: Cultural Dimensions of Globalization.* Minneapolis: University of Minnesota Press.

Archer, Margaret S. 1988. *Culture and Agency: The Place of Culture in Social Theory.* Cambridge: Cambridge University Press.

Aristotle. 1962. *The Politics.* Thomas A. Sinclair, Trans. Harmondsworth: Penguin.

Aron, Raymond. 1967. "What Is a Theory of International Relations." *Journal of International Affairs* 21: 185–206.

Ashley, Richard K. 1981. "Political Realism and Human Interest." *International Studies Quarterly* 25 (2): 204–236.

————. 1986. "The Poverty of Neorealism." In *Neorealism and Its Critics*, ed. Robert O. Keohane. New York: Columbia University Press.

————. 1989. "Living on Border Lines: Man, Poststructuralism and War." In *International/Intertextual Relations: Postmodern Readings of World Politics*, eds. James Der Derian and Michael Shapiro. Lexington: Lexington Books.

————. 1996. "The Achievements of Post-structuralism." In *International Theory: Positivism and Beyond*, eds. Steve Smith, Ken Booth and Marysia Zalewski. Cambridge: Cambridge University Press.

———— and R.B.J. Walker. 1990a. "Reading Dissidence/Writing the Discipline: Crisis and the Question of Sovereignty in International Studies." *International Studies Quarterly* 34(3): 367–416.

———— and R.B.J. Walker. 1990b. "Speaking the Language of Exile: Dissident Thought in International Studies." *International Studies Quarterly* 34(3): 259–268.

Austin, John L. 1962. *How to Do Things with Words*. Cambridge, Mass.: Harvard University Press.

Axford, Barrie. 1995. *The Global System: Politics, Economics and Culture*. Cambridge: Polity Press.

Baines, Erin K. 1999. "Gender Constructions and the Protection Mandate of the UNHCR: Responses from Guatemalan Women." In *Gender Politics in Global Governance*, eds. Mary K. Meyer and Elisabeth Prügl. Lanham: Rowman and Littlefield.

Baldwin, David A., ed. 1993. *Neorealism and Neoliberalism: The Contemporary Debate*. New York: Columbia University Press.

Barkdull, John. 1995. "Waltz, Durkheim, and International Relations: the International System as an Abnormal Form." *American Political Science Review* 89(3): 669–680.

Barnett, Michael N. 1998. *Dialogues in Arab Politics: Negotiations in Regional Order*. New York: Columbia University Press.

Barston, Ronald P. 1988. *Modern Diplomacy*. London: Longman.

Bartelson, Jens. 1995. *A Genealogy of Sovereignty*. Cambridge: Cambridge University Press.

Bartos, O.J. 1977. "Simple Model of Negotiation." *Journal of Conflict Resolution* 21(4): 565–579.

Bates, Robert H., Avner Greif, Margaret Levi, Jean-Laurent Rosenthal, and Barry R. Weingast. 1998. *Analytic Narratives*. Princeton: Princeton University Press.

Baylis, John and Steve Smith. 1997. *The Globalization of World Politics: An Introduction to International Relations*. Oxford: Oxford University Press.

Baynes, Kenneth. 1992. *The Normative Grounds of Social Criticism: Kant, Rawls and Habermas*. Albany: State University of New York Press.

Beauvoir, Simone de. [1952]1989. *The Second Sex*. New York: Knopf.

Behnke, Andreas. 1996. "Ten Years After: The State of the Art of Regime Theory." *Cooperation and Conflict* 30(2): 179–197.

Benedick, Richard E. 1992. "Perspectives of a Negotiation Practitioner." In *International Environmental Negotiation*, ed. Gunnar Sjöstedt. Newsbury Park: Sage.

Benhabib, Seyla. 1992. *Situating the Self: Gender, Community and Postmodernism in Contemporary Ethics*. Oxford: Polity Press.

————. 1999. "Sexual Difference and Collective Identities: The New Global Constellation." *Signs: Journal of Women in Culture and Society* 24(2): 335–361.

————, Judith Butler, Drucilla Cornell and Nancy Fraser. 1995. *Feminist Contentions: A Philosophical Exchange*. New York: Routledge.

Ben-Ze'ev, Aaron. 1995. "Is There a Problem in Explaining Cognitive Progress?" In *Rethinking Knowledge: Reflections Across the Disciplines*, eds. Robert F. Goodman and Walter R. Fisher. Albany: State University of New York Press.

Berger, Peter L. 1986. "Epilogue." In *Making Sense of Modern Times: Peter L. Berger and the Vision of Interpretive Sociology*, eds. James D. Hunter and Stephen C. Ainley. London and New York: Routledge and Kegan Paul.

—— and Thomas Luckmann. 1966. *The Social Construction of Reality: A Treatise in the Sociology of Knowledge*. New York: Anchor Books.

Berger, Suzanne and Ronald Dore, eds. 1996. *National Diversity and Global Capitalism*. Ithaca: Cornell University Press.

Bernauer, Thomas. 1993. *The Chemistry of Regime Formation: Explaining International Cooperation for a Comprehensive Ban on Chemical Weapons*. Geneva: UNIDIR.

Beyme, Klaus von. 1991. "Regierungslehre zwischen Handlungstheorie und Systemansatz." In *Regieren in der Bundesrepublik 3: Systemsteuerug und "Staatskunst": Theoretische Konzepte und empirische Befunde*, eds. H. Hartwich and G. Wewer. Opladen: Leske & Buderick.

Bhaskar, Roy. 1979. *The Possibility of Naturalism*. Brighton: Harvester Press.

Biersteker, Thomas J. and Cynthia Weber, eds. 1996. *State Sovereignty as Social Construct*. Cambridge: Cambridge University Press.

Bigo, Didier. 1996. *Polices en réseaux: l'experience europeenne*. Paris: Presses de la Fondation Nationale des Sciences Politiques.

Bildt, Carl. 1998. *Peace Journey: The Struggle for Peace in Bosnia*. London: Weidenfeld and Nicolson.

Bourantonis, Dimitris. 1993. *The United Nations and the Quest for Nuclear Disarmament*. Aldershot: Dartmouth Publishing.

Bourdieu, Pierre and Loic J.D. Wacquant. 1992. *An Invitation to Reflexive Sociology*. Chicago: University of Chicago Press.

Boyer, Robert and Daniel Drache, eds. 1996. *States Against Markets*. London: Routledge.

Brittan, Leon. 1997a. "Globalisation: Responding to New Political and Moral Challenges." *Address to the World Economic Forum*. Davos, January.

——. 1997b. *Globalization vs. Sovereignty?: The European Response: The 1997 Rede Lecture and Related Speeches*. Cambridge: Cambridge University Press.

Brock, Lothar. 1991. "The European Experience and its Meaning for Central America." In *Peace Culture and Society: Transnational Research and Dialogue*, eds. Elise Boulding, Clovis Brigagao, and Kevin Clements. Boulder: Westview Press

——. 1994. "Brüche im Umbruch der Weltpolitik." In *Frieden und Konflikt in den Internationalen Beziehungen: Festschrift für Ernst-Otto Czempiel*, eds. G. Krell and H. Müller. Frankfurt a.M.: Campus.

Brown, Chris. 1997. *Understanding International Relations*. Basingstoke: Macmillan.

Brown, Wendy. 1995. *States of Injury: Power and Freedom in Late Modernity*. Princeton: Princeton University Press.

Buchheim, Robert and Philip J. Farley. 1988. "The U.S.-Soviet Consultative Commission." In *U.S.-Soviet Security Cooperation: Achievements, Failures, Lessons*, eds. Alexander L. George, Philip J. Farley, and Alexander Dallin. Oxford: Oxford University Press.

Bueno de Mesquita, Bruce. 1981. *The War Trap*. New Haven: Yale University Press.

—— and David Lalman. 1992. *War and Reason: Domestic and International Imperatives*. New Haven: Yale University Press.

Bull, Hedley. 1969. "International Theory: The Case for a Classical Approach." In *Contending Approaches to International Politics*, eds. Klaus Knorr and James N. Rosenau. Princeton: Princeton University Press.

——. 1977. *The Anarchical Society: A Study of Order in World Politics*. New York: Columbia University Press.

——— and Adam Watson, eds. 1984. *The Expansion of International Society*. Oxford: Clarendon.

Bunch, Charlotte. 1990. "Women's Rights as Human Rights: Toward a Re-vision of Human Rights." *Human Rights Quarterly* 12(4): 486–500.

Bundy, McGeorge. 1988. *Danger and Survival*. New York: Random House.

Bunn, George. 1992. *Arms Control By Committee: Managing Negotiations with the Russians*. Stanford: Stanford University Press.

Butler, Judith. 1990. *Gender Trouble: Feminism and the Subversion of Identity*. New York: Routledge.

———. 1993. *Bodies That Matter: On the Discursive Limits of 'Sex.'* New York: Routledge.

———. 1997. *The Psychic Life of Power: Theories in Subjection*. Stanford: Stanford University Press.

Butterfield, Herbert. 1966. "The New Diplomacy and Historical Diplomacy." In *Diplomatic Investigations: Essays in the Theory of International Politic*, eds. Herbert Butterfield and Martin Wight. London: George Allen & Unwin.

Buzan, Barry. 1991. *People, States and Fear: An Agenda for International Security Studies in the Post-Cold War Era*. London: Harvester Wheatsheaf.

———, Ole Waever, and Jaap de Wilde. 1998. *Security. A New Framework for Analysis*. Boulder: Lynne Rienner.

Campbell, David. 1992. *Writing Security: United States Foreign Policy and the Politics of Identity*. Minneapolis: University of Minnesota Press.

———. 1993. *Politics Without Principles: Sovereignty, Ethics, and the Narratives of the Gulf War*. Boulder: Lynne Rienner.

———. 1996. "Political Prosaics, Transversal Politics, and the Anarchical World." In *Challenging Boundaries: Global Flows, Territorial Identities*, eds. Michael Shapiro and Hayward Alker. Minneapolis: University of Minnesota Press.

———. 1998a. "Epilogue." In *Writing Security: United States Foreign Policy and the Politics of Identity*, revised ed. Minneapolis: University of Minnesota Press.

———. 1998b. *National Deconstruction: Violence, Identity and Justice in Bosnia*. Minneapolis: University of Minnesota Press.

Carr, Edward H. 1964. *The Twenty Years' Crisis*. New York: Harper Torchbooks.

Carter, April. 1989. *Success and Failure of Arms Control Negotiations*. Oxford: Oxford University Press.

Cerny, Philip G. 1990. *The Changing Architecture of Politics: Structure, Agency and the Future of the State*. London: Sage.

———. 1996. "Globalization and Other Stories: The Search for a New Paradigm in International Relations." *International Journal* 51(4): 617–637.

——— and Mark Evans. 1999. "New Labour, Globalization and the Competition State." University of Leeds/University of York, mimeo.

Checkel, Jeffrey T. 1998. "The Constructivist Turn in International Relations Theory." *World Politics* 50(2): 324–348.

Chilton, Paul. 1996. *Security Metaphors: Cold War Discourse from Containment to Common House*. New York: Peter Lang.

Chin, Christine B. N. 1998. *In Service and Servitude: Foreign Female Domestic Workers and the Malaysian 'Modernity' Project*. New York: Columbia University Press.

Chodorow, Nancy J. 1995. "Gender as a Personal and Cultural Construction." *Signs: Journal of Women in Culture and Society* 20(3): 516–544.

Christiansen, Thomas, Knud Erik Jørgensen, and Antje Wiener. 1999. "Introduction." *Journal of European Public Policy* 6(4): 528–544.

Cohen, Raymond. 1981. *International Politics: The Rules of the Game*. London: Longman.

———. 1991. *Negotiating Across Cultures: Communication Obstacles in International Diplomacy.* Washington D.C.: United States Institute of Peace Press.

Cohn, Carol. 1987. "Sex and Death in the Rational World of Defense Intellectuals." *Signs: Journal of Women in Culture and Society* 12(4): 687–718.

Collin, Finn. 1997. *Social Reality.* London: Routledge.

Connell, Robert W. 1987. *Gender and Power: Society, the Person, and Sexual Politics.* Stanford: Stanford University Press.

Connolly, William E. 1983. *The Terms of Political Discourse*, 2nd ed. Princeton: Princeton University Press.

Cox, Robert W. 1981. "Social Forces, States and World Orders: Beyond International Relations Theory." *Millennium: Journal of International Studies* 10(2): 126–155.

———. 1986. "Social Forces, States and World Orders: Beyond International Relations Theory." In *Neorealism and its Critics*, ed. Robert O. Keohane. New York: Columbia University Press.

——— and Timothy Sinclair. 1996. *Approaches to World Order.* Cambridge: Cambridge University Press.

Cutler, Claire A., Virginia Haufler, and Tony Porter, eds. 1999. *Private Authority and International Affairs.* Albany: State University of New York Press.

Czempiel, Ernst-Otto. 1981. *Internationale Politik: Ein Konfliktmodell.* Paderborn: F. Schonigh.

———. 1986. *Friedensstrategien: Systemwandel durch Internationale Organisationen Demokratisierung und Wirtschaft.* Paderborn: F. Schonigh.

Dallmayr, Fred R. 1987. *Critical Encounters: Between Philosophy and Politics.* Notre Dame: University of Notre Dame Press.

Daly, Mary. 1978. *Gyn/Ecology: The Metaethics of Radical Feminism.* Boston: Beacon Press.

Davis, James, W. 1995. *The Forgotten Variable: The Role of Promises in Deterrence*, Ph.D. dissertation, Columbia University, New York.

Der Derian, James. 1989. "The Boundaries of Knowledge and Power in International Relations." In *International/Intertextual Relations: Postmodern Readings of World Politics*, eds. James Der Derian and Michael Shapiro. Lexington: Lexington Books.

——— and Michael Shapiro, eds. 1989. *International/Intertextual Relations: Postmodern Readings of World Politics.* Lexington: Lexington Books.

De Saussure, Ferdinand. 1974. *Course in General Linguistics.* London: Fontana.

Derrida, Jacques. 1981. *Positions.* Chicago: University of Chicago Press.

Dessler, David. 1989. "What's at Stake in the Agent-Structure Debate?" *International Organization* 43(3): 441–473.

Deudney, Daniel. 1995. "The Philadelphia System: Sovereignty, Arms Control, and the Balance of Power in the American States-Union, Circa 1787–1861." *International Organization* 49(2): 191–228.

Deutsch, Karl. 1957. *Political Community and the North Atlantic Area: International Organisation in the Light of Historical Experience.* Princeton: Princeton University Press.

Diebert, Ronald. 1997. *Parchment, Printing and Hypermedia: Communication in World Order Transformation.* New York: Columbia University Press.

Diez, Thomas. 1999. *Die EU Lesen: Diskursive Knotenpunkte in der britischen Europadebatte.* Opladen: Leske & Budrich.

Doty, Roxanne L. 1993. "Foreign Policy as Social Construction: A Post-Positivist Analysis of U.S. Counterinsurgency Policy in the Philippines." *International Studies Quarterly* 37(3): 297–320.

————. 1996a. *Imperial Encounters: The Politics of Representation in North-South Relations*. Minneapolis: University of Minnesota Press.

————. 1996b. "U.S. Colonialization of the Philippines." In *Post-Realism: The Rhetorical Turn in International Relations*, eds. Francis Beer and Robert Harriman. East Lansing: Michigan State University Press.

————. 1997. "Aporia: A Critical Exploration of the Agent-Structure Problematique in International Relations Theory." *European Journal of International Relations* 3(3): 365–392.

Druckman, Daniel and P. Terrence Hopmann. 1990. "Behavioral Aspects of Negotiations on Mutual Security." In *Behavior, Society and Nuclear War*, eds. Philip Tetlock, Jo L. Husbands, and Robert Jervis. New York: Oxford University Press.

Dunne, Timothy. 1995. "The Social Construction of International Society." *European Journal of International Relations* 1(3): 367–389.

————. 1998. *Inventing International Society: A History of the English School*. Basingstoke: Macmillan.

Dupont, Christopher and Guy-Olivier Faure. 1991. 'The Negotiation Process." In *International Negotiations. Analysis, Approaches, Issues*. ed. Victor Kremenyuk. San Francisco and London: Jossey-Bass.

Edelmann, Murray. 1985. "Political Language and Political Reality." *Political Science* 18(1): 10–19.

Edkins, Jenny. 1996a. "Legality with a Vengeance: Famines and Humanitarian Relief in 'Complex Emergencies.'" *Millennium: Journal of International Studies* 25(3): 547–575.

————. 1996b. *Facing Hunger, International Community, Desire and the Real in Responses to Humanitarian Disaster*. Paper presented to the annual conference of the British International Studies Association, Durham.

Elshtain, Jean B. 1995. "Exporting Feminism." *Journal of International Affairs* 48: 54–58.

Emig, Dieter, Christoph Hutting, and Lutz Raphael. 1992. *Sprache und Politische Kultur in der Demokratie: Hans Gerd Schumann zum Gedenken*. Frankfurt a.M. and New York: Peter Lang.

Enloe, Cynthia. 1990. *Bananas, Beaches and Bases: Making Feminist Sense of International Politics*. Berkeley: University of California Press.

————. 1993. *The Morning After: Sexual Politics at the End of the Cold War*. Berkeley: University of California Press.

Escobar, Arturo. 1995. *Encountering Development: The Making and Unmaking of the Third World*. Princeton: Princeton University Press.

European Commission. 1996. "Economic Communiqué: Making a Success of Globalization for the Benefit of All." *Bulletin of the EU* 6.

Featherstone, Mike, ed., 1990. *Global Culture: Nationalism, Globalization, and Modernity*. London: Sage.

Ferguson, James. 1994. *The Anti-Politics Machine: 'Development,' Depoliticization, and Bureaucratic Power in Lesotho*. Minneapolis: University of Minnesota Press.

Ferguson, Yale and Richard Mansbach. 1988. *The Elusive Quest: Theory and International Politics*. Columbia: University of South Carolina Press.

————. 1996. *Polities: Authority, Identities, Change*. Columbia: University of South Carolina Press.

Fierke, K.M. 1996. "Multiple Identities, Interfacing Games: The Social Construction of Western Action in Bosnia." *European Journal of International Relations* 2(4): 467–497.

————. 1997a. "At the Boundary: Language, Rules and Social Construction." In *The*

Aarhus-Norsminde Papers: Constructivism, International Relations and European Studies, ed. Knud Erik Jørgensen. Aarhus University: Department of Political Science.

―――. 1997b. "Changing Worlds of Security." In *Critical Security Studies*, eds. Keith Krause and Michael Williams. Minneapolis: University of Minnesota Press.

―――. 1998. *Changing Games, Changing Strategies: Critical Investigations in Security*. Manchester and New York: Manchester University Press and St. Martin's Press.

―――. 1999a. "Dialogues of Manoeuvre and Entanglement: NATO, Russia and the CEECs." *Millennium: Journal of International Studies* 28(1): 27–52.

―――. 1999b. "Besting the West: Russia's Machiavella Strategy." *International Feminist Journal of Politics* 1(3): 403–434.

―――. 2000. "Logics of Force and Dialogue: The Iraq/UNSCOM Crisis as Social Interaction." *European Journal of International Relations* 6(3): 335–371.

―――― and Nicholson, Michael. Forthcoming. "Divided by a Common Language: Formal and Constructivist Approaches to Games." *Global Society*.

Finnemore, Martha. 1996a. *National Interests in International Society*. Ithaca: Cornell University Press.

―――. 1996b. "Constructing Norms of Humanitarian Intervention." In *The Culture of National Security*, ed. Peter J. Katzenstein. New York: Columbia University Press.

―――― and Kathryn Sikkink. 1998. "International Norm Dynamics and Political Change." *International Organization* 52(4): 887–917.

Fischer, Markus. 1992. "Feudal Europe, 800–1300: Communal Discourse and Conflictual Practices." *International Organization* 46(2): 427–466.

Fisher, Roger and Scott Brown. 1989. *Gute Beziehungen: Die Kunst der Konfliktvermeidung, Konfliktlösung und Kooperation*. Frankfurt a.M.: Campus Verlag.

―――― and William Ury. 1988. *Das Harvard-Konzept: Sachgerecht verhandeln, erfolgreich verhandeln*. Frankfurt a.M.: Campus Verlag.

Foerster, Heinz von et al. 1997. *Einführung in den Konstruktivismus*. München: Piper.

Foucault, Michel. 1977. *Discipline and Punish: The Birth of the Prison*. London: Allen Lane.

―――. 1980. *Power/Knowledge: Selected Interviews and Other Writing*, ed. Colin Gordon. New York: Pantheon Books.

―――. 1991. "Governmentality." In *The Foucault Effect: Studies in Governmentality*, eds. Graham Burchell, Colin Gordon, and Peter Miller. Chicago: University of Chicago Press.

Franck, Thomas M. 1990. *The Power of Legitimacy Among Nations*. New York: Oxford University Press.

Frost, Mervyn 1996. *Ethics in International Relations*. Cambridge: Cambridge University Press.

Fuller, Steve. 1988. *Social Epistemology*. Bloomington: Indiana University Press.

Garnett, John C. 1984. *Common Sense and the Theory of International Politics*. London: Macmillan.

Garthoff, Raymond L. 1985. *Détente and Confrontation: American-Soviet Relations From Nixon to Reagan*. Washington D.C.: Brookings Institution.

Geertz, Clifford. 1973. "Thick Description: Toward an Interpretive Theory of Culture." In *The Interpretation of Cultures: Selected Essays*. New York: Basic Books.

Gehring, Thomas. 1995a. *International Environmental Governance: A Plea for Theory Integration*. Paper for the ECPR Joint Session of Workshops, Workshop 18: European Multilateralism, 27 April to 2 May, Bordeaux.

―――. 1995b. "Regieren im internationalen System: Verhandlungen, Normen und Internationale Regime." *Politische Vierteljahresschrift* 36(2): 197–219.

George, Alexander L. 1988. "Factors Influencing Security Cooperation." In *U.S.-Soviet Security Cooperation: Achievements, Failures, Lessons*, eds. Alexander L. George, Philip J. Farley, and Alexander Dallin. Oxford: Oxford University Press.

George, Jim. 1994. *Discourses of Global Politics: A Critical (Re)Introduction to International Relations*. Boulder: Lynne Rienner.

——— and David Campbell. 1990. "Patterns of Dissent and the Celebration of Difference: Critical Social Theory and International Relations." *International Studies Quarterly* 34(2): 269–293.

Gibson-Graham, J.K. 1996. *The End of Capitalism (as we knew it): A Feminist Critique of Political Economy*. Cambridge, Mass.: Blackwell Publishers.

Giddens, Anthony. 1984. *The Constitution of Society: Outline of the Theory of Structuration*. Cambridge: Polity Press.

Gill, Stephen. 1995. "Globalisation, Market Civilisation and Disciplinary Neoliberalism." *Millennium: Journal of International Studies* 24(3): 399–423.

——— and James H. Mittelman. 1997. *Innovation and Transformation in International Studies*. Cambridge: Cambridge University Press.

Gilligan, Carol. 1982. *In a Different Voice. Psychological Theory and Women's Development*. Cambridge, Mass.: Harvard University Press.

Gilpin, Robert. 1981. *War and Change in World Politics*. Cambridge: Cambridge University Press.

Glaser, Barney and Anselm Strauss. 1967. *The Discovery of Grounded Theory: Strategies for Qualitative Research*. Hawthorne: Aldine Publishing.

Glasersfeld, Ernst von. 1987. *Wissen, Sprache und Wirklichkeit*. Braunschweig: Vieweg.

———. 1995. *Radical Constructivism: A Way of Knowing and Learning*. London: The Falmer Press.

Goldstein, Judith and Robert O. Keohane. 1993. *Ideas and Foreign Policy: Beliefs, Institutions, and Political Change*. Ithaca: Cornell University Press.

Gray, Colin S. 1986. *Nuclear Strategy and National Style*. Lanham: Hamilton Press.

Gregson, Nicky. 1989. "On the (Ir)relevance of Structuration Theory." In *Social Theory of Modern Societies: Anthony Giddens and his Critics*, eds. David Held and John B. Thompson. Cambridge: Cambridge University Press.

Greven, Michael Th. 1987. "Power and Communication in Habermas and Luhmann: A Critique of Communicative Reductionism." In *Political Discourse: Explorations in Indian and Western Political Thought*, eds. Bhiku Parekh and Thomas Pantham. New Delhi: Sage

———. 1991. "Macht und Politik in der 'Theorie des kommunikativen Handelns' von Jürgen Habermas." In *Macht in der Demokratie: Denkanstosse zur Wiederbelebung einer klassischen Frage in der zeitgenossischen politische Theorie*, ed. Michael Th. Greven. Baden-Baden: Nomos.

Gupta, Akkil. 1998. *Postcolonial Developments: Agriculture in the Making of Modern India*. Durham: Duke University Press.

Gutting, Gary. 1989. *Michel Foucault's Archaeology of Scientific Reason*. Cambridge: Cambridge University Press.

Haas, Ernst. 1982. "Words Can Hurt You: Or, Who Said What To Whom About Regimes." *International Organization* 36(2): 207–243.

———. 1990. *When Knowledge Is Power. Three Models of Change in International Organizations*. Berkeley: University of California Press.

Habermas, Jürgen. 1981. *Theorie des Kommunikativen Handelns*, vol. I+II: Frankfurt a.M.: Suhrkamp Verlag.

———. 1985. "Remarks on the Concept of Communicative Action." In *Social Action*,

eds. Gottfried Seebass and Raimo Tuomela. Boston: Reidel Publishing Company.
————. 1988. "Entgegnung." In *Kommunikatives Handeln: Beiträge zu Jürgen Haber-mas' "Theorie des kommunikativen Handelns,"* eds. Axel Honneth and Hans Joas. Frankfurt a.M.: Suhrkamp.
————. 1990. *Moral Consciousness and Communicative Action.* Cambridge: Polity Press.
————. 1992. *Faktizität und Geltung: Beiträge zur Diskurstheorie des Rechts und des demokratischen Rechtsstaats.* Frankfurt a.M.: Suhrkamp.
————. 1993. *Justification and Application: Remarks on Discourse Ethics.* Cambridge: Polity Press.
———— and Niklas Luhmann. 1971. *Theorie der Gesellschaft oder Sozialtechnologie: was Leistet die Systemforschung.* Frankfurt a.M.: Suhrkamp.
Hacker, Peter M.S. 1996. *Wittgenstein's Place in Twentieth Century-Analytical Philoso-phy.* Oxford: Blackwell Publishers.
Hall, Bruce R. 1997. "Moral Authority as a Power Resource." *International Organiza-tion* 51(4): 591–622.
———— and Friedrich Kratochwil. 1993. "Medieval Tales: Neorealist 'Science' and the Abuse of History." *International Organization* 47(3): 479–492.
Hansen, Lene. 1997. "Slovenian Identity: State-building on the Balkan Border." *Alter-natives* 21(4): 473–496.
Hart, Herbert L. A. 1968. *Punishment and Responsibility.* Oxford: Clarendon.
Hay, Colin. 1999. *The Political Economy of New Labour: Labouring Under False Pre-tences?* Manchester: Manchester University Press.
———— and Matthew Watson. 1999. "The Discourse of Globalisation and the Logic of No Alternative: Rendering the Contingent Necessary in the Downsizing of New La-bour's Aspirations for Government." University of Birmingham, Department of Po-litical Science and International Studies, mimeo.
Heikka, Henrikki. 1996. "Constructing Threat and Russian Foreign Policy: Some Theo-retical Spin-offs." Paper for the ISA Conference in San Diego, April 17–20.
Held, David, Anthony McGrew, David Goldblatt, and Jonathan Perraton. 1999. *Global Transformations: Politics, Economics and Culture.* Cambridge: Polity Press.
Higgott, Richard A. 1998. "Review of Globalisation," (prepared for the Economic and Social research Council). University of Warwick, Centre for the Study of Globalisa-tion and Regionalisation, Working Paper.
————. 1999a. "Economics, Politics and (International) Political Economy: The Need for a Balanced Diet in an Era of Globalisation." *New Political Economy* 4(1): 23–36.
————. 1999b. "Back from the Brink: The Theory and Practice of Globalisation at Cen-tury's End." ASEAN ISIS, 13th Asia Pacific Roundtable, Kuala Lumpar, 30 May–2 June.
Hirschman, Albert. 1977. *The Passions and the Interests: Political Arguments for Capi-talism before its Triumph.* Princeton: Princeton University Press.
Hirst, Paul and Grahame Thompson. 1996. *Globalization in Question: The International Economy and the Possibilities of Governance.* Cambridge: Polity Press.
Hobbes, Thomas 1990. *Behemoth: or the long Parliament,* Chicago: Chicago University Press.
Hoffman, Mark. 1987. "Critical Theory and the Inter-paradigm Debate." *Millennium: Journal of International Studies* 16(2): 231–249.
Hollis, Martin and Steve Smith. 1991. *Explaining and Understanding International Re-lations.* Oxford: Clarendon.
Holmes, Stephen. 1990a. "Political Psychology in Hobbes's Behemoth." In *Thomas Hobbes and Political Theory,* ed. Mary G. Dietz. Lawrence: University of Kansas

Press.

———. 1990b. "The Secret History of Self-Interest." In *Beyond Self-Interest*, ed. Jane Mansbridge. Chicago: Chicago University Press.

Holsti, Kal J. 1996. "Along the Road of International Theory in the Next Millennium: Three Travelogues." Mimeo, University of British Columbia.

Honneth, Axel. 1995. *The Fragmented World of the Social*. Albany: State University of New York Press.

——— and Hans Joas, eds. 1991. *Communicative Action: Essays on Jürgen Habermas' Theory of Communicative Action*. Cambridge: Polity Press.

Hont, Istvan. 1994. "The Permanent Crisis of a Divided Mankind: 'Contemporary Crisis of the Nation-State' in Historical Perspective." *Political Studies* 42 (special issue): 166–231.

Hooks, Bell. 1981. *Ain't I a Woman. Black Women and Feminism*. Boston: South End Press.

Hopf, Ted 1998. "The Promise of Constructivism in International Relations Theory." *International Security* 23(1): 171–200.

Hoy, David C. and Thomas McCarthy. 1994. *Critical Theory*. Oxford: Blackwell Publishers.

Hunt, Michael. 1987. *Ideology and U.S. Foreign Policy*. New Haven: Yale University Press.

Huysmans, Jeff. 1998. "Security! What Do You Mean? From Concept to Thick Signifier." *European Journal of International Relations* 4(2): 226–255.

Ikle, Fred C. 1964. *How Nations Negotiate*. New York: Praeger.

Jachtenfuchs, Markus. 1995. "Ideen und Internationale Beziehungen." *Zeitschrift für Internationale Beziehungen* 2(2): 417–442.

Jaeger, Hans-Martin. 1996. "Konstruktionsfehler des Konstruktivismus in den Internationalen Beziehungen." *Zeitschrift für Internationale Beziehungen* 3(2): 313–340.

Jensen, Lloyd. 1988. *Bargaining for National Security. The Postwar Disarmament Negotiations*. Columbia: University of South Carolina Press.

Jepperson, Ronald L., Alexander Wendt, and Peter J. Katzenstein. 1996. "Norms, Identity, and Culture in National Security." In *The Culture of National Security: Norms and Identity in World Politics*, ed. Peter J. Katzenstein. New York: Columbia University Press.

Jervis Robert. 1998. "Realism in the Study of World Politics." *International Organization* 52(4): 971–991.

Johnston, David. 1986. *The Rhetoric of Leviathan: Thomas Hobbes and the Politics of Cultural Transformation*. Princeton: Princeton University Press.

Johnston, Alastair Iain. 1995. *Cultural Realism: Strategic Culture and Grand Strategy in Chinese History*. Princeton: Princeton University Press.

Jönsson, Christer. 1983. "A Cognitive Approach to International Negotiation." *European Journal of Political Research* 11: 139–150.

———. 1991. "Cognitive Theory." In *International Negotiations: Analysis, Approaches, Issues*, ed. Victor Kremenyuk. San Francisco and London: Bossey and Bass.

———. 1993. "Cognitive Factors in Explaining Regime Dynamics." In *Regime Theory and International Relations*, eds. Volker Rittberger and Peter Mayer. Oxford: Clarendon.

Jørgensen, Knud Erik, ed. 1997. *Reflective Approaches to European Governance*. Basingstoke: Macmillan.

———, ed. 1998. *The Aarhus-Norsminde Papers: Constructivism, International Relations and European Studies*. University of Aarhus: Department of Political Science.

Kampelman, Max. 1986. "The Lessons of the Madrid CSCE Conference." In *Negotiating World Order: The Artisanship and Architecture of Global Diplomacy*, ed. Alan K. Henrikson. Wilmington, Del.: Scholarly Reseources.
Kandiyoti, Deniz. 1992. "Identity and its Discontents: Women and the Nation." *Millennium: Journal of International Studies* 20(3): 429–443.
Katzenstein, Peter J., ed. 1996. *The Culture of National Security: Norms and Identity in World Politics*. New York: Columbia University Press.
———. 1990. "Analyzing Change in International Politics: The New Institutionalism and the Interpretative Approach." Paper presented as a guest lecture at the Max-Planck-Institut für Gesellschaftsforschung, Köln, Germany.
———, Robert O. Keohane, and Stephen D. Krasner. 1998. "International Organization and the Study of World Politics." *International Organization* 52(4): 645–685.
Keck Margaret E. and Kathryn Sikkink. 1998. *Activists Beyond Borders: Advocacy Networks in International Politics*. Ithaca: Cornell University Press.
Keck, Otto. 1995. "Rationales kommunikatives Handeln in den internationalen Beziehungen." *Zeitschrift für Internationale Beziehungen* 2(1): 5–48.
———. 1993. *Information, Macht und gesellschaftliche Rationalität: Das Dilemma nationalen kommunikativen Handelns, dargestellt am Beispiel eines Internationalen Vergleichs der Kernenergiepolitik*. Baden-Baden: Nomos.
Keeley, James. 1990. "Towards a Foucauldian Analysis of International Regimes." *International Organization* 44(1): 83–105.
Kegley, Charles W. 1994. "How Did the Cold War Die? Principles for an Autopsy." *Mershon International Studies Review* 38(1): 11–42.
Keohane, Robert O. 1984. *After Hegemony: Cooperation and Discord in the World Political Economy*. Princeton: Princeton University Press.
———. 1988. "International Institutions: Two Approaches." *International Studies Quarterly* 32(4): 379–396.
———. 1989. *International Institutions and State Power*. Boulder: Westview Press.
———. 1991. "International Relations Theory: Contributions of a Feminist Standpoint." In *Gender and International Relations*, eds. Rebecca Grant and Kathleen Newland. Bloomington: Indiana University Press.
———. 1998. "Beyond Dichotomy: Conversations Between International Relations and Feminist Theory." *International Studies Quarterly* 42(1): 193–198.
Kier, Elizabeth. 1997. *Imagining War: French and British Military Doctrine Between the Wars*. Princeton: Princeton University Press.
King, Gary, Robert O. Keohane, and Sidney Verba. 1994. *Designing Social Inquiry: Scientific Influence in Qualitative Research*. Princeton: Princeton University Press.
Kissinger, Henry. 1982. *Years of Upheaval*. Boston: Little Brown.
Klein, Bradley. 1994. *Strategic Studies and World Order*. Cambridge: Cambridge University Press.
Klotz, Audie. 1995a. *Norms in International Relations. The Struggle Against Apartheid*. Ithaca: Cornell University Press.
———. 1995b. "Norms Reconstituting Interests: Global Racial Equality and U.S. Sanctions against South Africa." *International Organization* 49(3): 451–478.
——— and Cecelia Lynch. 1998. "Conflicted Constructivism? Positivist Leanings vs. Interpretivist Meanings." Paper presented at the International Studies Association Annual Meeting, Minneapolis.
——— and Cecelia Lynch. Forthcoming. *Constructing World Politics*. New York: Cornell University Press.
Kohler-Koch, Beate. 1989. "Zur Empirie und Theorie internationaler Regime." In *Regime in den internationale Beziehungen*, ed. Beate Kohler-Koch. Baden-Baden:

Nomos.

Koselleck, Reinhart. 1985. *Futures Past: On the Semantics of Historical Time.* Cambridge, Mass.: MIT Press.

Koslowski, Rey and Friedrich Kratochwil. 1995. "Understanding Change in International Politics: The Soviet Empire's Demise and the International System." In *International Relations Theory and the End of the Cold War*, eds. Richard N. Lebow and Thomas Risse-Kappen. New York: Columbia University Press.

Kowert, Paul. 1998. "Agent Versus Structure in the Construction of National Identity." In *International Relations in a Constructed World*, eds. Vendulka Kubálková, Nicholas Onuf, and Paul Kowert. Armonk, N.Y.: M.E. Sharpe.

——— and Jeffrey Legro. 1996. "Norms, Identity, and Their Limits: A Theoretical Reprise." In *The Culture of National Security: Norms and Identity in World Politics*, ed. Peter J. Katzenstein. New York: Columbia University Press.

Krasner, Stephen D., ed. 1983a. *International Regimes.* Ithaca: Cornell University Press.

———. 1983b. "Structural Causes and Regime Consequences: Regimes as Intervening Variables." In *International Regimes*, ed. Stephen D. Krasner. Ithaca: Cornell University Press.

Krass, Allan S. 1985. *Verification: How Much Is Enough?* London and Philadelphia: Taylor & Francis.

Kratochwil, Friedrich V. 1982. "On the Notion of Interest in International Relations." *International Organization* 36: 1–30.

———. 1984a. "Errors Have Their Advantage." *International Organization* 38: 305–320.

———. 1984b. "Thrasymmachos Revisited: On the Relevance of Norms for International Relations." *Journal of International Affairs* 37(2): 343–356.

———. 1987. "Rules, Norms, Values and the Limits of 'Rationality.'" *Archiv für Rechts- und Sozialphilosophie* 73: 301–329.

———. 1988a. "Regimes, Interpretation, and the 'Science' of Politics." *Millennium: Journal of International Studies* 17(2): 263–284.

———. 1988b. "The Protagorean Quest: Community, Justice, and the 'Oughts' and 'Musts' of International Politics." *International Journal* 43(2): 205–240.

———. 1989. *Rules, Norms, and Decisions. On the Conditions of Practical and Legal Reasoning in International Relations and Domestic Affairs.* Cambridge: Cambridge University Press.

———. 1993a. "The Embarrassment of Changes: Neo-realism as the Science of Realpolitik Without Politics." *Review of International Studies* 19(1): 63–80.

———. 1993b. "Contract and Regimes: Do Issue Specificity and Variations of Formality Matter?" In *Regime Theory and International Relations*, ed. Volker Rittberger. Oxford and New York: Clarendon Press and Oxford University Press.

———. 1993c. "Norms Versus Numbers: Multilateralism and the Rationalist and Reflexivist Approaches to Institutions—a Unilateral Plea for Communicative Rationality." In *Multilateralism Matters: The Theory and Praxis of an Institutional Form*, ed. John G. Ruggie. New York: Columbia University Press.

———. 1994a. "The Limits of Contract." *European Journal of International Law* 5: 465–491.

———. 1994b. "Citizenship: On the Border of Order." *Alternatives* 19(4): 485–506.

———. 1996. "Is the Ship of Culture at Sea or Returning?" In *The Return of Culture and Identity in IR Theory*, eds. Yosef Lapid and Friedrich V. Kratochwil. Boulder and London: Lynne Rienner.

———. 1997. *Constructivism as an Approach to International Law and International Relations.* Mimeo.

————. 1998. "Politics, Norms and Peaceful Change." *Review of International Studies* 24 (special issue): 193–218.
———— and Edward D. Mansfield, eds. 1994. *International Organization.* New York: Harper Collins.
———— and John G. Ruggie. 1986. "International Organization: a State of the Art on the Art of the State." *International Organization* 40(4): 753–775.
Krause, Jill. 1996. "Gendered Identities in International Relations." In *Identities in International Relations*, eds. Jill Krause and Neil Renwick. Basingstoke and New York: Macmillan and St. Martin's Press.
Krause, Keith and Michael C. Williams. 1996. "Broadening the Agenda of Security Studies: Politics and Methods." *International Studies Quarterly* 40(2): 229–254.
Kremenyuk, Victor. 1991. "The Emerging System of International Negotiations." In *International Negotiations. Analysis, Approaches, Issues*, ed. Victor Kremenyuk. San Francisco and London: Bossey and Bass.
Krohn, Wolfgang, Günter Küppers, and Helga Nowotny, eds. 1990. *Selforganization: Portrait of a Scientific Revolution.* Dordrecht: Kluwer.
Krugman, Paul. 1997. "We Are Not the World," *New York Times,* 13 February. Hyperlink "http://www.mtholyoke.edu/acad/intrel/krugman.htm."
Kubálková, Vendulka, Nicholas Onuf, and Paul Kowert. 1998. "Constructing Constructivism." In *International Relations in a Constructed World*, eds. Vendulka Kubálková, Nicholas Onuf, and Paul Kowert. Armonk, N.Y.: M.E. Sharpe.
Laïdi, Zaki. 1998. *A World Without Meaning: The Crisis of Meaning in International Politics.* London: Routledge
Lake, David. 1996. "Anarchy, Hierarchy, and the Variety of International Relations." *International Organization* 50(1): 1–33.
Lakoff, George. 1987. *Women, Fire and Dangerous Things: What Categories Reveal about the Mind.* Chicago: University of Chicago Press.
————. 1996. *Moral Politics: What Conservatives Know that Liberals Don't.* Chicago: University of Chicago Press.
———— and Mark Johnson. 1980. *Metaphors We Live By.* Chicago: University of Chicago Press.
Lapid, Yosef. Forthcoming. "Introduction." In *Identities, Borders, Orders: New Directions in IR Theory*, eds. Mathias Albert, David Jacobson, and Yosef Lapid.
————. 1989. "The Third Debate: On the Prospects of International Theory in a Post-Positivist Era." *International Studies Quarterly* 33(3): 235–249.
———— and Friedrich V. Kratochwil, eds. 1996. *The Return of Culture and Identity in IR Theory.* Boulder and London: Lynne Rienner.
Larsen, Henrik. 1997. "British Discourses on Europe: Sovereignty of Parliament, Instrumentality and the Non-Mythical Europe." In *Reflective Approaches to European Governance*, ed. Knud Erik Jørgensen. Basingstoke: Macmillan.
Lax, David A. and James K. Sebenius. 1986. *The Manager as Negotiator. Bargaining for Cooperation and Competitive Gain.* New York: Free Press.
Layne, Christopher. 1994. "Kant or Cant: The Myth of the Democratic Peace." *International Security* 19(2): 5–49.
Lebow, Richard Ned. 1981. *Between Peace and War: The Nature of International Crisis.* Baltimore and London: John Hopkins University Press.
———— and Janice Gross Stein. 1987. "Beyond Deterrence." *Journal of Social Issues* 43(4): 5–71.
———— and Janice Gross Stein. 1994. *We All Lost the Cold War.* Princeton: Princeton University Press.
Lecomte, A. 1986. "Espaces des séquences: Approche topologique et informatique de la

séquence." *Langages* 81(2): 91–109.

——— and J. Marandin. 1986. "Analyse du Discours et Morphologie Discursive." In *Research in Text Connectivity and Text Coherence: A Survey*, eds. Michel Charolles, Janos S. Petöfi and Emel Sözer. Hamburg: Helmut Buske.

Lewis, David K. 1969. *Conventions: A Philosophical Study*. Cambridge, Mass.: Harvard University Press.

Lincoln, Bruce. 1989. *Discourse and the Construction of Society: Comparative Studies of Myth, Ritual, and Classification*. New York: Oxford University Press.

Lipson, Charles. 1991. "Why Are Some International Agreements Informal?" *International Organization* 45(3): 495–538.

Litfin, Karen. 1994. *Ozone Discourses: Science and Politics in Global Environmental Cooperation*. New York: Columbia University Press.

Lose, Lars G. 1997. *Orden og Samarbejde i det anarkiske samfund: Om den teoretiske forklaring af multilaterale samarbejdsformer*. MA thesis, University of Aarhus, Department of Political Science.

Luhmann, Niklas. 1968. *Vertrauen. Ein Mechanismus der Reduktion sozialer Komplexität*. Stuttgart: Ferdinand Enke.

———. 1984. *Soziale Systeme*. Frankfurt a.M.: Suhrkamp.

———. 1992. *Beobachtungen der Moderne*. Opladen: Westdeutscher Verlag.

———. 1997. *Die Gesellschaft der Gesellschaft*, 2 vols. Frankfurt a.M.: Suhrkamp.

Lynch, Cecelia. 1999. *Beyond Appeasement: Interpreting Interwar Peace Movements in World Politics*. Ithaca: Cornell University Press.

Majone, Giandomenico. 1989. *Evidence, Argument, and Persuasion in the Policy Process*. New Haven: Yale University Press.

———. 1994. "The Rise of the Regulatory State in Europe." *West European Politics* 17(3): 77–101.

———. 1996. "A European Regulatory State?" In *European Union: Power and Policy-Making*, ed. Jeremy J. Richardson. London: Routledge

Manning, Charles A. W. 1962. *The Nature of International Society*. London: London School of Economics.

Mansbridge, Jane J. 1990. "The Rise and Fall of Self-interest in the Explanation of Political Life." In *Beyond Self-Interest*, ed. Jane J. Mansbridge. Chicago: University of Chicago Press.

Manzo, Kathryn. 1992. *Domination, Resistance and Social Change in South Africa: The Local Effects of Global Power*. Westport: Praeger.

Marchand, Marianne H. and Jane L. Parpart, eds. 1995. *Feminism Postmodernism Development*. London: Routledge.

Marcus, George. 1999. "Foreword." In *Cultures of Insecurity: States, Communities, and the Production of Danger*, eds. Jutta Weldes, Mark Laffey, Hugh Gusterson, and Raymond Duvall. Minneapolis: University of Minnesota Press.

Masco, Joseph. 1999. "States of Insecurity: Plutonium and Post-cold War Anxiety in New Mexico, 1992–96." In *Cultures of Insecurity: States, Communities, and the Production of Danger*, eds. Jutta Weldes, Mark Laffey, Hugh Gusterson, and Raymond Duvall. Minneapolis: University of Minnesota Press.

Maturana, Humberto R. 1970. *Biology of Cognition*. Urbana: University of Illinois.

——— and Francisco J. Varela. 1980. *Autopoiesis and Cognition: The Realisation of the Living*. Dordrecht: D. Reidel Publishing Company.

McNamara, K.R. 1997. "Globalization Is What We Make of It? The Social Construction of Market Imperatives." Annual meeting of the American Political Science Association, Washington DC, 28–31 August.

McSweeney, Bill. 1996. "Identity and Security: Buzan and the Copenhagen School."

Review of International Studies 22(1): 81–93.

Mead, George H. [1934]1965. *Mind, Self & Society. From the Standpoint of A Social Behaviourist.* Illinois: University of Chicago Press.

Mearsheimer, John J. 1995. "The False Promise of International Institutions." *International Security* 19(3): 5–49.

Mercer, Jonathan. 1995. "Anarchy and Identity." *International Organization* 49(2): 229–252.

———. 1996. *Reputation in International Relations.* Ithaca and London: Cornell University Press.

Meyer, Mary K. and Elisabeth Prügl, eds. 1998. *Gender Politics in Global Governance.* Lanham: Rowman and Littlefield.

Meyers, Reinhard. 1990. "Metatheoretische und methodologische Betrachtungen zur Theorie der internationalen Beziehungen." In *Theorien der Internationalen Beziehungen, Bestandaufnahme und Forschungsperspektiven,* ed. Volker Rittberger. Opladen: Westdeutscher Verlag.

Midgaard, Knut. 1983. "Rules and Strategy in Negotiations: Notes on an Institutionalist and Intentionalist Approach." *European Journal of Political Research* 11: 151–166.

Miller, David. 1994. "The Nation-State: a Modest Defence." In *Political Restructuring in Europe: Ethical Perspectives,* ed. Chris Brown. London: Routledge.

Milliken, Jennifer. 1996. "Prestige and Reputation in American Foreign Policy and American Realism." In *Post-realism: The Rhetorical Turn in International Relations,* eds. Francis A. Beer and Robert Hariman. East Lansing: Michigan State University Press.

———. 1999. "Intervention and Identity: Reconstructing the West in Korea." In *Cultures of Insecurity: States, Communities, and Danger,* eds. Jutta Weldes, Mark Laffey, Hugh Gusterson, and Raymond Duvall. Minneapolis: University of Minnesota Press.

——— and David Sylvan. 1996. "Soft Bodies, Hard Targets and Chic Theories: US Bombing Policy in Indochina." *Millennium: Journal of International Studies* 25(2): 321–360.

Milner, Helen. 1998. "Regional Economic Co-operation, Global Markets and Domestic Politics: A Comparison of NAFTA and the Maastricht Treaty." In *Regionalism and Global Economic Integration: Europe, Asia and the Americas,* eds. William D. Coleman and Geoffrey R.D. Underhill. London: Routledge.

Mohanty, Chandra Talpade. 1991. "Under Western Eyes: Feminist Scholarship and Colonial Discourses." In *Third World Women and the Politics of Feminism,* eds. Chandra Talpade Mohanty, Ann Russo, and Lourdes Torres. Bloomington: Indiana University Press.

Moon, J. Donald 1995. "Practical Discourse and Communicative Ethics." In *The Cambridge Companion to Habermas,* ed. Stephen K. White. Cambridge: Cambridge University Press.

Moon, Katherine H. S. 1997. *Sex Among Allies: Military Prostitution in U.S.-Korea Relations.* New York: Columbia University Press.

Moravcsik, Andrew. 1999. "Is There Something Rotten in the State of Denmark? Constructivism and European Integration." *Journal of European Public Policy* 6(4): 669–681.

Morgenthau, Hans J. 1967. *Politics Among Nations: The Struggle for Power and Peace,* 4th ed., New York: Alfred A. Knopf.

Mosse, George L. 1985. *Nationalism and Sexuality: Respectability and Abnormal Sexuality in Modern Europe.* New York: H. Fertig.

Müller, Harald. 1989. "Regimeanalyse und Sicherheitspolitik: Das Beispiel Nonproliferation." In *Regime in den internationale Beziehungen*, ed. Beate Kohler-Koch. Baden-Baden: Nomos.

―――. 1993a. *Die Chance der Kooperation. Regime in den internationalen Beziehungen*. Darmstadt.

―――. 1993b. "The Internalization of Principles, Norms and Rules by Governments: The Case of Security Regimes." In *Regime Theory and International Relations*, ed. Volker Rittberger. Oxford: Clarendon Press.

―――. 1993c. "Verrechtlichung, Innen- und Außenpolitik." In *Internationale Verrechtlichung Jahresschrift für Rechtspolitologie*, ed. Klaus Dieter Wolf. Pfaffenweiler: Centaurus.

―――. 1994a. "Internationale Beziehungen als kommunikatives Handeln: Zur Kritik der utilitaristischen Handlungstheorien." *Zeitschrift für Internationale Beziehungen* 1(1): 15–44.

―――. 1994b. "Institutionen und Internationale Ordnung." In *Frieden und Konflikt in den internationalen Beziehungen: Festschrift fur Ernst-Otto Czempiel*, eds. Gert Krell and Harald Müller. Frankfurt a.M.: Campus.

―――. 1995. "Spielen hilft nicht immer—Die Grenzen des Rational-Choice-Ansatzes und der Platz der Theorie kommunikativen Handelns in der Analyse internationaler Beziehungen." *Zeitschrift für Internationale Beziehungen* 2(2): 371–391.

Mutimer, David. 1999. *The Weapons State: Proliferation and the Framing of Security*. Boulder: Lynne Reinner.

Navari, Cornelia. 1982. "Diplomatic Structure and Idiom." In *The Community of States—A Study in International Political Theory*, ed. James Mayall. London: Allen & Unwin.

Neufeld, Mark 1993. "Interpretation and the 'Science' of International Relations." *Review of International Studies* 19(1): 39–61.

Neumann, Iver B. 1996. "Self and Other in International Relations." *European Journal of International Relations* 2(2): 139–174.

―――. 1998. "European Identity, EU Expansion, and the Integration/Exclusion Nexus." *Alternatives* 23(3): 397–416.

―――. 1999. *Uses of the Other: 'The East' in European Identity Formation*. Minneapolis: University of Minnesota Press.

―――― and Jennifer M. Welsh. 1991. "The Other in European Self-definition: An Addendum to the Literature on International Society." *Review of International Studies* 17(4): 327–348.

Nicholson, Linda. 1994. "Interpreting Gender." *Signs: Journal of Women in Culture and Society* 20(1): 79–105.

Nicholson, Michael. 1996. *Causes and Consequences in International Relations: A Conceptual Study*. London: Pinter.

Noguera i Hancock, Ramon 1998. *The Systems (R)evolution. Systems Theory, Social Evolution and International Relations*, Ph.D. thesis, University of Wales, Aberystwyth: Department of International Politics.

Nørager, Troels. 1993. *System og Livsverden: Jürgen Habermas' Konstruktion af det Moderne*. Aarhus: Anis.

Nullmeier, Frank. 1993. "Wissen und Policy-Forschung. Wissenspolitologie und rhetorisch-dialektisches Handlungsmodell." In *Policy-Analyse. Kritik und Orientierung PVS-Sonderheft 24*, ed. Adrienne Héritier. Opladen: Westdeutscher Verlag.

Nye, Joseph S., Jr. 1986. "The Diplomacy of Nuclear Nonproliferation." In *Negotiating World Order: The Artisanship and Architecture of Global Diplomacy*, ed. Alan K. Henrikson. Wilmington: Scholarly Resources.

―――. 1988. "Neorealism and Neoliberalism." *World Politics* 40(2): 235–251.

Ohmae, Kenichi. 1995. *The End of the Nation State: The Rise of Regional Economies.* London and New York: Harper Collins and Free Press.

—. 1999. *The Borderless World: Power and Strategy in the Inter-linked Economy,* revised edition. New York: Harperbusiness.

Onuf, Nicholas G. 1989. *World of Our Making: Rules and Rule in Social Theory and International Relations.* Columbia: University of South Carolina Press.

—. 1991. "Sovereignty: Outline of a Conceptual History." *Alternatives* 16(4): 425–446.

—. 1994. "The Constitution of International Society." *European Journal of International Law* 5(1): 1–19.

—. 1995. "Intervention for the Common Good." In *Beyond Westphalia? National Sovereignty and International Intervention,* eds. Gene M. Lyons and Michael Mastaduno. Baltimore and London: Johns Hopkins University Press.

—. 1997a. "A Constructivist Manifesto." In *Constituting International Political Economy,* eds. Kurt Burch and Raymond A. Denemark. Boulder: Lynne Rienner.

—. 1997b. "Hegemony's Hegemony in IPE." In *Constituting International Political Economy,* eds. Kurt Burch and Raymond A. Denemark. Boulder: Lynne Rienner.

—. 1998a. "Everyday Ethics in International Relations." *Millennium: Journal of International Studies* 27(3): 669–693.

—. 1998b. "Constructivism: A User's Manual." In *International Relations in a Constructed World,* eds. Vendulka Kubálková, Nicholas Onuf, and Paul Kowert. Armonk, N.Y.: M.E. Sharpe.

Opp de Hipt, Manfred and Erik Latniak, eds. 1991. *Sprache statt Politik?: Politikwissenschaftliche Semantik- und Rhetorikforschung.* Opladen: Westdeutscher Verlag.

Ostrom, Elinor. 1990. *Governing the Commons: Evolution of Institutions for Collective Action.* Cambridge: Cambridge University Press.

Ó Tuathail, Gearóid. 1996. *Critical Geopolitics: The Politics of Writing Global Space.* Minneapolis: University of Minnesota Press.

Outhwaite, William. 1994. *Habermas: A Critical Introduction.* Oxford: Polity Press.

Owen, John M. 1994. "How Liberalism Produces Democratic Peace." *International Security* 19(2): 87–125.

Pasic, Sujata C. 1996. "Culturing International Relations Theory: A Call for Extension." In *The Return of Culture and Identity in IR Theory,* eds. Yosef Lapid and Friedrich Kratochwil. Boulder: Lynne Rienner.

Peterson, V. Spike. 1992a. "Transgressing Boundaries: Theories of Knowledge, Gender and International Relations." *Millennium: Journal of International Studies* 21(2): 183–206.

—. 1992b. "Security and Sovereign States: What Is at Stake in Taking Feminism Seriously?" In *Gendered States: Feminist (Re)Visions of International Relations Theory,* ed. V. Spike Peterson. Boulder: Lynne Rienner.

—. ed. 1992c. *Gendered States: Feminist (Re)Visions of International Relations Theory.* Boulder: Lynne Rienner.

—. 1993. "The Politics of Identity in International Relations." *Fletcher Forum of World Affairs* 17(2): 1–12.

—. 1995. "Political Identity, Emancipatory Politics and Global Dynamics." Paper presented at the Annual Meeting of the International Studies Association, Chicago.

— and Anne Sisson Runyan. 1999. *Global Gender Issues.* Boulder: Westview Press.

Pettman, Jan J. 1996. *Worlding Women: A Feminist International Politics.* London: Routledge.

Pin-Fat, Veronique. 1997. *Language in International Relations Theory: A Grammatical*

Investigation. Ph.D. Manuscript, University of Wales, Aberystwyth, Department of International Politics.

Pleydell, Alan. 1982. "Language, Culture and the Concept of International Political Community." In *The Community of States—A Study in International Political Theory,* ed. James Mayall. London: Allen & Unwin.

Polkinghorne, Donald E. 1983. *Methodology for the Human Sciences.* Albany: State University of New York Press.

———. 1988. *Narrative Knowing and the Human Sciences.* Albany: State University of New York Press.

Price, Richard. 1997. *The Chemical Weapons Taboo.* Ithaca: Cornell University Press.

——— and Reus-Smit, Christian. 1998. "Dangerous Liaisons? Critical International Theory and Constructivism." *European Journal of International Relations* 4(3): 259–294.

Pruitt, Dean G. 1981. *Negotiation Behavior.* New York.

Prügl, Elisabeth. 1996. "Gender in International Organization and Global Governance: A Critical Review of the Literature." *International Studies Notes* 21(1): 15–24.

———. 1999. *The Global Construction of Gender: Home-Based Work in the Political Economy of the 20th Century.* New York: Columbia University Press.

Putnam, Robert D. 1988. "Diplomacy and Domestic Politics: The Logic of Two-Level Games." *International Organization* 42(3): 427–460.

Rapoport, Anatol. 1960. *Fights, Games, and Debates.* Ann Arbor: University of Michigan Press

Rehbein, Jochen, ed. 1985. *Interkulturelle Kommunikation.* Tübingen: Gunter Narr.

Reus-Smit, Christian. 1999. *The Moral Purpose of the State: Culture, Social Identity, and Institutional Rationality in International Relations.* Princeton: Princeton University Press.

Ringmar, Erik. 1997. "Alexander Wendt: A Social Scientist Struggling with History." In *The Future of International Relations. Masters in the Making,* eds. Iver B. Neumann and Ole Waever. London and New York: Routledge.

Risse, Thomas. 1997. "'Let's Talk!' Insights from the German Debate on Communicative Behavior and International Relations." Paper presented to the Annual Convention of the American Political Science Association, Washington D.C., Aug. 27–31.

———. 1998. "A Europeanization of Nation-state Identities?" Chapter prepared for *Europeanization and Domestic Change,* eds. Maria Green Cowles, James Caporaso and Thomas Risse.

———. 2000. "Let's Argue: Communicative Action in World Politics." *International Organization* 54: 1–39.

——— and Wiener Antje. 1999. "'Something Rotten' and the Social Construction of Social Constructivism: A Comment on Comments." *Journal of European Public Policy* 6(5): 775–782.

Risse-Kappen, Thomas. 1988. *Null-Lösung: Entscheidungsprozesse zu den Mittelstreckenwaffen 1970–1987.* Frankfurt a.M. and New York: Campus.

———. 1994. "Ideas Do Not Float Freely: Transnational Coalitions, Domestic Structures, and the End of the Cold War." *International Organization* 48(2): 185–214.

———. 1995a. "Democratic Peace—Warlike Democracies? A Social Constructivist Interpretation of the Liberal Argument." *European Journal of International Relations* 1(4): 491–517.

———. 1995b. "Reden ist nicht billig. Zur Debatte um Kommunikation und Rationalität." *Zeitschrift für Internationale Beziehungen* 2(1): 171–184.

———. 1995c. *Cooperation Among Democracies: The European Influence on US Foreign Policy.* Princeton: Princeton University Press.

————. 1996a. "Collective Identity in a Democratic Community: The Case of NATO." In *The Culture of National Security: Norms and Identity in World Politics*, ed. Peter J. Katzenstein. New York: Columbia University Press.

————. 1996b. "Exploring the Nature of the Beast: International Relations Theory and Comparative Policy Analysis Meet the European Union." *Journal of Common Market Studies* 34(1): 53–80.

Rittberger, Volker. 1983. "Global Conference Diplomacy and International Policy-making: The Case of UN-Sponsored World Conferences." *European Journal of Political Research* 11: 167–182.

———— and Michael Zürn. 1990. "Towards Regulated Anarchy in East-West Relations: Causes and Consequences of East-West Regimes." In *International Regimes in East-West Politics*, ed. Volker Rittberger. London: Pinter.

Robertson, Raymond. 1992. *Globalization: Social Theory and Global Culture*. London: Sage.

———— and Haque Khondker, Habib. 1997. "Discourses of Globalisation: Preliminary Considerations." *International Sociology* 13(1): 25–40.

Rorty, Richard. 1979. *Philosophy and the Mirror of Nature*. Princeton: Princeton University Press.

————. 1991. *Objectivity, Relativism and Truth*. Cambridge and New York: Cambridge University Press.

Rosamond, Ben. 1999. "Discourses of Globalisation and the Social Construction of European Identities." *Journal of European Public Policy* 6(4): 652–668.

Rosenau, James N. 1990. *Turbulence in World Politics: A Theory of Change and Continuity*. Princeton: Princeton University Press.

————. 1992. "Governance, Order, and Change in World Politics." In *Governance Without Government: Order and Change in World Politics*, eds. James N. Rosenau & Ernst-Otto Czempiel. Cambridge: Cambridge University Press.

———— and Mary Durfee. 1995. *Thinking Theory Thoroughly. Coherent Approaches to an Incoherent World*. Boulder: Westview Press.

Ruddick, Sara. 1989a. *Maternal Thinking: Towards a Politics of Peace*. Boston: Beacon Press.

————. 1989b. "Mothers and Men's War." In *Rocking the Ship of State. Toward a Feminist Peace Politics*, eds. Adrienne Harris and Ynestra King. Boulder: Westview Press.

Ruggie, John G. 1983. "International Regimes, Transactions, and Change: Embedded Liberalism in the Postwar International Order." In *International Regimes*, ed. Stephen D. Krasner. Ithaca: Cornell University Press.

————. 1986. "Continuity and Transformation in the World Polity: Toward a Neorealist Synthesis." In *Neorealism and Its Critics*, ed. Robert O. Keohane. New York: Columbia University Press.

————. 1989. "International Structure and International Transformation: Space, Time, and Method." In *Global Changes and Theoretical Challenges: Approaches to World Politics for the 1990s*, eds. Ernst-Otto Czempiel and James N. Rosenau. Lexington: Lexington Books.

————. ed. 1993. *Multilateralism Matters: The Theory and Praxis of an Institutional Form*. New York: Columbia University Press.

————. 1996. *Winning the Peace: America and World Order in the New Era*. New York: Columbia University Press.

————. 1998a. "What Makes the World Hang Together? Neo-Utilitarianism and the Social Constructivist Challenge." *International Organization* 52(4): 855–85.

————. 1998b. *Constructing the World Polity: Essays on International Institutionaliza-*

tion. London: Routledge.

Saco, Diana. 1997. "Gendering Sovereignty: Marriage and International Relations in Elizabethan Times." *European Journal of International Relations* 3(3): 291–318.

———. 1999. "Colonizing Cyberspace: 'National Security' and the Internet." In *Cultures of Insecurity: States, Communities, and Danger*, eds. Jutta Weldes, Mark Laffey, Hugh Gusterson, and Raymond Duvall. Minneapolis: University of Minnesota Press.

Said, Edward W. 1995. *Orientalism: Western Conceptions of the Orient*. London: Penguin Books.

Schmalz-Bruns, Rainer. 1995. "Die Theorie Kommunikativen Handelns—eine Flaschenpost?" *Zeitschrift für Internationale Beziehungen* 2(2): 347–370.

Schmidt, Siegfried J. 1987. *Der Diskurs des Radikalen Konstruktivismus*. Frankfurt a.M.: Suhrkamp.

———. 1991. *Neue Wege des Konstruktivismus*. Frankfurt a.M.: Suhrkamp.

Schneider, Gerald 1994. "Rational Choice und kommunikatives Handeln. Eine Replik auf Harald Müller." *Zeitschrift für Internationale Beziehungen* 2(1): 357–366.

Scholte, Jan Aart 1996a. "Globalization and Collective Identities." In *Identities in International Relations*, eds. Jill Krause and Neil Renwick. Basingstoke and New York: Macmillan Press and St. Martin's Press.

———. 1996b. "Beyond the Buzzword: Towards a Critical Theory of Globalization." In *Globalization: Theory and Practice*, eds. Eleonore Kofman and Gillian Youngs. London: Pinter.

———. 1997. "Global Capitalism and the State." *International Affairs* 73(3): 427–452.

Schütz, Alfred. 1967. *Collected Papers, Vol. 1: The Problem of Social Reality*, ed. Maurice Natanson. The Hague: Martinus Nijhoff.

Scott, Joan W. 1986. "Gender: A Useful Category of Historical Analysis." *American Historical Review* 91: 1053–1075.

———. 1988. "Deconstructing Equality-Versus-Difference. Or the Use of Poststructural Theory for Feminism." *Feminist Studies* 14(1): 33–50.

Searle, John. 1969. *Speech Acts: An Essay in the Philosophy of Language*. Cambridge: Cambridge University Press.

———. 1995. *The Construction of Social Reality*. London: Allen Lane.

Sebenius, James K. 1992. "Challenging Conventional Explanations of International Cooperation: Negotiation Analysis and the Case of Epistemic Communities." *International Organization* 46(1): 323–365.

Sen, Amartya. 1978. "Rational Fools: On the Behavioral Foundations of Economic Theory." In *Scientific Models and Men*, ed. Henry Harris. Oxford: Oxford University Press.

Senghaas, Dieter. 1992a. *Friedensprojekt Europa*. Frankfurt a.M.: Suhrkamp

———. 1992b. "Von Struktur- zur Regimeanalyse und zurück. Analytische Heuristik als Falle und das Erfordernis synthetischer Urteile. Kommentar zu Volker Rittberger und Michael Zürn: Transformation der Konflikte in den Ost-West-Beziehungen: Versuch einer institutionalistischen Bestandsaufnahme." *Politische Vierteljahresschrift* 33(1): 93–100.

Shapiro, Ian and Alexander Wendt. 1992. "The Difference that Realism Makes: Social Science and the Politics of Consent." *Politics & Society* 20(2): 197–223.

Shapiro, Michael J. 1988. *The Politics of Representation: Writing Practices in Biography, Photography and Policy Analysis*. Madison: University of Wisconsin Press.

———. 1989. "Textualizing Global Politics." In *International/Intertextual Relations: Postmodern Readings of World Politics*, eds. James Der Derian and Michael J. Shapiro. Lexington: Lexington Books.

————. 1992. *Reading the Postmodern Polity*. Minneapolis: University of Minnesota Press.

————. 1997. *Violent Cartographies: Mapping Cultures of War*. Minneapolis: University of Minnesota Press.

———— and Hayward R. Alker, eds. 1996. *Challenging Boundaries: Global Flows, Territorial Identities*. Minneapolis: University of Minnesota Press.

Shevardnaze, Eduard. 1991. *Die Zukunft gehört der Freiheit*. Reinbek.

Shklar, Judith. 1964. *Legalism*. Cambridge, Mass.: Harvard University Press.

Sjolander, Claire Turenne. 1995. "The Rhetoric of Globalization: What's in a Wor(l)d?" *International Journal* 41(4): 603–733.

Smith, Anthony D. 1986. *The Ethnic Origins of Nations*. Oxford: Basil Blackwell.

Smith, Steve. 1992. "The Forty Years' Detour: The Resurgence of Normative Theory in International Relations." *Millennium: Journal of International Studies* 21(3): 489–506.

————. 1995. "The Self-images of a Discipline. A Genealogy of International Relations Theory." In *International Relations Theory Today*, eds. Ken Booth and Steve Smith. Cambridge: Polity Press.

————. 1996. "Positivism and Beyond." In *International Theory: Positivism and Beyond*, eds. Steve Smith, Ken Booth, and Marysia Zalewski. Cambridge: Cambridge University Press.

————. 1997. "New Approaches to International Theory." In *The Globalization of World Politics*, eds. John Baylis and Steve Smith. Oxford: Oxford University Press.

————. 1999a. "Social Constructivisms and European Studies: A Reflectivist Critique." *Journal of European Public Policy* 6(4): 682–691.

————. Forthcoming. "International Theory and European Integration." In *International Relations Theory and the Politics of European Integration*, eds. Morten Kelstrup and Mike Williams. London: Routledge.

————, Ken Booth, and Marysia Zalewski. 1996. *International Theory: Positivism and Beyond*. Cambridge: Cambridge University Press.

Sokal, Alan. 1996. "Trangressing the Boundaries: Towards a Transformative Hermeneutics of Quantum Gravity." *Social Text* 46/47: 217–252.

———— and Jean Bricmont. 1998. *Intellectuial Impostures: Postmodern Philosophers' Abuse of Science*. London: Profile Books.

Sparr, Pamela, ed. 1994. *Mortgaging Women's Lives: Feminist Critiques of Structural Adjustment*. London and Atlantic Highlands, N.J.: Zed Books.

Spelman, Elisabeth V. 1988. *Inessential Woman: Problems of Exclusion in Feminist Thought*. Boston: Beacon Press.

Spencer-Brown, G. 1979. *Laws of Form*. New York: Dutton.

Steans, Jill. 1998. *Gender and International Relations: An Introduction*. New Brunswick: Rutgers University Press.

Steier, Frederick, ed. 1991. *Research and Reflexivity*. London: Sage.

Stein, Janice Gross. 1989. "Getting to the Table: The Triggers, Stages, Functions, and Consequences of Prenegotiation." In *Getting to the Table: The Processes of International Prenegotiation*, ed. Janice G. Stein. Baltimore and London: John Hopkins University Press.

Stienstra, Deborah. 1994. *Women's Movements and International Organizations*. London: Macmillan Press.

Strange, Susan. 1996. *The Retreat of the State*. Cambridge: Cambridge University Press.

Suganami, Hidemi. 1983. "The Structure of Institutionalism: An Anatomy of British Mainstream International Relations." *International Relations* 7(5): 2363–2381.

Sylvan, David, Corinne A. Graff and Elisabetta Pugliese. 1998. "A Pilot Study on the

Changing Meaning of Sovereignty in International Relations: Rationale, Methodology, and a Preliminary Example." Paper presented at the annual conference of the International Studies Association, Minneapolis.

———. 1994. *Feminist Theory and International Relations in a Postmodern Era*. Cambridge: Cambridge University Press.

———. 1998. "'Masculinity,' 'Femininity,' and 'International Relations': Or Who Goes to the 'Moon' with Bonaparte and the Adder?" In *The 'Man' Question in International Relations*, eds. Marysia Zalewski and Jane L. Parpart. Boulder: Westview Press.

Talbott, Strobe. 1988. *The Master of the Game: Paul Nitze and Nuclear Peace*. New York: Knopf.

Tarrow, Sidney. 1998. *Power in Movement: Social Movements and Contentious Politics*, 2nd edition. Cambridge: Cambridge University Press.

Taylor, Charles. 1978. "Interpretation and the Sciences of Man." In *The Philosophy of Society*, eds. Rodger Beekler and Alan R. Drengson. London: Methuen.

———. 1985. *Human Agency and Language*, vol. 1. Cambridge and New York: Cambridge University Press.

———. 1989. *Sources of the Self: The Making of Modern Identity*. Cambridge, Mass.: Harvard University Press.

Thomas, Daniel C. Forthcoming. *The Helsinki Effect: International Norms, Human Rights, and the Demise of Communism*. Princeton: Princeton University Press.

Thompson, John B. 1981. *Critical Hermeneutics: A Study in the Thought of Paul Ricoeur and Jurgen Habermas*. Cambridge: Cambridge University Press.

Thompson, Helen. 1997. "The Nation-State and International Capital Mobility in Historical Perspective." *Government and Opposition* 32(1): 84–113.

Tickner, J. Ann. 1992. *Gender in International Relations: Feminist Perspectives on Achieving Global Security*. New York: Columbia University Press.

———. 1995. "Revisioning Security." In *International Relations Theory Today*, eds. Ken Booth and Steve Smith. Oxford: Polity Press.

———. 1996. "Identity in International Relations Theory: Feminist Perspectives." In *The Return of Culture and Identity in IR Theory*, eds. Yosef Lapid and Friedrich Kratochwil. Boulder: Lynne Rienner.

Tracy, Brian. 1978. "Bargaining as Trial and Error." In *The Negotiation Process: Theories and Applications*, ed. I. William Zartman. Beverly Hills and London: Sage.

Unger, Leonard. 1986. "The International Role of the Association of Southeast Asian Nations." In *Negotiating World Order: The Artisanship and Architecture of Global Diplomay*, ed. Alan K. Henrikson. Wilmington: Scholarly Resources.

Useem, John, John D. Donoghue. and Ruth Hill Useem. 1963. "Men in the Middle of the Third Culture." *Human Organization* 22(3): 169–179.

Vasquez, John A. 1983. *The Power of Power Politics: A Critique*. New Brunswick, NY: Rutgers University Press.

Waever, Ole. 1995. "Securitization and Desecuritization." In *On Security*, ed. Ronnie D. Lipschutz. New York: Columbia University Press.

———. 1996a. "European Security Identities." *Journal of Common Market Studies* 34(1): 103–132.

———. 1996b. "The Rise and Fall of the Inter-paradigm Debate." In *International Theory: Positivism and beyond*, eds. Steve Smith, Ken Booth, and Marysia Zalewski. Cambridge: Cambridge University Press.

———. 1997. "Figures of International Thought: Introducing Persons Instead of Paradigms." In *The Future of International Relations. Masters in Making*, eds. Iver B. Neumann and Ole Waever. London and New York: Routledge

————. 1998. "The Sociology of a Not So International Discipline: American and European Developments in International Relations." *International Organization* 52(4): 687–727.

Walker, R.B.J. 1987. "Realism, Change and International Political Theory." *International Studies Quarterly* 31(1): 65–86.

————. 1993. *Inside/Outside: International Relations as Political Theory.* Cambridge: Cambridge University Press.

Wallace, William. 1990. "Introduction: The Dynamics of European Integration." In *The Dynamics of European Integration,* ed. William Wallace. London: Pinter/RIIA.

————. 1996. "Truth and Power, Monks and Technocrats: Theory and Practice in International Relations." *Review of International Studies* 22(3): 301–321.

Walt, Stephen M. 1987. *The Origins of Alliances.* Ithaca and London: Cornell University Press.

————. 1998. "International Relations: One World, Many Theories." *Foreign Policy* 110: 29–46.

Waltz, Kenneth. 1979. *Theory of International Politics.* Reading, Mass.: Addison Wesley.

Warnke, Georgia. 1995. "Communicative Rationality and Cultural Values." In *The Cambridge Companion to Habermas,* ed. Stephen K. White. Cambridge: Cambridge University Press.

Watson, Adam. 1982. *Diplomacy—The Dialogue Between States.* London: Eyre Methuen.

Watson, Adam. 1992. *The Evolution of International Society: A Comparative Historical Analysis.* London: Routledge.

Watson, Matthew. 1999. "Rethinking Capital Mobility, Re-Regulating Financial Markets." *New Political Economy* 4(1): 55–75.

Weber, Cynthia. 1994. "Good Girls, Little Girls, and Bad Girls: Male Paranoia in Robert Keohane's Critique of Feminist International Relations." *Millennium: Journal of International Studies* 23(2): 337–349.

————. 1995. *Simulating Sovereignty: Intervention, the State and Symbolic Exchange.* Cambridge: Cambridge University Press.

Weber, Steve. 1991a. *Cooperation and Discord in U.S.-Soviet Arms Control.* Princeton: Princeton University Press.

————. 1991b. "Interactive Learning in U.S.-Soviet Arms Control. "In *Learning in U.S. and Soviet Foreign Policy,* eds. George W. Breslauer and Philip E. Tetlock. Boulder: Westview Press.

Weir, Allison. 1995. "Toward a Model of Self-Identity: Habermas and Kristeva." In *Feminists Read Habermas: Gendering the Subject of Discourse,* ed. Johanna Meehan. New York: Routledge.

Weiss, Linda. 1997. "Globalization and the Myth of the Powerless State." *New Left Review* 225: 3–27.

Weldes, Jutta. 1996. "Constructing National Interests." *European Journal of International Relations* 2(3): 275–318.

————. 1999. *Constructing National Interests: The US and the Cuban Missile Crisis.* Minneapolis: University of Minnesota Press.

———— and Diana Saco. 1996. "Making State Action Possible: The United States and the Discursive Construction of 'the Cuban Problem,' 1960–1994." *Millennium: Journal of International Studies* 25(2): 361–395.

Wendt, Alexander. 1987. "The Agent-Structure Problem in International Relations Theory." *International Organization* 41(3): 335–370.

————. 1991. "Bridging the Theory/Metatheory Gap in International Relations." *Re-*

view of International Studies 17(4): 383–392.

———. 1992a. "Anarchy Is What the States Make of It." *International Organization* 46: 391–425.

———. 1992b. "Levels of Analysis vs. Agents and Structures: Part III." *Review of International Studies* 18(2): 181–185.

———. 1994. "Collective Identity Formation and the International State." *American Political Science Review* 88(2): 384–396.

———. 1995. "Constructing International Politics." *International Security* 20(1): 71–81.

———. 1996. "Identity and Structural Change in International Politics." In *The Return of Culture and Identity in IR Theory*, eds. Yosef Lapid and Friedrich Kratochwil. Boulder: Lynne Rienner.

———. 1999. *Social Theory of International Relations*. Cambridge: Cambridge University Press.

——— and Robert Duvall. 1989. "Institutions and International Order." In *Global Changes and Theoretical Challenges: Approaches to World Politics for the 1990s*, eds. Ernst-Otto Czempiel and James N. Rosenau. Lexington: Lexington Books.

White, Hayden V. 1987. *The Content of the Form. Narrative Discourse and Historical Representation*. Baltimore and London: Johns Hopkins University Press.

White, Stephen K. 1995. "Reason, Modernity and Democracy." In *The Cambridge Companion to Habermas*, ed. Stephen K. White. Cambridge: Cambridge University Press.

Whitworth, Sandra. 1994. *Feminism and International Relations: Towards a Political Economy of Gender in Interstate and Non-Governmental Institutions*. Basingstoke: Macmillan.

Wiener, Antje. 1998. *European Citizenship Practice. Building Institutions of a Non-State*. Boulder: Westview Press.

Wight, Martin. 1966. "Western Values in International Relations." In *Diplomatic Investigations: Essays in the Theory of International Politics*, eds. Herbert Butterfield and Martin Wight. London: George Allen & Unwin Ltd.

———. 1966. "Why Is There No International Theory?" in *Diplomatic Investigations. Essays in the Theory of International Politics,* eds. Herbert Butterfield and Martin Wight. Cambridge, Mass.: Harvard University Press.

Williams, Michael C. 1996. "Hobbes and International Relations: A Reconsideration." *International Organization* 50(2): 213–236.

Williamson, Jeffrey G. 1996a. "Globalization, Convergence and History." *Journal of Economic History* 56(2): 277–305.

———. 1996b. "Globalization and Inequality Then and Now: The Late Nineteenth and Twentieth Centuries Compared." *NBER Working Paper*, 5491.

Wind, Marlene. 1997. "Nicholas G. Onuf: The Rules of Anarchy." In *The Future of International Relations: Masters in the Making*, eds. Iver B. Neumann and Ole Waever. London and New York: Routledge.

Wittgenstein, Ludwig. [1921]1958. *Tractatus Logico-Philosophicus,* David F. Pears and Brian F. McGuinness, trans. London: Routledge and Kegan Paul.

———. [1953]1958. *Philosophical Investigation*, 2nd edition. Oxford: Blackwell.

Wolf, Klaus Dieter. 1991. *Internationale Regime zur Verteilung globaler Ressourcen. Eine vergleichende Analyse der Grundlagen ihrer Entstehung am Beispiel der Regelung des Zugangs zur wirtschaftlichen Nutzung des Meeresbodens, des geostationären Orbits, der Antarktis und Wissenschaft und Technologie*. Baden-Baden: Nomos.

Young, Iris Mairon. 1990. *Justice and the Politics of Difference*. Princeton: Princeton University Press.

Young, Oran R. 1994. *International Governance: Protecting the Environment in a Stateless Society.* London and New York: Cornell University Press.

Youngs, Gillian. 1996. "Dangers of Discourse: The Case of Globalization." In *Globalization: Theory and Practice*, eds. Eleonore Kofman and Gillian Youngs. London: Pinter.

Yuval-Davis, Nira and Anthias, Floya, eds. 1989. *Woman-Nation-State.* Basingstoke: Macmillan.

Zalewski, Marysia. 1993. "Feminist Standpoint Theory Meets International Relations Theory: A Reminist Version of David and Goliath?" *The Fletcher Forum of World Affairs* 17(2): 13–32.

———. 1998. "Where Is Woman in International Relations? 'To Return as a Woman and Be Heard." *Millennium: Journal of International Studies* 27(4): 847–867.

——— and Enloe, Cynthia. 1995. "Questions About Identity in International Relations." In *International Relations Theory Today*, eds. Ken Booth and Steve Smith. Cambridge: Polity Press.

——— and Jane L. Parpart, eds. 1998. *The 'Man' Question in International Relations.* Boulder: Westview Press.

Zartman, I. William 1989. "Prenegotiations: Phases and Functions." In *Getting to the Table: The Processes of International Prenegotiation*, ed. Janice G. Stein. Baltimore and London: John Hopkins University Press.

——— and Maureen R. Berman. 1982. *The Practical Negotiator.* New Haven: Yale University Press.

Zehfuss, Maja. 1998. "Sprachlosigkeit schränkt ein: Zur Bedeutung von Sprache in konstruktivistischen Theorien." *Zeitschrift für Internationale Beziehungen* 5(1): 109–137.

Zhao, Shanyang. 1991. "Metatheory, Metamethod, Meta-data-analysis: What, Why, and How?" *Sociological Perspectives* 34(3): 377–390.

Zürn, Michael. 1992. Interessen und. Institutionen in der internationalen Politik. Grundlegung und Anwendungen des situationsstrukturellen Ansatzes. Opladen: Leske & Budrich.

Index

action. *See* communicative action, strategic action, theory of action
Adler, Emmanuel 3, 45, 54, 106, 117, 121, 123, 125, 130, 133, 134, 171, 226
  constructivist inconsistencies 108–110
  middle ground 8, 142, 214
agency 44, 45, 59, 82, 83, 85, 86, 87, 88, 89, 90, 117, 118, 121, 124, 127, 128, 133, 137, 204, 206, 209, 213, 215, 218, 223, 224, 226, 230, 231, 234
agent-structure debate 106, 229, 231
Aristotle 34, 105, 251
  distinction between "voice" and "speech" 18
  intersubjective understandings 17–18
  pain and pleasure 26–28
Aron, Raymond 41
Ashley, Richard 3, 5, 115, 116, 120, 137, 140, 146, 147, 153, 158, 226, 243
Austin, J.L. 4, 31, 49, 66, 70
  deeds 61
autopoiesis/autopoietic 97–100, 103, 108, 251

Beauvoir, Simone de 77, 79
behavioralism 48
Benhabib, Seyla 83, 84, 185
Bhaskar, Roy 53
Berger, Peter 4, 5, 38, 40, 41, 44, 54, 58, 69, 70, 179
Bourdieu, Pierre 40, 44
Bull, Hedley 170, 189–190, 192, 197

Campbell, David 3, 7, 9, 41, 116, 117, 119, 120, 128, 134, 135, 145, 146, 156, 158, 226
  post-structural problematics 119–122
Carr, Edward H. 15, 21–22, 225
causality 117, 125, 225, 231–233
Checkel, Jeffrey 3, 7, 45, 48, 49, 54, 102, 106, 202, 203, 214
Cold War, end of 5, 6, 76, 78, 115, 119, 122, 124, 125, 126, 137, 128, 129, 131, 133, 134, 135, 144, 146, 147, 156, 157, 226
Collin, Finn 37, 38, 53
communication 5, 9, 30, 39, 46, 65–66, 68–70, 72–73, 98–100, 102, 104, 110, 145, 160–161, 164–165, 167, 176–179, 194–195, 198, 201, 217, 231
  constructivism 16
  governed by conventions/criteria 15
  in diplomacy 185–194
communicative action 9, 45, 65, 69, 160–178, 179–200, 230, 251
  distinct type of social action 183
  explanation of change 164
  Hedley Bull 190–192
  ideal type 163
  lifeworld 185–186
  mutual recognition 162, 194–185
  power 174
  See also theory of communicative action
constitutive 1, 29, 53, 55, 57, 62, 77, 87, 90, 98, 105, 118, 187, 189, 199–200, 215, 225, 227, 232, 239, 241, 245
  "domestic analogy" 24

281

constitutive *(continued)*
  language 4, 7, 126, 155, 217
  rules 38, 59, 62, 65
  theory 41
construction of 20, 37, 52, 54, 61, 62, 70,
    78, 84, 86, 87, 121, 124, 127, 131,
    134, 138, 140, 145, 150, 181,
    190–191, 196, 200, 201, 204, 213,
    214, 216, 233, 235, 236, 237, 241,
    246, 247, 248
  collective meanings 33
  gender 77, 241
  globalization 198
  identity 80, 116, 120, 196, 232
  languages 20, 148
  power 85, 91
  (social) reality 40, 59, 63, 71–73, 95,
    101, 145
  social facts 108, 164, 191
constructivism 3, 36, 52, 55, 57, 59, 61,
    63, 70, 71, 74, 76, 78, 83, 84, 85, 87,
    88, 89, 93, 95, 96, 101, 107, 111,
    115, 117, 118, 119, 121, 125, 126,
    129, 180–181, 187, 199, 201, 202,
    204, 206, 214, 227, 229, 234
  as an approach 13–35
  constructivisms (in the plural) 4, 5, 8,
    39, 41, 54, 94, 102, 103, 106, 107,
    108, 109, 116, 229, 231
  "critical theory" 20
  genealogies of 4–7
  mandarin detachment 254
  metatheory 42–46, 181
  philosophy 38–42
  politics of 236–254
  positive heuristics 24–33
  postmodernism 116, 231
  role of criticism 19–24
  theorizing 47–50, 180, 199, 217
  See also empirical research
constructivists 14, 21, 31, 41, 43, 47, 48,
    50, 51, 53, 63, 72, 76, 77, 78, 79, 80,
    81, 83, 84, 85, 88, 89, 91, 96, 102,
    116, 118, 119, 120, 121, 122, 123,
    130, 134, 136, 138, 180–181, 202,
    205, 207, 213, 223, 224, 227, 228,
    229, 230, 231, 234, 237, 240, 241,
    242, 243, 250, 253
  ancestries 76

constructivists *(continued)*
  conventional 7, 8, 43, 227, 229,
    231
  "core" argument 16–19
  debate with rationalists 3
  depicted as naïve utopians 6, 241
  emigration to Europe 9
  empirical "tests" 32
  globalization 201, 213
  identity 78–84
  language 120–121, 237
  ontological 18, 103, 106, 107
  poststructuralism 120–121, 123,
    125
  power 88–91
  radical 5, 108
  research agenda 113, 223
  Third Debate 46
conventions 15, 19, 52, 190, 202, 209
Cox, Robert W. 5, 20, 77, 85, 87, 116,
    205, 243
  purpose of theories 71
criteria 8, 15, 16, 29, 52, 68, 118,
    125–129, 131, 135, 136, 163–164,
    167–168, 172
  for claims about the world 127–129
  moral 64
critical theory 20, 88, 110
criticism, role of 19–23
culture 72, 78, 81, 105, 134, 153, 162,
    177, 197–198, 225
  European 156
  foreign policies 226
  political 87
  rationalist methodologies 36
  The Culture of National Security 6
  United States 149
  world 169

deconstruction 20, 120, 121, 122, 134,
    152–153, 228
deeds 59, 61, 248
Derrida, 5, 118, 135, 158, 227, 228
description, critical 123, 129, 133
diplomacy 22, 59, 146, 149, 248
  communicative action 180–200
  constructivist theory 8
  definition 189
  language 198

discourse 51, 65, 66–67, 77, 83, 86, 110, 124, 130, 131, 130, 136, 137, 147, 149, 150, 151–152, 153, 155, 156, 157, 158, 162–173, 184–187, 205, 210, 213, 214, 215, 217, 218, 219, 228, 229, 231, 232, 243, 244, 246, 247, 248, 249, 254
diplomatic 171, 196, 198
discourse analysis 7, 9, 50, 136
globalization 201
hegemonic 14, 15, 16, 139, 158
legal 67
nationalist 81
political 21, 64, 72, 73, 175
rational 162
systems of signification 137, 140–145
Doty, Roxanne Lynn 81, 120, 123, 139, 142, 146, 147, 151, 226, 228
Durkheim, Emile 76, 95, 227

empirical research 6, 7, 8, 37, 42, 51, 53, 78, 102, 118, 144, 147, 166, 206
empiricism 7, 17, 34, 52, 137
English School, the 43, 45, 170, 187, 195–196, 200, 227
epistemology 16, 29, 31, 32, 34, 38, 42, 47, 51, 55, 64, 93, 99, 101, 106, 217, 223, 224, 229, 233

facts 59, 67–68, 73, 127, 138
brute 40
institutional 30, 40
social 38, 106, 107
falsification 9, 125–126, 135
family resemblance 20, 120, 128–130, 196
feminism 8, 76, 84, 241
Finnemore, Martha 45, 49, 51, 85, 86, 87, 226
Foucault, Michel 4, 5, 34, 80, 118, 150, 152, 158, 227
functional differentiation 98, 103

game 23, 30, 45, 50, 128–133, 165–169, 177, 188, 198, 214, 226, 229
Cold War 124, 128–130, 131
game theory 70, 123, 161, 226, 234
two-level 209
Wittgenstein 68
See also language games

gender 8, 76, 77, 78, 79, 80, 81, 83, 89, 91, 230, 241
constructions 87
relations 85, 86
rules 90
Giddens, Anthony 4, 5, 40, 44, 51, 53, 55, 59, 62, 76, 123, 204
See also structuration theory
governance 35, 89, 151, 182, 188, 207, 214, 216, 218
grammar 132

Haas, Ernst 176
Habermas, Jürgen 4, 9, 49, 53, 65, 110, 161–164, 169, 196–177, 181–188, 173, 199, 200, 227, 230, 251
hermeneutics 36, 38
"Humean fork" 22, 31, 34

idealism 37, 38, 39, 48, 53
philosophical 37–40, 48, 53
political 48, 53, 175
identity/collective identities 33, 34, 43, 50, 51, 55, 57, 58, 72, 74, 78–82, 83, 87, 89, 91, 103, 116, 119, 120, 121, 122, 124, 135, 139, 155, 156, 186, 196–199, 223, 232, 233, 237, 225, 238, 240, 241, 243
politics 238–242
individualism 234
institutionalization 59, 83
institutions 8, 23, 32, 34, 41, 42, 61, 64, 66, 77–78, 181, 196, 202, 205, 226, 236, 242, 250
international 84–89
like promise or contract 31–32
self-help and power politics 56
intentionality 5, 17, 40, 64, 95–96, 128,182
collective 38
interests 8, 26, 34, 78, 85, 87, 132, 134, 163–164, 166–167, 172, 175, 177, 182–186, 188–190, 193–194, 196, 199–200, 224, 226, 239
construction of 26
diffuse reciprocity 168
diplomacy 190, 195–196
globalisation 203, 206–209, 211, 213, 215, 218–219

interests *(continued)*
  practice and identity 55–58, 78–80, 103, 116, 119, 180
  international organizations 84, 85, 86, 87, 90, 146, 148, 150
  International Relations 3, 4, 5, 6, 7, 8, 9, 14, 36, 54, 55, 58, 62, 64, 71, 72, 74, 76, 93, 115, 116, 121, 122, 135, 136, 160, 180, 201, 223, 236, 24, 240, 242
  international society 9, 43, 152, 160, 184, 187, 192, 193, 196, 198, 200, 202
  interpretation 15, 20, 35, 36, 60, 64, 66, 67, 68, 70, 118, 128, 133, 136, 143, 162, 173–174, 182–185, 187, 190–195, 198, 225, 229
  of Hobbes and self-interest 24–26
  multiple 69
interstate negotiations 190
intersubjective 27, 57–58, 65, 66, 82, 84, 116, 117, 118, 132
  context 64–65, 67–68, 70–71
  structure 6, 56, 183–186, 188
  understanding 17, 30, 57–58, 118, 124, 179, 199, 224, 232, 245

Kant, Immanuel 20, 155
Katzenstein, Peter 3, 4, 43, 46, 47, 54, 58, 69, 71, 72, 78, 87, 88, 106, 111, 116, 118, 134, 181, 183, 244
  "methodological non-issues" 51
Klotz, Audie 6, 9, 46, 72, 226, 234
Kratochwil, Friedrich 6, 9, 13, 30, 35, 49, 51, 53, 54, 63–68, 70, 71, 22, 75, 78, 83, 84, 92, 101, 111, 120, 122, 181, 183, 203, 226, 227, 231, 234, 240, 243, 244, 245, 246, 248, 250, 254
  application 73
  criticism of regime theory 43
  linguistic turn 7
  speech acts 72
Kulturwissenschaften 20

language 6, 8, 9, 16, 24, 25, 27, 55, 58, 58, 59, 63, 74, 80, 82, 84, 90, 100, 110, 111, 117, 118, 121, 123, 125, 127, 126, 128, 134, 137, 139, 145, 150, 162. 165, 171, 174–176, 176–177, 191–192, 198, 200, 224, 226, 249, 251, 252

language *(continued)*
  a "form of life" 20
  constitutive role 7, 19, 70, 127
  constructivists 227–228, 230, 234, 237, 245–248
  function or role 19, 69–71, 168, 224
  in Wendt's constructivism 67–71
  mirror of reality 4, 7, 9, 29, 68
  philosophy 15, 19, 161–162
  predicate analysis 141–142
  rule governed activity 34
language games 20, 121, 131, 132, 135, 204, 231
levels of analysis 43, 91
liberal 56, 85, 89, 127, 144, 146, 227, 252
  scholars 47
  vision in international law 22
liberalism 47, 90, 170, 207, 215, 231
lifeworld 162, 167–172, 185–187
linguistic turn 4, 7, 19–20
Luckman, Thomas 4, 5, 38, 40, 41, 44, 54, 58, 69, 70, 179
Luhmann, Niklas 4, 8, 40, 44, 46, 53, 93, 97, 99, 101, 104, 105, 107, 110, 168, 251
Lynch, Cecilia 49, 91, 226, 229

materialism 24, 42, 234
Maturana, Humberto 16, 99
metatheory 7, 37, 41, 42, 43, 110
  constructivism 42–46
Methodenstreit 248–252
Meyers, Reinhard 44
Morgenthau, Hans J. 22, 225
Müller, Harald 9, 69, 70, 160, 164, 171, 181, 191, 194, 231, 234, 251, 251

nationalism 79, 205, 208
neoliberal institutionalism 41, 89
neorealism 42, 43, 47, 56, 107, 202, 253
nongovernmental organizations 148, 209
"normal science" 51, 138,-140, 206, 233
norms 24, 47, 51, 53, 63, 65, 79, 85, 87, 88, 103, 117, 137, 140, 149, 164, 171, 182–191, 194–195, 197–199, 202, 216, 217, 226, 227, 228, 230, 231, 232, 233, 234, 248
  as speech acts 31, 66–73
  different conceptions 72

norms *(continued)*
  discourse 32
  English School 43
  Neumann, Iver B. 79, 82, 156

ontology 42, 51, 56, 78, 89, 93, 106, 158,
    203, 214, 226
  and substantive theories 41
  onsequences for epistemology 51
  of social facts 38
Onuf, Nicholas G. 6, 7, 9, 16, 40, 44, 47,
    54, 55, 58–62, 69, 70, 71, 74, 83, 84,
    88, 95, 119, 122, 181, 203, 204–205,
    214, 223, 236, 239, 254
  application 73
  speech acts 73
  World of Our Making 58, 62, 203
operative closure 97
othering 81

paradigms 46–48
patriarchy 90, 241
philosophy of language 4, 19
philosophy of science 37, 51, 74, 214
politics 14, 21, 24, 28, 29, 36, 49, 52,
    55, 61, 63, 73, 85, 90, 91, 135,
    155, 176, 203, 205, 211, 217, 223,
    224, 230
  American 144
  domestic 127, 147, 165, 209, 238
  emancipatory 47
  hegemony 154, 158
  identity 238–241
  international 6, 8, 15, 21, 22, 41, 45,
    46, 47, 56, 63, 64, 71, 78, 80,
    125, 161, 174, 175, 180–183,
    189, 193, 198–199, 226, 230,
    136, 138, 248
  of constructivism 237
  of language 245–249
  personal 252–254
  poststructuralists 120–121
  representation 136, 138, 248
  status 242–245
positivism 7, 8, 14, 32, 34, 46, 50, 53, 63,
    65, 66, 102, 106, 118, 125, 133, 158,
    226, 227, 228, 231, 232, 237
postmodernism 133
poststructuralism 8, 121

power 16, 18, 22, 24, 25, 26, 40, 56, 57,
    71, 78, 80, 83, 85, 86, 88, 89, 91,
    100, 104, 124, 127, 128, 138, 151,
    153, 162–163, 166–167, 169, 172,
    193, 205, 210, 213, 217, 219, 228,
    234, 235, 238, 241, 249
  balance of 130, 133
  communicative action 174–175
  marginalization of alternatives 121
  structures of 82, 116
  theorizing 90, 121
practices, social 56, 76, 87

rational choice theory 13, 240, 250, 251
  "law of the hammer" 13
realism 15, 21, 55, 73, 108, 115, 126,
    135, 169, 217, 227
  antirealism 53
  in International Relations 22, 46–47,
    76
  masculine 85
  philosophical 37–39
regimes, international 84, 87, 89, 150,
    164, 170, 175, 211, 226, 231
research programs 4, 21, 34, 51–52
rhetoric 15, 25, 135, 206, 211, 247
Risse, Thomas 3, 9, 48, 71, 78, 82, 91,
    106, 125, 181, 205, 226, 234
Ruggie, John G. 3, 5, 6, 45, 48, 54, 76,
    81, 84, 89, 101, 109, 158, 170, 177,
    203, 212, 226, 227, 243
  general theory of constructivism regime
    theory 43, 49, 78, 179
rules 16, 19, 23, 31, 47, 62, 65, 68, 70,
    71, 72, 74, 88, 90, 97, 117, 120, 123,
    127, 130, 132, 170, 181–197, 204,
    215, 227–231, 232, 233, 241–242,
    244, 248, 254
  behavioral regulation 164
  classical diplomacy 22
  definition 66
  games 123–125, 132–133
  indeterminate 66
  institutional 31
  regulative/constitutive 38, 59–60, 66

Said, Edward 40
Searle, John 4, 49, 53, 186
  criticism of antirealism 53

Searle, John *(continued)*
general theory of the ontology of social
facts and institutions 38, 41
speech acts 31, 49, 70, 95
semantics of Old Europe 20, 100, 99,
104–106, 108–109, 120
Smith, Steve 52, 55, 56, 63, 71, 74, 134,
169, 203, 205, 209
constitutive and explanatory theory 44
debates in International Relations 45
social movements 91, 217, 231
social systems 98, 142
Sokal, Alan 36, 52
speech acts 20, 49, 72, 95, 165, 167,
186, 192, 230, 231, 248, 254
building block of social reality 84
deeds, rules and reasoning 59–61
intersubjective context 69
norms 66
power 83
research program 34
social sciences 31
speech situations, ideal 183
See also John Searle, Jurgen
Habermas, J.L. Austin,
Nicholas Onuf and Friedrich
Kratochwil
strategic action 161–163, 167–168, 174,
252
structural coupling 99, 101, 109
structuration theory 44, 51, 53, 55, 59,
123
structures 9, 43, 77, 97, 99, 106, 122,
123, 130, 131, 132, 133, 135, 143,
155, 159, 164, 180–188, 194–195,
197–199, 203, 205, 210, 218, 223,
224, 230, 246, 250
Cold War 134
historical 130
institutions 87
intersubjective 6, 56, 180–181,
184–188, 195
mutual constitution 55
power 82, 116

structures *(continued)*
regulatory 211
signification 138, 140–141
social 48–49, 58, 97, 180–181, 233
subjective. *See* intersubjective
systems 16, 18, 63, 94, 98, 138, 140, 141,
142, 144, 145, 157, 158, 165, 173,
196–198, 215
systems theory 8, 49, 53, 54, 93, 95,
97–98, 107, 108–109, 240, 251

Taylor, Charles 26–27, 36, 37, 41, 83, 179
theory building 32, 34, 45, 49–52
theory of action 16, 160–161, 166, 174
theory of communicative action 9, 49, 65,
164, 181

verstehen 15, 117, 134
Vienna Circle 9, 123, 133, 249

Walker, R.B.J. 3, 5, 9, 23, 111, 115, 136,
137, 139, 147, 153, 243
Weber, Max 9, 66, 76, 78, 95, 134, 145,
170, 178, 226, 227
Wendt, Alexander 4, 7, 21, 41, 43,-44, 45,
47, 48, 49, 51, 63, 72, 74, 78, 82, 84,
87, 88, 111, 115, 116, 118, 123, 124,
134, 135, 158, 164–170, 180–182,
195, 202, 204, 217, 223, 227, 238,
240, 243, 244, 246, 247
agent-structure problem 5, 5, 55–57, 123
conception of constructivism 52–56
intersubjective context 69–70, 245
social ontologies 41
Wittgenstein, Ludwig 59, 69, 76, 116,
119, 122, 126, 131, 227, 231, 249,
250
linguistic turn 4–5, 20
philosophy of language 4–5
women 76, 77, 79, 81, 83, 84, 85, 86, 89,
134
world society 48, 98, 105, 202
Waever, Ole 3, 6, 47, 55, 63, 119, 137,
147, 253

Printed in Great Britain
by Amazon